Cognitive behavioural processes across psychological disorders:
A transdiagnostic approach to research and treatment

Allison G. Harvey
Department of Experimental Psychology, University of Oxford, Oxford, UK

Edward Watkins
School of Psychology, University of Exeter, Exeter, UK

Warren Mansell
Department of Psychological Medicine, Institute of Psychiatry, London, UK

and

Roz Shafran
Department of Psychiatry, University of Oxford, Oxford, UK

OXFORD
UNIVERSITY PRESS

OXFORD

UNIVERSITY PRESS

Great Clarendon Street, Oxford OX2 6DP

Oxford University Press is a department of the University of Oxford.
It furthers the University's objective of excellence in research, scholarship,
and education by publishing worldwide in

Oxford New York

Auckland Cape Town Dar es Salaam Hong Kong Karachi
Kuala Lumpur Madrid Melbourne Mexico City Nairobi
New Delhi Taipei Toronto Shanghai

With offices in

Argentina Austria Brazil Chile Czech Republic France Greece
Guatemala Hungary Italy Japan South Korea Poland Portugal
Singapore Switzerland Thailand Turkey Ukraine Vietnam

Published in the United States
by Oxford University Press Inc., New York

First published 2004
Reprinted 2004

A catalogue record for this title is available from the British Library

ISBN 0 19 852887 6 (Hbk)
ISBN 0 19 852888 4 (Pbk)

10 9 8 7 6 5 4 3 2

Typeset by Cepha Imaging Private Ltd, Bangalore, India

Printed in Great Britain

on acid-free paper by Biddles Ltd., King's Lynn, Norfolk

For our loved ones
(they know who they are!)

Preface

Three of us (Roz, Warren, and Allison) began our work as clinical psychologists and researchers specializing in anxiety disorders and one of us (Ed) worked mainly with patients diagnosed with depression. As time went on our interests diverged. Roz to eating disorders. Warren and Ed to bipolar disorder. Allison to insomnia. We were all struck by the similarities between the disorders in which we first specialized and our new interests. At the annual conference of the British Association for Behavioural and Cognitive Psychotherapy (BABCP), held in London in 2000, Warren organized a symposium entitled 'Cognitive processes across disorders'. Again, we were struck by the similarities in the processes that maintained different psychological disorders. Since then we have organized, presented in, and attended several 'across disorder' symposia in which clinical researchers working on the same cognitive or behavioural process, across a range of different psychological disorders, presented their research. The similarities across the disorders were confirmed, again and again. Hence, in the Spring of 2003 we decided to attempt to systematically determine the utility of an 'across disorder', or 'transdiagnostic' approach, to understanding cognitive behavioural processes in psychological disorders. This book is the output of our efforts.

Before sharing with you where we have got to in our thinking on this issue, we would like to acknowledge that we have all been very fortunate to have had the opportunity to interact with, and be influenced by, many distinguished clinical researchers who have taught us so much. We are grateful to them all but would particularly like to thank our close supervisors and mentors as they have carefully and thoughtfully tutored and nurtured us. They are Chris Brewin, Richard Bryant, David M. Clark, Padmal de Silva, Anke Ehlers, Christopher Fairburn, Paul Salkovskis, S. Rachman, and John Teasdale.

We would like to extend a special thanks to Philip Tata who, in his capacity as Chair of the Scientific Committee of the BABCP, granted us the freedom to organize discussions and presentations on transdiagnostic issues at each annual conference. We would also like to acknowledge the influence on our thinking of the groundbreaking work of Christopher Fairburn, Zafra Cooper, and Roz Shafran who outlined a transdiagnostic approach to eating disorders as published in Behaviour Research and Therapy (Fairburn *et al.* 2003).

Finally, there are several other people we wish to thank for their patience and support while we have been writing this book and/or for their willingness to brainstorm ideas. Thanks to Alison Bugg, John Campbell, Padmal de Silva, David and Matthew Gittleson, Emily Holmes, Melissa Ree, and Mark Williams.

Contents

Chapter 1

Introduction

The importance of cognitive and behavioural processes in psychological disorders has long been recognized by clinicians and researchers. As a result of research by Pavlov (1928), Watson and Raynor (1920), Wolpe (1958), Skinner (1959) and many others, the role of behavioural processes, such as conditioning and reinforcement contingencies, became widely recognized. This perspective led to a range of treatments and techniques that came to be known collectively as behaviour therapy. The recognition of behaviour therapy's limitations in treating certain client groups (Rachman 1997) left the field reasonably open and receptive to the novel ideas of clinician researchers such as Aaron T. Beck (1967) and Albert Ellis (1958). Beck and Ellis had a common proposal; that cognitive processes, including unhelpful beliefs, illogical thinking, and distorted perception, were crucial to understanding and treating psychological disorders. These ideas led to the birth of cognitive therapy. In the ensuing years, clinicians and researchers have combined the two approaches into cognitive behavioural therapy (CBT; Barlow 2001) or have practised relatively pure forms of either behavioural therapy (BT; Lindsay *et al.* 1997; Öst *et al.* 1997; Ito *et al.* 2001) or cognitive therapy (CT; Clark *et al.* 1994; Beck 1995; Greenberger and Padesky 1995).

Research on cognitive behavioural processes in psychological disorders is currently dominated by a 'disorder-focus'. That is, researchers have tended to target one specific disorder and have tried to understand its aetiology and maintenance so as to develop more effective strategies to treat the disorder. This approach has greatly advanced our understanding of, and ability to treat, several psychological disorders (Clark and Fairburn 1997). However, it is notable that this work is often done in relative isolation from parallel work on other psychological disorders. A striking trend to emerge from the disorder-focused research is the marked similarity in the cognitive behavioural processes identified as important across the different psychological disorders. Accordingly, our aim in writing this book is to examine the utility of shifting perspective away from a 'disorder-focus' towards an 'across disorder', or transdiagnostic, perspective. In this introductory chapter, we will discuss the potential advantages and disadvantages of adopting a transdiagnostic perspective. In addition, the method we will use for evaluating the utility of a transdiagnostic perspective will be outlined.

Before beginning, we would like to point out that it is feasible to conduct this exercise for both psychological (cognitive/behavioural) and biological processes. Readers familiar with biological theories of psychological disorders will know that similar brain structures and neurotransmitters are implicated across the disorders. For example, the amygdala has been implicated in depression (Bowley *et al.* 2002; Frodl *et al.* 2003), schizophrenia (Kosaka *et al.* 2002; Shenton *et al.* 2002), obsessive-compulsive disorder (OCD; Szeszko *et al.* 1999), and post-traumatic stress disorder (PTSD; Rauch *et al.* 2000), and serotonin has been implicated in depression (Drevets *et al.* 1999), OCD (Barr *et al.* 1993), eating disorders (Jimerson *et al.* 1990), and schizophrenia (Kapur and Remington 1996). Similarly, various social (e.g. the role of the family—Kuipers 1992; Wearden *et al.* 2000) and emotional (e.g. Kring and Bachorowski 1999; Kring 2001) processes may well be relevant across disorders. However, the focus of this book will be on psychological, specifically cognitive and behavioural processes, for three reasons. First, these processes underpin CBT, an approach that has a strong evidence-base and is the treatment of choice for a diverse and growing range of psychological disorders (see Clark and Fairburn 1997; Barlow 2001; Nathan and Gorman 2002). Second, these processes have their roots in experimental psychology. As such, they can be subject to scientific scrutiny. Processes that do not have their foundation in experimental psychology (e.g. therapeutic processes) are not addressed in this book. Third, cognitive behavioural processes are our primary interest; each of the authors of this book are practising cognitive behavioural therapists and each of us has been involved in research investigations of cognitive behavioural processes.

Another issue to highlight at the outset is that a transdiagnostic perspective may well be relevant to the processes involved in predisposing an individual to develop a disorder, in the processes involved in the aetiology of a disorder (i.e. the distal cause or the original cause), as well as in the processes involved in the maintenance of a disorder (i.e. the proximal cause or the perpetuating processes). As depicted in Box 1.1, the relative contribution of each of these processes is likely to vary over the course of a disorder with the predisposing factors (e.g. genetics) potentially making a contribution throughout the entire course of the disorder, the precipitating processes (e.g. a life event) making their greatest contribution at the point of onset but then often waning, and the perpetuating or maintaining factors taking hold and increasing as the disorder becomes established. In this book we will focus on the maintaining processes as this is where most research has tended to focus. While we recognize the value of engaging in a parallel exercise for predisposing and precipitating processes, there is considerably less research on such

Box 1.1 Schematic diagram of the contribution of predisposing, precipitating, and perpetuating processes to change in psychological disorders over time

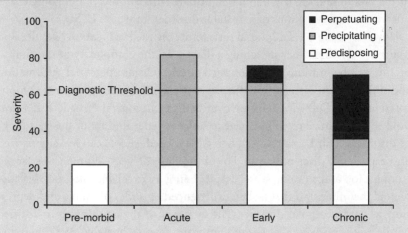

Adapted with permission from W. B. Saunders Co./Elsevier Science from Spielman, A.J., Caruso, L.S., and Glovinsky, P.B. (1987). A behavioural perspective on insomnia treatment. *Psychiatric Clinics of North America*, 10, 541–553.

processes, no doubt because of the difficulties in conducting long-term prospective studies requiring very large samples.

Classification

The dominant schemes for classifying psychological disorders are the Diagnostic and Statistical Manual of Mental Disorders (DSM; American Psychiatric Association) and the International Classification of Diseases (ICD; World Health Organization). The DSM is currently in its fourth edition (American Psychiatric Association 1994, 2001) and the ICD is in its 10th edition (World Health Organization 1992). Our discussion throughout this book will centre on the DSM as it is the system utilized by most of the research we will describe.

Classification systems provide several benefits in that they give us a common language to clearly communicate with other clinicians and researchers. Classification has also facilitated research. By studying a reasonably homogeneous group of people with a common set of symptoms it becomes possible to develop a picture of what might be contributing to the disorder and how the disorder can best be treated (Adams *et al.* 1977). Furthermore, being 'diagnosed' can be a relief for clients and their families. For example, an inpatient who was admitted to hospital following a severe leg and minor head injury, sustained during an assault, was given a leaflet outlining 'common reactions to trauma'. She was greatly relieved to read that the upsetting flashbacks of the assault and the frightening nightmares did not mean 'I'm going crazy' but were in fact symptoms of a treatable disorder known as PTSD.

However, there are substantial disadvantages to classification (Beutler and Malik 2002). First, when assigning a diagnosis, the complexity of the clinical picture can be minimized and important and relevant personal information about the patient lost. Second, the current classification systems are complicated with the DSM-IV defining over 350 psychological disorders. It seems unlikely that clinicians will manage to be knowledgeable about this vast range of disorders. Third, as a result of being diagnosed, clients can feel stigmatized and experience discrimination. For example, a 22-year-old man was sacked from his job at a clothing store, despite being an excellent salesman, because he told the other staff that he had experienced episodes of mania and depression, as part of bipolar disorder. The manager of the clothing store justified her decision by saying that she did not want anyone 'unstable' working in her store and that the other staff felt scared of him. Tragically, two days later the young man committed suicide. Unfortunately, many psychological disorders, including bipolar disorder, remain misunderstood, with sometimes devastating consequences. A fourth disadvantage of classification is that it is a categorical system that specifies a clear cut-off at an often arbitrarily defined point. The DSM considers each disorder as a discrete entity that is distinct from other psychological disorders and from 'normal behaviour'. Throughout this book it will be evident that a categorical conceptualization of disorders does not reflect the clinical reality and that most of the cognitive and behavioural processes we will discuss occur on a continuum. This dimensional view assumes that 'individuals assigned a DSM-IV diagnosis differ from "normal" persons only in the frequency and/or severity with which they experience the features that form the diagnostic criteria' (p. 22–23, Brown 1996). Finally, although claiming to be 'supported by an extensive empirical foundation' (p. XV, American Psychiatric Association 1994) there are several DSM diagnoses that have been criticized for being included without a sufficient rationale or evidence-base (e.g. depression—van Praag 1998; acute stress disorder—Harvey and Bryant 2002; personality disorders—Bornstein 2003; Widiger and Chaynes 2003).

The approach to classification adopted by the DSM and ICD systems is known as the 'syndromal approach' in that it uses groups of signs (what the clinician sees) and symptoms (what the patient reports) to identify disease entities (syndromes). These signs and symptoms are conceived as pointers to a disease with a known aetiology, course, and response to treatment. While this is realistic in some areas of medicine, this approach has been criticized for its use in the classification of psychological disorders because knowledge of psychological disorders is not sufficiently well-advanced for this ideal to be achieved. Yet the DSM is widely used and it dominates research programmes and often also treatment services (Follette and Houts 1996). As such, the DSM is a key driving force to the 'disorder-focus' that currently dominates the field. Despite the disadvantages of classification systems, many in the field point to their heuristic value (Brown and Chorpita 1996) and their utility (Kendell and Jablensky 2003).

Attempts are ongoing to improve on the syndromal approach. One alternative, born within the tradition of behaviour therapy, is the functional approach (for review see Haynes and O'Brien 1990). This approach relies on a thorough functional analysis, for each individual patient, involving (1) the identification of the client's problematic behaviour and the context in which it occurs, (2) formulation of the information gathered so as to identify causal relationships, (3) use of this formulation to collect additional information and finalize the formulation, (4) the development of an intervention based on Step 3, and then (5) implementation of the intervention and assessment of change. Then, if the treatment does not reduce the problematic behaviour, Step 2 is reconsidered. A number of problems with this approach have been highlighted (Hayes and Follette 1992). For example, it is difficult to replicate any one functional analysis and therefore the approach cannot be empirically verified. Relatedly, functional analysis relies heavily on clinical judgement. In response to these criticisms, Steven Hayes and his colleagues (1996) have proposed a different approach. Their proposal is that functional diagnostic dimensions, or common processes of aetiology or maintenance, should be the basis for research and clinical practice. Hayes *et al.* (1996) have demonstrated the utility of this approach with *experiential avoidance* by drawing on evidence suggesting that attempts to avoid internal experiences (thoughts, feelings, and sensations) is (1) a process that is common across disorders and is (2) implicated in the maintenance of disorders. Similarly, Ingram (1990) has proposed that self-focused attention is a common process across psychological disorders. Consistent with this hypothesis, Woodruff-Borden *et al.* (2001) found that the self-reported tendency to self-focus is common to several diagnostic groups (depression, panic disorder, other anxiety disorders) and that more self-focus was associated with more severe psychopathology (self-focused attention is discussed in more detail in Chapter 2). Thus, a case can be made that at least two cognitive and behavioural processes are functional diagnostic dimensions (Hayes *et al.'s* term) or transdiagnostic processes. This raises the possibility that there may be value in examining a wider set of processes across disorders.

Consistently, yet coming from a different theoretical tradition is the proposal that the current classification systems are a 'straitjacket for conceptual progress' (p. 767, van Praag 1998). Van Praag argues for an approach to depression research which involves the 'dissection of the prevailing syndrome(s) in its (their) component parts (i.e. a series of psychological dysfunctions). Those dysfunctions should be charted and measured, whenever possible, quantitatively' (p. 771, van Praag 1998).

Finally, Christopher Fairburn and his colleagues (2003) have convincingly argued that the various eating disorders that have been defined in the DSM (anorexia nervosa, bulimia nervosa, atypical eating disorder) are maintained by similar processes. On this basis Fairburn *et al.* proposed a transdiagnostic theory and treatment of eating disorders. Towards the end of their paper, Fairburn *et al.* highlight that their 'transdiagnostic approach to theory and treatment has implications beyond the field of eating disorders' (p. 524, Fairburn *et al.* 2003). It is these implications that we seek to explore in this book.

To summarize, the dominant classification systems are consistent with, and may well be key to driving the disorder-focus of most present day research. The alternative approaches involving functional diagnostic dimensions (Hayes *et al.* 1996), the identification of specific dysfunctions (van Praag 1998) and challenging the DSM-defined boundaries between disorders (Fairburn *et al.* 2003) are all consistent with, and encompass, the transdiagnostic perspective that will be evaluated in this book.

Advantages of a transdiagnostic perspective

In this section we will consider the potential advantages of a transdiagnostic perspective.

Comorbidity

Individuals seeking psychological services rarely present with a pure case of just one psychological disorder. The case of Bill, as described in Box 1.2, reflects the reality and complexity of much clinical practice. When assessing and treating Bill it would be necessary, as a minimum, to consider the following diagnoses: social phobia, PTSD, schizophrenia, psychosis, depression, and generalized anxiety disorder (GAD). One potential advantage of a transdiagnostic perspective is that it may provide an explanation for the high rates of comorbidity observed in clinical practice.

Box 1.2 The reality of clinical practice: a complex case

It is a hot July day as Bill walks hesitantly down his local high street. Today, like most days over the last two years, he expects to be attacked by a stranger when walking around outside. Most of the time when he is out he keeps his eyes to the ground. He does not want to meet eye-to-eye with another man incase the eye contact is taken as a provocation. A little later he notices that he is feeling hot and sweaty in his leather jacket. He thinks 'other people are thinking I'm an idiot wearing a leather jacket on a hot day like this'. He wants to take his jacket off 'But, if I take my jacket off...' he gets a fleeting image of himself fearful, wide-eyed, with thin and pasty arms, weak and vulnerable. This makes him feel anxious. Then he catches the turn of someone's head out of the corner of his eye and he speedily scans round at the people in his vicinity. He sees two men walking towards him and looking at him. His eyes meet their eyes and for a moment his gaze is transfixed, 'I'm in danger, I must get out of here' he concludes. Bill then looks around for an escape route 'Ah!—an alleyway!'. He swiftly turns down the alleyway and heads in the direction of home. When he gets home, memories of this frightening event flood back into his mind and he spends several hours worrying about whether the people he had seen would follow him home and attack him.

This description was provided by Bill, a 35-year-old man, during an assessment for therapy. Bill described this experience as typical for any occasion he ventures out of the house. Several months before the assessment he had been hospitalized with a diagnosis of paranoid psychosis. At the time he was admitted to hospital, he had thought that the people he passed on the street were shouting out his name and talking about him. These symptoms soon remitted and Bill was discharged and rediagnosed with social phobia, PTSD and major depression. Other information obtained during the assessment included that Bill had lost his job two years before, after being threatened and beaten up by a drunk colleague. His symptoms had emerged at this time. He experienced frequent, distressing memories and nightmares of the assault, and had become extremely wary of being attacked. He tried to push the memories of the assault out of his mind and he tried to convince himself that the assault had never happened. He had become very hopeless about his chances of ever getting better. He often asked himself why he always felt so bad and why he had so many more nasty experiences than everyone else in the world.

The results of the National Comorbidity Survey make a strong case for the relative rarity of 'pure' cases (Kessler *et al.* 1994). The National Comorbidity Survey was an epidemiological study, involving 65 244 adults in the United States between 15 and 54 years of age. As it was conducted during the early 1990s, the diagnoses were based on the DSM-III-R criteria (American Psychiatric Association 1987). The 12-month and lifetime prevalence of 14 DSM-III-R psychological disorders were assessed (see Box 1.3 for the list of disorders included). The term '12-month prevalence' refers to the percentage of participants meeting diagnostic criteria for one or more disorder anytime during the 12 months prior to the survey. The term 'lifetime prevalence' refers to the percentage of participants meeting diagnostic criteria for one or more disorder anytime during their lifetime. As can be seen in Box 1.4, almost 50% of respondents reported at least one lifetime disorder. The key result of interest is that the vast majority of the lifetime disorders (79.4%) were comorbid disorders (i.e. 25.5% had two lifetime disorders, 53.9% had three or more lifetime disorders). Further, 89.5% of severe disorders occurred in just 14% of the sample, with these people having a lifetime history of three or more

Box 1.3 The disorders assessed in the National Comorbidity Survey (Kessler *et al.* 1994)

Major depression
Mania
Dysthymia
Panic disorder
Agoraphobia
Social phobia
Simple phobia
Generalized anxiety disorder
Alcohol abuse
Alcohol dependence
Drug abuse
Drug dependence
Antisocial personality disorder
Nonaffective psychosis (a summary category that included schizophrenia, schizophreniform disorder, schizoaffective disorder, delusional disorder, and atypical psychosis)

Box 1.4. Results of the National Comorbidity Survey (Kessler et al. 1994)

No. of lifetime disorders	Proportion of sample	Proportion of lifetime disorders	Proportion of 12-month disorders	Proportion of respondents with severe 12-month disorders
0	52.0%	N/A	N/A	N/A
1	21.0%	20.6%	17.4%	2.6%
2	13.0%	25.5%	23.1%	7.9%
3+	14.0%	53.9%	58.9%	89.5%

Note. Severe 12-month disorders were defined as '(1) 12-month mania or non-affective psychosis, (2) lifetime mania or non-affective psychosis with 12-month treatment or role impairment, (3) 12-month depression or panic disorder with severe impairment (hospitalization or use of antipsychotic medication)'. (p. 9)

Adapted with permission from Kessler R.C. *et al.* (1994). Lifetime and 12-month prevalence of DSM-III-R psychiatric disorders in the United States. *Archives of General Psychiatry,* **51**, p. 13. Copyright 1994 by American Medical Association. All rights reserved.

disorders. Further highlighting the considerable comorbidity, Kessler *et al.* (1994) concluded that people who suffered from psychological disorders suffered, on average, 2.1 disorders per person. As already highlighted, 14 DSM-III-R disorders were assessed in the National Comorbidity Survey. As there are well over 200 adult disorders listed in the DSM-III-R, the patterns of comorbidity are likely to markedly change if different disorders, or a greater range of disorders, were assessed. Also, as only lifetime and 12-month prevalence were assessed, there is no guarantee that a person had more than one disorder at the same time. Hence, investigations of point prevalence are required to more fully examine the issue of comorbidity. The term 'point prevalence' refers to the number of participants meeting diagnostic criteria for one or more disorder at the time of the survey. But before moving on to consider investigations of point prevalence, it is important to emphasize that the National Comorbidity Survey is not alone in documenting the high rates of comorbidity. Similarly high rates have been reported in two other large studies; the Epidemiological Catchment Area Study (Regier *et al.* 1990; Robins *et al.* 1991) and in an international survey conducted in general health care (Ustun *et al.* 1995).

Moving on to studies of point prevalence, Timothy Brown and David Barlow (1992) investigated the point prevalence of anxiety disorders and depression among individuals presenting to a treatment clinic ($n = 468$). The rate of comorbidity was high with 50% of the participants with a principal anxiety disorder having at least one additional anxiety disorder or depression at the time of the assessment (Brown and Barlow 1992). A range of other studies of point prevalence uncovered similarly high rates of comorbidity among the anxiety disorders and depression (e.g. Sanderson *et al.* 1990; Carter *et al.* 2001). Box 1.5 presents data demonstrating that these high rates of comorbidity occur across a wide range of disorders.

Several accounts of the high rate of comorbidity among the psychological disorders have been proposed. First, they may reflect poor discriminant validity in that the DSM may distinguish between disorders that it would be better to combine (Blashfield 1990; Brown and Barlow 1992; Andrews 1996). However, Brown *et al.* (1998) have reported good discriminant validity for the anxiety disorders. Second, features of one disorder may act as risk factors for other psychological disorders. To give an example, insomnia is a well-established risk factor for the development of first-onset depression (e.g. Ford and Kamerow 1989), anxiety disorder (e.g. Breslau *et al.* 1997) and substance abuse (Weissman *et al.* 1997) so it is not surprising that insomnia is highly comorbid with these disorders (Harvey 2001*b*). Third, comorbidity may reflect a common vulnerability. Examples of factors implicated in vulnerability to develop an anxiety disorder include anxiety sensitivity (Reiss and McNally 1985),

Box 1.5. Examples of the high lifetime comorbidity across psychological disorders: a selective review

Psychological disorders	Comorbidity	Authors
Eating disorders and anxiety disorders	70–80%	Schwalberg *et al.* (1992)
GAD and depression	80%	Judd *et al.* (1998)
Insomnia and another psychological disorder	52%	Tan *et al.* (1984)
Drug-dependence and another psychological disorder	45%	Farrell *et al.* (2001)
Bipolar disorder and another psychological disorder	61%	Taman and Ozpoyraz (2002)
Schizophrenia and another psychological disorder	32%	Goodwin *et al.* (2003)

neuroticism (Eysenck 1973), and high trait anxiety and poor coping (Andrews 1996). A final possibility, and the one that is core to the aim of this book, is that perhaps psychological disorders co-occur because they share maintaining processes. Accordingly, we hypothesize that a transdiagnostic perspective has potential to provide a parsimonious account of comorbidity across the psychological disorders. This account is not necessarily inconsistent with the other accounts of comorbidity presented but it provides an additional explanation.

As an aside, we note that when a patient presents with one or more disorders, clinicians and researchers often try to identify the 'primary' disorder and treat it in the hope that the 'secondary' disorder/s will then spontaneously remit. However, there are significant problems in determining which is the 'primary' disorder leading some researchers to alter the terminology away from primary diagnosis versus secondary diagnosis towards principal diagnosis versus additional diagnosis (Brown and Barlow 1992). Klerman (1990) has highlighted three other approaches; the primary disorder could be the one that:

1. came first temporally (i.e. on the basis of chronology);

2. caused the other disorders (i.e. on the basis of causality);

3. is associated with the greatest distress or life interference (i.e. on the basis of symptomatic predominance).

Relying on chronology (point 1) requires reliance on the client's self-report as to which disorder occurred first. As we will discuss in Chapter 3, retrospective recall of symptoms can be inaccurate. Without the benefit of systematic prospective assessments, it seems unlikely that the original cause could be accurately determined (point 2). We agree with Brown and Barlow (1992) that if a clinician was to adopt one of these strategies, the third is the most viable as the disorder causing the most distress and impairment can be ascertained by asking the client[1] and then the treatment delivered will be one that addresses the client's prime concern. This is likely to increase the acceptability of the treatment to the patient. However, if a transdiagnostic perspective turns out to be viable, it may generate a fourth way to assess and treat patients presenting with comorbid disorders. The assessment and treatment would be targeted at the *processes* in common *across* the comorbid disorders. To summarize, we suggest that one advantage of a transdiagnostic perspective is that it may provide a fuller understanding of the high rates of comorbidity and, in turn, may provide a map for treating cases characterized by comorbidity.

Treatment development

A second advantage is that a transdiagnostic perspective would encourage greater transfer of theoretical and treatment advances between the disorders. This already happens to some extent. For example, early advances in the theory and treatment of OCD (Salkovskis 1985), panic disorder (Clark 1986) and hypochondriasis (Salkovskis and Warwick 1986) are evident in recent advances in the theory and treatment of psychosis (Morrison *et al.* 1995), social phobia (Clark and Wells 1995), body dysmorphic disorder (Veale *et al.* 1996), PTSD (Ehlers and Clark 2000), insomnia (Harvey 2002*a*) and depersonalization disorder (Hunter *et al.* 2003). However, perusal of the dates of these papers suggests that the transfer is relatively slow. Our hope is that the transdiagnostic perspective will lead to the more rapid transfer of advances to a broader range of disorders. Another possibility is that a transdiagnostic approach might lead the field to be able to specify a single treatment or treatment components that are effective across a wide range of disorders. Although it seems unlikely, given the reality of clinical practice, that there will ever be a 'one size fits all' treatment approach.

Response to treatment

A third advantage of a transdiagnostic perspective is that it has potential to explain some interesting findings. Most randomized controlled trials (RCTs)

---

[1] see Di Nardo *et al.* (1994) and Brown *et al.* (2001) for a method that systematically and reliably establishes level of distress and impairment present.

seek to treat one disorder. Thus, at the pre-treatment and post-treatment assessments, the presence and severity of this one target disorder is assessed. However, just a handful of RCTs have included pre-treatment and post-treatment assessments for a range of psychological disorders, even though the treatment was targeting just one disorder. The interesting result to have emerged from these studies is that the disorders that were not the prime target of the intervention can respond similarly to the treatment. For example, CBT targeting panic disorder and agoraphobia in 51 patients reduced the prevalence and/or severity of comorbid anxiety disorders and depression (Tsao *et al.* 2002). At the beginning of treatment, 31 of the participants (60.8%) had an additional diagnosis; 33% had a comorbid diagnosis of GAD, 16% had specific phobia, 18% had depression, 14% had social phobia, and 4% had a comorbid diagnosis of OCD. Immediately following the treatment, 39% of the participants who had a comorbid diagnosis prior to the treatment had fully remitted and the severity ratings of the comorbid disorders markedly reduced as a result of the treatment and were maintained 6 months later. A similar pattern of findings, with a variety of disorders, has been reported by several other research groups (e.g. Brown and Barlow 1992; Borkovec *et al.* 1995; Brown *et al.* 1995; Bélanger *et al.* in press).

There are at least two possible accounts of these findings. First, perhaps they reflect poor discriminant validity in the DSM system. That is, perhaps the DSM is discriminating between disorders that are not truly different (but as already noted, Brown *et al.* (1998) have demonstrated good discriminant validity for the anxiety disorders). Alternatively, it may be that the psychological disorders share common maintaining processes (an implication of the transdiagnostic perspective). It would then follow that a treatment that reverses the maintaining processes in one disorder should lead to an improvement in all disorders present. Given that we know that theoretical developments can lead to improvements in treatment outcome (Clark 1997), an interesting possibility is whether the positive treatment effects for comorbid disorders might be further maximized if the treatment was conceived of, and delivered, within a transdiagnostic perspective.

Disadvantages of a transdiagnostic perspective

One limitation of a transdiagnostic perspective is that it cannot explain why people with different psychological disorders can present so differently. For example, patients diagnosed with OCD (recurrent obsessions experienced as intrusive and inappropriate and compulsions such as hand washing and repeating words silently) present with very different symptoms relative to patients who present with insomnia (chronic difficulty initiating and maintaining sleep and daytime tiredness). Why is this? Accounting for the differences is likely to be a major challenge to a transdiagnostic perspective.

One possibility, that we will explore in the chapters that follow, is that the differences between psychological disorders may be, at least partly, accounted for by the different concerns inherent to each disorder. The idea of current concerns has been most developed within Eric Klinger's current concerns theory (1975, 1977, 1987, 1996). Klinger defines a current concern as a non-conscious (latent) processing state initiated when a person commits to pursue a specific goal, which lasts until the goal is either achieved or discarded, and which underpins the goal pursuit by sensitizing emotional responses to and cognitive processing of cues associated with that goal (Klinger 1996). As described in Box 1.6, several experimental studies indicate that thought content is triggered by, and reflects, ones' current concerns. To give a clinical example, anorexia nervosa is characterized by concerns about weight and shape. A woman with anorexia nervosa may be committed to the goal of preventing weight gain. In pursuing this goal, she would become more sensitive to the cues that are associated with this goal. For example, she would automatically be more attentive to any signs of weight gain which, if detected, would trigger emotional reactions such as fear or disgust. It is also likely that a patient suffering from anorexia nervosa would worry about her body weight and shape and spend time planning how to lose more weight. For further examples of the salient concerns of various psychological disorders see Box 1.7.

In this book, we will consider whether the cognitive and behavioural processes could be common across disorders and still produce disorder-specific presentations because the exact clinical presentation would depend upon the interaction between the processes and the concerns.

How will the transdiagnostic process perspective be evaluated?

The cognitive behavioural processes

The term 'process' literally means 'the progress or course of something', 'a natural or involuntary operation or series of changes' (p. 1065, Oxford English Dictionary; Pearsall and Trumble 1996). In this book we will use the term 'process' to refer more specifically to an aspect of cognition (e.g. attention, memory, thought, reasoning) or behaviour (e.g. overt or subtle avoidance) that may contribute to the maintenance of a psychological disorder.

In recent years there has been a proliferation of theoretical models focused on specific disorders that specify the cognitive and behavioural processes that maintain that particular disorder. Most of these derive from the pioneering

Box 1.6 Experimental studies of current concerns

Dichotic Listening Studies (Cox and Klinger 1988; Klinger and Kroll-Mensing 1995).

Participants: Student volunteers.

Task: During a dichotic listening task two different sets of auditory stimuli are presented simultaneously, one to each ear, using headphones. In these experiments participants were asked to simultaneously listen to two narratives, one of which included pre-identified personal concern words, the other of which included non-concern words.

Result: Participants spent more time listening to, recalled better and had more thought content related to the narrative with personal concern words inserted than the narrative with non-concern words inserted.

Conclusion: Current concerns influenced attention, memory, and thought content.

Dream Studies (Hoelscher *et al.* 1981; Nikles *et al.* 1998)

Participants: Normal volunteers.

Task: Current concerns were identified by prior interview. Participants were then presented with current concern or non-concern words, either as prompts before they went to sleep or during sleep. Participants were then woken during REM sleep and asked to report their dreams.

Result: Participants more often reported dreams related to concern-related than to non-concern-related cues.

Conclusion: The content of dream imagery reflected the content of the current concern words.

work of Aaron T. Beck on depression (Beck *et al.* 1979, 1985). For example, disorder-focused models have been proposed for panic disorder (Clark 1986; Barlow 1988), social phobia (Clark and Wells 1995; Rapee and Heimberg 1997), OCD (Salkovskis *et al.* 1998; Rachman 2002), bulimia nervosa (Fairburn 1997), insomnia (Lundh 1998; Harvey 2002*a*), PTSD (Foa and Kozak 1986; Brewin *et al.* 1996; Ehlers and Clark 2000), GAD (Wells 1995; Borkovec *et al.* 1998), impotence (Barlow *et al.* 1983; Barlow 1986), hypochondriasis (Salkovskis and Warwick 1986) and depersonalization disorder (Hunter *et al.* 2003). The aim of these disorder-focused models has been to specify how the cognitive behavioural processes operate within one specific psychological disorder. One reason for the proliferation in disorder-focused models is that

Box 1.7. Examples of salient current concerns for different psychological disorders

Psychological disorder	Current concern
Panic disorder	Changes in body sensations indicate an imminent physical catastrophe, such as suffocation or a heart attack (Clark 1986).
Specific phobia	The dangerousness of the phobic object and one's reactions to it (Arntz *et al.* 1993; Thorpe and Salkovskis 1995).
Social phobia	Being scrutinized, embarrassed, or humiliated in a social situation (American Psychiatric Association 1994, 2001).
OCD	Intrusive thoughts indicating responsibility for harm to others (Salkovskis 1985).
PTSD/ASD	Current threat of harm and concern about one's reactions to a past trauma (Ehlers and Clark 2000).
GAD	A non-specific range of possible dangers (American Psychiatric Association 1994, 2001). The consequences of worrying (Wells 1995).
Somatoform disorder	The negative consequences of potential illness (American Psychiatric Association 1994, 2001).
Eating disorder	Overconcern about body weight and shape (Fairburn 1997).
Sleep disorder	The consequences of inadequate quality and quantity of sleep. Concern about daytime performance being impaired by poor sleep (Harvey 2002*a*).
Psychotic disorder	Imminent attack or persecution by other people (American Psychiatric Association 1994, 2001). Holding culturally unacceptable beliefs (Morrison 2001).
Unipolar depression	Concerns about loss of acceptability and worth (American Psychiatric Association 1994, 2001).

theoretical models of disorders tend to generate systematic empirical research and, in turn, highly effective treatments (Salkovskis 2002).

A slightly different endeavour has been to try to specify how the cognitive and behavioural processes fit together more generally. Examples of theories that fall within this category are Interacting Cognitive Subsystems (ICS; Teasdale and Barnard 1993), Schematic Propositional Associative Analogue Representation Systems (SPAARS; Power and Dalgleish 1997), Self-Referent Executive Function Model (S-Ref; Wells and Mathews 1994), and work by Williams *et al.* (1988, 1997). At various points throughout this book, we will be referring to these general models, as well as the disorder-focused models. For now, we turn to introduce the processes to be discussed within this book by presenting the details of one disorder-focused model, the cognitive model of social phobia proposed by David Clark and Adrian Wells (1995; see also Rapee and Heimberg 1997 for a parallel conceptualization). To some degree the processes specified in the model of social phobia have been hypothesized as important in the majority of disorder-focused CBT models. So we are using the model of social phobia as an illustrative case to introduce the cognitive and behavioural processes of interest within this book.

The key cognitive and behavioural processes specified by Clark and Wells (1995) to maintain social phobia are summarized below in terms of the processes operating prior to entering a social situation, during a social situation, and on leaving a social situation.

1. Prior to entering a social situation

Clark and Wells (1995) suggest that, on anticipating a social situation, individuals with social phobia *selectively retrieve* negative information about how they think they are typically seen by others. They then dwell on or *ruminate* about this information before entering the situation. They ruminate about how to behave appropriately but they are insecure about their ability to do so, fearing that they will appear socially inept to others. Rumination serves to maintain the social anxiety because the content is dominated by past social failures and predictions of poor performance. It may lead the person to avoid the situation completely or to enter the situation in an already self-focused state.

2. During a social situation

The Clark and Wells model regards the process of *self-focused attention* as crucial to the maintenance of social phobia. Clark and Wells suggest that when in a self-focused state, individuals with social phobia use information from internal cues to derive information about how they are being (negatively) evaluated by others. They become trapped in a closed system in which most of the evidence for their fears is generated from internal cues. Examples of internal cues are feelings of trembling, sweating, blushing, tension, and subjective difficulty talking. These cues contribute to an impression of how the individual thinks he/she appears to others, which may occur as a 'felt sense' or as an image. An example of a felt sense is one patient's compelling feeling that the strong shaking sensations in her hands must mean that others could see her hands trembling violently. Whereas, in fact, other people could only see a mild tremor or nothing at all. In terms of images, individuals with social phobia typically view themselves from the perspective of the other people around them (i.e. observer perspective images). These *recurrent images* are thought to maintain social phobia because when in a social situation, individuals with social phobia pay relatively little attention to their external environment. Instead, they use information from distorted, negative images of themselves, from an observer perspective, to infer how they come across. The images contain exaggerations of their anxiety symptoms, such as streams of sweat or bright red blushing, or other distortions in appearance, such as a humiliated posture.

Avoidance of a feared social situation maintains social anxiety by preventing the disconfirmation of fears of rejection. Clark and Wells emphasize that avoidance during a social situation can be overt (e.g. leave a social gathering early) or more subtle (e.g. avoiding eye contact). These behaviours are called 'within-situation safety behaviours' or just 'safety behaviours' (Salkovskis 1989, 1991). In social phobia, safety behaviours are often intended to improve performance or hide a perceived inadequacy, thereby preventing a social catastrophe such as rejection. However, many safety behaviours actually make the person with social phobia feel more anxious and may make them appear distant or aloof to other people. For example, a patient who is worried that he may say something stupid will try to prevent this by comparing what he is about to say with everything he has said in the last few minutes. This safety behaviour will result in him appearing less involved in the conversation and will prevent disconfirmation of his belief that he is in danger of being seen as stupid. The safety behaviours used will be unique to each individual because they will be linked to specific feared outcomes. Taking another example, a patient feared that her trembling hands would be seen by others as a sign of weakness. In response, she would half-fill her glass and grip it tightly while drinking. Gripping the glass turned out, paradoxically, to increase the amount of trembling (Clark and Wells 1995).

3. On leaving a social situation

After leaving a feared social situation, individuals with social phobia *selectively retrieve* and dwell on the anxious feelings and negative self-perceptions from the conversation, leading the person to *interpret* the situation as overly negative. The individual with social phobia will then *ruminate* about how they came across. This has been called the 'post-mortem'. During the 'post-mortem', patients with social phobia often dwell on things that they did or said during the encounter which, in retrospect, they think indicated a serious social error. As a consequence, they conclude that things went even less well than they had thought when they first left the interaction. They may choose to avoid similar encounters in future, or to enter them and cope by adopting safety behaviours. Both of these actions would ultimately serve to maintain their social fears.

Summary

This theoretical conceptualization of social phobia specifies a role for several cognitive and behavioural processes:

- *Attentional processes*, particularly self-focused attention during a social situation, serves to heighten awareness of internal cues (e.g. trembling, sweating) which, in turn, confirm the patient's view that they are appearing socially inept to others.

- *Memory processes*, particularly selective retrieval of perceived social disasters in the past, serves to increase anxiety and self-focused attention prior to entering a social situation. Also, following a social situation clients with social phobia may selectively remember the anxious feelings and negative self-perceptions they experienced during the social situation. Recurrent images of past failures are also important in the maintenance of social phobia.

- *Reasoning processes*, such as the interpretative bias evident on leaving the social situation (i.e. 'that was a disaster and confirms that I'm a social misfit'), are also important in the maintenance of social phobia.

- *Thought processes*, particularly rumination, come to the fore prior to entering a social situation, when past failures are reviewed, and on leaving the social situation (the post-mortem).

- *Behavioural processes*, in the form of avoidance and safety behaviours, serve to prevent disconfirmation of the patients' beliefs and can also make a feared outcome more likely to occur.

Although we have reviewed these processes with respect to social phobia, an examination of other disorder-focused CBT models reveals that these different processes are included in many other models. Accordingly, in this book, we will take these five cognitive behavioural processes and examine the extent to which they are important *across* the psychological disorders. In Chapter 2 we will discuss the evidence pertaining to selective attention towards concern-related information in the external environment, particularly sources of threat and safety. We will also discuss the evidence for attention towards internal stimuli. In Chapter 3 we will consider memory processes, especially those that appear to enhance access to, and impair access to, concern-related information. In Chapters 4 and 5 we will review how reasoning processes and thought processes, respectively, operate across the disorders. Finally, in Chapter 6 we will discuss the role of behavioural processes including avoidance and safety-seeking.

The psychological disorders

Whilst reviewing the evidence for these five cognitive and behavioural processes across disorders, we have limited ourselves to the adult Axis 1 disorders specified by the DSM-IV. The categories of disorders that we have included in our survey of the literature are listed below, along with examples of the specific disorders that comprise each broad category.

1. Anxiety disorders: panic disorder with and without agoraphobia, specific phobia, social phobia, OCD, PTSD, ASD, and GAD.

2. Somatoform disorders: somatization disorder, conversion disorder, pain disorder, hypochondriasis, and body dysmorphic disorder (BDD).

3. Dissociative disorders: dissociative amnesia, dissociative fugue, dissociative identity disorder and depersonalization disorder.

4. Sexual and gender identity disorders: sexual dysfunction (e.g. orgasmic disorder, sexual pain disorder), paraphilias, and gender identity disorder.

5. Eating disorders: anorexia nervosa and bulimia nervosa.

6. Sleep disorders: primary insomnia and primary hypersomnia.

7. Impulse control disorders: gambling, kleptomania, and pyromania.

8. Mood disorders: major depressive disorder, dysthymic disorder, and bipolar disorder.

9. Schizophrenia and other psychotic disorders: schizophrenia, schizophreniform disorder, schizoaffective disorder, delusional disorder, and brief psychotic disorder.

10. Substance-related disorders: substance use disorders and substance-induced disorders.

We realize that by adopting the DSM system as our organizing structure that we are in fact adopting a perspective that is opposite (in being disorder-focused) to the one that is the motivation for this book (the transdiagnostic perspective). The disadvantages of this strategy are that we are bound to the system and will adhere to the disorders covered by the classification, sometimes excluding clinically interesting phenomena (e.g. anger, hostility) (Brown *et al.* 1998). The advantages of this strategy are that the research evidence that will be needed to evaluate the utility of a transdiagnostic perspective almost exclusively uses the DSM system. We have not discussed the child, adult Axis 2 disorders, and a handful of adult Axis 1 disorders (e.g. factitious disorders, delirium, dementia, and amnestic and other cognitive disorders) because there is less empirical research relating to cognitive behavioural processes in these domains.

Quality of evidence

As we began writing this book, it became clear that we needed a means of clearly and accurately summarizing the research conducted across the disorders for each of the cognitive behavioural processes. Accordingly, towards the end of each chapter we have included a summary table in which we indicate, for each cognitive behavioural process and each psychological disorder, the quality of the evidence that has accrued. Extending work by Chambless (1996), the three quality levels that we have used are explained below.

1. Good quality evidence

Good quality evidence is indicated in the table at the end of each of Chapters 2–6 by '***'. Good quality evidence is declared if the following criteria are met:

- Two or more studies have been conducted that:
  - have used a psychometrically validated instrument to diagnose a patient sample (e.g. Structured Clinical Interview for the DSM-IV, SCID; Spitzer *et al.* 1996) and;
  - have utilized more than one paradigm such that there is convergent evidence from two or more of the following: interview, self-report, experimental, or prospective studies and;
  - are methodologically strong (including consideration of power and appropriate comparisons groups) and;
  - have been reported by at least two independent research groups.

2. Moderate quality evidence

Moderate quality evidence is indicated in the table at the end of each of Chapters 2–6 by '**'. Moderate quality evidence is declared if the criteria for good quality evidence are not met but the following criteria are met:

- One or more studies have been conducted but:
  - the patient sample was not diagnosed using a psychometrically validated instrument and/or;

- only one paradigm has been employed (i.e. the finding has not yet been replicated with alternative methodology) and/or;
- only one research group has investigated the process and;
- at least one study is methodologically strong (including consideration of power and appropriate comparisons groups).

3. Tentative quality evidence

Tentative quality evidence is indicated in the table at the end of each of Chapters 2–6 by '*'. This level of evidence is declared if the conditions for good and moderate quality evidence are not met. Examples of scenarios when tentative quality evidence will be applied are:

- the studies are all based on non-patient (analogue) samples;
- a patient study has been conducted but there are methodological problems (i.e. inadequate power or absence of a comparison group);
- the study was a single case study.

Within the tables we have also included an indication of the findings for each cognitive behavioural process and each psychological disorder. The three levels, and their definition, are:

1. Positive evidence

Positive evidence is indicated in the table at the end of each of the chapters by '+' and is declared when *all* of the studies reported positive findings.

2. Negative evidence

Negative evidence is indicated in the table at the end of each of the chapters by '-' and is declared when *all* of the studies reported negative findings.

3. Mixed evidence

Mixed evidence is indicated in the table at the end of each of the chapters by '+/-' and is declared when a mix of findings, some positive and some negative, are reported.

We recognize at the outset that this categorization is somewhat crude. For example, we would have much less confidence in a finding reported by two studies, that would qualify for *** (good quality evidence), as compared to a finding reported by seven studies, that would also qualify for *** (good quality evidence). Similarly, we have declared mixed evidence (+/-) even if only one negative finding was reported in a sea of positive findings. While we justify this on the basis of the bias against the publication of negative findings, we realize that it may, in some cases, lead to an overly conservative conclusion.

Research samples

In this book we have generally limited ourselves to reviewing studies that have recruited people carefully diagnosed with a psychological disorder. Having said that, we recognize that there is likely to be a continuum between studies based on treatment seeking patient samples and studies based on non-patient samples who are manipulated into a 'state' that resembles the disorder of interest in some way (i.e. analogue samples). In between these two end points are studies based on patient samples who are not currently treatment-seeking (who may differ in some respects from their treatment-seeking counterparts) and studies based on non-clinical participants who do not fully meet criteria for the disorder but display sub-threshold levels of the key symptoms (e.g. high worry or high social anxiety). While we will be focusing on studies based on patient samples, we will occasionally refer to particularly notable analogue studies. One advantage of analogue studies is that they have allowed researchers to develop and test novel experimental paradigms and new concepts in an efficient and timely manner (Stopa and Clark 2001). As such, many of the ideas discussed throughout this book have attracted empirical investigation because of research initially conducted with analogue samples. Of course, the disadvantage of analogue research is that the general-izablity of the findings to treatment-seeking patient samples needs to be demonstrated.

Aims and summary

To summarize, our overall aim in writing this book is to examine the utility of a transdiagnostic process perspective. We begin by advancing the hypothesis that psychological disorders are more similar than different in terms of the cognitive behavioural processes that maintain them. We will test this hypothesis by reviewing the scientific literature across a range of adult Axis 1 disorders in order to determine which cognitive behavioural processes are common across the disorders, and which are distinct. We are encouraged to consider that this hypothesis is plausible by:

1. the high rates of comorbidity across the disorders and the finding that a treatment focused on one specific disorder can improve other comorbid disorders that were not the target of intervention.

2. research suggesting that experiential avoidance (Hayes *et al.* 1996) and self-focused attention (Ingram 1990) are processes common across disorders.

3. the consistent inclusion of attentional processes, memory processes, reasoning processes, thought processes, and behavioural processes in disorder-focused CBT models.

The potential implications of a transdiagnostic perspective, if found to have utility, include (1) that it may encourage rapid transfer of advances made in the context of one disorder to other disorders and (2) that it may encourage the emergence of a transdiagnostic treatment, or transdiagnostic treatment approaches, especially for patients with comorbid problems. However, we emphasize that there has been, and will continue to be, utility in the disorder-focused theories. We also emphasize the importance of not glossing over the differences between the disorders.

In the five chapters that follow we will take one set of cognitive behavioural processes at a time and examine them across each of the adult Axis 1 disorders with a view to establishing the extent to which each process is common across the disorders. For each process we will declare our level of confidence, based on the empirical evidence, that each process is transdiagnostic according to the following criteria:

1. A *definite transdiagnostic process* will be declared if the majority of evidence, which must be of at least moderate quality, indicates that the process is present in *all of the disorders* in which it has been investigated. As a minimum, the process must have been investigated in four or more disorders. Processes that meet this stringent definition will be referred to as a *definite transdiagnostic process*.

2. A *possible transdiagnostic process* will be declared if the evidence is suggestive, but more research is needed. This definition is satisfied if the majority of evidence, which must be of at least moderate quality, indicates that the process is present in *at least two disorders*. The process may be found to be absent in at least one disorder. Processes that meet this less stringent definition will be referred to as a *possible transdiagnostic process*.

In these definitions two terms need to be operationalized. The 'majority of evidence' is operationalized as the presence of '+' (as defined on page 22) in each disorder in which the process has been investigated. 'At least moderate quality evidence' is operationalized as the presence of '**', as defined on page 21.

Chapter 2

Attention

Harry was a 36-year-old man who had been diagnosed with schizophrenia in his late adolescence. He was troubled by thoughts with a sexual content. Whenever he experienced these thoughts, he became extremely anxious because he believed that other people could read his mind and were therefore disgusted by him. Often when Harry was in a situation with many other people, such as a bar, restaurant, or cinema, he would begin to get distracted by things around him. In particular, he would notice that strangers in the room were coughing, turning their head towards him, or saying things that related to him. He believed these were 'signals' that his thoughts had been broadcast into other people's minds. He would find himself noticing these signals even if he tried to ignore them. As he started to focus on them, he would find it very difficult to concentrate on what he was currently doing. For example, if he was having a conversation he would find it hard to follow what was said. He gradually became more convinced that his thoughts had been broadcast and so he would avoid looking at anybody for fear that they would approach him and attack him because they now knew he was a 'freak' and a 'pervert'; they had seen his disgusting thoughts and he was too afraid to look at them to see their response. He called this behaviour, of avoiding looking at anybody, 'going into his shell'. In order to avoid focusing on his environment, Harry's attention would be drawn inwards and towards his own disturbing thoughts. As he did this, he experienced a feeling of 'his mind opening up'. Following the intense anxiety of experiences of this kind, Harry would avoid going out of his home for several days, convinced that he would be attacked if he did so.

This clinical case demonstrates the processes of attention in a man diagnosed with schizophrenia. Harry showed *selective attention* for certain stimuli (e.g. coughs) at the expense of other stimuli (e.g. the conversation). As a consequence, he was particularly good at detecting certain stimuli (especially social cues that he thought were 'signals' that his thoughts were being broadcast). Later on, he switched to avoiding attending to his environment (attentional avoidance) and he focused on 'internal' stimuli (i.e. those going on in his own mind or his own body). This is typically known as *self-focused attention*.

The events to which Harry attends appear to be systematic rather than random; they are the stimuli that are personally significant for him. Sometimes he attends to sources of threat (other people sending out 'signals') and at other times he avoids the sources of threat in an effort to escape being attacked ('going into his shell'). At some moments he appears to choose what he attends to (e.g. avoiding looking at other people), whereas at other points he seems to find himself attending to a certain stimulus without intending to do so (e.g. people coughing). In other words, sometimes his attention is *controlled* and at other times it is *automatic.* It is also clear from this case that Harry's attention is very easily caught by different new events and he spends very little time attending to any one of these stimuli before his attention goes elsewhere. In other words he shows high *distractibility*.

This chapter will begin by defining the key concepts within attention research. Then the evidence across psychological disorders will be reviewed. In particular, we will focus on determining the extent to which attentional processes are truly transdiagnostic, and/or whether they are distinct to particular disorders.

What is selective attention?

Each moment in time our senses are bombarded by a vast array of information. Yet, our experience at any one point is dominated by some stimuli at the expense of others. The concept of selective attention goes back at least as far as the early psychologist, William James (1890/1950), who stated that 'my experience is what I agree to attend to' (p. 402). Thus, selective attention refers to a process by which specific stimuli, within the external and internal environment, are selected for further processing. The 'further processing' may be reasoning, thought, or the generation of a plan of action, and these processes, covered later in the book, are not to be confused with selective attention itself. Selective attention refers to the initial filtering of stimuli rather than their continued processing.

Several other terms have been used when investigating selective attention. An *attentional bias* refers to the observation that some groups of individuals, such as people with anxiety disorders, have a systematic tendency to attend to a particular class of stimuli. For example, patients with GAD appear to show an attentional bias to threatening words. A systematic tendency to avoid attending to certain stimuli (attentional avoidance) would also be regarded as an attentional bias. Hypervigilance is another term used to describe selective attention to threatening information in the anxiety disorders.

The processes of selective attention have been traditionally divided into automatic and controlled processes. Attention may occur in an automatic manner. That is, the person is either unaware that their attention has been drawn to a particular stimulus, or they may feel that their attention is out of their own control. An example is the experience of being distracted by a sudden moving object like a bird or a ball. Alternatively, selective attention may be a controlled process. That is, the person reports that they had consciously planned to attend to a specific stimulus. An example would be deliberately focusing on a person who is coming towards you on the street in order to work out who it is. While some cognitive theories suggest that automatic and controlled processes are qualitatively distinct (Norman and Shallice

1986), other theorists have suggested that they lie on a continuum that varies depending on the context (Neumann 1984). Indeed, it has been proposed that automatic and controlled processes can be closely related within the anxiety disorders and other forms of psychopathology (Mansell 2000). Importantly, both automatic and controlled processing are commonplace features of the human information processing system. For example, when driving we need to react instantaneously and automatically when encountering a red light, yet we are not always aware of this process. Examples of this kind are supported by detailed experimental research. This has led to the conclusion that most everyday behaviours are triggered, and often maintained, in an automatic manner such that they free up resources and thereby maximize the efficiency with which we operate in the world (Raichle 1997).

Self-focused attention

Self-focused attention has been defined as 'an awareness of self referent, internally generated information that stands in contrast to an awareness of externally generated information derived through sensory receptors' (p.156, Ingram 1990). As such, self-focused attention includes awareness of physical state, feelings, thoughts, emotions, and memories. As already highlighted in Chapter 1, self-focused attention is a common process across a range of psychological disorders (Ingram 1990; Wells 2000), particularly when the self-focused attention is excessive, sustained, and rigid. For example, Woodruff-Borden *et al.* (2001) found that the self-reported tendency to self-focus is common to depression, panic disorder, and other anxiety disorders and that greater the self-focus, the more severe the psychopathology.

Following Rick Ingram (1990), the term self-focused attention will be used in this book to refer to the initial attention to internally generated stimuli, such as bodily sensations and thoughts. The term will not be used to refer to the ongoing processes of thinking, ruminating, and reasoning about the self, which are discussed in Chapters 4 and 5. The term will also not be used to refer to the extent to which the person perceives himself or herself to be the subject of other people's attention, which is better described as 'public self-consciousness' or 'perceived social evaluation'.

How is selective attention measured?

Researchers have developed many different experimental paradigms to index attention in a standardized manner. Each relies on an indirect measure of selective attention and so each misses, to some degree, the complexities of a real-life situation. The degree to which the paradigm sensitively and reliably measures selective attention would reflect its internal validity, whereas the extent to which the paradigm applies to and captures everyday situations reflects its external (or ecological) validity.

Self-report measures

The simplest method to assess attention is to ask people. Self-report measures index how much the individual reports attending to the stimulus identified. Some of these scales are trait measures, asking people to report how much they tend to attend to the stimulus on a day-to-day basis. Other scales are state measures, enquiring about how much the individual has attended to the stimulus over a specific recent period of time. Box 2.1 provides some examples of self-report measures of selective attention.

There are at least two advantages of self-report measures. First, they are easy to use in clinical practice where other methods may not be available. Second, attention to certain stimuli, such as thoughts and bodily sensations, may be difficult to assess in other ways. However, there are many drawbacks to self-report measures. First, they tend to tap a broad range of processes other than attention. For example, the Private Self-consciousness Scale (Fenigstein *et al.* 1975) includes items such as 'I am always trying to figure myself out'. This seems to pertain to a style of thinking rather than the content of selective attention. Second, self-report scales are prone to biases and inaccuracies in memory because they are completed retrospectively. This is an issue we will return to in Chapter 3. Finally, self-report measures cannot provide information about automatic processes that are too quick or subtle for the person to notice.

The emotional Stroop task

The emotional Stroop task is one of the most commonly used methods to assess attention. In the original Stroop task (Stroop 1935), the participants were presented with a list of the names of colours, such as 'blue' and 'red'. The instruction was to read, out loud, the colour in which the words were printed and ignore the content of the word. Time taken to name the colour was compared in two conditions. In the first, the colour in which the word was printed was consistent with the colour content of the word (e.g. the word 'blue' was printed in blue ink). In the second, the two were inconsistent. That is, the word 'red' was printed in blue ink. Not surprisingly, the result was that participants took longer to name the colour when it was inconsistent with the content of the word. That is, participants were slower to say 'blue' when reading the word 'red' in blue ink. It has been proposed that the participants' selective attention to the content of the word interfered with their response to name the colour of the ink.

Box 2.1 Examples of self-report measures of selective attention

Name of measure	Description	Sample items
Private Self-consciousness Scale (Fenigstein et al. 1975)	This is a 10-item trait measure of *Inner State Awareness* and *Self-Reflectiveness*	'I am alert to changes in my mood' 'I am generally attentive to my inner feelings'
Focus of Attention Questionnaire (Woody 1996)	This 10-item scale has been used in social phobia. It is a state measure and has separate scales for *self-focused* and *other-focused* attention.	'I was focusing on what to do or say next' 'I was focusing on my level of anxiety' 'I was focusing on the other person's appearance or dress' 'I was focusing on what the other person was saying or doing'.
The Pain Vigilance and Awareness Questionnaire (McCracken 1997)	This 16-item scale assesses attention to pain over the last two weeks.	'I am quick to notice changes in pain intensity' 'I focus on sensations of pain' 'I notice pain even if I am busy in another activity'
The Somatosensory Amplification Scale (Barsky et al. 1990)	This 10-item scale includes items that assess attention, as well as fear of bodily changes.	'I am often aware of the various things happening within my body' 'I can sometimes hear my pulse or my heartbeat throbbing in my ear'
The Autonomic Perception Questionnaire (Mandler et al. 1958)	This 21-item scale assesses the general disposition to perceive a range of bodily sensations that are each rated on a line scale.	'Muscles becoming tense' 'Changes in heart action' 'Face becoming hot' 'Breathing becoming deeper'

In the 1980s and 90s the Stroop task was adapted by replacing the colour words with emotional words. The typical design involved selecting emotional words that were relevant to the disorder of interest and comparing the time taken to colour-name these words (e.g. 'death', 'blood', 'injury' for PTSD to the time taken to colour-name neutral words, matched for word length and frequency (e.g. 'ethic', 'tinted', 'formal'). Certain studies have included positive words to establish whether a participant is just responding to emotional words in general, regardless of valence (e.g. 'love', 'kind', 'happy'). Neutral words from a specific category (e.g. 'table', 'oven', 'stool') might also be included to rule out the possibility that the participant is just responding to words within a category rather than words with a particular meaning. In the first of many studies, Mathews and MacLeod (1985) found that people with GAD took longer to colour-name threat words than control words.

Clearly, it is significant that the presentation of an emotional word can significantly interfere with one's performance on a neutral task, such as colour-naming. However, it is not clear that this effect is actually a result of selective attention to the word, because the longer time taken to colour-name could be caused by other factors. First, the threatening words may create an emotional reaction, such as a startle, that inhibits any response and leads to longer reaction times. Second, the emotional Stroop effect may be capturing 'cognitive avoidance', in that the longer colour-naming latencies may simply reflect attempts by the individual to suppress the threatening meaning of the word (Ruiter and Brosschot 1994). A third possibility is that the emotional Stroop effect is reflecting mental pre-occupation with themes related to the emotional words (Wells and Matthews 1994).

A further adaptation of the emotional Stroop task has involved presenting the word cue very briefly (10–50 ms) and then immediately presenting a 'mask' of jumbled letters. The word cue is presented so briefly that the participants cannot consciously report or recognize seeing the words, and yet the content of the word has been shown to influence the time taken to name the colour of the mask. It is commonly thought that attentional paradigms involving these brief masked stimuli assess automatic attentional processes, whereas paradigms that involve presenting unmasked stimuli for a longer period (750–2000 ms) assess controlled processes (Mathews 1997; Mogg and Bradley 1998). In several studies the effects of the masked emotional Stroop are greater than the non-masked version (e.g. MacLeod and Hagan 1992; van den Hout *et al.* 1995), suggesting that this paradigm may be a more accurate reflection of the automatic processes of selective attention (Williams *et al.* 1996). Some studies have found that the masked and unmasked emotional Stroop effects are uncorrelated (e.g. Lundh *et al.* 1999), suggesting that they may measure different processes.

Detection tasks

If an individual selectively attends to a certain class of stimuli, then it follows that the person will be faster at detecting these stimuli. That is, detection is assumed to provide an index of selective attention. One commonly used detection task is the visual search task (e.g. Gilboa-Schectman *et al.* 1999). The participant is presented with an array of stimuli, and they must detect a target stimulus within this array as quickly as possible. The visual search task has also been adapted in an attempt to index the extent to which certain stimuli distract or capture attention. Selective attention is inferred from the extent to which the stimuli surrounding the target stimulus slow down the speed with which it is detected. See Box 2.2 for a more detailed explanation of the detection paradigm and the distraction paradigm.

Dichotic listening task

In the dichotic listening task the participants wear a pair of headphones and they read out loud a story that is being played to them through one ear—the

Box 2.2 The visual search task

The visual search task is used to assess selective attention in two different ways: detection and distraction.

Detection paradigm

Participants are presented with two kinds of arrays (shown below). One kind of array contains one negative target, whereas the other kind of array contains one neutral target. Each time, on each trial, the target is in a different position and on some trials no target is displayed within the array. The participant is asked to detect the target as fast as possible by pressing a button. Attentional bias to negative stimuli is inferred from faster reaction times to arrays with a negative target than arrays with a neutral target.

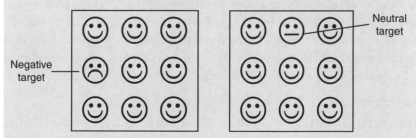

Box 2.2 **The visual search task** *(continued)*

Distraction paradigm

Participants are presented with two kinds of arrays (shown below). One kind of array contains negative distractors whereas the other kind of array contains neutral distractors. On each trial a discrepant stimulus is in a different position, and on some trials no discrepant stimulus is displayed within the array. Again, the participant is asked to detect a discrepant stimulus as fast as possible by pressing a button. Attentional bias to negative stimuli is inferred from slower reaction times to arrays with negative distractors than arrays with neutral distractors.

Negative Distractors

Neutral Distractors

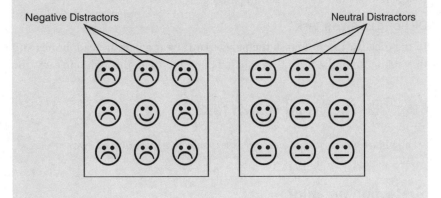

'attended channel' (e.g. Mathews and MacLeod 1986). However, threat and non-threat words are played on the 'unattended channel'. At the same time, the participant engages in a visual reaction time task in which they are asked to press a button as fast as possible as soon as they detect the word 'press' (the visual probe) on the computer screen in front of them. The visual probe is timed to appear on the computer screen immediately after the presentation of a word in the unattended channel. Attentional bias to threat words is indexed by a slower response to the visual probe when a threat word is played in the unattended channel, compared to the reaction time when a non-threat word is played in the unattended channel.

Dot-probe task

In both the emotional Stroop and dichotic listening tasks, greater selective attention to a particular stimulus is indexed by a longer time to respond. However, as already mentioned, there can be a variety of reasons, other than selective attention, for a longer response time. For this reason, Colin MacLeod and his colleagues (1986) adapted another task from cognitive psychology, known as the dot-probe task (Posner *et al.* 1980). The dot-probe task is regarded as a less ambiguous measure of selective attention because it is indexed by a *shorter* latency to respond (Dalgleish and Watts 1990). This task is displayed in Fig. 2.1. The participant is first instructed to fix his/her eyes on a cross presented in the centre of the screen for 1000 ms. Next, the cross is replaced by two word stimuli, typically one above the other. In early versions of this task, the cues included one emotional word and one neutral word. The participant's task is to read the top word out loud. Next, the pair of words is replaced by a dot that appears in the spatial location of one of the two words. The participant's task is to press the response button as fast as possible when s/he detects a dot on the computer screen. The response time to the dot is recorded. Then the next trial begins. The degree of selective attention to the emotional words is calculated by subtracting the time taken to respond to the dot-probes in the spatial location of the neutral word from the time taken to respond to the dot-probes in the spatial location of the emotional word. Thus, if the participant attends to the emotional word, rather than the neutral word, they would be quicker to respond to the dot-probes that appear in the same spatial location as the emotional word. Across the whole task, the spatial location of the emotional cue (upper vs lower) and the spatial location of the

1. Fixate on cross
(1000 ms)

2. Read top word out loud
(500 ms)

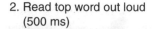

DEATH ◄

APRIL ◄

Neutral word

Emotional word

3. Press button as soon see
dot on the screen

4. Begin next trial

Fig. 2.1 Illustration of the modified dot-probe task.

dot-probe (upper vs lower) are balanced. Note that the dot-probe task is truly selective, in contrast to the emotional Stroop task, in the sense that two cues are presented simultaneously on a computer screen and the response time indicates preferential processing of one cue relative to the other cue.

The dot-probe task has been used extensively to assess selective attention in psychological disorders, and is probably the most direct and versatile measure of selective attention. It has been modified in many ways. For example, the presentation time of the cues has been varied to explore the time course of selective attention, including brief masked stimuli as used in the emotional Stroop (e.g. Mogg *et al.* 1995*a*). In this version of the task, the participant does not read the top word out loud. The cues have also been modified to improve the ecological validity of the task by including faces, other pictures, and 'internal' stimuli (e.g. the pain induced by a mild electric shock and displays of heart rate change).

Eye tracker (visual scanpath)

Most of the paradigms described thus far assess attention in a relatively indirect way. However, some researchers have used a more direct method involving an apparatus called an eye tracker. These kinds of studies are also known as visual scanpath studies (e.g. Loughland *et al.* 2002). The eye tracker directly assesses where, in a presented picture, people focus their eye gaze over time. Examples of the results of a visual scanpath study are shown in Fig. 2.2. This paradigm provides a very accurate way to measure the stimuli that are in the centre of one's vision (within the fovea of the eye). However, most of us have had the experience of being able to attend to things 'out of the corner of our eyes'. Therefore, one disadvantage of the eye tracker paradigm is that, unlike the other paradigms discussed, it cannot measure covert attention. That is, it cannot measure attention to a region of space that is independent of eye movement.

In summary, many different paradigms have been used in an attempt to index selective attention. Each of them has advantages and disadvantages. They vary to the extent that they have controlled for other factors and have incorporated ecologically valid stimuli within a real-world environment. In reviewing the literature, we will take care to sample convergent evidence from a variety of paradigms.

To what kind of stimuli do people selectively attend?

The cognitive psychology literature suggests a variety of external and internal stimuli to which people are more likely to attend. Across the modalities, stimuli that are novel are more likely to attract attention (e.g. Johnston *et al.* 1990).

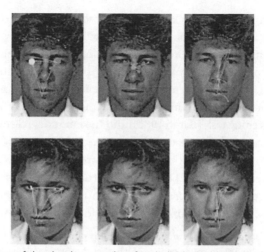

Fig. 2.2 Illustration of the visual scanpaths of an individual with no psychological disorder (left images), with schizophrenia (middle images) and with an affective disorder (right images). Dot size indicates number of fixations. (Reprinted from *Biological Psychiatry*, 52, Loughland, C.M., Williams, L. M., and Gordon, E. (2002), *Schizophrenia and affective disorder show different visual scanning behaviour for faces: a trait versus state-based distinction*, pp 338–48, Copyright 2002 with permission from Society of Biological Psychiatry.)

Stimuli that have certain physical properties attract attention, such as bright visual stimuli (Luck and Thomas 1999), moving stimuli (Washburn and Putney 1998), and intensely painful stimuli (Eccleston and Crombez 1999). If we take an evolutionary perspective, it makes sense that these kinds of stimuli would hold immediate meaning because they may indicate a source of reward, such as a nutritious food or a source of danger, such as a looming attacker. These kinds of stimuli have been described as 'prepared' in the sense that we have an innate sensitivity to detect and respond to these stimuli (Seligman 1971). Consistent with this view, several studies have shown that people generally attend to prepared stimuli that are both rewarding and threatening. For example, selective attention to food-related words is increased after fasting in non-patient participants (Lavy and van den Hout 1993; Mogg *et al.* 1998; Placanica *et al.* 2002). In terms of threatening stimuli, Mogg and colleagues have used the dot-probe task to demonstrate that non-patient populations selectively attend to images of highly threatening scenes more than images of mildly threatening scenes, which tend to be avoided (Mogg *et al.* 2000*a*). Others have demonstrated that angry faces are detected more quickly relative to happy faces in a visual search paradigm (Fox *et al.* 2000).

As already highlighted in Chapter 1, people also attend to their current concerns. That is, to the stimuli that are particularly personally meaningful to them at that time (Klinger 1996). Research using the dot-probe paradigm has shown that people selectively attend to previously neutral stimuli that has been conditioned to be threatening through being paired with an aversive outcome in the form of a loud white noise (Stormark *et al.* 1999). Studies using the dichotic listening task (Bargh 1982), and the emotional Stroop task (Bargh and Pratto 1986) have demonstrated that non-patient samples show selective attention to words that reflect concerns that are personally relevant to them. In the same vein, Dalgleish (1995) found that bird-watchers selectively attended to bird-related words. Edith Lavy and Marcel van den Hout (1994) provided a concise summary of the current evidence:

> attentional bias may occur for any stimulus that is of immediate personal relevance and that elicits an urge to act, regardless of whether this urge is related to (cognitive or motoric) approach or (cognitive or motoric) avoidance (p. 189, Lavy and van den Hout, 1994).

The above definition helps explain the observation that people may also direct their attention *away* from threat and towards sources of safety when they are attempting to escape danger. Kavin Mogg and Brendan Bradley and their colleagues have suggested that all clinical anxiety states may be associated with faster detection of possible threat stimuli and a subsequent avoidance of such information which, in turn, prevents habituation and objective evaluation of the stimuli (e.g. Mogg *et al.* 1997). This would lead the stimuli to maintain their propensity to evoke an anxiety reaction. Thus, people with an anxiety disorder would automatically attend to relevant threats in potentially dangerous environments, but seek to escape and avoid further danger as soon as they perceive it (probably in a controlled manner). The role of attentional avoidance, or attention to safety, in psychological disorders will also be assessed in this chapter.

To summarize, people attend to stimuli that are relevant to their current concerns either owing to their prepared nature or their acquired meaning, or both.

Selective attention

We will now turn to review the extent to which selective attention is transdiagnostic. In particular, we will focus on three processes that fall under the broad umbrella of selective attention: (1) attention to concern-relevant external stimuli, (2) attention to concern-relevant internal stimuli (self-focused attention) and (3) attentional avoidance and attention towards sources of safety. Note that throughout this chapter we use the term 'selective attention' interchangeably with the term 'attentional bias'. In the section that follows, we will seek to ascertain the extent to which the attentional biases tend to be automatic or controlled and whether these processes have been captured using ecologically valid designs.

Anxiety disorders

Panic disorder with and without agoraphobia

Several studies that have indexed performance on the emotional Stroop indicate that people with panic disorder are slower to name the colours of physical threat words such as 'collapse', 'coronary', and 'suffocate' (e.g. Ehlers *et al.* 1988; Hope *et al.* 1990), even when the words are masked (Lundh *et al.* 1999). Further, using the modified dot-probe task, one study has shown that people with panic disorder selectively attended to brief, masked physical threat words (Mathews *et al.* 1996). However, Lars-Gunnar Lundh and his colleagues found that a Stroop interference effect for masked threat words was related to general anxiety and depression rather than to the specific fear of bodily sensations (Lundh *et al.* 1999). Also, there have been failures to replicate the finding of an attentional bias to physical threat words (e.g. Horenstein and Segui 1997; Kampman *et al.* 2002). The literature is also mixed as to the specificity of the colour-naming bias, with some studies finding that people with panic disorder are also slower to name the colours of social threat words (Ehlers *et al.* 1988; Maidenberg *et al.* 1996), whereas other emotional Stroop studies have found the effect to be specific to physical threat words (e.g. Hope *et al.* 1990; Lundh *et al.* 1999). Two studies have investigated whether the attentional bias in patients with panic disorder is affected by context but no differential effects were identified; Hayward *et al.* (1994) examined the context of a public place and McNally *et al.* (1992) examined the context of elevated arousal.

It has been proposed that the primary concern of people with panic disorder is the threatening nature of their own internal physical sensations (Clark 1986). Therefore, studies have been designed to investigate attention to changes in these sensations in an ecologically valid manner. A self-report study found that patients with panic disorder reported greater vigilance to internal physical sensations than patients with social phobia and non-patient controls (Schmidt *et al.* 1997). An example of the kinds of sensations reported by people with panic disorder are the tingling fingers, dizziness, and unreality that can be induced by instructing people to hyperventilate (i.e. breathe deeply at a fast rate). A study that explored the effects of hyperventilatory sensations on performance on an attention-demanding task found no evidence of an attentional bias in panic disorder (Kroeze and van den Hout 2000*a*). However, these same researchers found that panic patients did selectively attend to a visual display of their heartbeat, relative to controls, in a modified dot-probe task (Kroeze and van den Hout 2000*b*). In an alternative modified probe paradigm (Ehlers and Breuer 1995), the participants were divided into four groups: panic disorder, specific phobia, infrequent panickers, and non-patient controls. The participants placed a finger of each hand on an apparatus that occasionally transmitted a small vibration. The participants were instructed to respond as fast as possible to each vibration (neutral probe). Intermittently, they were also subjected to a mild electric shock (physical threat cue) on either hand immediately prior to the onset of the vibration. In this study, both patient groups and the infrequent panickers selectively attended to the physical threat cue relative to the non-patient controls. Thus, panic disorder was associated with an attentional bias to a real physical threat stimulus, but it was not a specific feature of panic disorder. Similar results have been found using a paradigm in which participants are instructed to estimate their own heart rate. In a meta-analysis of this research, patients with panic disorder were more accurate than non-patient controls and patients with depression at detecting their heartbeats (van der Does *et al.* 2000). However, this analysis also indicated that accurate heart beat awareness is not common, even within panic disorder; only a minority of the patients actually had an accurate awareness of their heartbeat. Also, people with other anxiety disorders including social phobia, GAD, and specific phobia, also showed relatively higher levels of accuracy.

In summary, there is broad but not entirely consistent support for the view that people with panic disorder selectively attend to physical threat words reflecting their primary concerns. The two studies using masked stimuli suggest that these processes may be automatic. In some studies, people with panic disorder also show attention to social threat words, indicating that social threat may also be a concern for these patients. Although only a few studies have used more ecologically valid designs, these have indicated an attentional bias towards bodily sensations in patients with a range of anxiety disorders, not just panic disorder.

Specific phobia

Specific phobia is a good candidate for exploring attentional bias to threat, as the threatening object or situation is identified in the diagnosis. In some studies, people with spider phobia have shown longer colour-naming on the emotional Stroop task to concern-relevant words such as 'hairy', 'spider', and 'crawling' (e.g. Watts *et al.* 1986; Kindt and Brosschot 1997). Although one study found that the concern-relevant bias was also evident for masked concern-relevant words (van den Hout *et al.* 1997), another found the bias for unmasked but not masked words (Thorpe and Salkovskis 1997). Therefore, the evidence is mixed as to whether selective attention to concern-related words in specific phobia reflects an automatic process. There have also been failures to find evidence of an attentional bias for relevant words in blood-injury-phobia (Sawchuk *et al.* 1999) and driving phobia (Bryant and Harvey 1995*b*). Also, the only dot-probe study we found did not report evidence of an attentional bias to relevant threat words in students with mild clinical phobias (Wenzel and Holt 1999). Therefore, the evidence suggests that people with specific phobias selectively attend to words related to their fears but this may be absent in phobias of certain stimuli, or in mild clinical phobias. The evidence relating to whether the effect is automatic is mixed.

Several paradigms have directly assessed selective attention to more ecologically valid stimuli in the context of specific phobia. Kindt and Brosschot (1997) found that people with spider phobia took longer to colour-name pictures of spiders, relative to non-patient controls, on a modified emotional Stroop task. Using the visual search task, Öhman and colleagues found that spider fearful students were faster at detecting colour pictures of feared stimuli (spiders) relative to non-feared stimuli (snakes) in a visual array of fear-irrelevant stimuli, such as mushrooms and flowers (Öhman *et al.* 2001). Snake fearful students also showed faster detection of snakes relative to pictures of spiders. While this study used a creative ecologically valid design it has yet to be investigated in a patient sample.

Do people with specific phobia always selectively attend to signs of threat? Several studies indicate that in more real-world situations, patients with a specific phobia may be more motivated to avoid threat and direct their attention towards safety. For example, one study demonstrated that people with spider phobia were faster at responding to the presentation of the picture of a spider when this resulted in the immediate disappearance of the picture (Lavy *et al.* 1993*b*). The authors interpreted this finding as indicating that the faster response was motivated by the need to escape from the picture of the spider. In a particularly innovative study by Sue Thorpe and Paul Salkovskis (1998), people with spider phobia attended both to sources of threat and safety. This study is described in Box 2.3 and displayed in Fig. 2.3. A further example of avoidance was a study in which threatening stimuli were presented in a tachistoscope. Patients with spider phobia and blood injury phobia showed reduced viewing times to pictures relating to their specific fears, relative to control pictures, despite instructions to examine the pictures carefully in preparation for a subsequent recognition test (Tolin *et al.* 1999). The role of avoidance, escape, and safety-seeking behaviour is examined further in Chapter 6.

In summary, specific phobia may be associated with selective attention towards relevant stimuli, but most of the evidence is from the emotional

Box 2.3 Attention to threat and safety in a real phobic situation

The majority of studies of selective attention have used threat stimuli that are words, illustrations, or photographic images. Thorpe and Salkovskis (1998) developed a laboratory environment in which the stimulus was the real source of threat (a spider) and safety (a door to escape). People with a spider phobia were recruited to participate in this study. The hypothesis tested was that people with spider phobia would divide their attention between threat and safety, whereas controls would not show greater attention to either threat or safety.

Method

The participants were seated in a room in which the target stimulus (a light) was placed either by the door of the room or by the wall opposite the door. The participants were instructed to press a button as soon as they detected the light. Half of the participants carried out the task with a live Zebra Tarantula spider in the room. In one session the spider was by the door (threat and safety together) and in another session it was by the wall (threat and safety divided) (see Fig. 2.3).

Results

The findings indicated that the spider phobia group, but not the controls, were faster to detect the light when it occurred in the location where threat and safety were together, compared to when it occurred in the location where threat and safety were divided. The slowest reaction times for the spider phobia group were recorded in the condition in which the light was by the wall and the spider by the door.

Conclusions

The findings suggest that people with spider phobia attend to safety stimuli, as well as threat stimuli, in real life situations.

At home

Do you know anyone who is afraid of spiders? Where do they look when there is a spider in the room? Do they look for a way out? Or do they look for something to capture the spider in or kill the spider with? These would be examples of them attending to sources of safety. Do they look at the spider? If so, why?

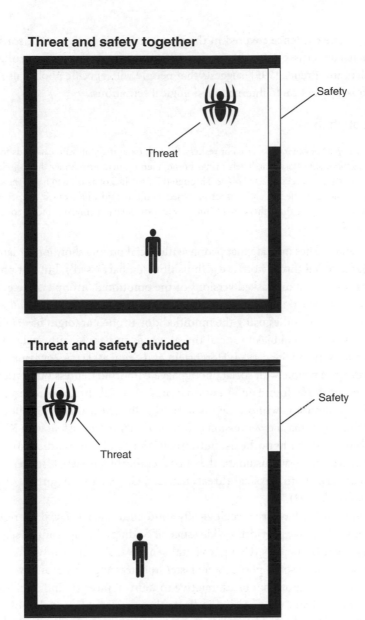

Fig. 2.3 Illustration of the Thorpe and Salkovskis (1998) study: Attention to threat and safety in spider phobia (see also Box 2.3).

Stroop paradigm. There have been difficulties in replicating the Stroop effect and in identifying selective attention using more stringent paradigms (e.g. dot-probe). Studies with greater ecological validity indicate that people with a specific phobia tend to avoid threatening stimuli and seek escape or safety. The evidence covered in the previous section on panic disorder, in which a specific phobia group was adopted as an anxious control group (Ehlers and Breuer 1995), suggests that people with specific phobia also show increased attention to internal physiological sensations.

Social phobia

> The eyes are generally averted or restless, for to look at the man who causes us to feel shame or shyness, immediately brings home in an intolerable manner the conscious-ness that his gaze is directed on us. Through the principal of associated habit, the same movements of the face and eyes are practised, and can hardly be avoided whenever we know or believe that others are blaming, or too strongly praising, our moral conduct. (p. 347, Darwin 1872).

Several studies indicate that people with social phobia show longer latencies to name social threat words (e.g. 'blushing', 'embarrassed'), but not physical threat words, on unmasked versions of the emotional Stroop task (e.g. Hope *et al.* 1990; Mattia *et al.* 1993; Maidenberg *et al.* 1996; Becker *et al.* 2001). However, two studies using the modified dot-probe paradigm have failed to find an attentional bias to social threat words in people with social phobia (Asmundson and Stein 1994; Horenstein and Segui 1997). A key issue may be whether the people with social phobia have comorbid depression. A modified dot-probe study found an attentional bias to social threat words in people with social phobia without depression, but this effect was absent in people with social phobia and depression (Musa *et al.* 2003). Consistent with Klinger's current concern hypothesis, patients with social phobia did not attend to physical threat words unless they had a comorbid anxiety disorder involv-ing concerns with physical threat; namely, GAD, panic disorder, or OCD (Musa *et al.* 2003).

Some studies have used ecologically valid cues, such as facial expressions. These studies have provided a wide range of findings that appear to depend on several subtle factors. Using a visual search task, one study has shown that people with social phobia were faster to detect angry faces and were more distracted by emotional faces, relative to neutral faces (Gilboa-Schectman *et al.* 1999). Thus, these studies indicate that people with social phobia may selectively attend to ecologically valid social threat cues. Further, this finding has been replicated using different experimental paradigms within analogue populations (Veljaca and Rapee 1998; Mogg and Bradley 2002).

In contrast to the above findings, observations such as those made by Charles Darwin and cited at the beginning of this section indicate that people with social phobia selectively avoid faces and other social cues. It is thought that avoidance serves to reduce social contact and therefore allows escape from a social catastrophe (Clark and Wells 1995; also see Chapter 6). Empirical research has confirmed these clinical observations. One study used a modified dot-probe paradigm in which photographs of face-object pairs were presented on a computer screen for 500 ms (see Fig. 2.4). People with social phobia selectively attended to the objects and away from the faces (Chen *et al.* 2002). A similar effect had been found in a sub-clinical socially anxious sample, although only to emotional faces, and only when the participants had been expecting to give a speech (Mansell *et al.* 1999). Supporting a similar conclusion, a visual scanpath study has demonstrated that people with social phobia avoid looking at facial features, particularly the eyes, compared to non-patient controls (Horley *et al.* 2003).

How can these studies be resolved with respect to one another? The studies finding evidence for an attentional bias towards threatening faces assessed the automatic stages of selective attention or they used detection paradigms which explicitly required participants to detect social threat. The studies that found

Fig. 2.4 Example of a negative (disgusted) face and a neutral object, similar to those used in the modified dot-probe study by Chen *et al.* (2002).

avoidance of threatening faces either (a) used longer display times, (b) induced a real social threat, or (c) assessed eye movement. Thus, a tentative conclusion is that when in non-threatening situations, people with social phobia may initially attend to threatening faces but avoid attending to them when they have sufficient time to move their eyes or where the social threat is more severe or enduring. Some further findings provide evidence for this view. Using a priming task, Nadir Amir and his colleagues found evidence for selective attention to social threat at 100 ms, followed by avoidance at 850 ms (Amir *et al.* 1998*b*). The same group of researchers found that the threat of a speech abolished the indications of selective attention towards social threat words, as measured by the emotional Stroop task (Amir *et al.* 1996).

The cognitive model of social phobia suggests that when people with social phobia selectively avoid social cues in their environment, their attention is drawn to internal stimuli (Clark and Wells 1995). A questionnaire-based study explored private and public self-consciousness in social phobia, panic disorder, OCD, and bulimia nervosa (Jostes *et al.* 1999). People with social phobia reported the highest levels of both public and private self-consciousness, with panic disorder and OCD scoring in between social phobia and the non-patient controls on these measures. Consistent with this evidence, people with social phobia report focusing attention on their own thoughts and behaviour during social situations more than non-patient controls (Woody and Rodriguez 2000), and this diminishes with successful treatment (Woody *et al.* 1997). Along with people with other anxiety disorders, patients with social phobia report being more aware of their bodily changes than non-patient controls (Edelmann and Baker 2002). In the meta-analysis of heart beat detection described earlier, a similar proportion of patients with social phobia as those with panic disorder were found to exhibit an accurate level of detection (van der Does *et al.* 2000). Further, two analogue studies that used novel paradigms have confirmed that high socially anxious individuals direct their attention away from external social threat and towards internal cues when faced with a socially threatening situation (Perowne and Mansell 2002; Mansell *et al.* 2003). However, in contrast to the evidence for heightened attention to internal cues in social phobia, a detailed study assessing participants' accuracy at detecting changes in their heart rate, sweating, and blushing during an anxiety-provoking conversation, found that people with social phobia were no more accurate than non-patient controls (Edelmann and Baker 2002).

In summary, the evidence suggests that people with social phobia may initially selectively attend to social threats in a potentially threatening social environment, such as other peoples' facial expressions. However, after a short time, or in clearly anxiety-provoking situations, they appear to attend away from other people. The evidence is also broadly consistent with the view that attention may be drawn to internal stimuli, such as thoughts and bodily reactions.

Obsessive compulsive disorder

Obsessive compulsive disorder is often characterized by checking behaviour (e.g. repeatedly looking at the controls on the oven to check that they are off). This clearly involves directing attention to stimuli in the environment that are related to patients' key concerns. However, the experimental evidence for a concern-related bias in OCD is mixed. Several emotional Stroop studies have found a specific attentional bias to concern-relevant threat words (e.g. Foa *et al.* 1993; Lavy *et al.* 1994), but other studies have not replicated these findings (e.g. Kyrios and Iob 1998; Kampman *et al.* 2002). One well-controlled study investigated selective attention to contamination words (e.g. 'dirty', 'infected') and social threat words using a modified dot-probe task in people with OCD, who had significant contamination concerns, and people with high levels of anxiety who were matched with the OCD group on mood (Tata *et al.* 1996). In support of the current concern hypothesis, the findings indicated a specific attentional bias for contamination words in the OCD group, and a specific attentional bias for social threat words in the high anxiety group.

Post-traumatic stress disorder

Elevated attention to signals of threat is one of the diagnostic features of PTSD (American Psychiatric Association 1994, 2001). Patients report that they are particularly aware of the dangers in their environment that remind them of their traumatic experience. So, for example, a person who developed PTSD after a road traffic accident would report being on the look out for possible dangers while driving.

Attentional bias to threat-related stimuli has been repeatedly demonstrated using the emotional Stroop in patients diagnosed with PTSD following rape (Foa *et al.* 1991), combat (McNally *et al.* 1993), ferry disaster (Thrasher *et al.* 1994), and road traffic accidents (Bryant and Harvey 1995*b*). However, there is some conflict in the literature as to whether the increased colour-naming latencies index automatic processes with one study identifying an automatic bias (Harvey *et al.* 1996), and two that have not (e.g. McNally *et al.* 1996; Paunovic *et al.* 2002). Also, mixed evidence exists as to whether selective attention is specific to trauma-related words. The majority of studies have provided evidence that the bias is specific (e.g. Foa *et al.* 1991; Thrasher *et al.* 1994; Kaspi *et al.* 1995; Vrana *et al.* 1995), whereas others have found indications of selective attention to general negative words (Buckley *et al.* 2002) and positive words (Paunovic *et al.* 2002). One study using the dot-probe (Bryant and Harvey 1997) and another assessing visual scanpaths (Bryant *et al.* 1995) found evidence for attention to relevant threat words. Overall, there appears to be reasonable evidence for attention to concern-related information in PTSD but there remains a lack of ecologically valid research. In one promising study, PTSD patients were found to be more easily distracted by trauma-relevant pictures than controls in a modified visual search paradigm (Chemtob *et al.* 1999).

Generalized anxiety disorder

People with a diagnosis of GAD worry about a wide range of different concerns. Therefore we would expect them to show selective attention to different kinds of threatening information. The evidence generally supports this conclusion. Early research using the emotional Stroop (Mathews and MacLeod 1985), the dichotic listening task (Mathews and MacLeod 1986) and the dot-probe task (MacLeod *et al.* 1986) indicated that people with GAD selectively attend to both social and physical threat words, compared to non-patient controls. These findings have been replicated (e.g. Becker *et al.* 2001). In further support of Klinger's (1996) current concern view, Mathews and MacLeod (1985) found that patients with worries about physical danger attended to physical threat words, although all patients selectively attended to social threat words.

The results suggest that the attentional bias in GAD may be automatic. For example, the participants who took part in the dichotic listening task made judgements about the words they had heard at chance level (Mathews and MacLeod 1986). Since then, this view has been supported in more thorough studies. For example, Karin Mogg and her colleagues found that people with GAD selectively attended to threat words that were presented for 14 ms and then masked (Mogg *et al.* 1995*a*). Nevertheless, the attentional bias may also be occurring in a controlled manner. A further study from this group of researchers used photographic pictures of facial expressions, instead of words, in a version of the dot-probe paradigm using stimulus durations of 500 ms and 1250 ms (Bradley *et al.* 1999). People with GAD selectively attended to angry, rather than neutral faces at both durations, in contrast to non-patient controls. In a subsequent study using an eye movement paradigm with a display time of 1000 ms, this finding was replicated for both angry and sad faces (Mogg *et al.* 2000*b*). The bias was not evident in people with GAD and concurrent depression, again indicating that comorbid depression may act to suppress biases in selective attention. Thus, it appears that GAD may be associated with automatic and controlled attention towards threat in the environment, such as angry reactions from other people. There appears to be no direct evidence that people with GAD direct their attention away from threat and towards sources of safety despite the extensive investigations using a paradigm (the dot-probe) that would have identified it. However, in Bradley et al.'s (1999) study, a bias towards happy faces emerged within the GAD group during the second half of the task, which could be interpreted as strategic attention to safe stimuli.

Few studies have investigated selective attention to internal stimuli in GAD, despite the importance of anxious feelings and worrying thoughts described by patients. Ehlers and Breuer (1992) found that GAD patients were more accurate at detecting their heart beats than non-patient controls. In an early study, patients with 'anxiety neurosis', along with patients with hypochondriasis, showed higher correspondence between their estimations of heart rate and an objective measure of heart rate, relative to participants with phobias (Tyrer et al. 1980). These findings suggest a heightened awareness of bodily function in GAD but it does not provide information specifically about attention to negative thoughts.

In summary, the evidence suggests that GAD is associated with attention to threatening words and face stimuli. There is also some evidence in support of attention to internal stimuli but mixed findings for attention to safety.

Somatoform disorders

Pain disorder

Evidence from a self-report study suggests that people with chronic pain who report attending to pain also report higher levels of pain intensity, emotional distress, and psychosocial disability (McCracken 1997). The Pain Vigilance and Awareness Questionnaire, as described in Box 2.1, was used in this study. The emotional Stroop paradigm has shown mixed results with respect to pain-related words in patients with pain disorders, although a meta-analysis of five studies indicated a significant effect (Roelofs et al. 2002). The only published dot-probe study we could identify found no evidence of an attentional bias, but there was an association between levels of general anxiety and attention to pain-related words (Asmundson et al. 1997). Another study indicated that the slower colour-naming of pain words on the emotional Stroop task was positively correlated with fear of pain (Snider et al. 2000).

One research group has explored attention to feelings of pain using a range of innovative experimental designs. Again, their evidence suggests that fear of pain is a more critical factor in selective attention than having pain disorder per se. Crombez and colleagues used a paradigm called the 'numerical interference test'. In this task, people are presented with two cards that each show an array of different quantities of digits (Crombez et al. 1999).

In the difficult version of the task, the participant must report the largest quantity of digits (e.g. seven) displayed on the two cards while ignoring the values of the digits (e.g. the number '8'). This is a demanding task that significantly taps attentional resources. Hence, decrements in performance are used to infer the degree of attention that is directed towards pain. Of course, like the emotional Stroop task, impaired performance could have an alternative explanation. Nonetheless, Crombez et al. (1999) reported that impaired performance on this task in a group of chronic pain patients was best predicted by an interaction between self-reported pain severity and pain-related fear. They developed a further task involving the detection of a tone while a mild pain-inducing shock was occasionally administered (Crombez et al. 2002). Among patients who experienced non-specific backpain, those who scored high on a measure of 'pain-catastrophizing' were slower to detect the tone when it followed the electric shock by 250 ms, but this effect disappeared (and non-significantly reversed) at 750 ms after the shock. This suggests that initial vigilance to the pain stimulus disappears over a short period of time.

While the above studies have not compared people with pain disorder to people without pain disorder, they provide evidence that anxiety concerning pain may show a similar pattern of attentional bias to that found in patients with anxiety disorders. Consistent with this view, instructions to distract from pain can lead to an increased tolerance of pain and less distress about pain in chronic pain patients (Harvey and McGuire 2000; Rode et al. 2001). The results of another study suggest that distraction may be more effective in managing the pain than attention towards pain in pain patients with low levels of health anxiety, but in patients with high levels of health anxiety the reverse occurs (Hadjistavropoulos et al. 2000). It appears that directing attention away from pain can be functional in some circumstances, although future research is necessary to determine the conditions under which attention towards or attention away from pain assists in pain management. In summary, several innovative experimental designs have been developed within the field of pain disorder, providing some evidence that fear of pain leads to selective attention to painful stimuli.

Hypochondriasis

People with medical conditions who report greater attention to somatic symptoms ('somatosensory amplification'—see Box 2.1) also show more discomfort and disability relating to their symptoms (Barsky et al. 1988). Self-reported attention to somatic symptoms (e.g. scanning body for aches and pains) was also found to be greater in a sample of people with hypochondriasis relative to a comparison sample of patients with a range of other psychological disorders (Barsky et al. 1990). Within this patient control group, the presence of clinical anxiety or depression was also associated with attention to somatic symptoms. This supports Ingram's (1990) view that people with psychological disorders have a general tendency to attend to internal stimuli. Nevertheless, the specific relationship between self-reported attention to somatic symptoms and hypochondriasis in this study remained, even when controlling for comorbid psychological disorders. One study demonstrated that instructing people with hypochondriasis to attend to their bodily sensations, led to even greater levels of symptom reporting (Haenen *et al.* 1996), providing evidence for a possible mediating role for attention. With regard to more objective measures, an early study of 'disease phobia' found that these individuals had lower thresholds for detecting the sensation of an electric shock before it was painful (Bianchi 1971). The study cited earlier by Tyrer *et al.* (1980) also indicated heightened bodily awareness in hypochondriasis. Similarly, a study of patients with mixed somatoform disorders found an increase in the accuracy of the perception of muscle tension relative to non-patient controls (Scholz *et al.* 2001). Thus, there is convergent evidence for attention to relevant internal stimuli in hypochondriasis, but little investigation of other attentional biases.

Body dysmorphic disorder

A common feature of body dysmorphic disorder (BDD) is a form of internally focused attention which involves extensive gazing at one's appearance in the mirror. In a self-report study, Veale and Riley (2001) found that patients with BDD engaged in longer and more frequent mirror gazing sessions than non-patient controls. During long sessions of mirror gazing, patients with BDD reported focusing more on their internal impression or feeling of how they appeared rather than their actual reflection. An emotional Stroop study found that people with BDD showed extended colour-naming latencies for emotional words compared to controls, but that the bias was greater for positive words relating to appearance (Buhlmann *et al.* 2002).

Sexual disorders

An interesting body of work exploring the effects of attentional focus on sexual arousal in people with sexual dysfunction has been developed by David Barlow and his colleagues. A key finding was that men with sexual dysfunction consistently underestimate the extent of their erections and are less accurate in their estimations relative to a group of non-patient controls (Sakheim *et al.* 1987). When encouraged to attend to their genital response, using video feedback, they became less aroused whereas non-patient controls become more aroused (Abramson *et al.* 1989). A similar finding occurs with external arousing stimuli, in that a film of a highly aroused woman led to less arousal in men with sexual dysfunction, but more arousal in the non-patient controls (Beck *et al.* 1983). One interpretation of these findings is that men with sexual dysfunction direct their attention away from internal and external arousing stimuli, possibly because their own lack of arousal is perceived as a threat to their sexual performance. Their reduced processing of arousing stimuli will feed into a vicious cycle of reduced sexual arousal.

Barlow (1986) has proposed that people with sexual dysfunction attend to non-sexual, task-irrelevant performance concerns (e.g. 'Am I doing it right?'). Therefore, one might expect men with sexual dysfunction to selectively attend to external threats to their performance, such as the evaluative facial expressions of their partner, and to focus internally on images about how they are seen by their partner or to negative thoughts about their performance, in a similar way to social phobia (Clark and Wells 1995). However, these studies have not been carried out. Further, no studies appear to have explored selective attention using better controlled paradigms (e.g. the dot-probe). Finally, we were not able to identify research on attentional bias in the paraphilias, where one would expect an attentional bias towards the sexual stimulus with which they were pre-occupied.

Eating disorders

The studies of attention have tended to group the different eating disorders together. Although the various eating disorders might exhibit common attentional processes (Fairburn 1997), grouping them in this way may obscure important differences. Several studies have indicated that people with an eating disorder show increased emotional Stroop interference for both food and body-shape related words (e.g. Perpina *et al.* 1993; Sackville *et al.* 1998). The findings have been replicated with body shape pictures (Walker *et al.* 1995). However, it should be noted that there have also been some failures to replicate the emotional Stroop effect (e.g. Fassino *et al.* 2002). Furthermore, a small body of evidence suggests that eating disorders are associated with an attentional bias to threatening self-relevant information beyond parameters of weight and shape. For example, an emotional Stroop study reported by Freda McManus and her colleagues (1996) found that people with bulimia nervosa were slower than controls to colour-name a range of different categories of threat words such as those relating to separation (e.g. 'isolated') and social anxiety (e.g. 'ridiculed'), but in particular those that reflected a threat to one's self-esteem (e.g. 'failure').

A better controlled measure of attentional bias has been used in one study of people with eating disorders. Reiger *et al.* (1998) explored selective attention to body shape and food words using a dot-probe paradigm. These researchers found that people with eating disorders (anorexia nervosa and bulimia nervosa) selectively attended towards words denoting a large physique but tended to avoid words denoting a thin physique. In a study based on an analogue population, Placanica *et al.* (2002) explored the effects of fasting on attentional bias to food words and body shape and weight words. All participants show an attentional bias towards high-calorie food words when they fasted. In addition, while in a non-fasted state, people with high scores on the Eating Disorder Inventory (EDI-2; Garner 1991) showed an attentional bias specifically for low-calorie food words. The authors suggested that the attentional bias reflected the cycle of high-calorie bingeing when hungry and low-calorie food selections when less hungry. These findings provide a more detailed analysis of attention than earlier emotional Stroop studies, and are encouraging for future research.

There is little evidence of attention to internal stimuli in eating disorders. Jostes *et al.* (1999) found that, unlike social phobia and OCD, people with bulimia nervosa did not differ from non-patient controls in private self-consciousness. To date, no studies appear to have explored attention to obviously relevant internal stimuli, such as thoughts about food, feelings of fullness, and parts of one's body. One exception is a study using an eye tracker, which demonstrated that patients spent more time looking at parts of their body with which they were dissatisfied, in contrast to non-patient controls (Freeman *et al.* 1991). However, the study did not directly assess whether attention was directed towards internal versus external stimuli.

Sleep disorders

One study found no evidence of emotional Stroop interference for sleep-related words in people with insomnia, relative to non-patient controls (Lundh *et al.* 1997), whereas another study found that emotional Stroop interference to sleep-related words was greater in people with persistent insomnia relative to those who had recovered from their insomnia (Taylor *et al.* in press). Other research suggests that attention to internal and external sleep-related threats is higher among individuals with insomnia relative to good sleepers (Harvey 2002*a*; Neitzert Semler and Harvey, in press-*a*,*b*). Examples of attention to internal sleep-related threats include muscle tension and rapid heart beat. An example of attention to external sleep-related threats include monitoring the clock to calculate how much sleep will be obtained.

Mood disorders

Unipolar depression

The study of selective attention in depression has tended to focus on whether there is an automatic bias or a controlled bias. Ian Gotlib and his colleagues have shown that people diagnosed with depression demonstrate increased emotional Stroop interference for depression-related and negatively-valenced words (e.g. Gotlib and McCann 1984; Gotlib and McCane 1987) and Andrew Matthews and his colleagues have shown an attentional bias to negative social words on the modified dot-probe task (Mathews *et al.* 1996). However, other studies have not shown these effects (e.g. Hill and Knowles 1991; Mogg *et al.* 1993). These mixed findings have led to the suggestion that selective attention to concern-related information is not reliably associated with depression (Williams *et al.* 1988, 1997). Indeed, some studies have shown that the presence of depression in people with an anxiety disorder results in failure to find the typical attentional bias to concern-relevant threat stimuli (e.g. Mogg *et al.* 2000*b*; Musa *et al.* 2003). Furthermore, if selective attention occurs in depression it may only be found using display times of over half a second (e.g. Gotlib and McCane 1987). In support of this view, using a modified dot-probe Karin Mogg and her colleagues (1995*a*) demonstrated an attentional bias for negative words in depression at display times of 1000 ms, but there was no attentional bias for negative words associated with depression using brief masked stimuli.

The evidence suggests that if depressed individuals do selectively attend to negative material it tends to be a more delayed, and possibly more controlled, process than in the anxiety disorders. It is also possible that people with depression have difficulty in controlling their attention sufficiently to disengage from negative material (Compton 2000). A range of studies using the Deployment-of-Attention Task (a similar paradigm to the modified dot-probe) suggests that people without depression attend away from negative stimuli and towards positive stimuli, whereas people with depression and people with elevated but non-clinical levels of depressed symptoms do not show this 'protective' bias (e.g. Gotlib *et al.* 1988; McCabe and Gotlib 1995; McCabe and Toman 2000). A lack of a protective bias has been replicated in patients who have recovered from depression, but only when they are in a sad, but not neutral, mood (McCabe *et al.* 2000). Interestingly, these studies have each presented stimuli for 730 ms or above, indicating that the bias may involve controlled processes. One study has also identified a form of attentional avoidance in unipolar depression. A visual scanpath study found that people with affective disorder[1] avoided scanning facial features relative to controls (Loughland *et al.* 2002; see Fig. 2.2).

---

[1] A group comprised of patients meeting diagnostic criteria for either unipolar depression or bipolar disorder.

There appear to be few studies on attention to internal stimuli in depression. Private self-consciousness is highly correlated with measures of depression in non-patient samples (Smith and Greenberg 1981; Ingram and Smith 1984), but as noted earlier, private self-consciousness is partly a measure of self-reflection rather than purely an index of awareness of internal states. Interestingly, in the meta-analysis of heart beat detection, no patients with depression were found to have accurate perception of their heart beats (van der Does *et al.* 2000), compared to 7.9% of non-patient controls and 17.9–25% of patients with anxiety disorders. Thus, there is mixed evidence to date. Unfortunately, no studies appear to have assessed attention to more relevant internal stimuli such as thoughts, aches, pains, and feelings of lethargy. Note that this research is not to be confused with evidence of dysfunctional self-relevant thinking in depression, for which there is strong evidence (as will be discussed in Chapters 4 and 5).

In summary, unipolar depression does not appear to be associated with an automatic attentional bias to specific kinds of stimuli. There is evidence of an attentional bias towards negative information at longer display times, and this may represent a difficulty in disengaging attention from the negative information. Further evidence suggests that depression may be associated with a reduction in the controlled avoidance of negative information and a reduction in the attention to positive information ('protective bias') that occurs in non-depressed individuals.

Bipolar disorder

An emotional Stroop study has indicated that two groups of people with a diagnosis of bipolar disorder, one group in a manic episode and one group in a depressed episode, were slower to colour-name depression-related words, but not euphoria-related words, compared to non-patient controls (Lyon *et al.* 1999). A neuropsychological study assessing participants' ability to respond and inhibit a response to positive and negative words found that patients in an episode of mania were faster to respond to positive words compared to controls, whereas depressed patients were faster to respond to negative words (Murphy *et al.* 1999). The authors concluded that the patients in a manic episode were selectively attending to positive stimuli. Clearly, research on selective attention in bipolar disorder is in its early stages and shows ambiguous findings.

Psychotic disorders

Patients with delusions show increased colour-naming latencies on the emotional Stroop for threatening words (Fear *et al.* 1996), paranoia-related words (Bentall and Kaney 1989), low and high-self-esteem-related words (Kinderman

1994) and words related to the specific delusion experienced (Leafhead *et al.* 1996). One interpretation of the findings is that people with delusions attend to stimuli that reflect their current concerns. Another body of evidence indicates a role for attention to internal stimuli in psychotic disorders. Smari *et al.* (1994) found that increased private self-consciousness was associated with paranoia in a group of males diagnosed with schizophrenia. In addition, using a self-report measure, Morrison and Haddock (1997*b*) found that patients with auditory hallucinations reported high private self-consciousness relative to patient and non-patient controls. However, as already highlighted, these findings are limited by the fact that private self-consciousness is partly a measure of self-relevant thinking. Evidence of attentional avoidance comes from eye tracking studies that indicate reduced processing of faces. More specifically, several researchers have found that people with schizophrenia show reduced attention to the eyes and other salient facial features (e.g. Phillips and David 1997; Streit *et al.* 1997; Williams *et al.* 1999). Figure 2.2 compares examples of the visual scanpaths of a patient with schizophrenia with that of a patient with an affective disorder, and non-patient volunteers (Loughland *et al.* 2002). In summary, patients with psychotic disorders may be characterized by attention away from social stimuli in the environment and towards concern-related thoughts, but future research is necessary to confirm this.

Substance-related disorders

Studies using the emotional Stroop have found that problem drinkers took longer to colour-name alcohol-related words (e.g. Johnsen *et al.* 1994; Sharma *et al.* 2001). In a more ecologically relevant dot-probe design, people with an opiate addiction selectively attended to pictures of drug-related stimuli (Lubman *et al.* 2000). Further, a modified dot-probe study, using word stimuli, found that selective attention to drug-related words was associated with the degree of intrusive 'craving' thoughts about cocaine within a group of patients diagnosed with cocaine abuse or dependence (Franken *et al.* 2000). These preliminary studies provide encouraging evidence for an attentional bias to concern-related information in individuals suffering from substance-related disorders.

Discussion

A summary of the research reviewed on selective attention across disorders is provided in Table 2.1. There is sufficient evidence across the psychological disorders to conclude that the following three attentional processes are definite transdiagnostic processes: (1) selective attention to concern-relevant external stimuli, (2) selective attention to concern-relevant internal stimuli

Table 2.1 Summary of findings across the psychological disorders (first column) and the attentional processes (top row)

	Selective attention to external stimuli		Selective attention to internal stimuli		Attentional avoidance or attention to safety		Reduced self-protective attentional bias	
Panic disorder with or without agoraphobia	***	+/–	***	+/–				
Specific phobia	***	+/–	***	+	***	+		
Social phobia	***	+/–	***	+/–	***	+		
OCD	***	+/–						
PTSD	***	+						
GAD	***	+	**	+	**	+/–		
Pain disorder	**	+/–	**	+				
Hypochondriasis			***	+				
BDD	**	+	**	+				
Dissociative disorder								
Sexual disorder					**	+		
Eating disorder	***	+/–	*	+/–				
Sleep disorder	**	+/–	**	+				
Unipolar depression	***	+/–	**	+/–	**	+/–	***	+
Bipolar depression	***	+/–						
Psychotic disorder	**	+	*	+	**	+		
Substance disorder	***	+						

Note. For each attentional process the left hand column presents an indication of the quality of the evidence as follows: *** = good quality evidence, ** = moderate quality of evidence, * = tentative quality of evidence (see page 21–22 for criteria for each) and the right hand column presents an indication of the findings as follows: + = positive findings, – = negative findings, +/– = mixed findings, black space = the memory process has not been researched in this disorder.

(self-focused attention), and (3) attentional avoidance or attention towards sources of safety. No possible transdiagnostic processes were identified. The evidence for a reduced self-protective bias is inconclusive as it has only been investigated in unipolar depression. No clearly distinct processes were identified. Each of these decisions will now be discussed in turn. But before moving on, as an aside it is perhaps interesting to note the evidence, as presented in Box 2.4, that there is a tendency for psychological disorders to be associated with heightened distraction by neutral stimuli.

Definite transdiagnostic processes

Selective attention towards concern-related external stimuli

The research that we have reviewed across the psychological disorders is consistent with the view from cognitive and social psychology that people

Box 2.4 Attentional deficits and distractibility

In addition to the studies on attentional *bias* that we have covered in this chapter, there are a wealth of studies on other types of attentional *deficits* in psychological disorders.

What is the evidence?

Many groups of patients have been found to be more easily distracted by *neutral* stimuli. There is evidence with patients with GAD (Dibartolo *et al.* 1997; Mathews *et al.* 1990), OCD (Veale *et al.* 1996; Clayton *et al.* 1999), PTSD (Vasterling *et al.* 1998), bipolar disorder (Clark *et al.* 2001; Liu *et al.* 2002), chronic pain (Rode *et al.* 2001), and people diagnosed with psychotic disorders (e.g. Fleck *et al.* 2001; Liu *et al.* 2002). In one study of patients with PTSD, the extent of re-experiencing symptoms correlated positively with the tendency to be distracted by neutral stimuli (Vasterling *et al.* 1998).

What is the explanation?

It is possible that the heightened distractibility to neutral stimuli is a function of the individual scanning their environment for *any* stimulus that is relevant to their concerns. For example, someone with PTSD following an assault is likely to be hypervigilant for sudden movements or noises. Also, we discussed evidence at the beginning of this chapter that neutral stimuli can capture attention through being previously paired with an aversive experience; thus what appear to be neutral stimuli to an observer may not be neutral when considering the learning history of that individual. Alternatively, it is possible that heightened distractibility may reflect a more trait-like vulnerability to psychological disorders that is independent of the patients' concerns.

Note that a range of studies have explored deficits in inhibition processes in selective attention that are beyond the remit of this book but see Hemsley (1987) for a conceptual review of this area of research in schizophrenia.

attend to stimuli that are relevant to currently active, personally relevant concerns. As can be seen in Table 2.1, these findings are perhaps clearest for the anxiety disorders, but also appear to be evident in pain disorder, BDD, eating disorders, insomnia, unipolar depression, bipolar depression, the psychotic disorders, and substance-related disorders. Admittedly, there have been several failures to replicate these findings. Also, the emotional Stroop task has been used in many studies and its findings are not easy to interpret owing to alternative explanations. Nevertheless, the balance of published evidence supports the view that selective attention towards concern-relevant external stimuli is a definite transdiagnostic process. Indeed, there is no convincing evidence that this process is absent in any one particular disorder. The evidence also suggests that selective attention to external stimuli may often involve an automatic attentional bias towards threatening stimuli, particularly in the case of GAD, specific phobias, and social phobia, with tentative evidence for panic disorder and PTSD. Preliminary evidence suggests that automatic attention to threat may also be found in patients diagnosed with psychotic disorders and pain disorder.

Selective attention towards concern-related internal stimuli

The evidence covered in this chapter also supports the view that self-focused attention is a definite transdiagnostic process (see also Ingram 1990). Several psychological disorders are associated with increased attention to concern-relevant internal stimuli, with particularly strong evidence from the anxiety disorders and moderate evidence in a range of other disorders (see Table 2.1). However, it is noted that this process is difficult to investigate in a thorough manner and most studies have used self-report measures that do not distinguish between attention and thoughts, feelings, and bodily sensations. Despite these methodological shortcomings, it is evident from Table 2.1 that most patient populations investigated appear to show elevated attention to internal stimuli relative to non-patient controls. The evidence also suggests that patients typically attend to internal stimuli that are perceived as threatening, such as pain, heart rate change, and illness symptoms. There has been very little research conducted to assess whether the internal bias is specific to the concerns of certain disorders (e.g. attentional bias to illness symptoms in hypochondriasis but not social phobia).

Attentional avoidance and attention to sources of safety

Table 2.1 suggests that attentional avoidance or attention to safety meet our criteria for a definite transdiagnostic process. The evidence is strongest for specific phobia and social phobia. There was indirect evidence in men diagnosed with sexual dysfunction. We also covered evidence of reduced scanning of facial features in depression, schizophrenia, and social phobia, which could be interpreted as a sign of avoidance of social engagement in these disorders.

The only disorder in which the majority of studies have failed to find attentional avoidance is GAD. Although attentional bias in GAD has been studied intensively, only one study has found an indication of attention to safety (Bradley *et al.* 1999). We do not know the explanation for this finding, but it may be because of a deficit in controlling attention (as will be discussed further below), because the participants attend to threat stimuli as a method of distracting themselves from other negative material (as we will discuss in Chapter 5) or because they cannot identify suitable sources of safety (as we will discuss in Chapter 6).

Distinct and inconclusive processes

The research on unipolar depression suggests that people diagnosed with depression show evidence of a reduced self-protective bias. However, it is important to note that this process has not been investigated in other psychological disorders and so we cannot draw a conclusion about whether it is a transdiagnostic process or a distinct process.

Do attentional processes play a causal role?

In order for the study of selective attention to be more fruitful, we need to identify that it has a causal role in maintaining or exacerbating psychopathology. Several studies have indicated a causal role within non-patient populations. For example, as described in Box 2.5, selective attention to threat appears to predispose people to become more distressed following a negative life event (MacLeod and Hagan 1992; Van den Hout *et al.* 1995). Further, a recent study has shown that people can be trained to automatically attend to negative information and that this increases the level of distress in response to a difficult task (MacLeod *et al.* 2002).

A further source of evidence for the causal role of attention in psychological disorders is to investigate the positive effects of re-directing attention. Experimental studies have explored how manipulating attention can reduce fear in individuals with sub-clinical phobias. For example, Mohlman and Zinbarg (2000) found that instructing spider-fearful participants to focus their attention on the spider and answer questions about its appearance and behaviour, resulted in greater fear reduction than spider fearful participants who did not focus on the spider, or those who focused on the spider without answering questions about its appearance and behaviour. In another creative study, Kamphuis and Telch (2000) carried out exposure therapy for students with fears of enclosed spaces. They compared exposure when the instructions asked the participants to focus on the external source of threat (e.g. an enclosing chamber) with exposure when the instructions asked the participants to distract from the source of threat. A third condition was included that involved exposure with no specific instructions. The results indicated that the

Box 2.5 Does attentional bias moderate the emotional reaction to a stressful life event?

Background

Although earlier studies had established that anxiety was associated with an attentional bias towards threat, no studies had established a causal role for the bias until MacLeod and Hagan (1992) tested the hypothesis that patterns of attentional bias moderates peoples' reactions to future stressful life events.

Design

Thirty-one women awaiting a cervical smear test were screened on a masked version and an unmasked version of the emotional Stroop test. Fifteen women later received a diagnosis of cervical pathology and reported how much emotional disruption they had experienced as a consequence of their diagnosis.

Results

The attentional bias toward threat words on the masked version of the emotional Stroop test was a significant predictor of their emotional reaction to the diagnosis. Moreover, it proved to be a better predictor, than the unmasked version, and compared to self-report measures of emotional vulnerability.

Conclusions

These results suggest that the automatic attentional bias toward threat indexes emotional vulnerability. The findings are consistent with the view that certain individuals were prioritizing attention to the threatening information, leading to an increased emotional reaction to a stressful life event.

condition involving attending to the feared stimuli was superior to the other conditions in reducing fear. Small-scale studies have evaluated the effects of training people with social phobia to focus their attention away from internal cues and towards their external environment during social interactions (Bogels *et al.* 1997; Wells and Papageorgiou 1998). For example, Adrian Wells and Costas Papageorgiou (1998) found that the attentional manipulation led to greater decreases in anxiety and social fear beliefs, relative to a control condition in which attention was not manipulated. Thus, the existing evidence tentatively suggests a causal role for attention in psychological disorders.

Theoretical issues

The current concern hypothesis, advocated by Eric Klinger, appears to be highly consistent with the studies reviewed in this chapter. People with psychological disorders selectively attend to internal and external stimuli that are related to their current concerns, including detecting and eliminating danger, pursuing reward, or detecting sources of safety. So, for example, a person with social phobia will attend to signs of negative evaluation from other people or internal signs of their own anxious appearance, whereas a person with hypochondriasis will be more likely to attend to aches and pains that signify a physical illness.

Despite the specificity noted above, we have also covered evidence of substantial overlap across disorders in the content of the stimuli to which people attend. For example, there is evidence of increased attention to social threat words in panic disorder, GAD, depression, bulimia nervosa, and social phobia. Other studies have identified evidence for selective attention to more general threat or other emotional words in GAD, PTSD, BDD, bulimia nervosa, depression, and psychosis. One possible explanation for these findings is that although attentional bias may often be concern-specific, some disorders may overlap in the concerns that relate to them. For example, it is likely that experiences of panic attacks in public places, awareness of one's body shape, and the symptoms of depression, may each increase concern about how one is being evaluated by other people and therefore activate concerns about social threat. It is also often the case that the degree of comorbidity has not been assessed in these studies and may help to account for the findings (Musa *et al.* 2003).

Three prominent models have been proposed to explain the role of selective attention in psychological disorders, although principally within the domain of anxiety disorders and depression. They are the model of Mark Williams and his colleagues (Williams *et al.* 1988, 1997), the Cognitive-Motivational Model (Mogg and Bradley 1998) and the Self-Regulatory Executive Function model (SREF; Wells and Matthews 1994).

Mark Williams and his colleagues have proposed that high levels of trait and state anxiety lead individuals to show an automatic attentional bias towards threatening stimuli (Williams *et al.* 1988, 1997). Hence, people with anxiety disorders would show such a bias by virtue of their high levels of trait and state anxiety. Depression is seen to be associated with biases in controlled processes, but not with biases in selective attention, which is conceptualized as an automatic process by Williams *et al.* (1988). The current data does indeed confirm the view that some anxiety disorders, especially GAD, are associated with an automatic attentional bias towards threat stimuli. However, the evidence of the existence of biases in controlled processes of attention in anxiety disorders indicates that attentional bias in anxiety is not only an automatic process. Further, we have also found evidence that people with psychological disorders often attend towards safety and away from threat. In addition, the model does not directly discuss attention to internal stimuli, although one might expect threat stimuli in the model to include internal stimuli, such as a rapid heartbeat in panic disorder. So although the suggestions made by Williams *et al.* (1988, 1997) provided a substantial grounding for studies of selective attention in psychological disorders, it cannot fully account for the evidence we have reviewed.

Mogg and Bradley (1998) propose that anxiety disorders are associated with an automatic attentional bias towards threat and that people with low levels of anxiety avoid threatening stimuli. They have explained this through the effects of motivation and appraisal. Specifically, they have proposed that the degree to which an individual attends to a stimulus will depend on their currently active goal and how they appraise the stimulus. So, for example, a person who believes they may be currently in danger would selectively attend to stimuli that they appraise as dangerous, such as the approach of a stranger. People with low levels of trait anxiety would appraise mildly threatening stimuli as non-threatening and therefore automatically avoid them. However, even low trait anxious individuals would attend to certain stimuli (e.g. grotesque images) if they appraised them as threatening. In addition, Mogg and Bradley (1998) suggest that depression suppresses these attentional biases because it entails the giving up of motivational goals of self-preservation (however, note that some theories of depression suggest that it involves a failure to relinquish unattained goals; Pyszczynski and Greenberg 1987). Mogg and Bradley (1998) briefly discuss avoidance of threat as a process involved in maintaining anxiety because it prevents the reappraisal of feared stimuli when they are not in fact dangerous. This model is consistent with many of the findings we have reviewed, including selective attention to current concerns, the suppression of an automatic attentional bias in people with comorbid depression, and the findings of attention towards safety and away from danger. The model also has the potential to help describe the role of attention in disorders in which the current concern may be rewarding (e.g. bipolar disorder, substance abuse disorders) because it states that all motivational goals can lead to biases in selective attention rather than anxiety per se. However, this model provides no explicit explanation for the convincing evidence of an attentional bias to internal cues. Also, it is important to note that much of the evidence described in this chapter was used to formulate the Mogg and Bradley (1998) model, and so it has received little independent testing since the hypotheses were derived.

Wells and Matthews (1994) proposed a model composed of an executive system, the S-REF, that engages in the controlled monitoring of 'low-level processing units' that are responsible for automatic processing. The monitoring behaviour of the S-REF is influenced directly by self-beliefs and procedural plans that are stored in long-term memory. The model proposes that people with emotional disorders engage in excessive monitoring of relevant information such as thoughts, bodily states, mood, and external threat. This process prevents attention to new information that may contradict negative beliefs, disrupts ongoing behaviour, and maintains the experience of distress. The model is consistent with the findings that psychological disorders are associated with a controlled process of attention to concern-related information and increased internally focused attention. It also helps to explain the findings that enhancing externally focused attention can lead to improvement in symptoms. It is also possible that enhanced distractibility is caused by the operation of plans to scan the environment, even for neutral stimuli, because they are regarded as threatening. However, the findings that the attentional bias is often automatic do not fit well with the S-REF model because it implicates a controlled process of monitoring. Nevertheless, the authors accept that the controlled processes can become automatized with repeated rehearsal. The model does not directly implicate attention to sources of safety and avoidance of threat in psychological disorders.

It appears that none of the prominent models can fully explain the processes of selective attention in the psychological disorders and none incorporate the possibility that people with certain psychological disorders, such as psychotic disorders and bipolar disorder, may have an underlying deficit in controlling their attention. The S-REF model represents a clinically useful model that provides a good fit to the existing data. However, a fully comprehensive model would have to accept several features of Mogg and Bradley's (1998) account. First, motivational states other than anxiety can influence selective attention in patients with psychological disorders. Second, the appraisal of certain stimuli as threatening can lead them to capture attention automatically even without repeated rehearsal (Mansell 2000). Third, avoidance of threat and attention to safety (and not just internally focused attention) are associated with psychological disorders. None of these features would seem to be incompatible with the S-REF model, but they are not currently incorporated within it. The S-REF model focuses on the processes that the authors perceive to be the key maintaining factors, namely internally focused attention and the perseverative processing of self-relevant information. The latter process, which represents a style of thinking, is covered in more detail in Chapter 5.

Clinical implications

Treatment research suggests that the attentional biases associated with psychological disorders are reduced following successful therapy. This pattern of findings has been reported for GAD (e.g. Mathews *et al.* 1995; Mogg *et al.* 1995*b*), social phobia (e.g. Mattia *et al.* 1993; Woody *et al.* 1997), specific phobia (e.g. Watts *et al.* 1986; Lavy and van den Hout 1993; van den Hout *et al.* 1997) and OCD (Foa and McNally 1986). Future research should explore the change in attentional bias following effective psychological therapy for other psychological disorders. It is not known whether these treatments work because attentional processes were modified directly through the therapy or whether the change in attentional bias is a secondary effect of targeting other cognitive and behavioural processes. Indeed, psychological treatments vary widely in their emphasis on modifying attention during therapy.

There are at least five possible ways in which selective attention may serve to maintain a psychological disorder. First, as we have seen, people attend to information that is consistent with their concerns. Such selective attention could often be counterproductive because it may cause the individual to miss information that could disconfirm his or her problematic beliefs. For example, a person with PTSD who believes that the world is a dangerous place would attend to people that look dangerous at the expense of attending to people that look innocuous or trustworthy. Accordingly, this person would continue to believe that the world is dangerous. A second effect of selective attention to a limited range of concerns is that, over time, it is likely to result in attention being directed away from other information in the internal and external environment that may be useful for learning skills, gaining knowledge, or improving social interactions. Thus, biases in selective attention may lead to objective decrements.

Turning to a third effect of selective attention, research from social psychology indicates that attention directed towards internal stimuli leads an individual to make more internal attributions for events (Hope *et al.* 1989). For example, when one experiences a major setback at work, the person who habitually focuses on his or her own thoughts, feelings, and actions would be more likely to blame him or herself for the setback, rather than take into account the role of colleagues, the competing firms, and other factors in the outside environment. These kinds of reasoning biases will be discussed further in Chapter 4. Fourth, selective attention may lead to the encoding of specific information within memory (e.g. Russo *et al.* 2001) which may then affect subsequent cognitive processing, as will be discussed in Chapter 3. Fifth, and finally, it is possible that the automatic nature of attentional biases may lead people to feel that their mind is not under their own control which would lead to fears of going mad or acting impulsively, although no studies have explicitly tested this idea.

The reviewed findings lead to several implications for therapy. As noted above, people with psychological disorders typically attend to information that is specifically related to their problematic concerns, and ignore information that is unrelated to them. The therapist must be aware of this bias, and help the patient broaden the range of stimuli to which they attend. We have also seen that certain disorders are associated with attention that is directed away from the social environment and towards internal stimuli. This process can have a direct effect on therapy because the patient may not fully process what the therapist is saying and how he or she is behaving towards the patient. Therefore, the therapist needs to generate conditions that can reduce internally focused attention, such as reducing eye contact with the patient to prevent them feeling scrutinized and jointly focusing on a neutral object, such as the diagram of their formulation. Of course, it may ultimately be in the patient's interest to tolerate being looked at by the therapist, but it would not be the first focus of therapy. The research also indicates that patients may have less voluntary control over their attention and therefore sometimes clients may agree at an intellectual level that they are paying excessive attention to concern-related information but have difficulty exerting control over this process. A technique known as attentional training (Wells 2000), which we will discuss in a moment, may help improve attentional control.

Several of the above points are also highlighted in the clinical case presented at the beginning of this chapter. Selective attention played a key role in the maintenance of Harry's delusional beliefs and his consequent anxiety. Harry and the therapist worked on the formulation collaboratively. The result of their efforts is illustrated in Fig. 2.5. Recall that while in a situation with other people, Harry would experience an intrusive thought of a sexual nature. His immediate response to the intrusion would be to think that his thought had been broadcast to other people. He then became vigilant for 'signals' that the thought had been broadcast. In particular, he would selectively attend to coughs, people turning their heads or people saying things that related to him. When outside he would selectively attend to signals from peoples' car horns. On detecting these 'signals', Harry would become increasingly convinced that his thoughts had been read by other people. At this point he switched his attention away from other people in an attempt to avoid being approached and attacked by them; he retired 'into his shell'. Unfortunately, by avoiding

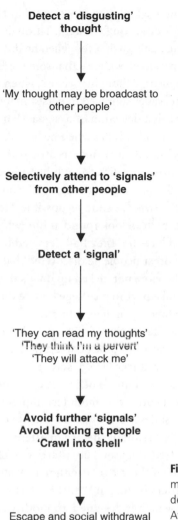

Fig. 2.5 Formulation of the maintenance of Harry's delusional beliefs. Attentional processes are displayed in bold.

other people, he was not able to find out whether the signals had occurred by chance or whether they did indicate he would be attacked. This formulation corresponds closely to the vigilance-avoidance model of attentional bias described earlier (Mogg and Bradley 1998).

When the formulation was discussed with Harry, he agreed that it might help explain some occasions when he had been mistaken. He said that he would feel safer if he did not believe that his thoughts would be broadcast and he was therefore willing to test out the belief using behavioural experiments. The role of attention was crucial in these experiments.

First, Harry was encouraged to attend to 'signals' in his environment when he was *not* experiencing a 'disgusting' thought. Through doing this, he realized that people were sending out 'signals' even when he did not have a thought to transmit to them. This provided evidence that some of the 'signals' he noticed were unrelated to a 'disgusting' thought. Second, when Harry did experience a 'disgusting' thought, he was encouraged to persist in looking for its effects on other people beyond the first detection of a 'signal'. For example, typically he would be afraid to look outside his flat when he heard a car horn for fear that it was directed towards him. By focusing his attention externally, Harry was able to see that the car horns were directed at other traffic. In another example, when Harry experienced a 'disgusting' thought, he would typically look away from other people on the street as soon as possible. He would be convinced that they had just been about to look round at him when he stopped looking at them, providing evidence that they had detected his intrusive thoughts. By persisting looking at other people he discovered that they typically did not look around, and had therefore not picked up on his thoughts.

Harry continued to take part in a college course during the therapy and towards the end of the therapy managed to attend seminars and even go to restaurants and cinemas. He continued to believe that on some occasions his thoughts were being broadcast to some people, but the range of situations that triggered this belief was reduced. He described the therapy as providing 'a chink in the huge black wall of the belief'. It is not possible to account for this client's improvement entirely through techniques that involve attention, but the two strategies just described illustrate the use of several helpful techniques. For a further discussion of the use of attentional techniques in the treatment of psychosis, (see Morrison 2001; Tarrier 2002; Williams 2002).

A prominent advocate of the use of attentional strategies in the treatment of psychological disorders is Adrian Wells. He has developed the method of attentional training which is designed 'to modify the perseverative self-relevant processing that is characteristic of emotional disorders' (p. 139, Wells 2000). The technique is summarized in Box 2.6. Attentional training is designed to promote the processing of disconfirmatory information and also to increase the voluntary, flexible control of attention so that patients can effectively disengage their attention from the stimuli that automatically capture their attention. The technique has been tested in small case series studies (e.g. Wells *et al.* 1997; Papageorgiou and Wells 1998, 2000) but awaits a published controlled evaluation. For a thorough description of the method, a review of case series that support the utility of the technique, and for a discussion of possible mechanisms underpinning the treatment see Wells (2000).

Box 2.6 What is attentional training?

Adrian Wells has developed a technique that is designed to counteract the attentional biases thought to maintain psychological disorders (e.g. Wells 2000). In essence, the procedure involves a series of attentional exercises in response to sounds. The patient is instructed to direct their attention to an increasing number of close and distant sounds for 10–15 min. The procedure is first practised in the therapy session and then repeated as homework. An important aspect of attention training is that it is practised when the patient is *not* in a state of anxiety, worry, or rumination, because it is not seen as a coping strategy but rather as a way of resetting maladaptive cognitive processes.

What does it involve?

The therapy is divided into several stages:

1. The therapist first provides a clear rationale for why reducing or interrupting self-focused processing may aid recovery.
2. The patient is asked to fixate on a visual stimulus (e.g. a mark on the wall) and then to focus attention for several moments on each of a series of different sounds (therapist's voice, tapping, clock). The patient is instructed to exclusively focus on each sound alone.
3. The patient shifts their attention rapidly between the set of sounds.
4. The patient attends simultaneously to all of the sounds, trying to be aware of as many sounds as possible.

As already discussed, the manipulation of attention during behavioural experiments is a technique that has been used successfully in the treatment of social phobia and specific phobia (e.g. Mohlman and Zinbarg 2000). In behavioural experiments sometimes it is helpful to enrich the environment to facilitate the patient to direct their attention. For example, patients with insomnia often monitor their bodily sensations for signs consistent and inconsistent with falling asleep (Harvey 2002*a*). In experimenting with directing attention away from sleep-related threats, one patient found it helpful to drip aromatherapy oils on her pillow. This gave her something novel and engaging in the environment to which to divert her attention outwards and away from her internal bodily sensations. Another way to enhance this intervention is to ask patients for detailed descriptions of their experience of focusing externally. By doing this it is possible to assess and reinforce the benefits of this technique. If patients can describe a situation in sufficient detail that a clear visual image occurs in the mind of the therapist, with no important details missing, the intervention is likely to have been helpful.

Three other therapies are noteworthy in this context. First, mindfulness training may well target attention (Segal *et al.* 2002). One key component of the intervention is to train people to be able to focus and sustain attention on one facet of their internal or external environment (e.g. their breath or a sound). Unfortunately, although this intervention is found to be effective in preventing relapse of depression in recovered but recurrently depressed patients, the role of attentional processes in the outcome has not yet been assessed. Second, cognitive rehabilitation for patients with schizophrenia, shows promising effects, and may improve attentional performance (Wykes *et al.* 2003). Finally, although only tested in analogue samples there is promising evidence that training anxious individuals, on a computerized task, to automatically attend towards non-negative stimuli may interfere with the tendency towards an attentional bias (MacLeod *et al.* 2002). However, it has yet to be evaluated in clinical trials with a patient population.

While the forms of therapy discussed above specifically target attention, several other techniques used in cognitive therapy may have the indirect effect of redirecting attention. First, the positive data log (Greenberger and Padesky 1995) aims to explicitly correct biases in attention, such as a tendency to only attend to negative information. The method requires patients to actively seek out and record positive information. For example, a patient with depression who notices only when she/he appears to be ignored or criticized would be asked to seek and record times when people did not ignore him/her (e.g. whether they said 'hello' or smiled) and instances when he/she was either not criticized or received praise. It is essential that the information-to-be-recorded is operationalized in precise detail (e.g. what exactly would count as being praised and not criticized). It can also be helpful to ask patients to actively seek and record previously ignored information which is not necessarily positive. For example, a patient with an eating disorder who only notices people who appear to eat less than him/her, might be encouraged to notice what everyone was eating, not just specific, selected individuals. Similarly, patients who tend to focus on how they are different from others, such as patients with body dysmorphic disorder (BDD), might be encouraged to actively look for how they are similar to other people. Second, automatic thought records (Beck 1995; Greenberger and Padesky 1995) may be helpful not just to identify unhelpful thoughts, examine the evidence for and against them, and to generate and evaluate alternative more functional thoughts, but they are also likely to encourage patients to attend to previously ignored information and consider issues from other perspectives. That is, with careful guided discovery, negative thought records can be used to demonstrate attentional bias and broaden the patients' perspective.

Future research

Although research on selective attention has progressed far in the last two decades, there are many areas of research that are lacking a thorough evaluation. The most advanced and thorough investigations have been based on samples diagnosed with GAD, panic disorder, specific phobia, social phobia, and unipolar depression. There are some persuasive emotional Stroop studies conducted on samples diagnosed with PTSD, OCD, eating disorders, substance abuse, and psychosis. There are virtually no studies on comorbid disorders, with the exception of anxiety with comorbid depression. In general, selective attention needs to be assessed across more psychological disorders using a wider range of well-controlled paradigms. In particular, it would be advisable to use paradigms that lead to less ambiguous interpretations. The emotional Stroop is very problematic in this regard, whereas the dot-probe and the eye tracker paradigms are more desirable.

Across the literature there is a paucity of ecologically valid research on selective attention. Researchers are yet to investigate attention to the kinds of stimuli that are specifically relevant for certain disorders. For example, studies could incorporate apparently contaminated objects for people with contamination-related fears in OCD, trauma-related images in PTSD, and voices in psychotic disorders. Naturally, close attention needs to be paid to the ethical viability of such studies. Selective attention to internal stimuli, especially intrusive memories has yet to be explored. Furthermore, as PTSD is defined by avoidance of stimuli that remind the patient of their traumatic experience, we might expect to find avoidance of ecologically valid threat stimuli in threatening situations, or when stimuli are presented for long periods of time.

There has been minimal study of the effects of the current context (e.g. threatening or safe situations) on selective attention within psychological disorders. Indeed, there are indications that selective attention to threat may be found under mildly threatening conditions, whereas selective attention towards safety and avoidance of threat may be found in more threatening situations. Furthermore, there are indications that it is the personal relevance of stimuli that affects attentional bias across the psychological disorders. Therefore, future research could test whether personal relevance accounts for differences in selective attention over and above the actual diagnosis that a person receives. This approach may be particularly useful for understanding selective attention in people with high levels of comorbidity.

Another important avenue for future research involves the interface between attentional bias and attentional performance. It appears that many different psychological disorders are associated with difficulties in the control of attention, in the sense that attention is more easily captured by 'neutral' stimuli (see Box 2.4), followed by a greater difficulty disengaging from the stimulus. These deficits appear to be more extreme in acute psychosis and mania, but also appear to be present in other disorders, such as PTSD and GAD. Further research could evaluate the extent and direction of the relationship between these difficulties and the attentional biases already identified, and whether treatments directed to improving attentional control can reduce the symptoms of psychopathology.

We need to remember that there is a possibility that selective attention may not necessarily be the key feature that distinguishes or exacerbates psychological disorders. The beliefs that motivate selective attention may be more important than attention per se. For example, attending to the experience of pain in order to assess the extent to which it is ruining one's life would appear to serve a very different role from attending to pain in order to reassess whether the pain is actually as bad as one thinks.

Finally, within the psychological literature, several other key properties of selective attention have been explored that researchers have not investigated to any great degree among patients with psychological disorders. They include the breadth of focus of attention (i.e. a wide or narrow spotlight of attention; Eysenck 1992), the mode of attention (i.e. to perceptual details or to meaningful objects; in an 'immersed' or 'detached' way; Lambie and Marcel 2002), and the degree of perceptual capacity (Lavie 1995). These important concepts are likely to have implications for psychological disorders that are yet to be realized.

Key points

1. The three attentional processes that can be regarded as definite transdiagnostic processes are: (a) selective attention to concern-relevant external stimuli, (b) selective attention to concern-relevant internal stimuli (self-focused attention), and (c) attentional avoidance or attention towards sources of safety.

2. It is not possible to draw a conclusion as to whether reduced self-protective bias is a distinct process or whether it is transdiagnostic because it has only been investigated in unipolar depression.

3. People with psychological disorders show attentional biases that are closely related to their current concerns, such as detecting relevant signals of danger, reward, and safety.

4. It has been proposed that an attentional bias towards particular classes of stimuli leads to the processing of information that confirms pre-existing beliefs and interferes with the processing of new information. Further, attentional avoidance and attention towards safety can prevent the habituation and reappraisal of stimuli perceived to be threatening.

5. Certain interventions target attentional processes including: reducing attention to negative stimuli, promoting attention to information that may disconfirm problematic beliefs and improving control over attention.

6. Future research needs to explore: attentional bias within ecologically relevant context, the effects of comorbidity, the effects of attentional bias on maintaining psychological disorders, and controlled clinical evaluations of attention-based therapies.

Chapter 3

Memory

A 29-year-old woman, Paula, was sitting in the passenger seat of the family car, next to her husband. Their two daughters, aged 5 and 8, were sitting in the back. Everyone was in good humour, telling jokes and laughing. The children were particularly excited in expectation of a day at the fair that had just arrived in a town 20 minutes down the motorway.

Five minutes onto the motorway their car was caught up in a road traffic accident involving a lorry and two other cars. Tragically, Paula's husband, who was 31 years old, died soon after impact. Paula, who was trapped in the front passenger seat, witnessed him struggling for breath whilst bleeding heavily. She desperately wanted to reach across to help him, or at least comfort him, but could not as she was trapped from the chest down. She described feeling terrified, helpless, and confused during the incident. At some stage, she was not sure when, she worked out that one of her children was critically injured (but recovered after several weeks in hospital). The other child escaped unharmed.

Three years after the accident, Paula made an appointment with a therapist. During the assessment session it became evident that Paula's memory of the accident was patchy. When she tried to describe what had happened her description was slow, disorganized, and unclear. She found it difficult to remember exactly how the accident had happened and her memory for several hours after the accident was unclear. For example, while Paula knew that she had spoken to the policeman at the scene of the accident, she was not able to describe all of the details of what they spoke about. Paula was not sure why her husband died. She said that she had attended a meeting with a doctor who explained the nature of the injuries but that she could not recall many of the details. She had a horrible feeling that her husband died by 'choking on his own blood'. This upset her terribly.

Paula's motivation for seeking therapy was to rid herself of the frequent vivid and lifelike flashbacks of the accident, particularly of her husband dying. Also, Paula was afraid to go to sleep because most nights she was plagued by nightmares that incorporated themes of the accident. Paula described feeling tortured by this excessive and relentless remembering, and she desperately wished she could forget the horrific scenes.

Paula also reported feeling chronically anxious and unsafe. She cited newspaper articles and television news reports as her source of information about danger; 'everytime you open a newspaper, yet another horrific story pops out. The world is filled with terror and unhappiness'. Paula avoided driving and taking buses and was strict with her children, not allowing them to travel in cars or buses. The former made it difficult for Paula to work (she left her last job, unable to cope, within three months of the accident). The latter was straining her relationship with her children who were constantly fighting for more independence.

Paula is suffering from post-traumatic stress disorder (PTSD). As evident from the clinical description, PTSD is characterized by both excessive remembering (e.g. Paula's flashbacks and nightmares) and difficulty remembering (e.g. Paula's memory for the details of the accident and the discussion with the doctor). In this chapter, our aim is to establish the extent to which memory processes, such as those characteristic of PTSD, are relevant to other psychological disorders. To begin, we will reflect on the nature of memory and define several concepts relevant to this chapter.

What is memory?

In many ways everyone knows what memory is; each of us use it constantly as we form memories of our day-to-day experiences and attempt to recall memories of past experiences. The human memory system is comprised of three stages of processing (Baddeley 1994, 1997). During *encoding*, we engage in the initial processing of novel information. The memory system would be incredibly inefficient, and the capacity filled up quickly, if we encoded every miniscule detail of our day-to-day lives. Instead, the memory system is highly *selective* in its operations. As we will see, there are many factors that govern the information that is selected for encoding. To take one example, we know that our picture of the world, or 'schema', based on past experience, is one important influence on the information selected for encoding (Bartlett 1932). The selective nature of memory can be disadvantageous as one's 'schema' may serve to bias or distort the memories that are encoded. To return to Paula, her traumatic experience had changed her picture of the world. For example, following the accident, Paula viewed herself as seriously unsafe. This led her to selectively encode information from her environment such that news of horrific events seemed to 'pop out' everywhere. That is, selective attention (the topic of Chapter 2) can lead to selective encoding that can, in turn, lead to selective remembering.

The second stage of memory is *storage* during which the encoded information is retained over time. The *limited storage capacity* of the memory system is apparent every time we try to remember all the jobs that need to be done before leaving the house and then walking out the door without remembering key tasks (e.g. feeding the poor cat!) or when we cannot recall the name of a friend who we have not seen for a while. The distinction between long-term memory and short-term memory is relevant here. Incoming information is thought to be held in temporary storage in short-term memory and, under certain circumstances, will be moved into long-term memory for storage (Parkin 1999). Some of the circumstances that govern the transfer of information into long-term memory storage will be discussed in a moment.

Early models of long-term memory proposed that it is formed from different subsystems. One useful distinction has been made between non-declarative and declarative memory (Cohen and Squire 1980; Squire 1994). Non-declarative memory is evident in behaviour that occurs without recollection of previous events. Examples include conditioning, associative learning, and procedural memory. Procedural memory refers to stored information that may not necessarily be consciously available about how to perform skills (e.g. driving or text messaging). Declarative memory, on the other hand, refers to factual information that is consciously available and is usually described in words. Declarative memory can be divided into semantic and episodic memory (Tulving 1983). Semantic memory refers to factual knowledge about the world, such as being able to name people, places, and objects and describe their properties (e.g. a truck is a large vehicle that transports goods). Episodic memory, on the other hand, refers to knowledge about personal incidents and events, such as the memory of what one ate for lunch yesterday. Later models of long-term memory have proposed that the operation of long-term memory can be explained through the operation of the encoding, storage, and retrieval processes rather than through different memory subsystems (e.g. Roediger and Blaxton 1987; Johnson and Hirst 1993).

During *retrieval*, the third stage of memory processing, attempts are made to access the information stored in long-term memory. In the clinical case, Paula retrieves the memories of her husband dying during the accident extremely clearly. In laboratory tasks, tests of recognition or recall of word stimuli are used to index retrieval processes. A *recognition test* involves asking the participant to pick out or recognize the words they had previously learned from a large list of words that includes the words learned, plus a set of distractor words not seen before. A *recall test* involves asking the participant to recall, without any prompts, the words learned. Recognition tests generate more correct responses than recall tests because 'presenting the word that has been learned facilitates access to its memory trace' (p. 7, Baddeley 1997).

As the three stages of processing (encoding, storage, retrieval) are closely interlinked it is difficult to separate their actions. For example, we cannot tell whether Paula's impaired, fragmented, and disorganized memory of the accident is because she did not fully encode the memories at the time or whether there are mechanisms operating that prevented her from fully retrieving the memories (see Box 3.1 for examples of impaired encoding and impaired retrieval). Much work remains to be done to isolate the effects of impaired encoding versus impaired retrieval.

Explicit and implicit memory

There are several other distinctions we will draw on during this chapter. First, tests of memory can be tests of explicit memory and/or tests of implicit memory. Explicit memory tests require participants to consciously retrieve previously presented stimuli. They can include free recall ('write down all the

Box 3.1 Impaired encoding and retrieval

An example of impaired encoding

The 'weapon focus' effect is when 'the weapon appears to capture a good deal of the victim's attention, resulting in, among other things, a reduced ability to recall other details from the environment, to recall details about the assailant, and to recognise the assailant at a later time' (p. 35, Loftus 1979).

Maas and Kohnken (1989) demonstrated weapon focus in a study in which the key experimental condition involved an experimenter entering the room with a hypodermic syringe. Participants confronted with the syringe were less likely to accurately identify the experimenter who carried the syringe, relative to a control group who were not confronted with the syringe.

Kramer *et al.* (1990) showed participants a series of slides. Some included a weapon and some did not include a weapon. For the slides that included a weapon, the participants had poorer memory for the other details of the slide, such as what the person carrying the weapon looked like.

An example of impaired retrieval

Case study reported by Christianson and Nilsson (1989, pp 290–1):

'On a light summer evening…a 23-year-old female (to be referred to as C.M.) was raped while she was out jogging close to her home…C.M. could not explain what had happened to her and she could not tell the identity of herself…Her memory of the course of events from the time she was found, onwards, however, was quite normal…Three weeks after the trauma…she was escorted by two policemen over the area in which the assault had occurred. During the walk…she appeared continually stressed…When C.M. was taken again to the scene of the assault one week later, she felt very uncomfortable at specific places, but had no recollection of the traumatic evening, except that the word "bricks"…crossed her mind…the explanation came later when they passed some crumbled bricks that were found on another small path beside her running route. Being confronted with this track on which pieces of the crumbled bricks were spread out C.M. showed intense emotional stress, and claimed that she associated the unpleasant feeling with the pieces of bricks on the track she was walking on. From the confession by the rapist a few days earlier the policemen knew, however, that this was the place where he had assaulted her and from which she had been forced out onto the small meadow where the actual rape took place.

Box 3.1 Impaired encoding and retrieval *(Continued)*

Her state of amnesia lasted until…11 weeks after the assault. On that day C.M. was out jogging again, for the first time after the trauma, but in a different surrounding…The cavities in the road where C.M. was running were filled with crushed bricks, which reminded her strongly of those bricks found in the vicinity of her recent experience…C.M. happened to stop at the entrance of another cottage, where a pile of bricks were placed. At that moment, images of the traumatic episode started to return to her…and within…10–20 min she was able to reconstruct the whole traumatic episode'.

words you can remember'), recognition ('from this list of words circle the ones you recognize'), or cued recall tasks ('these three letter stems are the beginning of some of the words that have just been presented, try to complete the word'; e.g. hap____ = happy, smi____ = smile). Implicit memory tests do not require conscious recollection of previously presented stimuli but assess the degree to which encoding of previously presented stimuli influence the subsequent response. They can include word stem completion ('please complete these three-letter stems with the first word that comes to mind') or tachistoscopic identification (participants are asked to name each of a series of words presented briefly, typically between 10 and 100 ms, followed by a pattern mask). Explicit memory tests are thought to be a measure of effortful or controlled memory processes while implicit memory tests are designed to measure automatic and unintentional memory processes (Williams *et al.* 1997). It is interesting to note that explicit memory can be involuntary (McNally 2003), as in the case of Paula's flashbacks of the car accident.

Perceptually-driven and conceptually-driven tasks

Another important distinction is between perceptually-driven and conceptually-driven memory tasks (Roediger and Blaxton 1987; Roediger and McDermott 1992). Perceptually-driven or data-driven tasks are those that require the processing of the perceptual features of word stimuli (an example of an encoding task is to count the number of 'e's in each word; an example of a retrieval task is to complete a word stem presented in exactly the same font as that presented earlier). Conceptually-driven tasks are those that require the processing of the conceptual features, or the meaning, of the words (an example of an encoding task is 'the opposite to summer is w____'; an example of a retrieval task is free recall). Roediger and Blaxton (1987) suggested that performance will be enhanced if the processing activities required by the retrieval task are similar to the encoding task (an effect known as transfer appropriate processing). This is a very important proposal because it means that on tests of implicit and explicit memory, the failure to find an effect may be due to a mismatch in the type of processing required by an encoding and retrieval task (rather than the absence of explicit or implicit memory). Conversely, significant effects on tests of implicit and explicit memory may be attributable to a close match in the type of processing required by encoding and retrieval tasks (rather than the presence of explicit or implicit memory). Particularly pertinent to this chapter, in studies that seek to measure differences in memory for differently valenced words (e.g. negative words vs positive words) the encoding task must be conceptually driven as the meaning of the word stimuli is crucial to testing hypotheses about valence (Williams *et al.* 1997). As will become evident during this chapter, the full implication of these proposals has yet to be realized in the literature relating to memory processes in psychological disorders. One example where it has been integrated is Ehlers and Clark's (2000) cognitive model of PTSD which predicts that a major influence on memory for trauma will be whether the trauma was encoded conceptually (i.e. relative clarity in thinking during the trauma enabling the meaning of the trauma to be fully comprehended) or perceptually (i.e. due to confusion in thinking during the trauma). Anke Ehlers and David Clark (2000) suggest that those who process the trauma perceptually will be most at risk of developing PTSD as the trauma memory will be difficult to intentionally access and more difficult to integrate with the existing store of autobiographical memories. Support for these proposals has been reported in an analogue sample (Halligan *et al.* 2002) and in cross-sectional and prospective studies of trauma survivors (Murray *et al.* 2002; Ehlers *et al.* 2003; Halligan *et al.* 2003).

Working memory

Various models of human memory function have been proposed over the years. One that has been particularly successful in generating research is Baddeley and Hitch's (1974) working memory model. Baddeley and Hitch proposed the term 'working memory' to describe the operations involved in the short-term storage and processing of information. A key element of working memory is the *central executive* which is a control and decision making mechanism. The central executive controls the actions of two subsystems. The first, the *articulatory loop*, stores and manipulates verbal material. The second, the *visuospatial sketchpad*, stores and manipulates visual and spatial material. This part of working memory is particularly active in patients with PTSD who report vivid flashbacks of their trauma (McNally 2003). Other ways in which this model is relevant to psychological disorders will become clear later in this chapter.

Verbally accessible and situationally accessible memories

A final distinction that we need to make before moving on has been proposed by Chris Brewin and his colleagues in the Dual Representation Theory of PTSD. Brewin *et al.* (1996) proposed a distinction between two types of memory of a traumatic incident. The first are called verbally accessible memories (VAMs). These are verbal or visual memories of a trauma that can be intentionally retrieved. VAMs were given sufficient conscious attention during the trauma and thus were encoded in a way that permits the interaction of the memory with the rest of the autobiographical memory system, making later memory search and retrieval relatively easy. In contrast, situationally accessible memories (SAMs) are subconsciously generated memories (e.g. Paula's flashbacks of the accident, particularly of her husband dying). SAMs are information that received minimal processing and are thereby encoded using a lower-level and largely perceptual system that does not interact with the rest of the autobiographical knowledge base. The distinction between VAMs and SAMs will be returned to later in this chapter.

What kind of stimuli do people selectively remember?

As for attention (as discussed in Chapter 2), it is clearly the case that some stimuli are more memorable than others and that the stimuli that are most memorable to one person may not be the stimuli most memorable to another. What factors govern the stimuli that are, and are not, remembered? As discussed in Chapter 2, we tend to preferentially attend to stimuli pertinent to our survival. It is also likely that such 'prepared' stimuli influence memory. Further, as we have seen earlier in this chapter, one's 'schema', or picture of the world, will influence memory (Bartlett 1932). Note that this notion is core to Beck's (Beck *et al.* 1979, 1985) and Bower's (1981, 1987) theories of the interaction between cognition and emotion, although we recognize that the term 'schema' lacks clarity in several ways (see Chapter 9 in Williams *et al.* 1997).

Various aspects of an individual's internal (i.e. in the body) and external environment (i.e. contextual/environment factors) are also likely to be important. For example, the mood a person is in is a major influence on memory. *Mood-congruent memory* is defined as the selective encoding or retrieval that occurs 'while individuals are in a mood state consistent with the affective tone of the material' (p. 194, Ellis and Moore 1999). An example of mood-congruent memory would be that during a sad mood (e.g. induced due to conflict with one's partner) it is easier to recall sad information (e.g. the death of a loved one 6 years ago, friends who have moved away). *Mood-dependent memory* is defined as 'the increased likelihood of remembering material that was learned in a particular mood state' (p. 196, Ellis and Moore 1999). An example of mood-dependent memory would be that during a happy mood (e.g. induced due to a productive day at work) it is easier to recall information that was encoded during a previous happy mood (e.g. the details of conversations that took place during an enjoyable party 6 months ago). Using mood manipulations (see Box 3.2), the consensus to emerge from studies of mood-congruent memory and mood-dependent memory is that

Box 3.2 Feel like being moody? Induce a mood by:

The Velten procedure (Velten 1968)

Participants read 30 cards containing one self-statement each. For the depressed mood induction the self-statements include:

Looking back on my life I wonder if I have accomplished anything really worthwhile

I feel downhearted and miserable

Every now and then I feel so tired and gloomy that I'd rather just sit than do anything

For the happy mood induction the self-statements include:

Life is so full and interesting it's great to be alive!

I feel so good I almost feel like laughing

If your attitude is good, then things are good

Hypnosis (Gilligan and Bower 1984)

Highly hypnotisable participants are recruited and hypnotized for 10–15 minutes and then asked to develop a happy or sad mood by 'reviving a personal experience in which that mood was prominent' (p. 548, Gilligan and Bower 1984). The patients are asked to relive this episode in their imagination. Then they are asked to 'forget about the specific content of the revived memory and instead simply concentrate on reviving the accessed emotional state' (p. 548, Gilligan and Bower 1984).

> **Box 3.2 Feel like being moody? Induce a mood by:** *(continued)*
>
> ## Success or failure at computer games (Isen *et al.* 1978; Experiment 2)
>
> The computer game, 'Star Trek', involves 'you, in the Starship Enterprise, will be in a battle with a Klingon Battle Cruiser' (p. 5, Isen *et al.* 1978). In fact, the outcome of each move is determined by the experimenter. At the end of the game the participant is given feedback about victory (to induce a positive mood state) or defeat (to induce a negative mood state).
>
> ## Music
>
> Stein *et al.* (2000) presented eight minute segments of classical music. To induce a positive mood Delibes's Coppelia was played. To induce a neutral mood Faure's Ballad for Piano and Orchestra (Opus 19) was played.
>
> Williams *et al.* (2002) presented Prokofiev's 'Russia under the Mongolian Yoke', recorded at half speed, to induce a negative mood and Brahm's second and third movements from the third symphony to induce a neutral mood.

while mood-congruent memory is a robust effect, the evidence is mixed for mood-dependent memory (Eich 1995; Williams *et al.* 1997; Ellis and Moore 1999). A wide range of other state/context influences on memory have been demonstrated including being in pain (Kuhajda *et al.* 2002; Pauli and Alpers 2002) and intoxication with alcohol (Lister *et al.* 1987; Erblich and Earleywine 1995) or marijuana (Hooker and Jones 1987). It is also notable that catastrophizing and rumination, topics that will be discussed in Chapter 5, can enhance encoding and recall (Spanos *et al.* 1979; Lefebvre and Keefe 2002).

In addition to the effects of mood, people are also likely to preferentially encode and recall information that is particularly personally meaningful to them. Thus Klinger's (1996) current concern model, as discussed in Chapter 1, is also relevant to memory processes. For example, someone who is currently deciding which car to buy, and is acutely aware of how much a new car costs, will preferentially encode information about this current concern. Prior to deciding to buy a car this same information would have passed by without encoding. Similarly, when conversing with a couple who have recently become parents, the memories retrieved by the couple during the conversation are often dominated by their current concern (their new baby). In this chapter we will examine the extent to which the concept of current concerns is relevant to memory in individuals with psychological disorders.

Having now mapped out the background, we move on to pursue the main purpose of the chapter, to review the various memory phenomena found to be characteristic of psychological disorders, with a view to establishing the extent to which each memory process is transdiagnostic.

Selective memory

Two competing hypotheses relating to selective memory have been evaluated. Most research has tested the hypothesis that people with psychological disorders selectively remember information relevant to their current concerns. For example, in the clinical case presented at the beginning of this chapter, Paula described selective memory relevant to her current concerns; information about danger. This prediction originates from Beck's schema model (Beck *et al.* 1979) and Bower's associative network model (Bower 1981, 1987). The theory is that when a schema (for the former model) or node (for the latter model) is activated, aspects of information processing will be biased towards material that is congruent with the activation. However, several studies have evaluated the opposite hypothesis; that people with psychological disorders avoid concern-related information such that they should then have *poorer* memory for concern-related information. As will be described in more detail later, the vigilance-avoidance hypothesis proposed by Karin Mogg and her colleagues (1987) provides a theoretical context for this second hypothesis. In this section we will evaluate the first of these hypotheses, with the second being discussed later in this chapter. In the following disorder-by-disorder review of the selective memory literature it should be noted that studies that have used an encoding task that was a test of attention, such as the emotional Stroop or the dot probe, have mostly been omitted due to the concern that adequate and equal encoding of all stimulus materials cannot be ensured under such conditions (Coles and Heimberg 2002).

Most of the studies reviewed in this section have employed a task that requires the participant to encode a list of words that vary in their relevance to the disorder of interest. For example, in investigations of depression the words presented would include depression-related words (e.g. misery, sad). In addition, control words (typically neutral words) are presented as a comparison. To encode the words, participants might be asked to listen to each word, read each word silently, or read each word and then create a visual scene involving themselves and the word (the latter has been called 'incidental learning'). Then explicit and/or implicit memory is tested (see page 75 and 77 for a reminder of methods used to index explicit and/or implicit memory).

Anxiety disorders

Panic disorder with or without agoraphobia

In panic disorder, with or without agoraphobia, the vast majority of the findings indicate an explicit memory bias for concern-relevant words (e.g. McNally *et al.* 1989; Cloitre and Leibowitz 1991; Lundh *et al.* 1997; Becker *et al.* 1999), although note that there have been null findings reported (e.g. Ehlers *et al.* 1988). For implicit memory, the findings are mixed with some studies reporting an implicit memory bias (e.g. Cloitre *et al.* 1994; Amir *et al.* 1996) and others not reporting an implicit memory bias (e.g. Rapee *et al.* 1994; Lundh *et al.* 1997; Banos *et al.* 2001).

Social phobia

The majority of studies have failed to show any explicit memory bias among people diagnosed with social phobia (e.g. Rapee *et al.* 1994; Cloitre *et al.* 1995; Becker *et al.* 1999). However, as will be discussed below, some studies that have employed a more ecologically valid design have identified an explicit memory bias in social phobia. While a handful of studies have demonstrated an implicit memory bias (Amir *et al.* 2000; Lundh and Öst 1997 for non-generalized social phobia only), Rapee *et al.* (1994) reported a null result for implicit memory.

Obsessive-compulsive disorder

Selective memory for concern-relevant words in obsessive-compulsive disorder (OCD) has been minimally investigated. In the only study we uncovered, Foa *et al.* (1997) investigated implicit and explicit memory in people diagnosed with OCD who reported contamination fears. An explicit memory bias was not demonstrated. For implicit memory, the results were inconclusive because *both* the OCD and the control group demonstrated an implicit memory bias for threat. More recent studies have explored selective memory in individuals diagnosed with OCD within an ecologically valid design. These will be discussed below.

Post-traumatic stress disorder

Paunovic *et al.* (2002) reported an explicit memory bias for trauma-related words in PTSD, although it should be noted that the encoding task in this study was the emotional Stroop. As such, there are concerns that the adequate and equal encoding of all stimulus materials cannot be ensured (Coles and Heimberg 2002). The earlier findings have been more mixed. For example, Vrana *et al.* (1995) found enhanced memory for emotional words (but not trauma-related words) on a free recall test. In terms of implicit memory, McNally and Amir (1996) reported no implicit memory for trauma words in people diagnosed with PTSD but Amir *et al.* (1996) found implicit memory for trauma-related sentences. It is possible that by presenting sentences, as opposed to individual words, a clearer context was provided and this better captured the effect.

Generalized anxiety disorder

The majority of studies suggest that there is no explicit selective memory bias in generalized anxiety disorder (GAD) (e.g. Mogg *et al.* 1989; Bradley *et al.* 1995; Becker *et al.* 1999). Only one study known to the authors has reported positive results. Using a novel methodology, Friedman *et al.* (2000) demonstrated a clear explicit memory bias in people diagnosed with GAD. The method employed involved a conditioning procedure whereby a coloured dot (yellow or green) was presented in the centre of a computer screen and was followed by either a threat or a non-threat word. The colour of the dot was consistently paired with either a threat word or a non-threat word that was presented for 8 s. Participants were asked to read each word silently. A memory bias was evident in a subsequent free recall task during which the GAD group recalled more threat words than non-threat words. In addition, the GAD group recalled more threat words than the control group. Given the number of negative findings reported in the literature, it will be important that a replication of this study is attempted. Friedman *et al.* suggested that the positive results may be attributable to 'protracted, passive viewing...(that) may have overridden the avoidant aspects of worry' (p. 752, Friedman *et al.* 2000).

Moving onto the literature concerning implicit memory, although two studies have reported an implicit memory bias in GAD (Mathews *et al.* 1989; MacLeod and McLaughlin 1995), two others have failed to confirm it (Otto *et al.* 1994; Mathews *et al.* 1995). Mathews and his colleagues highlighted that in their 1989 study the word stimuli were elaboratively encoded (i.e. imagine yourself in a scene suggested by each word) whereas for the 1995 study the words were structurally encoded (i.e. count the number of 'es' in each word). Consistent with the previous discussion of perceptually versus conceptually-driven tasks, Mathews and colleagues raised the possibility that implicit memory effects 'are more dependent on semantic processing than we had previously assumed' (p. 9, Mathews *et al.* 1995).

Real world experiments in the anxiety disorders

Several accounts of the mixed findings relating to selective memory in the anxiety disorders have been proposed (McNally 1997; Coles and Heimberg 2002). One particularly plausible possibility is that the traditional paradigms used to investigate selective memory (i.e. words presented on a screen) do not adequately capture the processes of interest. Hence, the goal of recent studies has been to increase ecological (external) validity by establishing real life situations that capture the memory phenomena of interest. Five particularly original 'real world' studies are summarized in Box 3.3. The results of these studies suggest that when more ecologically valid paradigms are employed,

Box 3.3 'Real world' investigations of selective memory in the anxiety disorders

Lundh and Öst (1996)

Participants: People with and without social phobia.
Task: To rate a series of faces in photographs as either critical or accepting.
Result: During a subsequent recognition test, the social phobia group demonstrated a memory bias for critical faces.

Lundh *et al.* (1998)

Participants: People with and without panic disorder with agoraphobia.
Task: To rate a series of faces in photographs as safe (could be relied on if help was needed) or unsafe (could not be relied on if help was needed).
Result: During a subsequent recognition test, the panic disorder group demonstrated a memory bias for safe faces.

Mansell and Clark (1999)

Participants: People scoring high and low in social anxiety.
Task: Prior to an encoding task, half of the participants were told that they would have to give a speech immediately following the task while the other half were not given a speech threat. The encoding task involved public self-referent words ('How well does the word describe what someone who knows you or had just met you would think of you?'), private self-referent words ('How well does the word describe you?'), and other-referent words ('How well does the word describe your next-door neighbour at college?').
Result: During a free recall task, the high socially anxious group recalled less positive public self-referent words. But this bias was evident only in the speech threat condition.

Radomsky and Rachman (1999)

Participants: People with OCD, an anxious control group, and a normal control group.

Box 3.3 'Real world' investigations of selective memory in the anxiety disorders
(continued)

Task: Watching carefully as the experimenter touched objects on a table with one of two tissues. One tissue was described as clean and unused whereas the other tissue was described as having been found on the floor somewhere in the hospital (i.e. not clean!). Twenty five objects were touched and contaminated and 25 objects were touched but not contaminated.

Result: The OCD group displayed superior memory for contaminated objects than clean objects but they were not able to more accurately identify the contamination origin (i.e. dirty or clean) of the objects. That is, the OCD group showed a memory bias on a free recall task but not a recognition task.

Note: In an attempt to replicate these findings with a larger sample comprised of OCD-washers, OCD-checkers, patients with social phobia and non-anxious controls, Ceschi *et al.* (2003) found a memory bias for the OCD-checkers (but not the other groups) on the recognition task but not the free recall task.

selective explicit memory bias is found in social phobia (Lundh and Öst 1996), panic disorder (Lundh *et al.* 1998) and OCD (Radomsky and Rachman 1999; Ceschi *et al.* 2003). Future research is needed to ensure that the memory processes that are tapped by these kinds of experiments are identical to those captured by the traditional laboratory paradigms. It is also important to note that not all attempts to capture selective memory in the real world have generated significant results (e.g. Rapee *et al.* 1994, Experiment 3; Perez-Lopez and Woody 2001).

PTSD: a different angle on selective memory

Before leaving our discussion of the anxiety disorders a slightly different set of investigations, indicating the presence of selective memory, has been conducted in the context of PTSD. These studies have involved interviewing participants soon after a trauma and then re-interviewing them several years later. The results indicate that at two years posttrauma there was a significant positive correlation between the severity of PTSD and (1) the degree of distortion in the recollection of the trauma (Southwick *et al.* 1997), (2) the estimated amount of trauma exposure (Roemer *et al.* 1998), and (3) the recall of the number of symptoms experienced soon after the trauma (Harvey and Bryant

2000). That is, the more severe the PTSD, the greater the magnification and distortion of some aspects of the memory of the trauma. These findings reflect selective memory and mood-congruence. One implication of the findings is that although studies based on prospectively collected data are increasing, much of our knowledge about the role of the early trauma response is based on ret-rospective recall (e.g. McFarlane 1986; Solomon 1989; Marmar *et al.* 1994; Bremner and Brett 1997). Given that the recall of symptoms is influenced by the symptoms experienced at the time of the trauma, studies that report results based on retrospective recall are best regarded as preliminary until they are replicated with a study in which the data is collected prospectively. Importantly, the findings highlight that trauma memories are not fixed and indelible, an issue that has been at the centre of the false memory debate, as discussed in Boxes 3.4 and 3.5.

Box 3.4 The false memory debate

Issue: Is it possible for adults to 'remember' childhood trauma, especially child sexual abuse, after having had no recollection of the event for many years?

Viewpoint 1: The experience of trauma can be so devastating that an indi-vidual may use dissociation and repression to block out the memory (Terr 1991; van der Kolk 1994). The traumatic memory is not available for conscious recall but may still influence the person's current state (Brown *et al.* 1988). The memories can be accurately retrieved at a later date (Terr 1994).

Viewpoint 2: Memory is a constructive and selective process. There are many variables that can affect memory retrieval including mood, selective attention, and high levels of current symptoms. There is robust evidence that recollections of past events are subject to bias and error over time (Kihlstrom 1995; Hyman and Loftus 1998; Schacter 1999). Hence, so called 'repressed memories' are likely to be false memories.

Middle ground: It is likely that some reports of recovered memories are false, but possible that some reports of recovered memories are true (Nash 1994; Brewin and Andrews 1998).

Clinical implication: 'Recalling one's past is not like playing a videotape of one's life in working memory. When we remember an event from our past, we reconstruct it... There are very few instances in which remembering resembles reproducing' (p. 35, McNally 2003).

Box 3.4 The false memory debate *(continued)*

As therapy relies on a client's recall of events all memories recalled are best regarded as narrative truth (as opposed to historical truth). These memories are likely to be rich in information about the client's current state and view of the world but are unlikely to be exact replicas of the historical truth (Spence 1982; Nash 1994).

Therapists should take care not to advertently foster the development of false memories. We know that authoritative suggestions from a trusted source and repetition of the suggestions are conditions under which false memories are highly likely to be retrieved (Lindsay and Read 1994). As such, clinicians should avoid making explicit suggestions that an event must or might have occurred (Kihlstrom 1998). The use of techniques, such as hypnosis and age regression, to facilitate the search for traumatic memories have been identified as particularly likely to result in the recall of distorted or false memories, and thus should be avoided (Loftus 1993; Kihlstrom 1995; Hyman and Loftus 1998).

Somatoform disorders

Pain disorder

A memory bias for pain-related words has been investigated in several studies in patients with pain disorder. Pearce and colleagues reported that following the presentation of a mixed list of words, pain patients recalled more pain words (e.g. stinging, burning, paralyzing) relative to a non-patient control group (Pearce *et al.* 1990, Experiment 1). This effect was also present on a delayed recall test. Another study examined the effect of comorbid depression by comparing pain patients with or without depression, depressed patients without pain, and healthy controls. Only pain patients with minimal or no symptoms of depression selectively recalled pain adjectives (Edwards *et al.* 1992). A later study clarified this result by showing that depressed pain patients show a memory bias for negative pain words, but only when encoded as self-referential (i.e. as applying to themselves; Pincus *et al.* 1995). Interestingly, following successful surgery for the pain, there is evidence that the selective memory bias disappears (Edwards *et al.* 1995). This result raises the possibility that selective memory for pain-related words is a secondary consequence of the pain, rather than a trait factor.

A study by Pauli and Alpers (2002) is notable for investigating a broader range of somatoform disorders. The four groups tested were (1) a group

Box 3.5 Empirical investigations of false memory; the example of recovered memories of child sexual abuse and the example of recovered memories of alien abduction

Clancy *et al.* (2000)

Participants: Four groups of women were tested:

Recovered memory group; Women who report recovering memories of child sexual abuse.

Repressed memory group; Women who believe they were sexually abused as a child but have no memory for the abuse.

Continuous memory group; Women who were sexually abused as a child and have always remembered the abuse.

Control group; Women with no history of abuse.

Procedure: Based on the Deese/Roediger-McDermott paradigm, a list of words were presented, one at a time, on a computer screen. An example of one of the word lists was: sour, candy, sugar, bitter, good, taste, tooth, nice, honey, soda, chocolate, heart, cake, tart, and pie. All of these words are clearly associated with the word 'sweet' (the 'lure'), but the word 'sweet' was not actually presented. The key measure was whether the participants recalled or recognized the word 'sweet' as having been presented during the subsequent memory tests. A tendency to recall false memories was inferred from the number of times the 'lure' (e.g. sweet) was recalled.

Result: The participants in the recovered memory group were more prone to the false recognition of the 'lure' relative to each of the other three groups. That is, 'women who report recovered memories of sexual abuse are more prone than others to develop certain types of illusory memories' (p. 30).

But, the authors were concerned that they were unable to definitively establish whether the memories retrieved by the recovered memory group were true or false. So they conducted a followup study...

Clancy *et al.* (2002)

Participants: Three groups of people were tested:

Recovered memory group; People reporting recovered memories of alien abduction.

Repressed memory group; People who believed they were abducted by aliens but had no memory of it.

Box 3.5 Empirical investigations of false memory; the example of recovered memories of child sexual abuse and the example of recovered memories of alien abduction *(continued)*

Control group; People who denied being abducted by aliens.

That is, the first two groups believed that they had experienced a traumatic event that was unlikely to have occurred.

Procedure: Identical to Clancy *et al.* (2000) except that presentation of word cues was via a tape recorder.

Result: The participants who reported recovered and repressed memories of alien abduction were more prone to recall and recognized the 'lure' falsely compared to the group who denied being abducted by aliens.

Conclusion: The recovered and repressed memory groups were the most prone to false memories. Also, individuals who have a tendency to develop false memories in the laboratory are also those who have a tendency to develop false memories in the real-world.

diagnosed with pain disorder *and* hypochondriasis, (2) a group diagnosed with pain disorder only, (3) a group diagnosed with hypochondriasis only, and (4) a group recruited from the same general practice without pain disorder or hypochondriasis. The word groups presented during the encoding task were positive, negative, pain-related, and neutral. By selecting these word categories the experimenters were testing for the presence of a pain-related memory bias, not a hypochondriasis-related memory bias. The results indicated that those participants who had both hypochrondriasis and pain disorder showed a memory bias in favour of pain words. That this effect was not evident in the pain disorder alone group is inconsistent with the studies reviewed in the previous paragraph. One explanation for this inconsistency is that by recruiting the sample from general practice, as opposed to pain clinics, the sample employed by Pauli and Alpers may have been less severe and less likely to have been in pain at the time of the study. Another possibility, given that the studies reviewed above did not report assessing for the presence of comorbid disorders, is that the pain disorder group in previous research may have included individuals with comorbid hypochrondriasis.

Memory for the sensations of pain has been another interesting area of investigation. In an early study, Rachman and Eyrl (1989) assessed people suffering from episodes of headache pain and menstrual pain. Participants first monitored their pain levels for a period of time. Then, after a 4-week gap, the participants were asked to recall the pain experienced during the monitoring period.

The participants recalled their pain as significantly worse than it actually was. Extending this finding, Richard Bryant (1993) assessed forty people with chronic lower back pain both prior to and following a pain management programme. At the end of the treatment, those who reported an increase in their pain or depression over the course of the treatment overestimated their pre-treatment pain and depression levels. In other words, like we saw for PTSD, it appears that the recall of pain is influenced by current symptoms. Future research is necessary to determine the variables that influence the relationship between recall of pain and current pain levels. In Chapter 2 we reviewed evidence that fear of pain and catastrophizing about the pain was associated with a stronger effect on selective attention to pain stimuli relative to pain disorder per se. Within research on memory, studies have established a role for catastrophizing about the pain in that catastrophizing is associated with better recall of the pain, even after controlling for actual pain (e.g. Lefebvre and Keefe 2002). Based on findings that catastrophizing is associated with superior somatic awareness, Lefebvre and Keefe suggested that people who catastrophize may have enhanced memory for their pain because the pain is more salient to them and therefore better encoded. Wright and Morley (1995) examined the presence of pain-congruent memory by asking participants with and without chronic pain to recall autobiographical memories of pain and non-pain events. Pain patients retrieved more memories of themselves in pain and the memories of pain were recalled significantly faster than non-pain memories. These findings suggest that pain-state may distort the memories retrieved. Future research must rule out the possibility that the patient group had more concern-related experiences to remember.

Eating disorders

Hermans *et al.* (1998) compared people diagnosed with anorexia nervosa and non-dieting control participants. The encoding task comprised four word types: anorexia-related (e.g. diet, thighs), positive, negative, and neutral. The participants were then given an explicit (cued recall) and an implicit (word stem completion) memory test. There was an explicit memory bias for anorexia-related words among people diagnosed with anorexia nervosa but not for the control group. No bias in implicit memory was observed. But note that each group was comprised of 12 individuals. As such, this study may have been insufficiently powered to detect differences.

A study by Sebastian *et al.* (1996) compared a heterogeneous group of people diagnosed with an eating disorder (10 with anorexia, 10 with bulimia, and 10 with an eating disorder not otherwise specified) with a weight-pre-occupied group and a non-weight pre-occupied group. The encoding task involved the presentation of fat (e.g. heavy, plump), non-fat (e.g. build, stature), and neutral (e.g. post, pear) words. For each word the participants were asked to imagine themselves in a past, present, or future scene that involved themselves and a scene related to the cue word. On a free recall test, the eating disorder group selectively recalled more fat words relative to non fat and control words, and compared to both control groups. Finally, Hunt and Cooper (2001) endeavoured to correct for two methodological weaknesses inherent to the previous studies; the absence of controls for the emotionality of the words and the presence of depression. Three groups of women were compared including a group diagnosed with bulimia nervosa, a group diagnosed with depression, and a group with neither bulimia nervosa nor depression. Positively and negatively toned weight/shape words, food words, emotional words, and neutral body words were presented in a self-referential encoding task ('imagine a scene involving yourself and the word'). On a free recall test, the bulimia nervosa group demonstrated a bias in the recall of positive and negative weight/shape words relative to emotional words (but not relative to neutral nouns or body words). A memory bias for food-related words was found in both the bulimia nervosa group and the depression group.

Mood disorders

Unipolar depression

Unipolar depression is the most thoroughly researched disorder in the selective memory literature. Early research involved exploring the effects of experimentally manipulating sad mood on memory in analogue samples (see Box 3.2 for methods used to manipulate mood). However, during the late 1970s and early 1980s the crucial concern was to establish the extent to which the analogue findings reflected processes inherent to depression. In a now classic study, David Clark and John Teasdale (1982) addressed this question by recruiting people diagnosed with depression who experienced diurnal variation in their mood (i.e. marked changes in mood throughout one day). The participants were then tested at two different time points during one day; when feeling significantly more depressed and when feeling significantly less depressed. At each testing session, the participants were asked to retrieve past real-life experiences to a series of neutral stimulus words. The results indicated that memories involving unhappy experiences were more likely to be retrieved on the more depressed occasion and memories involving happy experiences were more likely to be retrieved on the less depressed occasion. That is, mood-congruent memory was demonstrated. In addition, this study elegantly showed that the mood congruence found in non-clinical participants were analogous to processes operating in depressed samples. Further, the findings suggest that memory biases in depression are influenced by state factors such as changes in mood, an effect that has subsequently been replicated (e.g. Fromholt *et al.* 1995).

In a meta-analysis of studies that have investigated memory for positive and negative words or sentences (Matt *et al.* 1992) three noteworthy results emerged. First, control participants recalled 8% more positive words compared to negative words. Second, the bias towards positive words was eliminated in university students who scored high on the Beck Depression Inventory (BDI). Third, people with depression recalled 10% more negative than positive words. In other words, selective memory for negative words is a robust finding in unipolar depression and it has been replicated many times over since the publication of the meta-analysis (e.g. Denny and Hunt 1992; Bradley *et al.* 1995; Power *et al.* 2000—Experiment 3). Further, the results from this meta-analysis suggest that the selective memory effects occur on a continuum with the university students who score high on the BDI falling midway between non-clinical participants and samples diagnosed with depression. One final implication is that in investigations of selective memory in other disorders, it is important to control for the effects of depression. As will become evident, this guide has rarely been followed.

In an extension of these investigations, Ridout and colleagues (2003) investigated memory for sad, happy, and neutral facial expressions among individuals with depression and non-patient controls. While the two groups did not differ in the identification of the emotion in the faces presented, the patients with depression displayed better memory for the sad faces but poorer memory for the happy faces, compared to both the neutral faces and the non-depressed control group. This study demonstrates that the findings of an explicit memory bias using word and sentence stimuli are replicable using more ecologically valid stimuli. The authors speculated that this bias in memory for emotional faces may interfere with interpersonal relationships which rely on accurate perception of facial expressions and may also delay recovery from depression.

> Thus, if a woman has a greater chance of remembering the facial expressions of her husband and children when they are sad, then she might conclude that her family are generally unhappy, which in turn could be interpreted by her as evidence of her being a failure as a wife and mother. Such beliefs could further undermine the individual's self-confidence resulting in feelings of guilt and hence maintain or even intensify the depressed mood (p. 119, Ridout *et al.* 2003).

While there is clear evidence of an explicit selective memory bias in depression, most studies have not detected an implicit bias (Denny and Hunt 1992;

Watkins *et al.* 1992, 1996; Banos *et al.* 2001). The one exception is a recent study by Philip Watkins *et al.* (2000) who administered one of four implicit memory tests to a group diagnosed with depression and a group of non-depressed controls. The novel aspect of the study was that two of the implicit memory tests were perceptually-driven tasks and the other two were conceptually-driven tasks (see page 77 for a definition of these terms). An implicit memory bias for negative words was demonstrated in just *one* of the conceptually-driven tests (word retrieval involving the presentation of a definition, the participant had to provide the word the definition described). Hence, it appears that 'conceptually-driven tests may be necessary but do not appear to be sufficient for demonstrating implicit mood congruent memory in depression' (p. 288, Watkins *et al.* 2000).

Bipolar disorder

Lyon *et al.* (1999) reported that during an encoding task involving the presentation of trait words, a control group and a currently manic group endorsed more positive trait adjectives as 'describing me' relative to negative trait adjectives, whereas the currently bipolar-depressed group endorsed more negative than positive trait adjectives. However, when later asked to recall as many trait words as possible, the control group recalled more positive than negative words, whereas the bipolar-depressed and manic groups both recalled more negative words than positive words. Although limited by the lack of comparison group, the results for the currently manic group were particularly interesting. This group endorsed a high number of positive words, yet recalled a high number of negative words, suggesting that the underlying memory processes may be similar across manic and depressed states. In a small sample of people diagnosed with rapid-cycling bipolar disorder, Eich *et al.* (1997) found evidence for mood-congruent memory in that more positive memories were recalled during a manic or hypomanic mood and more negative memories were recalled during a depressed mood. Further, more memories were recalled when the participant was in a mood that was congruent with their mood during the encoding task (i.e. mood-dependent memory).

Substance-related disorders

Consistent with Goldman and colleagues' proposal that memory processes contribute to drinking decisions among problem drinkers (Goldman *et al.* 1991), several empirical studies have reported an implicit (Zack *et al.* 1999) and explicit (Zack *et al.* 2002) memory bias for alcohol-related words in problem drinkers. Further, Zack *et al.* (2002) reported that state anxiety predicts explicit memory for alcohol-related cues in problem drinkers. This finding is consistent with the proposal that conditioned alcohol-related responses are encoded in memory and that when this memory is activated, the conditioned response (drinking) is prompted (Zack *et al.* 1999; Stein *et al.* 2000). That is, cravings to drink alcohol, for problem drinkers, are increased when the associated cues that are stored in memory (e.g. anxiety) are activated.

Summary

Much has been learned about selective memory for concern-related stimuli. Taking the results of the word cue task and the real world experiments together, there is one or more study reporting evidence for an explicit memory bias for concern-related stimuli in panic disorder, social phobia, OCD, PTSD, GAD, somatoform disorder, eating disorder, unipolar depression, bipolar disorder, and alcohol use disorder. The evidence is least strong for social phobia, OCD, and GAD. However, it is possible that these disorders are less amenable to laboratory-based investigations and that real-world paradigms better capture the effect (as evident in Box 3.2). Accordingly, the evidence indicates that explicit selective memory for concern-related information is a definite transdiagnostic process. The caveat on this conclusion is the need to establish that the real world paradigms tap identical processes to those captured by the word cue task.

Much less research has been devoted to investigations of implicit memory and the evidence has been mixed. As such, implicit selective memory meets our criteria for a possible transdiagnostic process because one or more positive findings have been reported for panic disorder, social phobia, PTSD, GAD, unipolar depression, and substance abuse. An important guide to future research is the work by Philip Watkins and his colleagues (2000) suggesting that an implicit memory test must be conceptually driven (i.e. involving processing of the meaning of the stimuli), as opposed to perceptually-driven (i.e. involving processing of the perceptual features of the stimuli). Further, it is possible that the implicit memory effects may be easier to capture if a fuller context is provided (e.g. by using sentences rather than single words; Amir *et al.* 1996).

Studies on PTSD and pain disorder have indicated that memories are not indelible and that they can be distorted. There is also evidence that current symptoms influence the recall of symptoms experienced in the past. Further, current symptoms of PTSD were shown to influence the recall of the trauma. These are examples of state-dependent memory. The state of being in pain or being traumatized appears to distort memory in a way that amplifies the concerns of patients.

How specific are these findings to the concerns of each patient group? Only a handful of studies have addressed this issue. Radomsky and Rachman (1999, see Box 3.3) compared a group of patients with OCD and a mixed anxious comparison group. The OCD group showed selective memory for contaminated stimuli, the mixed anxious comparison group did not. In a particularly nice example, Ceschi *et al.* (2003, see Box 3.3) reported that OCD-washers displayed superior memory for contaminated items relative to clean items. This effect was not evident for OCD-checkers or patients with social phobia. Lundh and colleagues (1999) administered panic-related, interpersonal threat and neutral words to a group of patients with panic disorder and an age and sex-matched comparison group. On a tachistoscopic identification task, the group of patients with panic disorder identified more panic words than the controls. The two groups did not differ on interpersonal threat words or neutral words. Finally, the explicit selective memory bias in depression appears to be content specific in that it is found for depression-related words but not negative words in general (e.g. Mathews and Bradley 1983; Watkins *et al.* 1992). These studies are consistent with Klinger's current-concern hypothesis (1996) in that they suggest that the selective memory bias is specific to disorder-related concerns, although further research that includes a range of patient groups and a range of concern-relevant stimuli is needed to fully address the specificity of the concerns.

Overgeneral memory

Autobiographical memories are the memories 'a person has of his or her own life experiences' (p. 19, Robinson 1986). In 1986, Mark Williams and Keith Broadbent made an important discovery related to autobiographical memories. Their discovery involved distinguishing between two types of memory; namely, *specific memories* or events that happened at a particular place, at a particular time, and took no longer than one day versus *generic memories* or memories where the time period was not referred to or was greater than one day. Williams and Broadbent noticed that people admitted to hospital, following a suicide attempt, found it difficult to retrieve specific autobiographical memories. In fact, relative to a control group, people who had attempted suicide recalled significantly more generic memories, especially in response to positive cue words. The test Williams and Broadbent administered, now known as the autobiographical memory test, involved presenting a series of cue words, one at a time. For each word, the participant is asked to recall a specific memory that is triggered by the cue word. The participant is then given 60 s to retrieve the specific memory. If the participant's response is not a specific memory (i.e. something that happened at a particular place and time) the participant is prompted again 'can you think of a specific time—one particular event'. To give an example, if the cue word is 'happy' a specific memory would be 'when I went to the beach last Saturday' and a response that is generic would be 'when I go to the beach for holidays'. This finding has triggered considerable research interest as it raises the possibility that psychological disorders might be, at least partly, maintained because of inadequate access to the store of specific knowledge, which is necessary to adequately operate in the world.

Williams and Dritschel (1988) observed that generic memories typically take one of two forms; categoric memories that are summary memories or categories of memories (e.g. my visits to the beach) and extended memories that are events that lasted for more than one day. Compared to participants without a psychological disorder, people with depression retrieved significantly more categoric memories but did not differ in the recall of extended memories. That is, an increase in the recall of categoric memories appears to be associated with psychopathology (Williams and Dritschel 1988). In the following disorder-by-disorder review we will endeavour to establish the extent to which overgeneral memory is common across the disorders.

Anxiety disorders

Social phobia

Wenzel et al. (2002) tested a group of individuals with social phobia, along with a non-anxious control group. The word stimuli were 15 social threat words and 15 neutral words. By including social threat words Wenzel et al. altered the original paradigm, employed with depressed and suicidal patients, so as to increase its relevance to social phobia. However, no differences were detected between the groups for the extent to which the participants retrieved specific memories.

Obsessive-compulsive disorder

Wilhelm et al. (1997) found that people with OCD had difficulty retrieving specific memories, but these results were attributable to comorbid depression, rather than OCD. However, it should be noted that in this study the original paradigm was not altered to enhance its relevance to OCD (by using cue words relevant to OCD concerns).

Post-traumatic stress disorder and acute stress disorder

Two studies by Richard McNally and his colleagues (McNally et al. 1994, 1995) have found evidence for overgeneral memory in Vietnam veterans with PTSD. In the study reported in 1994, the possibility that the effect might be attributable to depression was examined via correlational analyses. A significant positive correlation between the tendency to recall generic memories and PTSD symptoms remained even when the effects of depression were partialled out. Another study compared road traffic accident survivors who either did or did not meet criteria for ASD (Harvey *et al.* 1998). When the influence of depression was entered as a covariate, participants with ASD retrieved fewer specific memories to positive cue words than non-ASD participants. Further, poorer recall of specific memories within one month of the trauma was predictive of PTSD severity, as assessed 6-months posttrauma. Finally, Wessel *et al.* (2002) found elevated overgeneral memory in people in their 60s, often with diagnoses of PTSD following war-related atrocities experienced as children, compared to aged matched controls.

Generalized anxiety disorder

Burke and Mathews (1992) presented a group of people diagnosed with GAD, and a group of controls, with a series of neutral cue words. For each cue word, participants were asked to retrieve either an anxious or a non-anxious memory. While patients with GAD recalled more memories that were later judged as 'nervous', they did not retrieve more generic memories. However, note that the sample size in this study was on the small side ($n = 12$ per group).

Eating disorders

Tim Dalgleish and his colleagues (2003) compared patients with an eating disorder, including patients with a diagnosis of anorexia nervosa and bulimia nervosa, in their ability to retrieve a specific memory to five pleasant and five unpleasant cue words, relative to a non-patient control group. The eating disorder group retrieved more overgeneral memories relative to the non-patient control group. Further, for the group with an eating disorder, the severity of self-reported parental abuse (indexed with the Measure of Parenting Style; Parker *et al.* 1997) was positively correlated with the number of overgeneral memories recalled to negative cue words. This correlation was not found for the non-patient control group.

Mood disorders

Unipolar depression

A robust finding in the literature is that people with unipolar depression, along with those who have recently attempted suicide, find it difficult to recall specific autobiographical memories. Instead, they produce generic memories that are categoric (e.g. Moore *et al.* 1988; Williams and Scott 1988; Puffet *et al.* 1991; Kuyken and Dalgleish 1995). This effect is also observed in postnatal depression (Croll and Bryant 2000) but is not observed in people with seasonal affective disorder (Dalgleish *et al.* 2001*a*). The authors of the latter study suggested that the absence of the effect in seasonal affective disorder reflects the strong biological underpinnings of the disorder, related to seasonal light–dark changes, rather than psychological processes, such as life events (Dalgleish *et al.* 2001*a*). Further, Willem Kuyken and Chris Brewin (1995) found that women with depression who reported childhood sexual abuse produced more overgeneral memories than women with depression with no reported history of child sexual abuse. Self-reported avoidance of the intrusive memories of childhood physical or sexual abuse was positively correlated with the number of overgeneral memories recalled.

The functional significance of overgeneral memory in depression has received some research attention. Several studies have documented a significant positive correlation between an overgeneral memory and ineffective problem-solving in people diagnosed with depression or those admitted to hospital following an attempted suicide (Schotte and Clum 1987; Evans *et al.* 1992; Goddard *et al.* 1997; Sidley *et al.* 1997). How might these findings be explained? There are at least two advantages of retrieving specific events from memory. First, it may allow a person to think of an event in a different way. For example, if a man has a memory of being deliberately ignored by another person, he may reappraise this memory as less negative when he remembers that the other person was walking on the other side of the street so may not have noticed him. Second, access to specific memories may assist in planning and making changes to future behaviour. In the above example, the man may decide that next time he could approach the person.

Several studies suggest that overgeneral memory has an impact on later functioning in that increased categoric recall is associated with poorer long-term outcome in depression (Brittlebank *et al.* 1993; Scott *et al.* 1995; Mackinger *et al.* 2000; Peeters *et al.* 2002) and seasonal affective disorder (Dalgleish *et al.* 2001*a*). However, it should be noted that Brewin *et al.* (1999) did *not* replicate these effects (although Dalgleish *et al.* 2001*a* suggest that this null finding may be attributable to the measure of depression). Research conducted in the context of ASD, as will be discussed below, adds to the findings suggesting that overgeneral memory has an impact on later functioning.

Although overgeneral memory has traditionally been conceived of as an enduring trait (e.g. Williams and Dritschel 1988), three recent studies provide evidence suggesting that autobiographical memory may be modifiable. Two such demonstrations were experimental studies (Watkins *et al.* 2000; Watkins and Teasdale 2001) and one, which will be discussed more fully later in this chapter, was a treatment study (Williams *et al.* 2000).

Bipolar disorder

Jan Scott and her colleagues (2000) reported a study in which people diagnosed with bipolar disorder, but who were remitted (i.e. not within an episode of either mania or depression), recalled more overgeneral memories on the auto-biographical memory test relative to a group of healthy controls. Consistent with the findings for unipolar depression, the bipolar group were less able to generate solutions to social problem solving tasks.

Psychotic disorders

Kaney *et al.* (1999) compared a group of people diagnosed with delusional disorder, a group of people diagnosed with depression, and a group of normal controls. Relative to the control group, the group diagnosed with delusional disorder demonstrated overgeneral memory, especially for categoric memories. However, the depressed group did not show overgeneral memory. In accounting for the latter finding, the authors speculated that the people included in the depression group may have been less severely depressed relative to the depressed groups included in previous studies. However, as the group diagnosed with delusional disorder were less depressed relative to the depression group, the results are unlikely to be solely attributable to comorbid depression.

Summary

This section has reported empirical evidence indicating that overgeneral memory is characteristic of people with current depression and remitted bipolar depression, people who have attempted suicide, those diagnosed with ASD and PTSD, patients diagnosed with an eating disorder and patients diagnosed with delusional disorder. Overgeneral memory was not found, in the absence of depression, among people diagnosed with OCD, social phobia, or GAD. It remains possible that these null findings are attributable to the word stimuli insufficiently priming concerns specific to the disorder (i.e. Burke and Mathews presented neutral cue words to a GAD sample; Wilhelm *et al.* presented positive and negative word cues used in the depression studies; but Wenzel *et al.* did alter the word cues to social threat words). However, until this issue is clarified in future research overgeneral memory is best classified as a possible transdiagnostic process.

Convergent evidence indicates that overgeneral memory is associated with a history of trauma. In addition to the evidence from the studies reported by Kuyken and Brewin (1995) and Dalgleish *et al.* (2003), as well as the studies involving patients with PTSD, Henderson *et al.* (2002) found elevated overgeneral memory in a non-clinical sample of women with a reported history of child sexual abuse. Further, de Decker *et al.* (2003) have reported that exposure to war trauma among adolescents growing up in Bosnia is associated with elevated overgeneral memory, compared to chronic stress (growing up near Chernobyl) or growing up in Belgium (the control group). Future research will need to determine how the form (e.g. emotional, physical, or sexual), age of the person at the time and severity of the trauma influence the degree of overgeneral memory.

There are likely to be several implications of overgeneral memory retrieval. In depression, it is strongly associated with a problem solving deficit. Also, one study with an ASD sample (Harvey *et al.* 1998) and several studies with depressed samples (e.g. Brittlebank *et al.* 1993) indicate that the tendency towards overgenerality is prognostic of a poorer outcome. Finally, it appears that what has been considered a long-term cognitive style may, in fact, be modifiable (e.g. Watkins and Teasdale 2001). This is a point that we will return to in the discussion of clinical implications below.

Avoidant encoding and retrieval

Retaining the theme of access to memory, people suffering from psychological disorders, particularly those disorders that involve exposure to trauma, are thought to adopt an avoidant encoding and retrieval style in an attempt to distance themselves from and cope with the traumatic information. At the outset, it is worth noting that there is likely to be a link between the research reviewed in the previous section and the research reviewed in the present section as some accounts of overgeneral memory, most notably Williams (1996), have conceptualized overgeneral memory as an avoidant retrieval style which functions to reduce the recall of upsetting specific memories (see also Raes *et al.* in press).

Research relating to dissociation is relevant to this section. Dissociation describes the process by which strategies are used to reduce the awareness and control of cognition which causes 'disruption in the usually integrated functions of consciousness, memory, identity, or perception of the environment' (p. 766, American Psychiatric Association 1994). Dissociation is thought to be employed by an individual in an attempt to cope with, avoid, or minimize the adverse emotional consequences of trauma (Janet 1907; van der Kolk and van der Hart 1989). The memory impairment that is characteristic of dissociation may take the form of complete amnesia or a reduction in awareness for an event (Spiegel 1993). Cognitive theorists have emphasized that reduced access to memories of a trauma, due to avoidance or dissociation, serves to maintain disorders such as ASD and PTSD because they function to prevent the processing and resolution of the trauma memory (Foa and Hearst-Ikeda 1996) and prevent change to excessively negative appraisals of the trauma (Ehlers and Clark 2000).

Several conceptual issues within this literature remain to be tackled. First, the term 'dissociation' has been criticized as being too broad. Second, it is not yet clear whether dissociation affects the encoding of memories, the retrieval of memories or both (see Box 3.1 for further discussion of impaired encoding and retrieval). Third, it is not yet clear that dissociation is in fact different from attentional avoidance. Further, as noted by Halligan et al. (2003), dissociation appears to overlap conceptually with perceptual or data-driven processing. Fourth, while we refer to dissociation and other forms of avoidant encoding and retrieval as 'strategies', they do not 'always have an intentional quality. They may be performed in a habitual or reflexive fashion' (p. 328, Ehlers and Clark 2000). This last point means that the empirical investigation of dissociation is particularly challenging.

Problems aside, avoidant encoding and retrieval has been studied using a variety of methodologies. This chapter will focus on those studies that have utilized methodologies involving (1) prospective studies of the predictive power of reports of avoidance and dissociative symptoms, (2) the recall of discrete autobiographical memories, (3) the analysis of the way in which the memories recalled are organized, and (4) the directed forgetting paradigm. Before embarking on our disorder-by-disorder check for avoidant encoding and retrieval processes, the directed forgetting paradigm needs some explanation.

Drawn from the cognitive psychology literature (MacLeod 1989; Johnson 1994), the directed forgetting paradigm has two forms. The *item method* involves the presentation of a word followed by a cue to remember or to forget that word. In participants without a psychological disorder, initial free recall is better for to-be-remembered than to-be-forgotten stimuli, suggesting differential encoding of to-be-remembered and to-be-forgotten stimuli. This is known as the directed forgetting effect. The *list method* involves participants being asked to remember a list of words. Half way through the list they are instructed to forget the first half and to instead remember the second half. As for the item method, initial free recall is better for the to-be-remembered than the to-be-forgotten stimuli. Theoretically, the item method is thought to be sensitive to encoding processes and the list method to be sensitive to retrieval processes. However, it should be noted that the list method has been criticized for confounding memory and recency. That is, the enhanced recall of to-be-remembered items may be a function of recency effects as this list is always presented just prior to retrieval (Moulds, 2002). While this paradigm has mainly been of interest to researchers of psychological disorders thought to be characterized by avoidance of the encoding or retrieval of aversive experiences, more recently it has been extended to explore other aspects of memory (e.g. Power *et al.* 2000; Amir *et al.* 2001).

Anxiety disorders

Specific phobia

Watts *et al.* (1986) explored the cognitive avoidance hypothesis (e.g. Mogg *et al.* 1987); that people with spider phobia will exhibit *poorer* memory for phobia-related stimuli because they avoid focused attention on phobia-related stimuli. The phobic stimuli in these experiments were dead spiders of various sizes mounted on cards. The participants were instructed to 'look at the spiders'. In a first study, the hypothesis that poorer memory for phobia-related stimuli would be present was supported, but only when the stimuli were large spiders. However, in a second study these results did not clearly replicate (Watts *et al.* 1986). Pursuing the hypothesis further, Watts and Coyle (1993) asked participants to watch for one minute as the experimenter handled a live spider. Then the participants were asked to listen to a list of spider-related and neutral words. The results indicated that memory was impaired for words describing an anxiety response (e.g. repelled, recoil) but not for words describing the features of a spider (e.g. fangs, hairy). Watts and Dalgleish (1991) exposed participants with and without a spider phobia to either a dead or alive spider prior to the memory task. The participants were 'encouraged to put one hand as close as possible to the spider. When they stopped moving their hand they were encouraged to go further if they possibly could' (p. 320). The results showed that the spider phobia group had poorer memory for the spider words, but only following exposure to the live spider.

Social phobia

In a recent study, Wenzel and Holt (2002) asked people with social phobia and a non-patient control group to read two social-threat and two neutral passages of prose. The passages of prose were selected in preference to word cues in an attempt to 'provide detailed contextual information…which…would activate relevant fear structures to a greater degree than would single words' (p. 75, Wenzel and Holt 2002). After reading the passage, the participants were asked to recall what they could remember from the passage. The social phobia group were *poorer* at remembering the social-threat passages relative to the control group. This finding was interpreted as supportive of the cognitive avoidance hypothesis.

Post-traumatic stress disorder and acute stress disorder

In the clinical case presented at the beginning of this chapter, when Paula tried to describe her car accident her description was slow, disorganized, and unclear. In an attempt to empirically investigate these organizational aspects of trauma memory, Edna Foa and colleagues collected detailed recollections of the trauma prior to and after exposure-based treatment for PTSD (Foa et al. 1995a). Each phrase within each narrative was coded for various features including fragmentation, disorganization, thoughts, feelings, and actions. Reduced PTSD symptoms following treatment was associated with an increase in the occurrence of organized thoughts and a decrease in fragmentation within the memory narrative. Although it is not possible from this correlational study to draw conclusions about causality, these results are consistent with the hypothesis that a cohesive and organized traumatic memory is important for the resolution of posttrauma symptoms (Foa and Kozak 1986). In a later study, Harvey and Bryant (1999) recruited people who did and did not meet criteria for ASD following a motor vehicle accident. Participants' audiotaped recollections of their memory for the accident were coded in terms of disorganized structure, dissociative content, and perception of threat. The recollections of ASD participants were characterized by more disorganization and dissociation relative to those of non-ASD participants. Further suggesting the importance of disorganization, Halligan et al. (2003) found that disorganization within the trauma narrative predicted subsequent PTSD. Box 3.6 presents a trauma narrative to illustrate disorganization and dissociation. There has been a welcome attempt in subsequent studies to increase the objectivity of the scoring of trauma narratives (Amir et al. 1998; Zoellner et al. 2002), although this issue requires further research attention.

As we have already discussed, reliance on retrospective recall may yield inaccurate data as current symptoms have been shown to influence retrospective reports (Southwick et al. 1997; Harvey and Bryant, 2000). Accordingly, prospective studies are necessary to examine the extent to which the symptoms and processes present soon after a trauma predict the presence of later PTSD. Such studies have indicated that the presence of dissociation (e.g. Shalev et al. 1996, 1997; Halligan et al. 2003), avoidance (e.g. Ehlers et al. 1998; Dunmore et al. 2001), and perceptually-driven or data-driven processing (e.g. Halligan et al. 2003) at the time of the trauma, or soon after, predicts the presence of later PTSD.

Two studies have investigated avoidant encoding and retrieval using the directed forgetting paradigm in individuals diagnosed with ASD and PTSD. McNally et al. (1998) tested three groups of women; adult survivors of child sexual abuse with PTSD, adult survivors of sexual abuse without PTSD, and

Box 3.6 Trauma narrative excerpt demonstrating disorganization and dissociation, characteristic of patients diagnosed with ASD and PTSD

...come down to an intersection I could see I was safe to go through I thought I was safe to go through...I just continued on at the same speed approximately 50–60 miles per hour...and I saw this truck start to pull out in front of me...from nowhere from nowhere...I knew it was too late to do anything I knew I was going to hit him I just screamed out noooooo... I don't believe this is going to happen... a feeling of ah inevitability...that there is nothing I can do to change this...and that its serious from the second it started happening I know it was serious uhm...during it time stood still...everything was in slow motion it was like I was caught in a terrible dream...this is happening to me...I thought everything came back onto me I think oh no I'm dead...stupid so stupid always so careful always so careful I was hanging out over the front had my eyes open...my face almost hit the van and started my car started going backwards I came back away again...my insides were exploding I'm going to die for sure

Note. ... = pauses of 3 seconds or more

women with neither abuse histories or PTSD. The item method was used. That is, a word cue was followed by an instruction to remember or to forget. The word cues included trauma words (e.g. molested), positive words (e.g. confident), or categorized neutral words. Contrary to the hypothesis that PTSD, especially following child sexual abuse, would be characterized by an avoidant encoding style, no deficits were detected for either the to-be-remembered or the to-be-forgotten trauma words.

Michelle Moulds and Richard Bryant (2002) compared two groups of people who had recently experienced trauma; those who met diagnostic criteria for ASD and those who did not. In addition, a non-traumatized control group was tested. Like McNally *et al.'s* (1998) study, the item method was employed with trauma, positive or neutral word cues being followed by the instruction to either remember or forget. On a subsequent recall test, the ASD group displayed poorer recall of the to-be-forgotten trauma-related words compared to non-ASD participants. This suggests that people with ASD display a superior ability to forget aversive material. How can these findings be reconciled with the null findings reported by McNally *et al.* (1998) for people with PTSD? The PTSD and ASD diagnoses differ in that to meet diagnostic criteria for ASD an individual must have experienced at least three out of five dissociative symptoms. As it is possible to be diagnosed with PTSD without experiencing any dissociative symptoms, Moulds and Bryant (2002) suggested that by requiring the presence of dissociation ASD may be more strongly associated with avoidant encoding than PTSD.

Dissociative disorders

Given the latter interpretation of the Moulds and Bryant study, we would expect that studies of directed forgetting in people diagnosed with a dissociative disorder would show a directed forgetting effect. However, to date, only one study has been conducted with individuals diagnosed with dissociative disorder and no evidence was reported for directed forgetting of trauma-related stimuli. In fact, in the group with a dissociative disorder, being told to forget a cue word actually enhanced memory for that cue word (Elzinga *et al.* 2000).

Summary

A handful of studies have found poorer memory for concern-related stimuli in two anxiety disorders; specific and social phobia. These findings have been interpreted, in line with Mogg *et al.'s* (1987) vigilance-avoidance hypothesis, as reflecting an avoidance of the discomfort associated with the elaborative processing of threat. The vigilance-avoidance hypothesis suggests that individuals with an anxiety disorder will initially attend to threat (to facilitate the detection of danger) but then avoid elaborative processing of threat to minimize the discomfort associated with prolonged exposure causing poorer memory for certain information.

Although the findings from the directed forgetting paradigm are mixed, the finding that trauma memories are fragmented and disorganized is consistent with the proposal that ASD and PTSD are characterized by avoidant encoding and retrieval processes. However, firm statements about causality cannot be made based on these results given that the findings are correlational. The link with poorer treatment outcome in one study (Foa *et al.* 1995*a*) is interesting and consistent with cognitive models of PTSD that predict that impaired access to traumatic memories will impede the recovery process by preventing traumatic memories from being activated and modified (e.g. Foa and Kozak 1986).

Overall, it is worth acknowledging that avoidant encoding and retrieval of memories may take a variety of forms including dissociation, disorganization, and probably also overgeneral memory recall. If we consider all of these phenomena to reflect avoidant processing of memories, then avoidant encoding and retrieval meets our criteria for a possible transdiagnostic process.

There are many questions to resolve in future research. What is the relationship between these different forms of avoidance? Do they act together or are they mutually exclusive? For example, does a patient who dissociates also exhibit overgeneral memory or does one memory process preclude the other? What determines which particular aspect of processing is altered?

Perhaps avoidant encoding and retrieval will be a process common to all patients with a traumatic history. As traumatic experiences have been highlighted in the development of a range of psychological disorders, including depression (Weiss *et al.* 1999), psychosis (Neria *et al.* 2002), OCD (De Silva and Marks 1999*b*; 2001), panic disorder with nocturnal panic (Freed *et al.* 1999), sexual disorders (De Silva 2001), and eating disorders (Wonderlich *et al.* 2001), avoidant encoding and retrieval may well turn out to be a definite transdiagnostic process. Although it should be noted that the tentative null finding for dissociative disorders (tentative because there is only one study published at the time of writing) runs contrary to this hypothesis, as dissociative disorders are thought to arise partly from traumatic experiences in childhood.

Recurrent memories

This section discusses investigations of recurrent intrusive memories. In this chapter we are primarily concerned with intrusive images that are linked to memories. Intrusive memories and imagery are thought to be rich with meaning as well as highly informative for understanding strong emotion (Greenberger and Padesky 1995).

Anxiety disorders

Agoraphobia

Day *et al.* (in press) asked 20 patients with agoraphobia and 20 matched controls to describe any recurrent images they experienced in agoraphobic situations, and also any associated memories. All patients with agoraphobia, but no control participants, reported having distinct recurrent images that were typically linked with past memories of distressing events, such as being neglected or abused at home and being attacked.

Social phobia

During a social situation, research indicates that people with social phobia experience negative and distorted observer perspective images (outside the situation looking on) in which they see themselves in a social situation and from an external point of view (Hackmann *et al.* 1998). These images are thought to maintain social phobia because when in a social situation, individuals with social phobia pay relatively little attention to their external environment (as already discussed in Chapters 1 and 2). Instead, they use information from detailed self-observation and monitoring and from the distorted, negative images of themselves from an observer perspective to infer how they come across (Clark and Wells 1995).

In a nice extension of these ideas, both Wells *et al.* (1998) and Coles *et al.* (2001) reported evidence that people with social phobia remember social situations from an observer perspective. In a particularly impressive experimental study, Meredith Coles and her colleagues (2002) controlled for the limitation inherent to previous studies of asking participants to recall a *past* situation, a strategy that precludes control over differences inherent to the situation recalled or the length of time since the situation occurred. Instead, Coles and her colleagues asked participants about their memory for two social situations role-played in the lab. The participants were questioned immediately following the two role-played situations and three weeks later. This methodologically enhanced study replicated the previous finding; at both time points the social phobia group reported more observer perspective memories of the role-played situations relative to controls.

In a novel but uncontrolled study, Ann Hackmann *et al.* (2000) interviewed 22 people with social phobia. All of the participants reported spontaneously occurring imagery. The finding relevant to the current context was that most of these images were linked to memories of an adverse social event. The image and the linked memory were remarkably similar in content such that the 'image appeared to correspond to the abstracted essence of the memory' (p. 606). Raising the possibility that imagery may be involved in the development of social phobia, there was a relationship between when the linked memory occurred and the onset of the social phobia; 41% said it occurred in the same year.

Taking this line of work a step further, Colette Hirsch and her colleagues (in press) investigated whether the negative self-images of performing poorly, when in feared social situations, contaminates the social interaction. High socially anxious participants took part in two conversations with another volunteer. During one conversation, the participant was trained to hold in mind a negative self-image, while during the other conversation the participant was trained to hold in mind a less negative (control) self-image. The results indicated that when holding the negative image the participants rated their anxiety to be higher, used more safety behaviours and rated that they performed more poorly. That is, negative self-images, based on memory of past social situations, did contaminate social interactions.

As we will discuss in more detail later in this chapter, two recent studies indicate a causal role for negative observer perspective self-images in the maintenance of social phobia; one in a patient sample (Hirsch *et al.* 2003*a*) and one in an analogue sample (Spurr and Stopa 2003).

Post-traumatic stress disorder

Although intrusive memories, also known as flashbacks, are considered a hallmark symptom of PTSD (American Psychiatric Association 1994), they have been subjected to relatively little empirical scrutiny. Two very interesting studies significantly progress our knowledge about flashbacks. In the first, Anke Ehlers and her colleagues (2002) interviewed a range of trauma survivors who either did or did not have PTSD. An Intrusion Questionnaire was administered as an index of the quality and content of the intrusive memories experienced. Visual intrusions were the most commonly reported intrusive memories. Importantly, they typically consisted of stimuli that were present immediately before the trauma happened or shortly before the moment that had the largest emotional impact. This finding led Ehlers and her colleagues to advance the *warning signal hypothesis*. This hypothesis states that intrusive memories acquire the status of warning signals through their temporal association with trauma. If this is the case, it represents a major step forward in understanding the role of intrusions in PTSD and provides an explanation as to why intrusions trigger such a strong sense of current threat (Ehlers and Clark, 2000).

As discussed earlier in the chapter, Brewin and his colleagues (1996) proposed that memories of a trauma can be VAMs or SAMs (see page 79 for definitions). Dual Representation Theory would predict that the experience of intrusive memories should be reduced by a concurrent visuospatial task because it would compete for resources with SAMs (Brewin and Holmes 2003). Conversely, a concurrent verbal task would have the opposite effect, and increase the frequency of intrusive memories. Holmes *et al.* (in press) have confirmed these predictions using a series of well-controlled laboratory-based studies. In a further test of the distinction between VAMs and SAMs, Hellawell and Brewin (2002) theorized that a SAM should mainly occupy the visuospatial loop of the central executive within working memory (see page 78 for a reminder of the definition of working memory). They predicted that during the experience of a SAM, performance on a test of visuospatial processing should be impaired. The task involved participants with PTSD completing either a visuospatial task or a verbal task during a flashback (SAM) and an ordinary memory (VAM). The method used to elicit SAMs and VAMs was to ask participants to write a detailed description of the trauma.

At various points during the writing the participant was asked 'are you currently experiencing a flashback?' (which had been defined prior to beginning of the experiment). Then two cognitive tasks were administered. The visuospatial task required the participants to complete the trail making test which involves drawing lines to connect consecutively numbered points on a page without lifting the pen. The verbal task required the participants to count backwards by threes. As predicted, the SAMs were specifically associated with poorer performance on the visuospatial processing task. This study is novel for introducing a self-report (analysis of narrative descriptions) and behavioural (the visuospatial task) test that is sensitive to differences between VAMs and SAMs. However, future research needs to ensure that interrupting a flashback or ordinary memory does not interfere with the flow of the memories such that the cognitive task is simply indexing the aftermath of the memory, rather than the memory itself.

Mood disorders

Unipolar depression

Following several studies showing that people diagnosed with unipolar depression commonly experience intrusive visual memories (e.g. Kuyken and Brewin 1994; Brewin *et al.* 1996), Reynolds and Brewin (1999) compared the intrusive memories reported by a group of people with PTSD and a group of people with depression. This is a particularly interesting comparison given that the intrusive memories and flashbacks experienced by people with PTSD are commonly assumed to be unique. With a semi-structured interview, Reynolds and Brewin (1999) asked the participants about stressful life events and whether these had triggered intrusive memories. For the stressful life events the PTSD group were more likely to have experienced personal illness or assault and the depression group were more likely to have experienced family death, illness, and interpersonal events. Other than this, there were few differences between the groups. Each memory was coded for the presence of anger, sadness, fear, helplessness, and guilt. The only difference to emerge was that helplessness was mentioned more by the PTSD group. No differences were detected between the groups for how long the memories lasted, the physical sensations associated with the memories, and whether a sense of reliving was associated with the memories. In other words, the intrusive memories experienced by people with depression and PTSD appear to be remarkably similar.

Bipolar disorder

One study has identified recurrent memory in bipolar disorder (Mansell and Lam, in press). The participants were asked to recall a memory in response to negative and positive cue words. Compared to a control group, the remitted bipolar group rated the negative memory as more recurrent in everyday life. The memories were rated as vivid and distressing and included themes of personal failure and the experience of depression.

Psychotic disorders

In 1976, Aaron T. Beck suggested that the images experienced by people with psychotic symptoms were important for unlocking the meaning of the symptoms. This is a bold proposal, even today, when the dominant explanation and treatment for psychosis is biologically orientated. To begin the process of testing these ideas, Tony Morrison *et al.* (2002) administered a semi-structured interview to 35 people who were experiencing hallucinations and/or delusions. Seventy five percent of the interviewees reported images. Of these, 71% reported the image to be associated with a past memory. To give the flavour of the findings, four examples are given in Box 3.7. Each example includes the image reported by the participant, the associated psychotic symptom, and the associated memory. The results support Beck's proposal that the images and memories, linked to symptoms, are rich sources of information.

Box 3.7 Case examples of the link between psychotic symptoms, imagery, and a past memory (Morrison *et al.* 2002)

Image: Being chopped up with axes
Psychotic symptom: Persecutory delusion
Associated memory: Being physically assaulted in a pub

Image: Man with beard shouting
Psychotic symptom: Voices criticizing self
Associated memory: Being raped as an adult and sexually abused as a child

Image: Being led away to prison by two large policemen, crowds watching.
Psychotic symptom: Paranoia (when he believes he is responsible for a world disaster)
Associated memory: Believing he was responsible for his grandfather's death

Image: Self-rocking in a psychiatric hospital
Psychotic symptom: Voices and paranoia
Associated memory: I am going mad

These findings require replication in a study that includes a patient control group and a non-patient control group.

Summary

Studies have indicated the presence of recurrent intrusive memories in all of the disorders investigated including agoraphobia, social phobia, PTSD/ASD, depression, and psychosis. As such, recurrent memory appears to be a definite transdiagnostic process. In PTSD, the recurrent memories may have become a warning signal and in psychosis some symptoms appear to link with past memories. In addition, it appears that the recurrent memories reported by individuals with depression are similar to those reported by individuals with PTSD. Observer perspective images are present in individuals with social phobia.

Working memory

Investigations of working memory in psychological disorders have, to date, been mainly limited to studies based on analogue populations. To give one of the most novel examples, Ron Rapee (1993) tested undergraduate students on one of four tasks. The first task utilized the phonological loop only (repeat the word 'one' once per second). The second task utilized both the phonological loop and the component of the central executive concerned with the phonological loop (generate a random letter of the alphabet once per second). The third task utilized the visuospatial sketchpad (strike a keypad, once per second, in an S-shaped pattern). The fourth task utilized both the visuospatial sketchpad and the component of the central executive concerned with the visuo-spatial sketchpad (strike random keys, once per second, on the keypad). Whilst performing one of these four tasks, the participant was asked to worry. The prediction tested was that the four tasks would differ in their ability to interfere with worry. Specifically, on the basis of the evidence that worry is primarily verbal (an issue that will be discussed in Chapter 5) it was predicted that the tasks utilizing the phonological loop would be more successful in blocking worry. Indeed, the task in which the participants generated a random letter of the alphabet once per second interfered with worry the most, followed by the task involving repetition of the word 'one' (but non-significantly so). This result has at least two implications; it provides evidence for the utility of Baddeley and Hitch's (1974) model and it adds support to the proposal that worry is primarily verbal, an issue that will be discussed in Chapter 5. Additionally, these findings suggest that worry involves the phonological loop of the central executive of working memory. The extent to which these findings generalize to patients with GAD (characterized by chronic worry) remains to be established.

Memory distrust

David Tolin and his colleagues (2001) found that when people with OCD are repeatedly exposed to 'unsafe objects' (e.g. simulated blood and faeces) their confidence in their memory for the objects progressively declined over successive trials. In contrast, confidence remained high for the anxious controls and non-anxious controls. This is an interesting result that is consistent with other research in the area (McNally and Kohlbeck 1993; Zitterl *et al.* 2001) and it provides a possible account for why people with OCD engage in repeated checking; they need to continue checking because they have less confidence in their memory the more often they are exposed to the feared stimuli. Further studies should explore the mechanism for this effect. We will discuss memory confidence further in Chapter 5.

Discussion

The aim of this chapter has been to establish the extent to which memory processes are relevant across the disorders. As summarized in Table 3.1, the quality of the evidence that has accrued can be improved for virtually every memory process. Further, memory processes have not yet been investigated in several disorders. Nonetheless, the processes that meet our criteria for a definite transdiagnostic process are explicit selective memory and recurrent memory. The processes that meet our criteria for being a possible transdiagnostic process are implicit selective memory, overgeneral memory, and avoidant encoding and retrieval. For working memory and memory distrust, too little research has been conducted across disorders to draw conclusions. We will now move on to elaborate on these decisions and discuss their theoretical implications.

Definite transdiagnostic processes

Explicit selective memory

Although the findings for explicit selective memory in social phobia, OCD, and GAD using the traditional word cue task were weak, the positive findings to emerge from studies that have used real world designs raise the possibility that positive results have not been forthcoming for these disorders because the traditional word cue paradigm has not sufficiently captured the phenomena of interest. In support of this view, the more ecologically valid studies have turned up positive results for OCD and social phobia. Accordingly, the

Table 3.1 Summary of findings across the psychological disorders (first column) and the memory processes (top row)

	Explicit selective memory	Implicit selective memory	Overgeneral memory	Avoidant encoding and retrieval	Recurrent memory	Processes of working memory	Memory distrust
Panic disorder with or without agoraphobia	*** +/–	** +/–			** +		+
Specific phobia							
Social phobia	*** +/–	** +/–	** –	** +/–	*** +		
OCD	** +/–	** –	** –	** +			** +
PTSD/ASD	** +/–	** +/–	*** +	*** +/–	*** +		
GAD	*** +/–	** +/–	* –				
Pain disorder	** +/–					* +	
Dissociative disorder				* –			
Sexual disorder							
Eating disorder	** +	* –	** +				
Sleep disorder							
Unipolar depression	*** +	** +/–	*** +/–		** +		
Bipolar depression	** +		** +		** +		
Psychotic disorder			** +		* +		
Substance disorder	** +	** +					

Note. For each memory process the left hand column presents an indication of the quality of the evidence as follows: *** = good quality evidence, ** = moderate quality of evidence, * = tentative quality of evidence (see page 21–22 for criteria for each) and the right hand column presents an indication of the findings as follows: + = positive findings, – = negative findings, +/– = mixed findings, black space = the memory process has not been researched in this disorder.

evidence that has accrued to date suggests that explicit selective memory for concern-related information is a definite transdiagnostic process.

Theoretically, a number of predictions have been made about the role of selective memory biases. Although differing in many details, a prediction in common between the schema model (Beck *et al.* 1979) and the associative network model (Bower 1981, 1987) is that when a schema (for the former model) or node (for the latter model) is activated, attention and memory will be biased towards material that is congruent with the activation. That is, these models predict that psychological disorders should be characterized by better encoding and recall for concern-related information.

In 1988 and 1997, Williams *et al.* concluded that the accruing data did not support the predictions made by Beck and colleagues and Bower. In making sense of the data, Williams and his colleagues drew on Schneider and Shiffrin's (1977) distinction between automatic processes that are fast, operate without awareness and are not affected by capacity limitations, and strategic or elaborative processes that are capacity limited and slow. Their proposal, regarding memory, is that encoding and retrieval utilize both automatic and strategic processes and that these can operate independently from each other (i.e. if a bias in automatic processes is present it does not necessarily mean that a bias in strategic processes will be present). Williams *et al.* suggest that the data may be explicable if different emotional states turn out to affect automatic and strategic processes differently. For example, the data reviewed by Williams *et al.* (1988) led them to suggest that people with anxiety disorders might not be characterized by a bias in elaborative processes (accounting for the negative findings on the explicit memory tests), but might be characterized by a bias in automatic processes (accounting for the positive findings on implicit memory). That is, patients with an anxiety disorder may show an (early) automatic processing bias whereby they selectively attend to threats relevant to their concerns, but not a (later) elaborative processing bias (protecting the person from having to endure excessive fear). For people with depression, the data reviewed by Williams *et al.* appeared to be in the opposite direction. People with depression appear to exhibit a bias in elaborative processing (accounting for the positive findings on explicit memory tasks), but not a bias in automatic processing (accounting for the negative findings on implicit tasks). These proposals were broadly supported in both the 1988 and 1997 reviews (Williams *et al.* 1988, 1997). However, since then more ecologically valid experiments (e.g. Radomsky and Rachman 1999; Creschi *et al.* 2003) and studies controlling for conceptually-driven versus perceptually-driven processing tasks (Watkins *et al.* 2000) have been published. Including these more recent studies the evidence appears to be more consistent with the schema and associative network theories; that there is a selective memory bias across disorders. However, this conclusion clearly depends on the results of further research and on the assumption that the more ecologically valid studies tap the same memory processes as the traditional word cue paradigm. Also, other problems inherent to the schema model and the associative network model remain, as elegantly summarized by John Teasdale and Phil Barnard (1993).

Earlier we drew a distinction between *mood-congruent memory* (preferential memory for information that is consistent with the person's current mood state) and *mood-dependent memory* (preferential memory for information that was learned in a particular mood state when that mood state is reinstated) and said that in the cognitive psychology literature mood-congruent memory had been easier to demonstrate than mood-dependent memory. As most of the studies reviewed in this chapter did not specifically index the mood state of participants during the experiment these memory phenomena have been addressed by only a handful of studies. Mood-congruent memory was reported in depression (Clark and Teasdale 1982), bipolar disorder (Eich *et al.* 1997), and chronic pain (Wright and Morley 1995). Mood-dependent memory was observed in bipolar disorder (Eich *et al.* 1997). Also, mood-congruence was one potential explanation of the finding that patients with PTSD and chronic pain tend to magnify their recall of previous symptoms and events in a way that is consistent with their current symptoms (e.g. Southwick *et al.* 1997; Harvey and Bryant 2000).

Recurrent memories

Recurrent intrusive memories occur in a range of disorders including agora-phobia, social phobia, PTSD, depression, bipolar disorder, and psychosis. Accordingly, the evidence to date suggests that recurrent memories meet our criteria for being a definite transdiagnostic process. The content of the memories relate to concerns that are specific to each disorder. In the PTSD literature recurrent memories have been conceptualized as reminding the person of the need to integrate and make sense of the traumatic information that is incompatible with the view of the world held prior to the trauma (Foa and Kozak 1986; Horowitz 1986). A more recent, not inconsistent, contribution is the evidence suggesting that recurrent memories may operate as a warning signal (Ehlers *et al.* 2002). This proposal was based on the finding that the content of recurrent memories in patients with PTSD typically reflects events that occurred just prior to the trauma. It would make evolutionary sense that humans have a capacity whereby they are regularly reminded to avoid future trauma by way of these continual warning signals. While this may be adaptive if the threat is ongoing (e.g. ongoing war), the warning signals will trigger unnecessary anxiety and distress if the trauma has past (e.g. a motor vehicle accident). There is a need to establish whether recurrent memories are present across disorders because (1) trauma history is common across disorders (e.g. de Silva and Marks 1999b, 2001; Neria et al. 2002) or because (2) the conceptualizations of the PTSD theorists (e.g. Horowitz 1986) have relevance across disorders. Note that the onset events recalled by individuals with social phobia do not appear to reflect trauma in the same sense as that required for a diagnosis of PTSD because the images reported by social phobia patients involve embarrassment, ridicule, or humiliation rather than threat of physical harm.

It should be noted that many of the recurrent memory studies reviewed above are interview studies. While a clear advantage of interview studies is that they are a rich source of information they also suffer obvious limitations; they rely on self-report, retrospective memory, and as discussed earlier, will be influenced by the current symptoms of the participant. Hence, the move toward experimental studies is welcome (e.g. Holmes et al. in press).

Possible transdiagnostic processes

Implicit selective memory

The results for implicit selective memory are more tentative than the explicit memory findings. However, given that there are positive findings for panic disorder, social phobia, PTSD, GAD, unipolar depression, and problem drinking, implicit selective memory for concern-related information meets our criteria for a possible transdiagnostic process. The theoretical discussion included under the heading 'explicit selective memory' in the previous section encompasses these findings as implicit memory effects reflect automatic processes (Schnieder and Shiffrin 1977).

Overgeneral memory

Overgeneral memory is evident in PTSD/ASD, eating disorders, unipolar and bipolar depression, and psychosis (although note the one negative finding by Kaney et al. 1999 for unipolar depression). To date, overgeneral memory has not been found to be characteristic of individuals diagnosed with social phobia, OCD, or GAD. However, these are tentative findings as there has only been one published study that has investigated autobiographical memory in each disorder. Further, as already discussed, it may be important to adapt the paradigm to more fully capture the concerns of the target disorder. Given this level of evidence, we have concluded that overgeneral memory is a possible transdiagnostic process.

The extent to which a previous trauma history is necessary and/or sufficient for the development of an overgeneral retrieval style is an important issue. History of trauma has been incorporated into the leading theory of the development of an overgeneral retrieval style, as proposed by Mark Williams in 1996. This theory draws on work by Martin Conway and colleagues who propose, as illustrated in Fig. 3.1, that autobiographical knowledge is structured in a hierarchy comprised of lifetime periods at the upper level, general events at the middle level, and event-specific knowledge at the lowest level (Conway and Rubin 1993). Accessing autobiographical knowledge at one level is thought to facilitate access to knowledge stored at the next level. For the successful retrieval of a specific memory, the retrieval process must not be aborted before the lowest level is accessed. Further, memories of general events need to be inhibited at some stage in the retrieval process so that a specific memory can be retrieved (Williams 1996).

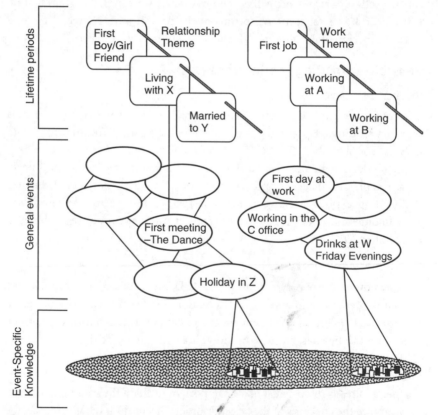

Fig. 3.1 Conway's (1996) memory hierarchy of lifetime events, generic memories, and specific memories. From Conway, M.A. (1996). 'Autobiographical memories and autobiographical knowledge'. In D.C. Rubin, ed. *Remembering our past: studies in autobiographical memory* (p. 68). England: Cambridge University Press. Copyright 1996 by Cambridge University Press. Reprinted with permission.

With this background in mind, Williams (1996) suggested that the ability to exert control over an overgeneral memory, such that a specific memory can be retrieved, develops when children are 3–4 years of age (Nelson and Gruendel 1981). If living in conditions of chronic stress in childhood, Williams has suggested that the child learns that recalling a specific memory is aversive and punishing (due to the negative affect experienced). Accordingly, when cued to recall a negative autobiographical memory, an overgeneral memory is retrieved in order to begin the process of accessing a specific memory. But, before a specific memory can be retrieved, the search is aborted due to prior learning that specific memories are aversive. This search process is initiated again and again; attempts to retrieve a specific memory followed by aborting the process at the general memory level. The result of this process is that the negative overgeneral descriptions become overelaborated and chronically activated. Williams (1996) coined the term 'mnemonic interlock' to describe this overgeneral encoding-retrieval cycle that blocks retrieval of specific memories due to excessive access to overgeneral memories. As we highlighted earlier in this chapter, empirical support for a link between overgeneral memory and trauma is increasing (Kuyken and Brewin 1995; Henderson et al. 2002; de Decker et al. 2003; Dalgliesh et al. 2003), although Ineke Wessel and her colleagues (2001) found that a diagnosis of depression, but not reported childhood trauma, predicted overgeneral memory in patients with depression, patients with anxiety disorders, and non-patient controls.

Evidence that overgeneral memory acts as a form of cognitive avoidance is less well-established. In support of the affect regulation hypothesis proposed by Williams (1996), a recent analogue study found that individuals who tended to recall specific memories experience more subjective stress following a failure feedback task relative to individuals who tended to recall overgeneral memories (Raes et al. in press).

Avoidant encoding and retrieval

Various paradigms have been developed to index the presence of an avoidant encoding and retrieval style. This issue has been of particular interest in those disorders that involve a history of exposure to trauma. As seen in Table 3.1, there is some evidence for the presence of an avoidant encoding and retrieval style in ASD and PTSD, but not dissociative disorders. In addition, there is evidence of avoidant encoding in specific phobia and social phobia. As such, the state of the evidence is that avoidant encoding and retrieval qualifies as a possible transdiagnostic process. The theoretical relevance of these findings is best discussed in two parts.

To take the results for ASD and PTSD first, both dissociative theory (e.g. Spiegel 1993) and cognitive theory (e.g. Foa and Hearst-Ikeda 1996) predict that avoiding the encoding and/or retrieval of trauma-related material protects the individual from the distress and arousal associated with remembering and allows the person to distance themselves from, and therefore cope with, the traumatic memories. However, avoiding or dissociating from memories of trauma prevents the processing and resolution of the traumatic memories and hence maintains trauma-related symptoms (Foa and Kozak 1986). Given this theoretical account, it is surprising to note the null finding for dissociative disorders.

To move onto the findings for specific and social phobia, these are best interpreted in terms of Mogg et al.'s (1987) vigilance-avoidance hypothesis. As discussed in Chapter 2, this theory suggests that individuals with an anxiety disorder will initially attend to threat (to facilitate the detection of danger) but then avoid elaborative processing of threat to minimize the discomfort associated with prolonged exposure. This serves to maintain the anxiety as the individual will be unable to retrieve information related to the past threats they encountered so that they can more realistically appraise stimuli in their environment.

Distinct processes and inconclusive processes

No clearly distinct processes were identified although more research is needed to establish how the components of working memory operate across disorders. Similarly, memory distrust has only been examined in OCD and the findings indicate that memory confidence progressively declines with repeated exposure to OCD-relevant stimuli (Tolin et al. 2001). Again, further research is required before conclusions can be drawn about the extent to which memory distrust is a process that is present across disorders.

Do memory processes play a causal role?

Many of the studies reviewed in this chapter are self-report or experimental manipulations that capture a memory process without examining the impact of the process on symptomatology. As such, few studies comment on the causal role of memory processes. The studies most suggestive of a causal role are the prospective studies showing that dissociation, avoidant coping style, and perceptually-driven processing, at the time of a trauma or soon after, predicts subsequent PTSD (e.g. Shalev et al. 1997; Ehlers et al. 1998, 2003). In addition, there are a number of studies indicating that overgeneral memory is predictive of subsequent depressive symptoms (e.g. Brittlebank et al. 1993; Mackinger et al. 2000) and one study reporting that overgeneral memory is predictive of subsequent PTSD (Harvey *et al.* 1998). As will be discussed further in Chapter 4, prospective studies are a less reliable indicator of causality relative to experimental studies. As such, a challenge for researchers has been to work out methods whereby memory processes can be manipulated in an ecologically valid way. Several creative studies have done just this.

A recent attempt at manipulating memory processes is described by Philippot *et al.* (2003). In two studies, non-clinical participants were primed to recall autobiographical memories in either a specific or an overgeneral mode, prior to a mood induction (mental imagery in the first study, films in the second study). In both studies, priming for a general memory mode, prior to the induction, resulted in more change in mood relative to priming a specific mode. This finding suggests that the type of memories retrieved can influence affect. If shown to generalize to a patient population, these findings would suggest a causal role for memory in influencing symptoms. Further, Spurr and Stopa (2003) reported that giving a speech while using the observer perspective produced more negative thoughts, safety behaviours, and more negative self-evaluation than giving a speech while using the field perspective. Although this was an analogue study comparing university students high and low in social anxiety, it raises the possibility that observer perspective images of social situations serve a causal role in perpetuating the symptoms of social phobia. In another analogue study, as already described, Colette Hirsch and her colleagues (in press) showed that holding negative self-images in mind during a social situation contaminated the social situation. Finally, in the only study we could identify that has tested the causal role of memory processes in a patient group, Hirsch *et al.* (2003*a*) asked patients diagnosed with social phobia to participate in two conversations with a stranger; one while holding their usual negative self-image in mind and one while holding a control self-image in mind. The results indicated that whilst holding a negative self-image in mind the patients with social phobia rated that they experienced more anxiety, felt their anxiety to be more visible and rated their performance as poorer, relative to when they held the control self-image in mind. Further, blind ratings indicated that when holding a negative self-image in mind the patients with social phobia appeared more anxious and behaved less positively. That is, this clever study provides evidence that self-imagery plays a causal role in the maintenance of social phobia.

Theoretical issues

Over the course of this chapter we have seen that the memory processes relate to the concerns of each patient group. For example, Radomsky and Rachman (1999) showed the presence of selective memory for contamination in patients with OCD but not in an anxious comparison group and Lundh *et al.* (1999)

reported that patients with panic disorder selectively remember panic-related words but not interpersonal threat words. In other words, patients demonstrate memory biases towards their current concerns (Klinger 1996). The implication is that this memory bias towards one's current concerns is likely to impede the encoding and storage of a broader range of information and, instead, enhance the storage of those memories that confirm pre-existing beliefs.

In the previous section we worked through each memory process, one-by-one, discussing theoretical accounts of the empirical findings. Can we go further? Is there an account that spans and encompasses the range of findings reviewed? If there is, we suggest that the key theme of such an account should be *access to memory* for concern-related information. The empirical data we have reviewed indicates evidence for both poorer access to memory (the over-general memory and avoidant encoding and retrieval findings) *and* superior access to memory (the selective explicit/implicit memory and recurrent memory findings). As the demonstrations of superior access are for information consistent with the patient's current concerns, these demonstrations can be viewed as indicative of a restriction on access to the full store of memories. That is, preferential access to some memories (those related to concerns) at the expense of access to other memories. Accordingly, we suggest that a distinguishing feature of patients with psychological disorders is that access to their store of memories is impoverished because: (1) access to the store of specific memories is impeded, (2) dissociation and avoidance impair encoding and/or retrieval, and/or because (3) of the dominance of current concerns.

There are at least six reasons why this poor access to the broad store of memories is likely to contribute to the maintenance of psychopathology across disorders. First, a bias in implicit and/or explicit memory towards disorder-congruent concerns and recurrent disorder-related memories will increase access to information that confirm the necessity of the concern. Second, increased access to concern-related information will bias reasoning processes, which are influenced by the availability of memories, as we will discuss in Chapter 4. Third, current symptoms seem to distort retrieval (Southwick *et al.* 1997; Harvey and Bryant 2000) in a way that confirms current concerns. Fourth, poor access to the store of specific memories is likely to block emotional processing resulting in the maintenance of current concerns (Foa and Kozak 1986). Emotional processing and its relationship with thought processes will be discussed in Chapter 5. Fifth, poor access to the broadest range of (specific) memories will prevent spontaneous alteration of unhelpful beliefs and appraisals (Ehlers and Clark 2000). Finally, reduced access to specific memories is associated with poor problem solving (Williams 1996).

Given the likely importance of access to memory processes in the maintenance of psychological disorders, we need to consider what determines access. Both encoding and retrieval processes will obviously be important. What determines whether encoding takes place and, if it does, what the quality or depth of encoding is? First, the person's current concerns will influence the information that is encoded, as evident in the selective memory section of this chapter. Consistently, recent accounts of autobiographical memory emphasize that personal goals play a major role in the formation, access, and construction of personal memories (Conway and Pleydell-Pearce 2000). Second, based on the weapon focus effect (described in Box 3.1), the presence of threat stimuli will contribute to selective encoding. Third, based on the evidence reviewed in patients with chronic pain (Spanos *et al.* 1979; Lefebvre and Keefe 2002) thought processes, such as rumination and catastrophizing lead to stronger, but more selective memory. Thought processes will be discussed further in Chapter 5. Finally, the extent to which the information is processed conceptually (i.e. in terms of the meaning) versus perceptually (i.e. just fragments and impressions) will influence access to memory with conceptual processing resulting in a better quality memory (Ehlers and Clark 2000).

In terms of retrieval processes that determine later access to memory, current concerns are again going to be important (Conway and Pleydell-Pearce 2000). Second, retrieval will be impaired by the tendency towards overgeneral retrieval (e.g. Williams 1996), which in turn appears to be sensitive to the cognitive state prevailing prior to autobiographical memory recall (Watkins *et al.* 2000; Watkins and Teasdale 2001). Indeed, Watkins and colleagues found that reducing analytical rumination reduced overgeneral memory in patients diagnosed with depression, suggesting that overgeneral memory recall is a dynamic process dependent on the mode of processing at retrieval. Third, current symptoms reduce access to the broadest range of memories (Southwick *et al.* 1997; Harvey and Bryant 2000). Finally, retrieval will be adversely affected if a memory is fragmented and disorganized (Foa *et al.* 1995*a*; Harvey and Bryant 1999). Where does dissociation fit in? The jury is still out as to whether dissociation affects encoding or retrieval, but it is fairly clear that dissociation contributes to reduced access to memory.

Why is access restricted? How might restricted access be functional? We suggest that restricted access to memory can be understood as an attempt at affect regulation. Such an interpretation is consistent with proposals made by Williams (1996) in the context of overgeneral memory. Perhaps the most interesting issue is that we do not yet know whether one patient will show all of the memory processes that we have reviewed in this chapter. If not, what might determine the presence of one memory process over another?

One possibility is that the memory process/es present may be influenced by learning history, including the experience of trauma. Another possibility is that the various memory processes that we have reviewed operate as a hierarchy such that an individual who has a low need to regulate affect might exhibit one memory process and an individual with a high need to regulate affect might exhibit another memory process.

To summarize, we suggest that many of the memory processes reviewed in this chapter can be conceived as causing impaired access to the broadest range of memories and that this impaired access, in turn, contributes to the maintenance of psychological disorders. Several of the findings we have reviewed can be understood to be the by-products of impaired access. For example, perhaps obsessional rumination impairs access to memory, causing memory distrust in OCD. The recurrent memory findings may also be viewed as a by-product of impaired access. If access to memory is poor it will be difficult to process and resolve recurrent memories. This view is consistent with Horowitz's (1986) proposal that the function of recurrent memories is to bring the information into awareness so as to provide an opportunity for the individual to integrate the information contained within the memory. As already highlighted, an issue that remains to be resolved is the extent to which impaired access to memory is independent of or explained by trauma history. Further, the relationship between the memory processes and their role in affect regulation requires clarification.

Clinical implications

Avoidant encoding and retrieval

Several strategies are likely to be important for the treatment of avoidant encoding and retrieval. First, it is helpful to educate the client about the potential adverse consequences of prolonged avoidance. Ehlers and Clark (2000) make use of analogies. For example, to explain the concept of a disorganized memory and to provide a rationale for exposure treatment, the following metaphor is used:

> imagine 'a cupboard in which many things have been thrown in quickly and in a disorganized fashion, so it is impossible to fully close the door and things fall out at unpredictable times. Organizing the cupboard will mean looking at each of the things and putting them into their place. Once this is done, the door can be closed and remains shut' (p. 337).

Another approach is to conduct, within a session, an experiment in which the client is asked to close their eyes and try very hard not to think about a big white fluffy polar bear. This experiment was conducted with Paula (the clinical case presented at the beginning of the chapter) who reported that the suppression of white bear images was impossible and that she spent the whole time thinking about the polar bear (see Chapter 5 for further discussion of the thought suppression literature). For Paula the experience of trying to suppress big white polar bears was a compelling example of the adverse consequences of trying to avoid remembering her accident. In the subsequent discussion, the concept of avoidance was broadened from cognitive avoidance to avoidance of places and people who reminded Paula of her car accident. Hence, this in-session task laid the ground work for exposure therapy.

Second, as discussed earlier, Foa *et al.* (1995a) found an increase in the organization of trauma memories following exposure therapy. This result suggests that exposure treatment may be useful for correcting the disorganization and fragmentation of the trauma memory. Exposure therapy typically involves an imaginal component and an *in vivo* component. Imaginal exposure requires the individual to vividly imagine the trauma, including all details, both sensory and affective, for prolonged periods. Ehlers and Clark (2000) suggest starting imaginal exposure by asking the client to review the entire sequence of the events surrounding the trauma. At various points during this review the level of distress experienced is recorded. This process will assist in identifying the most distressing parts of the trauma, called the 'hot spots' (Richards and Lovell 1999). Focusing on these 'hot spots' in further imaginal exposure sessions, and in the discussion before and after each session, can assist in identifying and correcting unhelpful appraisals of the trauma. The process of cognitive restructuring within exposure has been described in some detail by Grey *et al.* (2002) who nicely demonstrate how the technique can be applied not only to memories associated with fear but also to hot spots involving intense guilt, shame, or disgust. Therapy may also incorporate *in vivo* exposure that involves live graded exposure to the feared trauma-related stimuli (see Foa and Meadows 1997; Harvey *et al.* 2003a). During the exposure component of therapy with Paula it was important to start with imaginal exposure as this increased her confidence in her ability to cope with recalling the memories. As Paula gained confidence, *in vivo* exposure commenced.

Third, to clarify the sequence of events it may be important to obtain factual information from various sources including eyewitnesses and police and ambulance records. Paula and her therapist consulted the police reports and discovered the exact location of the accident. They then went back to the scene of the accident to work out how the accident happened. They also met with a doctor to discuss how Paula's husband died. The cause of death turned out to be head injury. Paula was distressed during the meeting but expressed some relief on hearing that he was unconscious (i.e. not aware) and that he did not die by choking on blood, as she had feared. In other words, therapy can focus on restructuring the memory in order to incorporate the factual information that is known about the incident and thereby reduce distress.

Recurrent memories and imagery

Moving onto recurrent memories, the treatment approaches discussed above are well documented to assist in reducing the occurrence of intrusive flash-backs. Given that flashbacks may be a 'warning signal', the therapist may need to make sure that a clear distinction is made between the harmless (current) trigger for an intrusion and the original (past) trigger that was part of the trauma (Ehlers *et al.* 2002). Therapy time should be devoted to assisting the patient to spot triggers to intrusions following which 'detailed discussion of the similarities and differences between the present and the past ... can be used to facilitate stimulus discrimination' (p. 341, Ehlers and Clark 2000). Paula also experienced recurrent memories in the form of nightmares. Empirically supported treatment approaches for nightmares include writing down the nightmare, changing it in any way the patient wishes, writing down the changed dream and rehearsing it in the imagination and in the waking state for 10–15 min a day (Krakow *et al.* 2001; see Harvey *et al.* 2003*b* for review). Treating Paula's nightmares was attempted after she had made progress with imaginal and *in vivo* exposure. As Paula's insomnia seemed to be fuelled by fear of going to sleep due to fear of having a nightmare, the intervention for the nightmares quickly led to better sleep which, in turn, led to an enhanced sense of coping during the day.

Moving onto a discussion of images more generally, therapists should consider routinely asking clients about the experience of intrusive memories and imagery. It might be necessary to set, as one goal for therapy, a reduction in the frequency of images or the distress associated with images (Morrison *et al.* 2002). Ann Hackmann (1997) has described various techniques that can be employed when working with images. These include unlocking the meaning of images through traditional cognitive therapy techniques such as socratic questioning, guided discovery, and behavioural experiments. For highly traumatic memories, Hackmann (1997) recommends actively reconstructing the traumatic image so as to incorporate the new perspectives discovered during the therapy sessions (see also Layden *et al.* 1993). Modifying the content or meaning of the image may require the creative use of role plays involving characters associated with the image. For example, Paula was constantly fearful for the safety of her children who, at the time of therapy, were 8 and 11 years of age. This fear was fuelled by occasional horrific images of their mangled bodies in mangled cars. Her fears led her to declare a close to total ban on travelling in cars and buses, causing a great deal of conflict within the family. In-session role plays, where Paula and the therapist took turns to play 'the mother' and 'the daughters', helped Paula to discover a new perspective; that her daughters were safe, healthy, and well. Further, she discovered that they were sensible and mature for their age and had a good sense of safe and unsafe situations. These new perspectives gave Paula an alternative response to the horrific images ('no, they're both safe and well') and removed much of the distress associated with the images. This accompanied a marked decrease in the frequency of the image. In addition, Paula felt more confident in granting her children freedoms appropriate for their age.

Recent research confirms the utility of directly modifying negative observer perspective self-images in patients with social phobia, as recommended by some cognitive therapy programmes (e.g. Clark and Wells 1995). Hirsch *et al.* (2003*a*) showed that it was possible to replace a negative self-image with a less negative one in patients with social phobia and that this reduced anxiety and improved performance. The technique used was an adaptation of the video feedback method described by Clark and Wells (1995) and empirically examined by Harvey et al. (2000). Also, recall that earlier we described an analogue study in which Spurr and Stopa (2003) reported that giving a speech while using the observer perspective produced more negative thoughts, safety behaviours, and more negative self evaluation than giving a speech while using the field perspective. This raises the possibility that it may be helpful to train patients with social phobia (and perhaps others who adopt an observer perspective) to adopt a field perspective during a social situation. Here is an extract from Spurr and Stopa's procedure for promoting a field perspective during a speech:

> As you are speaking, focus your attention on your surroundings. For example, if you were giving a presentation to an audience, as you usually would be, you might observe people's expressions and actions or notice details about their appearance.... Try as much as possible to be aware of the environment, rather than yourself. Try not to think about yourself, try not to monitor your own behaviour or reactions (p. 9, Spurr and Stopa, 2003).

Overgeneral memory

Overgeneral memory retrieval should also be targeted in therapy. Given the association with problem-solving and the possible prognostic significance there is an urgent need for treatments that specifically seek to help patients access their store of specific memories. A first step in treating patients who tend to retrieve overgeneral memories is to recognize that a 'patient's difficulty in being specific [is not] a deliberate attempt to frustrate the thera-peutic process' (p. 246; Williams 1996). It is possible that the use of negative automatic thought diaries and the process of cognitive reappraisal that these encourage may be one method to reduce overgeneral memory (Beck 1995; Watkins *et al.* 2000). Another approach is based on the preliminary evidence that mindfulness-based cognitive therapy (MBCT) may help reduce overgen-eral memory. MBCT involves paying attention in a particular way, on purpose, in the present moment and non-judgementally (Kabat-Zinn 1994). During the treatment, mindfulness meditation is practised by a combination of formal exercises (sitting and breathing exercises) and informal exercises (focusing attention during everyday activities, increased awareness of here and now). This is combined with the strategies typically used in CBT for depression (for full details see Segal *et al.* 2002). Teasdale and his colleagues (2000) recruited people who were not currently depressed but who had experienced at least two previous episodes of depression and randomly allo-cated them to either treatment as usual or to MBCT. MBCT was found to significantly reduce depressive relapse over a year compared to treatment as usual. The finding of relevance to our discussion here was that the group who received MBCT showed a significant reduction in the number of overgeneral memories retrieved following therapy (Williams *et al.* 2000). No equivalent change was noted for participants in the treatment as usual group. This finding suggests that MBCT may reduce the tendency towards an overgeneral retrieval style. However, it should be noted that as this study was conducted with a subgroup of people who had previously suffered from depression (i.e. those who had two or more episodes of depression), we are yet to discover whether the increase in the recall of specific memories is generalizable to other people with depression and to people suffering from other psychological disorders. Also, it should be noted that other therapies have not yet been assessed for their ability to enhance specific memory retrieval.

Memory distortion

The fact that memory is distorted by mood, current symptoms, and current concerns means that all memories that we or our patients retrieve are best regarded as the *narrative* truth but not necessarily the *historical* truth (Spence 1982). That is, memories retrieved may be firmly held as true but may not be historically true. Nonetheless, all memories reported by clients need to be respectfully received and assessed for their potential clinical importance regardless of whether they reflect the historical truth. Of course, one should keep in mind that it is possible that the memories reported are the historical truth (Nash 1994; Brewin and Andrews 1998). As discussed in Boxes 3.4 and 3.5, particular care must be taken to not create false memories during the course of therapy. For example, hypnosis and age regression techniques are well-known to result in the recall of distorted or false memories (e.g. Loftus 1993; Kihlstrom 1995). Relatedly, clinicians have also been warned against making explicit suggestions that an event may have occurred (Kihlstrom 1998).

The possibility that the recall of past symptoms may be magnified (e.g. Bryant 1993) may be an important maintaining process in some psychological disorders. To take the example of chronic pain, if a person recalled the severity of his or her back pain last week as worse than it was, then it would be understandable for the person to avoid any exertion. This, in turn, may serve to maintain the pain as if the person does not exercise then his or her muscles will waste, and this will increase the risk of further injury. Further, if the person never attends social gatherings, due to fear of exertion, support networks will break down and the person will become more socially isolated and perhaps develop depression. These ideas are consistent with Rachman and Artnz's (1991) theoretical paper that draws attention to the tendency for people to overpredict how much pain they will experience and the role this might play in promoting fear of pain. One way that exaggerated recall of pain can be addressed in therapy is via a behavioural experiment. Keeping a diary of pain levels three times a day for one week and then, at a later date, asking the patient to accurately recall the levels for each day is likely to provide a clear demonstration that the belief that 'it is possible to accurately recall my pain symptoms' is inaccurate. Then discussion can take place to determine how this new information could change moment-by-moment choices about the activities engaged in. Such behavioural experiments are also likely to be important in the treatment of memory distrust in OCD. The great strength of real world experiments, as conducted by Tolin *et al.* (2001), is that they can be adapted for completion within the therapy session. By replicating Tolin and colleagues' method within the session it will be possible to give the client an experience that shows them that continual checking only serves to reduce confidence.

Future research

As evident in Table 3.1, many gaps in our knowledge-base on memory processes across disorders exist. Memory processes are yet to be investigated in several psychological disorders including sexual disorders and sleep disorders. In addition, dissociative disorders, eating disorders, and substance disorders have received minimal investigation. It will be important to conduct research with the broadest range of psychological disorders in order to provide a true evaluation of the relevance of memory processes across disorders. But immense care will be needed to design appropriate paradigms to fully capture the memory phenomena of interest, especially to ensure the adequate encoding of the stimuli and the ecological validity of the paradigms adopted.

One potential criticism of the existing investigations of memory processes is that even though the methods attempt to ensure that the participants have encoded information in the same way, there is no guarantee that they have done so. It is possible that encoding varies across participants because of different associative connections with their knowledge base or, in the incidental learning paradigm, participants may imagine themselves in connection with the word to different degrees. Developing paradigms that ensure equivalent encoding is an important future direction. Perhaps the only way to guarantee a retrieval bias is to show that the bias is affected by state dependent factors at recall (e.g. Clark and Teasdale 1982).

While a handful of researchers interested in memory and psychological disorders have begun the process of taking account of the distinction between perceptually-driven and conceptually-driven tasks (Cloitre and Leibowitz 1991; Williams *et al.* 1997; Ehlers and Clark 2000; Watkins *et al.* 2000), much research remains to be done to discover its implications for the selective memory literature reviewed in this chapter. For example, it will be important to vary the use of perceptually-driven and conceptually-driven processing tasks during encoding and retrieval (Eysenck and Byrne 1994; Nugent and Mineka 1994). Having said that, Williams *et al.* (1997) conclude that the distinction between perceptually-driven and conceptually-driven processing 'might account for some failure to find implicit or explicit memory effects in some studies [but] cannot account for the positive results that have been found' (p. 296, Williams *et al.* 1997).

Despite the extensive research into memory biases in psychological disorders, few studies have paid close attention to the context during encoding and retrieval and, as a result, may not have fully activated the core concerns of the patients. Increasing the ecological validity of paradigms to investigate memory processes is a priority for all future research in this area. Experiments that involve the presentation of word lists may activate relevant concepts but not their fuller meaning. Some paradigms may not be adequate to activate the elaborative processing that is required for memory tasks (Wenzel and Holt 2002). A memory bias for concern-relevant information may only be observed when the participants perceive themselves to be confronting, or about to confront, a real concern. For example, having a spider in the room during the memory task in investigations of specific phobia (Watts and Dalgleish 1991) and telling the participants they will have to give a speech immediately follow-ing the memory task for investigations of social phobia (Mansell and Clark 1999). As noted earlier, for disorders such as GAD, where the target concerns are likely to be broad, it is difficult to develop one paradigm that is suitable for all patients. It is possible that an idiosyncratic approach, involving slight adap-tations to the experimental protocol to increase the relevance to each partici-pant, may be fruitful (e.g. Salkovskis et al. 1999). Overall, we emphasize that the future of research into memory processes lies in providing an appropriate context for the experiments. In the case of substance abuse, for example, the situation would be the presence of the drug to which the individual is addicted.

It is worth noting that people can also show mood-incongruent memory in the context of naturally occurring moods, for example, recalling happy mem-ories in a sad mood induced by cloudy weather or sad memories in a happy mood induced by bright weather (Parrott and Sabini 1990). These effects can be respectively explained as mood repair and attempts to consider 'unfinished business' (see Teasdale and Barnard 1993 for further discussion). These results suggest that people may recall different memories to naturally occurring memories compared to experimentally induced moods. However, other than an analogue study demonstrating that reflective self-focus increases mood-incongruent recall to negative moods, whereas ruminative self-focus increases mood-congruent recall to negative moods (McFarland and Buehler 1998), the relevance of mood-incongruent memory to psychological disorders has not been examined. Future research may profitably examine whether patients with psychological disorders differ from each other and from non-patient controls in mood-incongruent memory.

Future research requiring patients to retrospectively recall situations or symptoms should be interpreted with care given the evidence that recall is distorted by a range of variables, especially current symptoms. Instead, prospective designs should be used where possible. However, given the sparse research focusing on the cognitive behavioural processes involved in the original development of psychological disorders it is recognized that retrospective designs are sometimes necessary to generate hypotheses that can be tested later with prospective designs (e.g. Hofmann et al. 1995). Another implication of the memory distortion findings is the importance of taking account of current symptoms in experiments designed to index memory processes. A particularly impressive way in which to control for current symp-toms was adopted by Kuhajda and colleagues (2002). These researchers tested pain patients twice; when they were and were not currently in pain. The par-ticipants contacted the experimenter, via beepers, at the onset of a headache. They were then immediately tested.

The sensations of pain (or any other condition) are likely to grab attention and thereby consume cognitive capacity. Hence, comparing patients who are currently experiencing symptoms with patients who are currently not experiencing symptoms is important to rule out the possibility that the effects are simply secondary to the neuropsychological deficits that may be inherent to the disorder. There is a broader issue here about the neuropsychological sequelae of current symptoms. A range of studies have shown memory deficits across a range of psychological disorders (e.g. PTSD—schizophrenia—Dolan *et al.* 1997; OCD—Savage *et al.* 2000; Golier *et al.* 2002; Greisberg and McKay 2003). Accordingly, there is a need to reconcile the many findings reviewed in this chapter of superior memory for concern-related stimuli across the disorders with the findings of an overall decrement in performance on memory tests that do not involve concern-related stimuli. It may be that the high level of cognitive resources devoted to the processing of concern-relevant information causes impairment to the processing of non-concern information. A practical implication of this is that when conducting a neuropsychological assessment it is important to assess for current symptoms and to take them into account when interpreting the results of the assessment to rule out the possibility that memory deficits are simply the result of symptoms present *during* testing (e.g. pain, depression, anxiety).

Few studies in the literature have assessed for, or taken account of, comorbidity. Given the strength of the memory findings for depression (especially selective memory and overgeneral memory) and that depression is highly comorbid with a range of psychological disorders, it is particularly important to assess for the presence of depression. However, it should be remembered that taking into account comorbid conditions, via statistics, is rarely possible. While analysis of covariance (ANCOVA) is a tempting statistical strategy to hold the severity of depression 'constant' or to 'partial out' the effects of depression, in many experimental designs this method is inappropriate (Miller and Chapman 2001). Alternative statistical methods are available (Cohen and Cohen 1983; Maxwell and Delaney 1990) but perhaps the best solution is to design the study as a comparison between a group with the disorder of interest who *has* the comorbid disorder and a group with the disorder of interest who *does not have* the comorbid disorder.

Finally, further research is necessary to determine the links between the memory processes discussed in this chapter with the other processes discussed in this book. First, attentional processes are going to be a crucial influence on memory processes. The emerging evidence as to the circumstances under which people attend versus avoid information processing has potential to enhance our understanding of the circumstances under which people have enhanced versus poorer memory for concern-related information. Second, in Chapter 5 we will see that people with a range of psychological disorders attempt to suppress thoughts relating to their core concerns. The evidence indicates that many attempts to suppress are not successful and instead fuel the thoughts. Hence, it is possible that the paradoxical effects of thought suppression may enhance selective memory for concern-related stimuli. Alternatively, perhaps thought suppression impairs the elaboration of some aspects of a memory. For example, if a person consistently attempts to suppress the worst aspects of a traumatic event and has some success with this by distracting from the worst aspects onto other less traumatic aspects of the trauma, their memory for the worst aspects may be impaired. Finally, the relationship between selective encoding and selective attention is yet to be determined. Giving some clue as to the likely relationship are the findings reported by Holmes *et al.* (in press) who showed a traumatic film to an analogue sample. The results indicated that at the points of the film that subsequently became distressing, intrusive images were characterized, during encoding, by periods of slowed heart-rate or bradycardia. Bradycardia is known to be associated with orientating towards threatening stimuli.

Key points

1. The two memory processes that can be regarded as definite transdiagnostic processes are: explicit selective memory and recurrent memory.
2. Implicit selective memory, overgeneral memory, and avoidant encoding and retrieval meet our criteria for a possible transdiagnostic process.
3. There is currently inconclusive evidence for working memory, and memory distrust.
4. The memory biases observed relate to, and are specific to, the concerns of each patient group.
5. A theme to emerge is that impoverished access to the full store of memories is characteristic across the disorders and serves to maintain them. The possibility that impoverished access may play a role in affect regulation has been highlighted.
6. A range of strategies are available to tackle memory processes that maintain psychological disorders including: education, in session and between session behavioural experiments, imaginal and *in vivo* exposure and working with the 'hot spots' in memory.

7. Future research should aim to (a) develop methods to ensure adequate encoding, (b) examine the impact of perceptually-driven and conceptually-driven encoding and retrieval, (c) the effect of context, (d) the effect of symptoms present during encoding and retrieval, and (e) the relationship between memory processes and the other cognitive and behavioural processes discussed in this book.

Chapter 4

Reasoning

Jane is a 23-year-old woman who works as a personal assistant. Jane was referred for psychological treatment by her GP. She needed help with severe anxiety and depressed mood. Jane presented as smartly dressed but very shy, avoiding eye contact during the first few sessions. During the assessment, it was clear that Jane met criteria for social phobia, manifesting as extreme anxiety in social settings, with a concern that people stare at her and think that she looks odd. She was particularly concerned that people will see her blushing or shaking when she is anxious and then think that this means that she is crazy. She can manage to go to work, where her interactions are relatively structured but she is extremely uncomfortable and self-conscious around people when going out socially. Jane avoids talking as much as possible when around other people, and tends to stay at the back of groups, looking at the floor. Because of her concerns about shaking, she always tries to sit down and often fiddles with objects in her handbag. When talking about her interactions with other people, it became clear that Jane anticipates that future dealings with people will be difficult and she expects people to judge her as odd-looking and very anxious. When Jane feels anxious, she is sure that her anxiety will be noticed and judged by other people and because of the anxiety, Jane believes that she is coming across very badly. Jane thinks that if she is anxious there is potential threat of humiliation. Furthermore, Jane is extremely sensitive to possible signs of anger or disapproval in other people, and usually judges that conversations with other people have gone badly. For example, if someone looks at her, Jane will think that they are staring at her because she is looking strange. Each evening when Jane thinks back to the events of the day, she tends to dwell on the events that confirm her view that she has come across badly. When trying to explain how well she gets on with people, Jane attributes any pleasant interactions to luck or to other people just being nice, whilst blaming any unpleasant interactions on her own deep-seated personal inadequacy and strangeness. Jane's social phobia started during adolescence and she described herself as a sensitive and shy child. Her father was verbally abusive and critical, calling her weak and pathetic. Furthermore, she has vivid and distressing memories of several occasions when she was bullied and picked on by classmates. Jane has a vivid and distorted self-image of herself as looking extremely shaky and with a beetroot-red blushing face.

This case description illustrates a number of ways that reasoning processes can become biased so as to both reflect and contribute to a psychological disorder. Reasoning is defined here as thinking that is concerned with deducing conclusions, generating judgements, and testing hypotheses in a logical and coherent way. A reasoning bias occurs when thinking about the world tends towards particular conclusions in a systematic and regular manner, across time and different contexts (Alloy and Abramson 1988). For example, Jane consistently estimates that there is a very high likelihood of her being embarrassed or humiliated in public, she regularly uses her emotional state to judge threat and always interprets social situations negatively. Biased reasoning is often (but not necessarily) erroneous in that the conclusion drawn differs from objective reality. For example, Jane judges that people are likely to think badly of her anxiety, but objectively most people would not notice and even if they did, they would not care nor think badly of her because of it. Reasoning biases are a common, normal, and universal phenomenon, which can occur whenever we attempt to make sense of, understand, or predict the world around us (Kahneman *et al.* 1982). Indeed, biases in reasoning are not necessarily dysfunctional and some biases in reasoning may have real benefits. In particular, biases known as 'self-serving biases' promote self-esteem and motivation in non-clinical populations (Taylor and Brown 1988). The aim of this chapter is to examine to what extent the processes that drive reasoning biases are common across different psychological disorders. We will also consider whether these reasoning biases play a causal role in the onset and/or maintenance of disorders and whether reasoning in psychological disorders is biased in qualitatively different (in kind), quantitatively different (in degree) or thematically different ways (same process but different content) from non-patient controls. Box 4.1 presents a summary of each of the reasoning processes that we will consider in this chapter. These processes have been selected because they have been subject to empirical investigation.

Box 4.1 Summary of reasoning processes discussed in this chapter

Interpretative reasoning involves reaching a conclusion as to the meaning of an ambiguous or open-ended situation.

Attributional reasoning is the process by which people infer the causes for why particular outcomes occurred.

Expectancy reasoning involves the processes used to predict the likelihood of future events and to predict the outcomes that might result from particular actions or situations. A number of reasoning shortcuts or heuristics have been implicated in expectancy reasoning.

Detection of covariation is the ability to detect that two events tend to co-occur in a regular and consistent way.

Hypothesis testing is the reasoning process used when evaluating whether explanations and beliefs are accurate or need to be revised in the light of new information. In general, there is a confirmation bias, such that people tend to be biased towards validating pre-existing beliefs.

Cognitive models of psychological disorders emphasize the importance, in terms of aetiology and maintenance, of how people interpret events, how people explain the causes of events and how people predict future events (e.g. Beck 1976; Clark 1986, 1988; Clark *et al.* 1999). Thus, the reasoning processes involved in making interpretations, inferring the causes for events (attributional reasoning) and judging the likelihood or expectancies of events are all likely to be important in psychological disorders. Furthermore, cognitive distortions, such as catastrophizing, personalizing, overgeneralizing, and selective abstraction, which are considered to be critical targets to identify and challenge in cognitive therapy (e.g. Beck *et al.* 1979), parallel the output of biased reasoning processes. Box 4.2 defines the different cognitive distortions and indicates which reasoning processes could produce each distortion.

In practice, cognitive distortions often overlap and have proved hard to distinguish (Krantz and Hammen 1979). Similarly, it is sometimes hard to separate the different reasoning processes, since interpretations, attributions, expectancies, and judgements often overlap at a practical and functional level. Thus, distinctions between the different forms of reasoning processes may be somewhat arbitrary, particularly as the reasoning processes are probably not independent processes but, instead, feed into and fuel each other. For example, judgements about the likelihood of events happening (expectancy reasoning) are likely to interact with the interpretation of ambiguous situations (interpretation reasoning) in that expecting a negative outcome and interpreting an ambiguous situation as negative are complementary processes. Nonetheless, for ease of comprehension and in order to reflect previous distinctions we will review each bias separately, whilst acknowledging that there is considerable practical and functional overlap between them.

Current concerns

To continue a theme that has emerged throughout the book so far, in this chapter we will see that reasoning processes reflect the important personal concerns of the individual. In particular, biases in reasoning tend to reflect the predominant concerns and priorities inherent to each psychological disorder. As such, the operation of cognitive biases in people with psychological disorders seems to be an extension of the suggestion that cognitive biases in non-patient controls reflect their current concerns (Klinger 1996).

Interpreting ambiguous stimuli

In day-to-day life, much of the information we receive is inherently ambiguous. Clear-cut answers to questions such as 'How well am I doing on

Box 4.2 Examples of cognitive distortions and potentially related reasoning processes

Arbitrary inference involves drawing unwarranted conclusions in the absence of evidence (e.g. Jane deciding that a man was looking at her because she looked overanxious). Arbitrary inference could be a product of biases in interpretative reasoning, hypothesis testing, judgements of expectancy, or covariation bias.

Selective abstraction involves focusing on a detail out of context whilst ignoring other important features of the situation (e.g. Jane thinking that she came across badly because she felt anxious, without considering the interest and smiles from the people to whom she was speaking). Selective abstraction could be a product of biases in hypothesis testing, judgements of expectancy, or interpretative reasoning.

Overgeneralization involves drawing a general rule or conclusion on the basis of one or more isolated incidents and applying the concept across the board to related and unrelated situations (e.g. Jane thinking that because one person was unpleasant towards her that everyone did not like her). Overgeneralization could be a product of biases in attributional reasoning (in particular adopting an internal, stable, global style), hypothesis testing, or in judgements of expectancy.

Magnification/Catastrophization involves exaggerating the significance or importance of an event in a negative direction (e.g. Jane thinking that blushing will lead everyone to stare and laugh at her). Magnification could be a product of biases in interpretation, attributional reasoning, hypothesis testing, judgements of expectancies, or covariation bias.

Personalization involves inappropriately relating external events to oneself (e.g. Jane judging that someone cut a conversation short because of something she did). Personalization could be the product of biases in interpretation, attributional reasoning, or hypothesis testing.

Dichotomous thinking (black and white thinking) is categorizing all experience into one of two extreme categories, e.g. all good or all bad. Dichotomous thinking could be the result of biases in heuristic reasoning (representativeness).

this task?' and 'What does that person's facial expression mean?' are rarely available. How people disambiguate these sources of information is important for how they respond to the world. In general, the evidence suggests that people suffering from psychological disorders show clear differences from non-patients in their interpretation of ambiguous information that is relevant to their current concerns. A range of stimuli can be ambiguous, including performance on tasks, physical sensations, and social cues, such that the interpretation of ambiguity can potentially have a far-reaching impact on day-to-day life.

Self-report paradigms

Initial studies examined the self-reported response to vignettes that could be interpreted in more or less threatening ways. For example, Butler and Mathews (1983) presented vignettes such as 'You wake up with a start in the middle of the night, thinking you heard a noise but all is quiet'. Participants were then asked to select from a range of predetermined resolutions (e.g. 'it was a cat / burglar') to disambiguate the vignette (Butler and Mathews 1983; McNally and Foa 1987; Baptista *et al.* 1990). However, these studies raise questions concerning the potential role of demand effects.

Cognitive-experimental paradigms

To minimize the impact of limitations inherent to self-report paradigms, cognitive-experimental approaches were developed to examine the interpretation of ambiguous stimuli. In the homophone spelling task, participants listened to homophones (words with the same sound but different spellings) that were presented through headphones. The homophones have both disorder congruent (e.g. for anxiety 'die', for eating disorder 'weight') and positive/neutral meanings (e.g. 'dye' or 'wait'). The task required the participants to spell each word. The number of disorder-congruent spellings is used as an index of the bias in interpreting ambiguous stimuli (Eysenck *et al.* 1987; Mathews *et al.* 1989).

In the lexical priming task, participants are presented words on a computer screen. The first word presented is the prime word, which is then followed by the target stimulus, which can be a proper English word (e.g. 'disease') or a non-word (e.g. 'dasiese'). Participants are asked to press a response key as soon as they decide whether the target stimuli is a proper English word or not. This paradigm is known as a lexical decision task. The time to decide whether the target stimulus is an English word is reduced if the stimulus is preceded by a prime word with which it is semantically associated (Neely 1977). Richards and French (1992) adapted the lexical priming task to investigate interpretations of ambiguity by using ambiguous homographs as the critical prime words (e.g. 'growth' as in 'getting larger' or as in 'cancerous tumour'). Ambiguous homographs are words with the same spelling that have both positive and negative meanings. Within the course of the study, the ambiguous primes were repeated, with half the presentations followed by target words related to their neutral meaning, and half the presentations followed by target words related to their threatening meaning. If a participant has a bias towards a negative interpretation of ambiguity, then the threatening meaning of the homograph will be used, such that the lexical decisions (i.e. is this a proper word or a non-word) will be faster when the target words with threatening meanings are presented after the prime, relative to when the neutral target words are presented after the prime (Richards and French 1992). For example, if the prime is 'growth' and the participant makes a threatening interpretation of this word, then they will be faster to decide that the target word 'disease' is a proper word than to decide that the target 'larger' (the neutral target word) is a proper word.

Another paradigm developed to investigate the interpretation of ambiguous stimuli is the recognition memory task. In this task participants are presented with an ambiguous sentence that is related to their current concern. After some intervening time, the participants are asked to choose which of a choice of several sentences is most closely related to the original sentence. For example, an ambiguous statement for patients with eating disorders might be 'After exercising for two hours at a health club, you catch a glimpse of the shape of your hips as you pass by a mirror'. The participant is then asked to choose which of the following two sentences is most closely related to their recall of the original sentence: 'you get a glimpse of your large hips' or 'you get a glimpse of your toned hips' (Jackman *et al.* 1995).

Even for these paradigms, the selection of the more negative interpretation could reflect a response bias rather than an interpretative bias. For example, for a patient with an anxiety disorder the bias could simply reflect an anxiety-linked response bias rather than a genuine interpretative bias. So although the participant may be aware of both meanings, there may be a tendency to select the more threatening as it is congruent with the anxiety state. To rule out this possibility, more sophisticated designs have been used, such as online text comprehension (MacLeod and Cohen 1993) and visual blink measures (Lawson *et al.* 2002). In the online text comprehension task paradigm, participants read sentences presented on a computer. After reading the sentence the participant presses a button to indicate that they are ready to read the next line of text. The time taken to understand the completion of a sentence is determined by measuring the time taken between button presses. Sentences that are consistent with the expected interpretation will be read faster than sentences that are not consistent. For example, if the following sentence was presented 'it was early when the building was lit' and the person interpreted the sentence as the building being set on fire, then they would read this sentence 'the flames could be seen from a distance' faster than they would read this sentence 'the lights could be seen from a distance'.

In the visual blink task, the key measure is the blink reflex, which involves measuring contractions of the orbicularis oculi muscle (a muscle surrounding the eye) in response to an unexpected burst of white noise. Research has established that the magnitude of the reflex is mood-dependent in that whilst imagining negative scenarios, the blink reflex is larger than when imagining neutral scenarios. Taking this paradigm further, Lawson *et al.* (2002) demonstrated that imagining a situation in response to an ambiguous auditory stimulus derived from sounds common to negative and neutral words (e.g. 'rief' from grief and brief) was associated with a greater blink reflex when preceded by cues that facilitated negative interpretations (e.g. 'church ceremony' for 'grief') rather than the neutral interpretation (e.g. 'very short' for 'brief'). Thus, the blink reflex is modified by the valence of the interpretation that individuals impose on ambiguous stimuli.

Having reviewed the paradigms used to investigate interpretations of ambiguous stimuli, we will now examine the evidence for the presence of this reasoning process across the psychological disorders.

Anxiety disorders

Patients with anxiety disorders tend to show negative interpretations of ambiguous stimuli relevant to their particular fear concerns.

Panic disorder with or without agoraphobia

Using a range of self report measures, a number of studies have found that patients with panic disorder with or without agoraphobia exhibit more negative and concern-specific interpretations of ambiguous stimuli, relative to non-patient controls (Stoler and McNally 1991; Harvey *et al.* 1993; Clark *et al.* 1997; Kamieniecki *et al.* 1997; Richards *et al.* 2001).

Social phobia

A number of studies have found that patients with social phobia make more negative disambiguations compared to non-patient controls. This result has been reported using self-report tasks where participants were asked to report their open-ended response and then select predetermined interpretations in response to an ambiguous situation (Harvey *et al.* 1993; Stopa and Clark 1993,

2000; Amir *et al.* 1998*a*; Constans *et al.* 1999). This result has also been reported using the homophone spelling task (Amir *et al.* 1998*b*). The negative disambiguations seem to be specific to social concerns. For example, patients with social phobia made more negative interpretations of self-relevant socially ambiguous material but did not make negative interpretations in other ambiguous situations. In contrast, patients with obsessive-compulsive disorder (OCD) did not make negative interpretations of socially ambiguous situations (Amir *et al.* 1998*b*). In another example, using a real world design, patients with social phobia were found to evaluate their social performance as significantly worse relative to non-patient controls. This was true for both successful and unsuccessful social interactions (Wallace and Alden 1997) and for an impromptu speech (Rapee and Lim 1992).

Hirsch and Mathews (1997, 2000) made a distinction between a negative interpretative bias that occurs 'on-line', that is, at the time that the ambiguous situation is first encountered and a negative interpretative bias that occurs as the result of anticipatory or retrospective thinking about a social situation. That is, an interpretative bias could reflect reasoning that occurs during the situation ('on-line') or could reflect thinking before or after the situation. Using a modified lexical decision task for words presented within the context of stories about social situations, Hirsch and Mathews (2000) found that non-patient controls tended to make positive 'on-line' inferences for ambiguous social situations, whereas patients with social phobia did not make any 'on-line' inferences either positive or negative. This lack of a positive 'on-line' bias may render patients with social phobia more prone to make negative interpretations about their social performance. More recently, Hirsch *et al.* (2003*b*) demonstrated that holding a negative self-image in mind removed the positive 'on-line' inference in low anxious participants, suggesting that negative self-images in social phobia interferes with on-line reasoning (see Chapter 3 for a further discussion of self-images).

Post-traumatic stress disorder

Amir *et al.* (2002) found that people who had experienced trauma and who had PTSD showed less inhibition of the threat meanings of trauma-related homographs (as indexed by response times for semantic judgements) than did people who had experienced trauma and who did not have PTSD. This finding suggests that PTSD, rather than the experience of trauma per se, leads to threatening interpretative biases.

Generalized anxiety disorder

Several studies have found that patients with GAD make more threatening interpretations of ambiguous stimuli than non-patient controls on the homophone task (Mathews *et al.* 1989) and on the recognition memory task

(Eysenck *et al.* 1991). Using the lexical priming paradigm with an analogue sample, Richards and French (1992) found that high trait anxious participants were quicker to correctly decide that target words with threatening meanings were English words than low trait anxious participants. In an online text comprehension task with an analogue population, MacLeod and Cohen (1993) showed that high trait anxious participants, but not low trait anxious participants, demonstrated faster comprehension latencies for continuation sentences that were consistent with the threatening interpretation of the ambiguous sentence. For example, for the ambiguous sentence 'The doctor examined little Emily's growth', high trait anxious participants were faster to read the sentence 'Her tumour had changed little since last visit', compared to low trait anxious participants. The interesting results that have emerged from comparisons of high versus low trait anxious individuals require replication with patients diagnosed with GAD to determine their applicability to patient groups.

Somatoform disorders

Pain disorder

Pincus *et al.* (1994) found that chronic pain patients responded to ambiguous homonyms with more health-related associations than both controls and physiotherapists. The physiotherapists were included as a control for frequency of exposure to pain language. Pincus *et al.* (1996) found that chronic pain patients interpreted ambiguous homophones as more illness and pain-related relative to matched controls. Edwards and Pearce (1994) found that individuals with chronic pain made more pain-related completions of word stems (e.g. ten-der/ten-t) than controls.

Hypochrondriasis

Using self-report questionnaires, patients with hypochrondriasis were found to falsely identify harmless physical sensations as a symptom of a catastrophic disease (Haenen *et al.* 1997) and define good health as the absence of any physical symptoms (Barsky *et al.* 1993). Also based on self-report is the finding that patients with somatoform disorders favour illness interpretations rather than benign causes for physical sensations (Garcia-Campayo *et al.* 1997; Rief *et al.* 1998; Haenen *et al.* 2000).

Eating disorders

Williamson *et al.* (2000) found that compared to controls, patients with eating disorders made more negative and 'fat' interpretations of ambiguous body-related situations but not of ambiguous health-related situations. Furthermore, patients with anorexia nervosa and bulimia nervosa interpreted ambiguous negative self-referent scenarios (Cooper 1997) and ambiguous homophones (e.g. 'weight'/ 'wait') as having more weight, shape or food-related meanings than controls (Vitousek *et al.* 1995 cited in Vitousek, 1996). To take an example of one item from the Cooper (1997) study, the scenario 'friends are being uncomplimentary about you' is more likely to be interpreted as 'this means that I am fat and unattractive'. It is worth noting that the Vitousek *et al.* 1995 cited in Vitousek, 1996 study demonstrates the importance of demand effects on the homophone paradigm. Post-experimental inquiry revealed that the eating disorder participants were more aware of the study's purpose than controls, presumably because they guessed that it was related to their psychological condition. When non-patient controls were told that the study was about eating disorders, they also produced more food and weight-related interpretations of ambiguous stimuli. Finally, some studies have investigated whether the cognitive biases associated with eating disorders are related to the current concern of maintaining personal control. Shafran *et al.* (2003) found that patients with eating disorders interpreted ambiguous scenarios that described symptoms of severe dietary restraint (e.g. feeling hungry, feeling dizzy, or weak) in terms of personal control significantly more than a non-patient group.

Mood disorders

Patients with depression endorsed more negative interpretations of ambiguous textual scenarios than controls (Butler and Mathews 1983; Nunn *et al.* 1997). However, on more sophisticated paradigms, the findings are less consistent. For example, Lawson and MacLeod (1999) failed to find that patients diagnosed with depression were significantly faster at naming negative disambiguations of primed words. Although note that it is possible that this paradigm is insensitive to cognitive processing in patients with depression because of the variability of response latencies in depression (Byrne 1976). In an analogue study, Lawson *et al.* (2002) found that compared to low Beck Depression Inventory (BDI) scorers, high BDI scorers had greater eye blink reflexes for ambiguous stimuli, but not for unambiguous (neutral or negative) stimuli. This result suggests that people who are dysphoric have a tendency to make more negative interpretations of ambiguous material.

Psychotic disorders

Hemsley's (1993) model of schizophrenia predicts that ambiguous or degraded sensory input is more likely to be misinterpreted among people with schizophrenia, perhaps leading to the experience of hallucinations. However, this hypothesis has not been experimentally investigated, other than the demonstration that presenting meaningful auditory stimulation (e.g. interesting passages of prose) resulted in fewer hallucinations in patients with schizophrenia relative to when meaningless sounds and white noise were presented (Margo *et al.* 1981).

Substance-related disorders

Stacy and colleagues have found that heavier drinkers are more likely than light drinkers to associate alcohol-related meanings to ambiguous verbal stimuli (e.g. 'pitcher'; Stacy 1995, 1997; Ames and Stacy 1998). In addition, Earleywine (1994) found that women who tend to drink more alcohol construed more words that could have alcohol or non-alcohol-related meanings (e.g. 'shot' 'bar') to be alcohol-relevant, compared to women who tend to drink less. As several of these studies have used non-patient samples, such as female undergraduates, questions about the generalizability of these findings to the relevant patient groups remain to be answered.

Summary

Biased interpretation of ambiguous stimuli appears to be common across all psychological disorders that have been tested to date. Accordingly, biased interpretation meets our criteria for a definite transdiagnostic process. The information that is biased tends to reflect the current concerns of the patients. However, except for MacLeod and Cohen's (1993) use of comprehension latencies and Lawson *et al.* (2002) use of the visual blink reflex (and these were both analogue studies), all of the positive findings discussed could potentially be the result of demand or response biases. Accordingly, further research with more sophisticated paradigms that exclude demand and response biases are required.

Attributions

When people seek to explain why good or bad events have happened to them, they attribute the outcome to particular causes. An extensive literature has developed examining the types of attributions that people provide to explain particular events. The attributions that people use to explain why a particular outcome occurred differ across three principal dimensions:

1. The degree to which the cause is predominantly internal (i.e. principally caused by the individual) or external (i.e. principally caused by the environment).

2. The degree to which the cause is predominantly stable (i.e. not likely to change such as a personal trait) or transient (e.g. a one-off occurrence or short-lived state such as tiredness).

3. The degree to which the cause is predominantly global (i.e. relevant to other situations) or local (i.e. specific to this event only).

Repeated studies have indicated that people typically have a self-serving bias, whereby negative events tend to be attributed to external, transient, and local causes (e.g. 'it's not my fault, I was unlucky') and positive events tend to be attributed to internal, stable, and global causes (e.g. 'I am clever') (Taylor and Brown 1988). Ross (1977) also identified the fundamental attributional error where people tend to attribute another person's behaviour to their personal disposition, while overlooking situational causes or transient influences. For example, an outburst from a colleague may be taken as a sign that he is 'a threatening person' rather than as a consequence of his currently high levels of stress at work. The converse of the self-serving bias is a *pessimistic attributional style*, characterized by attributing negative events to internal, stable, and global causes, whilst attributing positive events to external, transient, and local causes. For example, a person with this pessimistic style would attribute a recent failure on an exam to being stupid and success at another exam as down to chance or the fact that it was too easy. Research evidence relating to the pessimistic attributional style will be discussed in the section below. Note that in many of the studies reviewed below, attributional style has typically been measured with the Attributional Style Questionnaire which is a self-report measure in which people are asked to indicate, for a series of hypothetical positive and negative scenarios, how internal–external, stable–transient and global–local the causes are within each scenario (Peterson *et al.* 1982).

Anxiety disorders

It is difficult to reach a firm conclusion about whether patients with anxiety disorders have a pessimistic attributional style because of mixed findings and because of a number of limitations in the current evidence. First, as we will discuss in more detail in a moment, the evidence indicates that comorbid depression is important in determining a pessimistic attributional style (Heimberg *et al.* 1987, 1989). However, few studies have controlled for levels of depression. Second, most studies have used the standard Attributional Style Questionnaire rather than modifying the vignettes to examine attributions for events that are congruent with the specific concerns of the disorder (e.g. vignettes about social embarrassment for patients with social phobia). As such, it is possible that the null findings are due to the items not adequately indexing the process of interest.

Using the standard Attributional Style Questionnaire, Heimberg *et al.* (1987) found that patients with anxiety disorders (panic, specific phobia, social phobia, GAD) had a pessimistic attributional style compared to non-patient controls, but only if they were also depressed. However, by using such a heterogeneous sample of patients diagnosed with anxiety disorders, this study was not able to determine whether any particular anxiety disorder exhibits a specific bias in attributional style. In a follow-up study, Heimberg *et al.* (1989) found that patients with dysthymia, patients with social phobia, and patients with agoraphobia all had a more pessimistic attributional style than non-patient controls, but did not differ from each other. Further, patients with panic disorder attributed negative outcomes to more stable and global causes than non-patient controls, but did not differ on attributions to internal causes. In this study, the patients with anxiety disorders were still significantly more pessimistic than non-patient controls when levels of depression were controlled for, although the level of significance decreased. However, the different groups in this study were not matched for age or gender, which may potentially influence attributional style.

John Riskind and his colleagues (1989) found that patients with GAD were not as pessimistic in their attributional style as patients with depression, when coding the causal explanations from patients' thought records, although this study did not include a non-patient control group. Michelson *et al.* (1997) found that in patients with agoraphobia, a pessimistic attributional style was associated with depression but not with agoraphobia severity. Similarly, Falsetti and Resick (1995) found no difference on attributional style between under-graduates who had and had not been victims of crime, with and without symp-toms of PTSD, using the standard Attributional Style Questionnaire. However, note that a limitation of this study was that it did not determine whether the participants met diagnostic criteria for PTSD. However, Mikulincer and Solomon (1988) found that for soldiers who had suffered a combat stress reaction, attributing bad events to more stable and uncontrollable causes was associated with more intense symptoms of PTSD. However, this study did not determine whether the participants met diagnostic criteria for PTSD, did not control for level of depressed symptoms and used the standard Attributional Style Questionnaire, rather than items specifically related to combat.

Several studies suggest that examining attributions for the specific concerns of each disorder may be more likely to uncover a bias in attributional style in patients with an anxiety disorder. For example, as memories of more anxious past social situations were recalled, the attributions for social performance in the recalled situation became more internal, stable, and global for patients with social phobia but less internal, stable, and global for non-patient controls (Coles *et al.* 2001). Further, Tolin *et al.* (2002) found that patients with OCD reported more internal, negative attributions for failure to suppress thoughts on the white bear test (see Chapter 5), compared to patients with social phobia and non-anxious controls.

Somatoform disorders

Compared to anxious and non-anxious controls, patients with hypo-chrondriasis were found to attribute physical symptoms to somatic or illness causes rather than to psychological or emotional causes (MacLeod *et al.* 1998; Brosschot and Aarsse 2001), particularly for those symptoms congruent with their main concerns.

Sexual disorders

A number of studies have found that internal attributions for negative events specific to the concerns of the disorder (e.g. poor sexual performance) are related to symptoms in men with sexual dysfunctions, especially erectile difficulties. Both Fichten *et al.* (1988) and Simkins-Bullock *et al.* (1992) found that men presenting with sexual dysfunction gave internal attributions for their difficulties. Weisberg *et al.* (2001) reported that compared to men with erectile difficulties, sexually functional men identified more external factors that might have interfered with their ability to get an erection. Further, Weisberg *et al.* (2001) reported work conducted in 1998, in which the Attributional Style Questionnaire was modified for sexual events. On this modified Attributional Style Questionnaire, men with erectile disorder rated their attributions of negative sexual activities as significantly more internal and stable than sexually functional men.

Eating disorders

Several studies have found that compared to non-patient controls, patients with anorexia nervosa and bulimia nervosa (Dalgleish *et al.* 2001*b*), women with binge eating disorder (Watkins *et al.* 2001) and women with bulimia nervosa (Goebel *et al.* 1990; Schlesier-Carter *et al.* 1989) have a pessimistic attributional style. However, in those studies that controlled for level of depression, the differences between patients with eating disorders and non-patient controls on attributional style were significantly reduced or completely lost, suggesting that the pessimistic attributional style was due to depressed mood (Schleiser-Carter *et al.* 1989; Dalgleish *et al.* 2001*b*). Consistent with the possibility that attributional style is associated with depression, Metalsky *et al.* (1997) found that patients with bulimia nervosa and depressed symptoms had a pessimistic attributional style, whereas patients with bulimia nervosa but no depressed symptoms did not have a pessimistic attributional style. One limitation of all these studies is that the versions of the Attributional Style Questionnaire used were not specific to the particular concerns of patients with eating disorders (e.g. vignettes about gaining weight).

Impulse control disorders

In patients with a gambling problem, an exaggerated self-serving bias has been found, with a tendency to attribute wins to dispositional factors (e.g. skills, abilities) and to attribute losses to chance or bad luck (Ross and Sicoly 1979; Ladouceur and Mayrand 1986; Wagenaar 1988; Gadboury and Ladouceur 1989).

Mood disorders

Consistent evidence indicates that patients with major depression have a pessimistic attributional style that is associated with hopelessness and reduced motivation (Abramson *et al.* 1978; Sweeny *et al.* 1986; Seligman *et al.* 1988; Heimberg *et al.* 1989; Abramson *et al.* 1989*b*; Robins and Hayes 1995; Joiner 2001). Interestingly, Reilly-Harrington *et al.* (1999) found that there were no differences in the attributional style exhibited by non-patient controls, patients with unipolar depressed and patients with bipolar disorder. However, this study examined attributional style in patients with lifetime diagnoses so that not all patients were tested during a current episode of depression or mania. Therefore, this study would have missed effects reliant on current psychological symptoms.

Lyon *et al.* (1999) tested the hypothesis that bipolar patients have a covert pessimistic attributional style, by comparing explicit and implicit attributions. They found that bipolar patients in a manic episode showed a self-serving bias on the Attributional Style Questionnaire (as did the non-patient controls), whilst bipolar patients in a depressed episode had a pessimistic style on the Attributional Style Questionnaire. A more implicit incidental recall task (The Pragmatic Inference Test) was also administered. In this task, participants are presented with self-referent vignettes containing both internal and external causes for outcomes. They were then asked to answer, from memory, several multiple-choice questions about the story, including making a choice as to whether the vignette reflects an internal or external attributional cause. Bipolar patients in both depressed and manic episodes selected more internal causal inferences for negative events than for positive events, leading Lyon *et al.* to suggest that bipolar disorder patients have an implicit pessimistic attributional style.

Psychotic disorders

Patients with schizophrenia and patients with persecutory delusions make more stable and global attributions for negative events compared to controls. However, compared to depressed patients and non-patient controls, patients with schizophrenia who had delusions and patients with delusional disorder excessively attribute negative events to external rather than internal causes (Kaney and Bentall 1989; Candido and Romney 1990; Lyon *et al.* 1994; Fear *et al.* 1996; Sharp *et al.* 1997; Martin and Penn 2002). In particular, patients with schizophrenia who have paranoid delusions tend to make external-personal (because of someone else's actions) rather than external-situational (because of circumstances) attributions for negative events (Kinderman and Bentall 1997*b*). Bentall *et al.* (1991) found that patients with schizophrenia who had paranoid delusions made excessive external-personal attributions for explaining negative events that happened to a third party. However, this finding was not replicated by Young and Bentall (1997), suggesting that the external-personal attributional style may be limited to explaining negative events that are relevant to the self.

The evidence regarding attributional style for positive events in patients with schizophrenia is less clear. Silverman and Peterson (1993) and Candido and Romney (1990) reported that patients with schizophrenia excessively attribute positive events to internal causes compared to both non-patient controls and patients with depression. However, this exaggerated self-serving bias was not found in patients with schizophrenia compared to non-patient controls in a number of other studies (Lyon *et al.* 1994; Fear *et al.* 1996; Sharp *et al.* 1997; Kinderman and Bentall 1997*b*). Thus, on balance, patients with schizophrenia do not seem to have a greater tendency than non-patient controls to attribute positive events to internal causes.

Richard Bentall and his colleagues (Bentall and Kinderman 1998; Bentall *et al.* 2001) suggested that the external attribution for negative events might serve a defensive function, since patients with paranoid schizophrenia implicitly have an internalizing style for negative events but explicitly report an external attributional style (e.g. Lyon *et al.* 1994). This argument has prompted much debate (see Garety and Freeman 1999) and is far from resolved, particularly as the covert internalizing style has not been replicated by Peters *et al.* (1997), Bentall and Kaney (1996), Krstev *et al.* (1999) and Martin and Penn (2002).

Research suggests that patients with schizophrenia also demonstrate an external attributional style for internal events, such as thoughts and images. There is a growing theoretical view that hallucinations are the result of private mental events being misattributed to an external source, possibly as a result of cognitive deficits (Frith 1992; Hemsley 1993) and/or cognitive biases (Bentall 1990; Morrison *et al.* 1995; Garety *et al.* 2001). The first step in this misattribution seems to be a deficit in self-monitoring and source monitoring in patients with schizophrenia. The proposal is that patients with schizophrenia, who suffer from hallucinations, have a breakdown in self-monitoring.

One empirical result that supports this view is that patients with schizophrenia who experience hallucinations fail to perceive a difference between self-generated and experimenter-generated tactile sensations (touches to the hand). In contrast, non-patient controls and patients with affective disorders were found to experience self-generated tactile sensations as less intense than experimenter-generated sensations (Blakemore *et al.* 2000).

Source monitoring is the ability to remember the origin of where memories, knowledge, and other information were obtained and in particular, to determine whether the information came from an external source (e.g. an event that actually occurred) or was generated internally (e.g. an imagined event). Considerable evidence suggests that patients with schizophrenia who suffer from hallucinations exhibit impaired source monitoring, in that they find it difficult to detect whether a mental event or action was self-generated, compared to non-patient controls (Harvey 1985; Harvey *et al.* 1988; Vinogradov *et al.* 1997; Keefe *et al.* 1999). Following this difficulty in self-monitoring, patients with schizophrenia who experience hallucinations may then be more likely to misattribute the source of self-generated thoughts and actions to external sources in the environment. Compared to patients with schizophrenia who do not hallucinate, patients with schizophrenia who do hallucinate were more likely to misattribute the source of self-generated words, in a word association task, to the experimenter than to him or herself (Bentall *et al.* 1991; Morrison and Haddock 1997*a*; Baker and Morrison 1998). Thus, these patients are explaining an internal event by making an external attribution. Ensum and Morrison (2003) found that increasing self-focused attention in patients with schizophrenia who experience auditory hallucinations increased the misattribution of self-generated words to an external source. For a patient with schizophrenia, this process might mean that a spontaneous intrusive thought or memory, such as a self-criticism, may not be detected as self-generated. It is then attributed to an external source, leading to the phenomenological experience of auditory hallucinations or thought insertion.

Substance-related disorders

Using the standard Attributional Style Questionnaire, Dowd *et al.* (1986) found that patients receiving treatment for alcohol dependence made less global and less stable attributions for positive events than non-patient controls and than patients who had recovered from alcohol dependence. No difference was found in attributions for negative events. However, this study did not control for level of depression and did not examine attributions for events related to drinking.

A pessimistic attributional style has been linked to the rule violation or abstinence violation effect (Marlatt and Gordon 1985) in substance-related disorders. The abstinence violation effect is when a small infringement of a self-imposed rule, such as a lapse in abstinence (e.g. having a drink), leads to abandoning any attempts at self-control, progressing to a full relapse. The abstinence violation effect theory predicts that internal, stable and global attributions for the cause of a lapse will increase feelings of guilt and loss of control and increase the probability of a return to regular substance abuse. A number of empirical studies have confirmed the predictions of the abstinence violation effect model.

Summary

The research reviewed in this section suggests that biases in attributional style are found in patients with depression and patients with psychotic disorders. However, the nature of the biased attributional style is different between these disorders: depression is characterized by a pessimistic attributional style with negative events explained by internal, stable, and global causes, whereas in schizophrenia, negative events are explained by an external attributional style. Whilst biases in attributional style have been found in a number of other disorders (e.g. anxiety disorders, hypochrondriasis, eating disorders, sexual disorders, and substance-related disorders), it may be that these biases are secondary to depression. When levels of depression are controlled, the differences in attributional style between patient and non-patient controls disappears in some anxiety disorders and in eating disorders. Studies examining attributional style need to adequately control for level of depression. Furthermore, the majority of studies have used the unmodified Attributional Style Questionnaire, rather than examining attributions for disorder-relevant events. We propose that examining attributions for disorder-relevant events may more fully capture the processes of interest. Indeed, those studies that have used more disorder-relevant material, for example attributions for sexual dysfunction, have found that patients differ from controls. Nonetheless, based on the evidence to date, attributional reasoning meets our criteria for a possible transdiagnostic process. But note the caveat that the different styles of attribution found in depression and schizophrenia could either reflect (1) attribution processes operating differently across the disorders or (2) the same process operating to produce different styles because of the different current-concerns of each disorder. For example, an external attribution in schizophrenia may reflect concerns about others being dangerous, whilst an internal attribution in depression may reflect concerns about personal inadequacy. Future research is required to separate these two possible accounts.

Expectancies and heuristics

A crucial aspect of reasoning is making judgements about uncertain events such as predicting the likelihood of future events (expectancies), judging how likely it is that certain actions will lead to particular outcomes or that certain responses will follow particular situational cues. Such predictions could influence the investment of effort and energy towards relevant goals and behavioural choices. As such, expectancy judgements are likely to play an important role in the maintenance of psychological disorders (Kirsch 1997, 1999). To give some examples, expecting that a substance will lead to a desired outcome (e.g. increased relaxation) predicts substance abuse (Jones *et al.* 2001). Similarly, expecting that negative events are likely to happen exacerbates avoidance and anxiety (Constans and Mathews 1993; MacLeod and Campbell 1992). A well-established literature in cognitive psychology indicates that judgements of uncertainty, including expectancies, are commonly biased in everyone (i.e. patients and non-patients) by the use of heuristic rules (useful rules of thumb) (Kahneman *et al.* 1982; Tversky and Kahneman 1973, 1974; Kahneman and Tversky 2000). The principal heuristic rules that have been identified include:

1. the availability heuristic: judgements influenced by what comes easily to mind;
2. the representativeness heuristic: judgements influenced by what is seen as typical;
3. emotional reasoning heuristic: judgements based on emotional feelings.

These heuristics are approximately accurate and effective much of the time, with the benefit of being rapid, economical, and relatively effortless (Gigerenzer *et al.* 1999). However, they lead to consistent biases in judgements, particularly with reference to underestimating abstract and statistical information. All of these heuristics tend to ignore how often or frequent a particular event typically occurs (base rate information). For example, the influence of horoscopes partly relies on the fact that people do not consider the high likelihood that most people will experience the kind of events described for each star sign. We are interested in these heuristics because of the possibility that they are specific mechanisms influencing reasoning processes. We now turn to define these heuristics in more detail.

Availability heuristic

The availability heuristic is the tendency for the estimation of the likelihood or frequency of an event to be influenced by the relative availability/accessibility of related memories. A subtype of the availability heuristic is the simulation heuristic where the expectancies are influenced by the relative ease of imagining mental simulations of related or similar events. The greater the availability or accessibility of a related event in memory, or the greater the ease of imagining the event happening, the more likely/frequent an event is considered to be. Amos Tversky and Daniel Kahneman (1973, 1974) have conducted numerous and classic empirical investigations of these phenomena (see Boxes 4.3, 4.4

Box 4.3 Experimental studies of heuristic biases—part 1

This box contains a 'mock-up' of some of the studies used by Kahneman and Tversky to examine the different heuristic biases. To get a flavour of the studies, try working through the items below without reading ahead.

Read each of the following lists of names as quickly as possible.

List A: Madonna, James Brolin, Jodie Foster, Nigel Bruce, Frederic Forrest, Catherine Zeta-Jones, Nicole Kidman, Tom Skerritt, Roger Livesey, Joel McRae, Kate Winslet, David Farrar, Cameron Diaz, Kevin McCarthy, Meg Ryan, Robert Newton, Meryl Streep, John Reilly, Julia Roberts.

List B: Russell Crowe, Karen Black, Harrison Ford, Laura Regan, Lillian Gish, Mel Gibson, Kevin Spacey, Veronica Lake, Al Pacino, Celia Johnson, Tom Cruise, Joanne Samuel, Brad Pitt, Clint Eastwood, Margaret Dumont, Sean Connery, Cathy Moriaty, Claire Trevor, Susan Harrison.

Now, try the following exercise. Read the following description and then write down on a piece of paper how likely you think each of the following statements is, rating 1 for most probable and 10 for least probable.

'Linda is 31 years old, single, outspoken and very bright. She studied philosophy at university. Linda is very concerned about issues of discrimination and social justice. She has participated in several anti-nuclear marches'

A. Linda is a teacher in a primary school

B. Linda works in a bookstore

C. Linda is active in the feminist movement

D. Linda is a psychiatric social worker

E. Linda is a bank-teller

F. Linda sells insurance

G. Linda is a bank-teller who is active in the feminist movement.

Box 4.4 Experimental studies of heuristic biases—part 2

Without looking back at Box 4.3, from memory decide whether List A or List B had more women's names than men's names? Which did you choose?

If you thought that there were more women's names than men's names in List A, this is an example of the availability heuristic in action, as found by Kahneman and Tversky's classic 1973 study. In fact, list A had fewer women's names than men's names and list B had more women's names than men's names. However in List A, the women's names were more famous than the men's names, whereas in List B, the men's names were more famous than the women's names. The more famous names should be easier to remember, biasing the judgement of frequency, such that List A would seem to have more women's names.

Turning to the judgements of likelihood for Linda, did you rate statement G as more likely than statement E? If you did, this is an example of the representativeness heuristic in action. Because Linda's description is seen as being typical of a feminist but not a bank-teller, Kahneman and Tversky found that people generally give increased likelihood ratings for C and G, and reduced likelihood ratings for E. Of course, on basic probabilities, G should be less likely than E, since the combination of two events (a bank-teller and active in feminist movement) is less likely than any one event on its own (just a bank-teller).

and also MacLeod and Campbell 1992). The availability heuristic causes people to be influenced by familiarity, vividness, recency, and salience of memories and images, such that recent information (hearing about an accident that befell a friend) or vivid images (recalling a traumatic accident) will have particular sway on judgements (likelihood of accidents). An important form of the simulation heuristic concerns counterfactuals. Counterfactual reasoning involves generating alternative simulations of past events in the form of 'What ifs' or 'If onlys' (e.g. 'If only I had not worked late, I would not have been mugged', for review see Roese 1997). Counterfactuals are often generated in response to negative events, and can influence subsequent behaviour, judgement (Galinsky and Moskowitz 2000) and emotion (Niedenthal et al. 1994; Roese 1997).

Consistent with the availability and simulation heuristics, Greening et al. (1996) showed that students' personal experience and imagery of weather disasters were significant predictors of their personal estimates of the risk of weather disasters. Similarly, Sherman *et al.* (1985) found that participants who imagined contracting a disease whose symptoms were considered 'easy-to-imagine', rated the disease as more likely to occur, relative to participants who imagined a disease whose symptoms were considered 'hard-to-imagine'. Likewise, Brown *et al.* (2002) showed that in pregnant women, the better the mental simulation of entering labour and arriving safely at hospital, the higher the likelihood estimates for a positive outcome.

Patients' ability to generate examples of particular classes of event has been used as an index of the availability/accessibility of these events, although for positive and negative events, this approach might be confounded with strategic attempts to control mood. Within this domain, the Future Thinking Task (MacLeod *et al.* 1993) is an important paradigm. The Future Thinking Task involves asking participants to generate possible positive ('looking forward to') and negative ('not looking forward to') events over several future time periods (next week, next year, next 5–10 years). The number of events generated in a limited time period provides some measure of the availability of these events.

Representativeness heuristic

The representativeness heuristic occurs when judgements about expectancy, causality, or categorization are based on the extent to which a specific event is seen as typical of a large group of events. See the second example in Boxes 4.3 and 4.4 for a demonstration of the representativeness heuristic. Another example is the 'gambler's fallacy', where it is wrongly believed that each gambling event in a game of chance (e.g. toss of a coin) is not independent but rather that deviations in one direction (a run of heads) will be corrected by a converse deviation (a run of tails). The gambler's fallacy occurs because people see sequences that are balanced and alternating (e.g. Head-Tail-Head-Tail-Tail) to be more representative of chance than prolonged sequences of one outcome (e.g. Head-Head-Head-Head-Head). Consistent with a representativeness heuristic account for the gambler's fallacy, undergraduates tend to generate erroneous sequences that do not reflect the independence of events, when asked to generate random sequences of heads and tails (Ladouceur *et al.* 1996).

Emotional reasoning heuristic

The emotional reasoning heuristic occurs when feelings are used as a source of information in making evaluative judgements ('How do I feel about it'; Schwarz and Clore 1983, 1988). Schwarz and Clore (1983) demonstrated that current mood influenced judgements of one's current life situation (e.g. life judged as less satisfactory if in a sad mood) and that this effect of mood on judgements was eliminated when participants were induced to attribute their current mood to situational factors (e.g. bad weather). An extensive 'mood as input' literature has also found that mood can provide information about how well a job is being done or information about how enjoyable a task is depending on the particular context and on the rules used when interpreting mood (Martin *et al.* 1993; Martin and Stoner 1995). The emotional reasoning heuristic, as studied in psychological disorders, is also known as 'ex-consequentia reasoning' (Arntz *et al.* 1995).

Arntz *et al.* (1995) examined whether specifying the degree of anxiety experienced during various more and less objectively threatening vignettes would influence the estimate of danger. For a description of the method see Box 4.5. This experiment demonstrated that patients with a range of anxiety disorders have an emotional reasoning style with respect to anxious mood states. In this study, patients tended to conclude that there must be danger merely because they feel anxious (i.e. ex-consequentia reasoning). This effect was not specific to the type of threat scenario, indicating that the emotional reasoning bias was a common process across at least four anxiety disorders.

Having described the expectancy biases and heuristics, their relevance to psychological disorders will now be reviewed. But at the outset note that it is important to state that both positive and negative expectancies can be clinically meaningful. Positive expectancies may be associated with the uptake of problem behaviour. For example, judgements that using alcohol or drugs will be pleasurable or relaxing may increase drinking or drug use.

Anxiety disorders

Panic disorder with or without agoraphobia

Andrew MacLeod and his colleagues (1997) found that compared to controls, patients with panic disorder generated more future negative events and rated negative events as more likely to happen. Arntz *et al.* (1995) found that patients with panic disorder showed emotional reasoning, with information about experiencing anxiety leading to increased estimates of danger. Patients with panic disorder also overestimate the level of fear that they will experience and the likelihood that they will panic when exposed to a fear-evoking situation (Rachman and Lopatka 1986*a–d*; Rachman *et al.* 1988). This phenomenon is called overprediction of fear and is clinically observed before the initial trial of exposure during a course of exposure therapy (Rachman 1994).

Box 4.5 Investigating emotional reasoning in anxiety disorders

Arntz *et al.* (1995)

Participants: Patients with panic disorder ($n = 41$), patients with spider phobia ($n = 52$), patients with social phobia ($n = 38$), patients with a mix of anxiety disorders ($n = 31$; 13 OCD, 5 GAD, 5 PTSD, 5 phobia, 3 atypical) and non-patient controls ($n = 24$).

Task: Participants read scenarios that had endings that differed on two dimensions; whether there was or was not objective information about safety or danger and whether there was or was not information about a fear response (symptoms of anxiety). Hence, for each scenario, there was an objective safety-no anxiety response ending, an objective safety-anxiety response ending, an objective danger-no anxiety response ending and an objective danger-anxiety response ending. Participants rated the dangerousness of the situation on visual analogue scales. Specific scenarios were constructed for each anxiety group. An example for patients with panic disorder would be being stuck in a lift. Following an initial description of being in an overcrowded lift, the statement 'All of a sudden, the lift becomes stuck between floors. Two people faint. Suddenly, you become very anxious' would be presented. This example combines both objective danger and anxiety response information.

Result: Compared to controls, all of the anxious patient groups were influenced by the anxiety response information in that information about an anxious response increased ratings of danger in all anxiety groups, across all situations, but did not influence controls. In general, anxious patients rated that there was more danger even when objective safety information was given compared to controls.

Specific phobia and social phobia

Patients with agoraphobia (McNally and Foa 1987), patients with claustrophobia (Öst and Csatlos 2000), and patients with social phobia (Gilboa-Schechtman *et al.* 2000), all overestimate the likelihood of negative events happening to themselves, compared to non-patient control groups. The increased negative expectancies tend to be specific to the particular concerns of each disorder. Patients with spider phobia overestimate the likelihood of being bitten by spiders compared to controls (Lavy *et al.* 1993a; Jones and Menzies 2000) and a diagnosis of claustrophobia is associated with overestimating claustrophobic but not other negative events (Öst and Csatlos 2000). Social phobia is associated with greater estimates for negative social events but not for negative non-social events (Lucock and Salkovskis 1988; Foa *et al.* 1996). Finally, patients with spider phobia were found to exhibit emotional reasoning (Arntz *et al.* 1995).

Obsessive-compulsive disorder

Patients with OCD have been found to overestimate the likelihood of negative outcomes (Rachman and Hodgson 1980). More recently, it has been established that checking and rituals are performed until it 'feels just right' to stop or until a rule under the control of internal sensations has been satisfied (e.g. Leckman *et al.* 1994; Miguel *et al.* 2000; Wells 2000). In an analogue sample, Coles *et al.* (2003) found that 'not just right' experiences were positively related to sub-clinical symptoms of OCD. These observations suggest that patients with OCD may display some form of emotional reasoning bias for judging threat, although this has not been explicitly tested in a sample of patients of OCD. Consistent with this possibility, Emmelkamp and Aardema (1999), in a large community sample, found that obsessive-compulsive behaviours were strongly correlated with self-reported beliefs of emotional reasoning (the beliefs measured 'inverse inference', which is another term for ex-consequentia reasoning referring to the use of feelings to judge risk, e.g. 'Whenever I feel anxious, it must mean that danger is near'). Note also that patients with OCD were the largest contributing group to the mixed anxiety disorder group, in which Arntz *et al.* (1995) found evidence of emotional reasoning (see Box 4.5).

Post-traumatic stress disorder and acute stress disorder

Warda and Bryant (1998) found that patients with acute stress disorder (ASD) have elevated expectancies for negative events happening to them compared to controls. Adapting the emotional reasoning paradigm, Engelhard *et al.* (2001) demonstrated that patients with PTSD also infer danger from the presence of anxiety symptoms and from the presence of intrusive thoughts, compared to non-patient controls.

Generalized anxiety disorder

Gillian Butler and Andrew Mathews (1983) found that patients with GAD tend to expect negative outcomes and predict greater likelihood of negative events happening in the future compared to non-anxious controls. Furthermore, worry, a defining characteristic of GAD, is associated with elevated subjective probabilities of negative events, perhaps as a result of increasing the availability of negative events (MacLeod *et al.* 1991). A series of studies with the Future Thinking Task have found that a high anxiety group, including those meeting criteria for GAD, tend to generate more negative future events but not fewer positive future events, relative to low anxiety controls (MacLeod and Byrne 1996; MacLeod *et al.* 1997). Byrne and MacLeod (1997) compared participants with anxiety alone (some meeting diagnostic criteria for GAD), with mixed anxiety and depression and without either anxiety or depression. Both the anxious alone and the mixed anxious-depressed groups provided more reasons for, relative to reasons against, negative events occurring and rated these negative events as more likely to happen. Conversely both anxious and mixed anxious-depressed groups provided more reasons against, relative to reasons for, positive events happening and estimated positive events as less likely to happen. This pattern of findings is consistent with the operation of the availability heuristic. The increased availability of negative future events in patients with GAD, coupled with increased expectancies of negative events, is consistent with an availability heuristic account of negative expectancies.

Moving on to emotional reasoning, patients with GAD were among the mixed anxiety disorder group displaying emotional reasoning in the Arntz *et al.* (1995) study, although the numbers were small. However, consistent with the possibility that GAD is characterized by emotional reasoning, Gasper and Clore (1998) found that a high trait anxiety group found it harder to ignore the influence of their anxious feelings when making likelihood judgements. In particular, attributing anxiety to a situational cause (e.g. an upcoming examination), which should seem irrelevant to non-examination-related judgements, reduced likelihood estimates for other risks (e.g. having something stolen) for low trait anxious people more than for high trait anxious people. Gasper and Clore (1998) also found that attributing anxiety to a particular situational cause ('thinking about a negative event') only reduced the effects of anxiety on likelihood estimates for other risks when the participants were instructed to make judgements based on their factual knowledge. When participants were instructed to make judgements based on their emotions and feelings, attributing anxiety to the situational cause 'thinking about a negative event' did not reduce the effects of anxiety on likelihood estimates for other risks, regardless of the level of trait anxiety. These results suggest that high trait anxiety is associated with the use of feelings to judge expectancies of negative events.

Somatoform disorders

Pain disorder

Crombez *et al.* (1996) found that patients with chronic low back pain initially overestimated the pain they would experience during exercise. However, the expected pain did not predict the actual pain experienced during exercise and these overestimates were corrected on repeated exercise. Nonetheless, the overestimation of pain was associated with greater fear of injury and with reduced exercise performance, perhaps as a consequence of avoidance of effort during exercise. Cipher and Fernandez (1997) found that in patients with chronic pain, expectations of the ability to tolerate pain predicted actual tolerance, whilst expectancies that pain signals damage predicted avoidance.

Hypochrondriasis

Patients diagnosed with hypochrondriasis overestimate their risk of developing diseases and the negative outcomes of health-related scenarios but not the risk of non-health-related negative events (accidents or criminal assault) compared to controls (Haenen et al. 2000; Barksy et al. 2001). The perceived risk was reported to be associated with the self-reported tendency to amplify benign bodily sensations.

Sexual disorders

Sakheim et al. (1987) found that, for the same objective level of erectile response, men who have difficulty maintaining an erection under-estimated the size of their erections, compared to men with no difficulties. Cranston-Cuebas et al. (1993) gave placebo pills to sexually functional and sexually dysfunctional men, informing them that the pills either acted to increase their erections, decrease their erections or were a placebo. The 'erection-decreasing' pills had no effect on the sexually functional men, but reduced erections in the sexually dysfunctional men, whereas the 'erection-increasing' pills increased erections in the sexually dysfunctional men. This pattern of results was interpreted as indicating that men who have difficulties maintaining an erection have negative expectancies of their performance except when provided with external sources of confidence (van den Hout and Barlow 2000).

Eating disorders

Cooper (1997) found that eating disorder patients estimate negative events as likely to happen to them as a consequence of their weight or shape. Hohlstein et al. (1998) found that patients with bulimia nervosa are more likely to expect that eating helps manage negative moods and reduces boredom and have a greater expectancy that dieting and thinness will lead to self-improvement, relative to non-patient controls. Patients with anorexia nervosa had a stronger expectancy that thinness will lead to positive outcomes and a reduced expectancy that eating will lead to a positive outcome.

Impulse control disorders

Problem gamblers have the expectation that they will win their bets (Corney and Cummings 1985) and that gambling will lead to positive outcomes (e.g. in prison inmates, Walters and Contri 1998). The gamblers' fallacy is an example of the representativeness heuristic (see page 156 for definition) and is pervasive in non-patient samples when tested on games of chance, although the fallacy is more pronounced in problem gamblers (Coulombe *et al.* 1992; Ladouceur *et al.* 1995).

Mood disorders

Experimental studies, using a variety of methods, have demonstrated that people with depression are more pessimistic in their prediction of future outcomes than non-depressed controls (Alloy and Ahrens 1987; Pyszczynski *et al.* 1987; Dunning and Story 1991). Research indicates that patients with depression make higher estimates of the likelihood of negative events happening to them (Kaney *et al.* 1997) and lower estimates of the likelihood of positive events, relative to non-patient controls (Andersen *et al.* 1992). Furthermore, in depression, these predictions about the future are made relatively automatically, with attentional load (holding a six-digit number in memory) not increasing depressed people's response time to endorse whether negative or positive events will occur, but increasing response time for controls (Andersen *et al.* 1992; Andersen and Limpert 2001). These findings suggest that people with depression have highly available/accessible representations of negative events, whilst representations of positive events are much less accessible. On the Future Thinking Task, depressed parasuicidal patients (MacLeod *et al.* 1993), parasuicidal patients (MacLeod *et al.* 1997*a*), and patients with depression (MacLeod *et al.* 1997*b*; MacLeod and Salaminiou 2001) all show reduced generation of positive future events but not elevated generation of negative future events, compared to controls. Byrne and MacLeod (1997) found that compared to controls, people with elevated anxiety and depression provided more reasons for, relative to reasons against, negative events occurring and rated these negative events as more likely to happen. Conversely, anxious and depressed people provided more reasons against, relative to reasons for, positive events occurring and estimated positive events as less likely to happen. The combined finding of reduced positive expectancies and reduced generation of future positive events is consistent with an availability heuristic/simulation heuristic account of expectancies in depression.

Psychotic disorders

Kaney *et al.* (1997) found that patients with schizophrenia, with and without persecutory delusions, have greater estimates of the likelihood of negative events happening to themselves, relative to non-patient controls. In this study, patients with schizophrenia and persecutory delusions also reported greater estimates of the likelihood of negative events happening to other people, indicating a generally negative world-view.

Substance-related disorders

Patients with problems relating to substance abuse make higher estimates of the likelihood of specific positive outcomes (relaxation, arousal) related to the use of drugs or alcohol (Stacy 1997; Goldman 1999; Wiers *et al.* 2002) relative to non-patient controls. These positive expectancies predict prospective substance abuse and treatment response (Jones *et al.* 2001).

Summary

Biased expectancy appears to be a common process across all the psychological disorders studied and therefore meets our criteria for a definite transdiagnostic process. The biases in likelihood estimations reflect the specific concerns of each disorder. However, it is worth noting that since likelihood estimates are typically assessed by self-report methods, these findings could be due to demand biases. The availability heuristic appears to operate in the same way across patients with GAD, patients with panic disorder, depressed patients, and non-patient controls, and is associated with judgements of expectancies. Accordingly, since our criteria for a definite transdiagnostic process requires the presence of four or more disorders, the operation of the availability heuristic is a possible trans-diagnostic process. Emotional reasoning is a process common across at least five different anxiety disorders making it a definite transdiagnostic process. However, we note that this conclusion needs to be treated with caution, since emotional reasoning has only been examined within the anxiety disorders.

We will now move on to review the final two reasoning processes: covariation bias and hypothesis testing. Although both of these biases depend on expectations and could be subsumed under the rubric of expectancy biases (van den Hout and Barlow 2000), we are separating them because they have previously been investigated separately, and in the interests of clarity.

Detecting covariation and illusory correlation

Covariation detection is the ability to detect that two events tend to co-occur in a regular and consistent way. Detecting covariation is important for understanding and predicting the world, for example, by learning what cues signal forthcoming reward or punishment. However, it is important to distinguish between temporal contiguity, when two events occur within a short space of time of each other and covariation when two events predominantly occur together and do not tend to occur independently and thus, may be dependent on each other. The covariation bias occurs when people find an illusory correlation between two categories of events that, in reality, are correlated to a lesser extent or even correlated in the opposite direction (Chapman and Chapman1967; Alloy and Tabachnik 1984). Covariation bias is a well-documented effect in the cognitive psychology literature, with humans being more likely to perceive events as co-occurring if there is a prior expectation that they will occur together, such that the heuristic biases can contribute to covariation bias (Chapman and Chapman 1967; Tversky and Kahneman 1973). One example of the covariation bias is the tendency for people to over-estimate the frequency of co-occurrence for word pairs that are semantically associated (e.g. 'bacon-eggs'), when presented with lists of word-pairs that occur at different frequencies. Covariation bias is involved in social stereotyping, impaired clinical judgement, impaired interpretation of test results (Chapman and Chapman 1982), and belief in the paranormal (Schienle *et al.* 1996). Covariation bias can be studied by examining the ability to detect contingency between the repeated presentation of two sets of stimuli. For example, by presenting word-pairs or by presenting descriptions of different situations and groups and asking people to estimate how often they occur together. We will now move on to briefly review the literature on covariation bias across the psychological disorders. As will become evident, most research on covariation bias has been conducted on patients with an anxiety disorder.

Anxiety disorders

One paradigm used to study illusory correlations involves participants being shown slides that are randomly paired with either an aversive outcome (or unconditioned stimulus, in conditioning terms) such as loud noise or mild electric shock or with a neutral outcome (e.g. nothing happening). The slides could be neutral fear-irrelevant stimuli (e.g. mushrooms, flowers) or specific emotionally related stimuli, for example slides of snakes, angry faces, or emergency situations. The extent of the illusory correlation is measured by asking participants to rate what they expect after each slide. That is, they are asked to judge the overall contingency or, in other words, the proportion of trials where the target stimulus is followed by an aversive stimulus. Covariation bias occurs when participants markedly overestimate the contingency between the fear-relevant stimulus and the shock, but not between the neutral stimuli and the shock. Compared to non-patient controls, a fear-relevant covariation bias has been found in panic disorder (Pauli *et al.* 1996; Wiedemann *et al.* 2001), spider/snake phobia (Tomarken *et al.* 1989; de Jong *et al.* 1992; Tomarken *et al.* 1995; de Jong *et al.* 1995*a*; de Jong and Merckelbach 2000) and flight phobia (Pauli *et al.* 1998). Importantly, there was no difference between patients with spider phobia and controls for fear-related stimuli other than spider stimuli. Likewise, the illusory correlation in panic disorder was only found for the panic-related stimuli (i.e. for slides of emergency situations). Thus, the illusory correlation appears to be specific for the main fear concern of each disorder. In a number of these studies, prior expectancies significantly correlated with the covariation bias.

However, no difference was found in an analogue sample between people with high and low fear of blood-injury in their judgements of covariation between blood-injury-related slides and shocks (Pury and Mineka 1997). Similarly, no difference was found between high and low social anxiety groups in their judgements of covariation between slides of angry faces and shocks (de Jong *et al.* 1998). In both of these analogue samples, both high and low fear participants showed the covariation bias.

Impulse control disorders

Using self-report measures, problem gamblers are found to be prone to correlating salient features of the environment with both wins and losses, even if such associations are non-contingent. For example, using the day of the week as a cue to success of betting (Gaboury and Ladouceur 1989; Griffiths 1994).

Psychotic disorders

Brennan and Hemsley (1985) found that patients with paranoid schizophrenia reported particularly strong illusory correlations for word pairs that were relevant to their paranoid delusions, compared to patients with non-paranoid schizophrenia and non-patient controls. However, Chadwick and Taylor (2000) found that patients with paranoid schizophrenia did not seem more prone to illusory correlations on neutral word-pairs than patients with depression, nor than previously established normative data. However, it should be noted that this study only used neutral stimuli, and was limited by the small sample size ($n = 10$ for each group).

Summary

Covariation bias is clearly observed across specific phobia and panic disorder and there is a tentative suggestion that it may occur for gambling disorders and psychotic disorders. Again, the covariation bias seems to be limited to the particular fear or emotional concerns of each patient group. Based on our criteria, covariation bias is a possible transdiagnostic process. Future research is warranted because covariation bias has potential to explain the maintenance of negative responses to particular stimuli (e.g. extreme fear to a spider), even when the majority of experiences associated with that stimuli are not negative.

Hypothesis testing and data gathering

An important aspect of day-to-day reasoning is formulating explanations and accounts for why things happen and then being able to revise these accounts in the light of new information. Such hypothesis testing usually has a confirmation or belief bias, that is, a tendency to agree with conclusions that fit prior beliefs (whatever their actual logical status), and to gather evidence that confirms our beliefs rather than evidence that challenges them (Evans *et al.* 1993; Nickerson 1998). Prior expectancies have been found to influence the search for information in a manner that is consistent with the expectancy (Bodenhausen 1988). Accordingly, expectancies will influence what people expect to occur and, thereby, contribute to the belief bias. Confirmations of prior expectations are overvalued, whereas disconfirmations of prior expectations are downplayed.

Belief bias is often tested on syllogistic reasoning tasks (Evans *et al.* 1983) in which participants are presented three statements, two serving as the premises of an argument (e.g. 'No fast vehicles are safe', 'Some cars are safe') and the third serving as the conclusion of the argument (e.g. 'Therefore, some cars are not fast vehicles'). Participants must decide whether the conclusion is a valid deduction from the first two premises. That is, assuming that the first two statements are true, does the third statement logically follow? Actual reasoning on syllogistic tasks is determined both by the logical argument contained within the two premises and by people's real-world experience. Specifically, when the logical deduction from the premises is inconsistent with people's beliefs about the world, people make more mistakes in determining whether the conclusion is logically correct or not. Thus, these tasks demonstrate the effect of a belief bias. When the conclusion is logically invalid but believable and consistent with expectations and knowledge about the world (e.g. such as the conclusion 'Therefore, some fast vehicles are not cars' for the premises above), people will make more mistakes. Conversely, when the conclusion is logically valid but unbelievable, people will make more mistakes. An example of a conclusion that is logically valid and believable for the premises above is 'Therefore, some cars are not fast vehicles'.

Beliefs can also take the form of conditional rules, where there is an 'If …then' structure. For example, 'If I feel anxious, then danger is present'. Importantly, reasoning is often context-specific and guided by the perceived usefulness of falsifying or confirming information (Manktelow and Over 1991; Kirby 1994; Evans and Over 1996; Evans 2002). For example, in response to potential threat, one could adopt a danger rule ('If the lion approaches then danger') or a safety rule ('If the lion moves away then safe'). In response to objective dangers, information that confirms a danger rule and information that falsifies a safety rule are of greater utility. Such information would have survival value, since it is better to have many unnecessary concerns about danger rather than miss one real danger. Indeed, non-patient participants tend to select verifying information for danger rules and falsifying information for safety rules in response to objective dangers (de Jong *et al.* 1997*a*, 1998).

Biases in confirmation or falsification of conditional rules are typically tested by the Wason selection task (see Box 4.6), which investigates the type of strategy people employ in response to conditional rules. The other aspect of hypothesis testing of interest in psychological disorders is the amount of information that people gather before deciding to confirm or reject a hypothesis. It is possible that people with psychological disorders could be over or under cautious in reaching conclusions. Probabilistic tasks such as the 'beads in jars' task assesses the degree of data gathering before a decision is reached. On this task, participants are given coloured beads (red or blue) one at a time and asked to guess whether the beads came from a jar with a 85:15 ratio of red to blue beads or from a jar with a 15:85 ratio of red to blue beads. The number of beads drawn before deciding which jar the beads came from is an index of data gathering.

Having outlined the basic methodology for investigating hypothesis testing and confirmation bias, we will move on to review the findings across the psychological disorders to determine the extent to which these reasoning processes are transdiagnostic.

Anxiety disorders

Specific phobia

de Jong *et al.* (1997*a*) found that patients with spider phobia, but not non-patient controls, showed a danger-confirming reasoning strategy for spiders on an emotionally-relevant Wason selection task. Thus, in this study patients with spider phobia tended to gather evidence consistent with their beliefs that spiders are dangerous. Interestingly, both patients with spider phobia and non-patient controls showed a danger-confirming strategy for general objective

Box 4.6 Investigating conditional reasoning—the Wason selection task

The Wason selection task is a deductive reasoning problem, which asks participants to search for information that can falsify a conditional rule. Participants are first presented with the conditional rule. For example,

'If you suffer from a headache, then you may have a brain tumour'

Participants are then presented with 4 cards that display, on one side, whether the antecedent of the rule is true or false and, on other side, whether the consequence is true or false. The cards are presented such that at least one of each antecedent and consequence is displayed.

For example, the participants would see the following cards (with reverse side in parentheses):

– positive antecedent: 'I have a headache' (I do not have a brain tumour)

– negative antecedent: 'I do not have a headache' (I do not have a brain tumour)

– true consequence: 'I have a brain tumour' (I have a headache)

– false consequence: 'I do not have a brain tumour' (I have a headache)

Participants indicate which card/cards they definitely need to turn over to determine whether the rule is true. Selecting the true consequence card is a verifying strategy, whilst selecting the false consequence card is a falsifying strategy.

By summing up the different choices across a number of scenarios, one can determine which strategy people prefer.

To make the Wason selection task more meaningful, some versions do not present the information as statements of facts, but rather as questions and answers that can be obtained from talking to people (Smeets *et al.* 2000).

threats. So rather than showing a general strengthening of the threat confirmation bias, patients with spider phobia demonstrate a specific extension of the normal danger-confirming strategy to their feared stimuli.

On a syllogistic reasoning task, female patients with spider phobia demonstrated an enhanced belief bias compared to non-patient controls, with this enhanced belief bias occurring more for neutral themed syllogisms rather than phobia-relevant themed syllogisms (de Jong *et al* 1997*b*). The phobia group were significantly slower at responding to mismatches between logical validity and believability for syllogisms than controls, indicating an impact of belief bias on judging the statements. This pattern of results suggests that women with spider phobia have an exaggerated belief bias in general, and not just for fear concerns, compared to controls. Such a tendency may make this group less able to correct unhelpful beliefs when exposed to disconfirming information. Accordingly, theoretically the exaggerated belief bias could be involved in maintaining the disorder.

Obsessive-compulsive disorder

Several studies have found that patients with OCD gather more information than non-patient controls and patients with GAD before reaching a conclusion on probabilistic tasks, such as the 'beads in jars' task (Fear and Healy 1997; Pelissier and O'Connor 2002). Pelissier and O'Connor (2002) found that patients with OCD did not differ from non-patient controls or patients with GAD on a neutral Wason Selection task, nor on a syllogistic reasoning task. This finding suggests that there was no difference in the basic belief bias for neutral themes. However, on tasks of inductive reasoning, participants with OCD took longer than patients with GAD and non-anxious controls to generate a link between two arbitrary unrelated statements and demonstrated reduced conviction about an arbitrary statement after generating reasons to support this statement. This finding suggests that when patients with OCD generate reasons to support an argument, inductive reasoning increases their doubts.

Dar *et al.* (2000) attempted to account for the doubt, reduced confidence and repeated checking, characteristic of patients with OCD, by speculating that patients with OCD may have a weakened confirmation bias compared to controls. To date, this interesting hypothesis has not been tested using disorder-relevant material.

Generalized anxiety disorder

Pelissier and O'Connor (2002) found that patients with GAD did not differ from non-patient controls on a Wason selection task with neutral content, on a neutral syllogistic reasoning task or on the 'bead in jars' task. However, in a non-patient sample, Ladouceur *et al.* (1997) found that increased intolerance of uncertainty, a characteristic of patients with GAD (as will be discussed in Chapter 5), is positively correlated with gathering more information before making a decision on an inference task.

Somatoform disorders

In both patients with hypochrondriasis and non-patient controls, health threats have been found to activate a danger-confirming strategy on a modified emotionally-relevant Wason selection task (de Jong *et al.* 1998). However, the instructions used in this task referred to participants being worried about the danger, which in itself may have activated a danger-confirming strategy. With this confound removed, for general threat, non-patient controls and the hypochrondriasis group both used a threat-confirming reasoning pattern, but only the hypochrondriasis group showed a threat-confirming reasoning pattern for health threat stimuli (Smeets *et al.* 2000).

Mood disorders

Several studies show that patients with depression do not differ in hypothesis testing for neutral information compared to non-patient controls. For example, Bentall and Young found no difference between patients with depression and non-patient controls when selecting from a range of pre-supplied strategies to test what caused positive and negative outcomes (Bentall and Young 1996) or when solving visual discrimination problems (Young and Bentall 1995). Several studies have found that patients with depression do not differ from non-patient controls in data gathering on the 'beads in jars' task (Dudley *et al.* 1997*a*; Peters *et al.* 1997) or on a probabilistic reasoning task incorporating both neutral and emotionally salient material (Dudley *et al.* 1997*b*). However, Young and Bentall (1997) found that patients with depression had fewer draws before reaching a conclusion on the 'beads in jar' task than controls.

Dudley *et al.* (1998) found no difference between patients with depression and non-patient controls on a series of Wason Selection tasks, whether neutral or more realistic in content. However, Silberman *et al.* (1983) reported that depressed patients were impaired on a discrimination-learning problem, compared to non-patient controls, as a result of an inability to narrow down the set of possible hypotheses.

Psychotic disorders

In patients with schizophrenia, there is evidence for a bias in information-gathering in that people with delusions tend to seek less information before reaching a decision. Using the 'beads in jar' task, Huq *et al.* (1988) and Garety *et al.* (1991) found that patients with schizophrenia, who had delusions, guessed which jar the beads came from after fewer trials than mixed patient controls or non-patient controls. If the pattern of beads removed was first consistent with the beads coming from one jar and then altered to be more consistent with the beads coming from the other jar, the patients with delusions more readily changed their hypothesis. This result is consistent with a bias towards gathering less data before reaching a conclusion and suggests that if anything, patients with schizophrenia change their hypotheses too easily. Note that patients with delusions do not have a deficit in estimating the probabilities for beads to come from each jar when asked directly (Dudley *et al.* 1997*b*). Accordingly, the bias seems to be towards gathering less data before reaching a conclusion. This data gathering bias has been replicated in patients with delusions, irrespective of a diagnosis of schizophrenia or delusional disorder, compared to non-patient controls, mixed patient controls, patients with depression and patients with OCD (e.g. John and Dodgson 1994; Fear and Healy 1997; Peters *et al.* 1997; Young and Bentall 1997).

Hypothesis testing in patients with persecutory delusions (schizophrenia or delusional disorder) was found to be no different from non-patient controls and depressed patients when participants were supplied with a range of options to assess the causes of positive and negative events (Bentall and Young 1996). Likewise, patients with delusions did not differ from controls in probability estimates, when they were provided with all the information required rather than when they were left to decide whether they had sufficient information (Dudley *et al.* 1997*b*). On Wason Selection tasks, patients with schizophrenia who had delusions did not differ from patients with depression and non-patient controls, when the task content was abstract (Dudley *et al.* 1998). However, as the task material became more realistic, the patients with schizophrenia, who had delusions, became impaired at the task relative to the two control groups. Dudley *et al.* (1997*b*) found that all groups (non-patient controls, depressed controls, and patients with schizophrenia) requested less information before making a decision on a probabilistic task when the content of the task was more emotionally salient. There was a trend for this effect of emotional material to be stronger in patients with schizophrenia. Thus, hypothesis testing may be poorer in patients with schizophrenia when personally relevant information is involved.

The tendency to gather less data before reaching a conclusion is less evident when patients make probability estimates on a fixed number of trials (Dudley *et al.* 1997*a*), suggesting that the data gathering bias is not due to an impulsive response or limitations in working memory (for a definition of working memory see Chapter 3). Furthermore, when given a range of options, or a choice of different experiments to test hypotheses, patients with persecutory delusions make sensible decisions (Bentall and Young 1996).

Summary

General hypothesis testing for neutral material appears to be normal across a range of psychological disorders. The notable exception is schizophrenia, where patients show a tendency to gather less data before reaching a conclusion. It also appears that patients with OCD may gather more data before reaching a conclusion. Thus, data gathering may be a process that is distinct across different psychological disorders. Threat confirmation biases are found in both specific phobias and hypochrondriasis, with the bias being specific to the concerns of each disorder. Accordingly, given that the threat confirmation bias appears to operate across a range of disorders, it meets our criteria for a possible transdiagnostic process. There is a tentative suggestion that specific phobias are associated with an increased general belief bias. However, studies of hypothesis testing and belief bias for emotional material (e.g. disorder-relevant syllogisms) and tests of disorder-relevant confirmation bias (e.g. modified Wason Tests with disorder-congruent conditional rules) are lacking in nearly all psychological disorders. Accordingly, it is not currently possible to determine whether belief bias is or is not a transdiagnostic process. At a clinical level, the threat confirmation biases closely parallel Beck's (1976) description of cognitive distortions, most notably catastrophizing and jumping to conclusions, and may provide a more detailed description of how these cognitive distortions occur.

Discussion

The aim of this chapter has been to establish the extent to which reasoning processes are relevant across the disorders. The results are summarized in Table 4.1. As evident in the table, biases in interpretations appear to be common across the majority of disorders studied. Hence, according to the criteria outlined in Chapter 1, interpretative reasoning appears to be a definite transdiagnostic process. There is evidence that attributional reasoning is biased in depression and schizophrenia, although the attributional style is in contrasting directions. There is also evidence of pessimistic attributional reasoning in sexual disorders, anxiety disorders, and eating disorders, although some of these effects, such as in eating disorders and generalized anxiety disorder, are secondary to depression. Accordingly, the evidence to date indicates that attributional reasoning meets our criteria for a possible trans-diagnostic process. Biases in judgements of expectancies appear to be common across all the disorders studied. Hence, expectancy reasoning is a definite transdiagnostic process. Results consistent with the operation of the heuristic biases considered to underlie the judgement of expectancies (the availability heuristic and the emotional reasoning heuristic) have been found in all the disorders studied. The availability heuristic has been investigated in GAD, panic disorder, and depression, thus it meets our criteria for a possible trans-diagnostic process (that is, it has not been investigated in more than three disorders). Likewise, emotional reasoning has been demonstrated in at least five disorders (specific phobias, social phobia, panic disorder, PTSD, and

OCD), meeting our criteria for a definite transdiagnostic process, although emotional reasoning has only been studied in one cluster of disorders, the anxiety disorders. This is a point to which we will return in Chapter 7 when we discuss the limitations of the criteria we set for the definition of a definite and possible transdiagnostic process. Covariation bias has been demonstrated across panic disorder, specific phobias, and psychotic disorder making it a possible transdiagnostic process. Hypothesis testing can be subdivided into (1) confirmation or belief bias processes and (2) data gathering processes. Confirmation or belief bias processes have been tested on syllogistic reasoning tasks which test pre-existing beliefs about the world and on Wason selection tasks that examine conditional rules, typically about judging threat. Confirmation bias for threat rules has been demonstrated in both specific phobias and hypochrondriasis but has not been studied in any other disorders. Accordingly, confirmation bias for threat rules is a possible transdiagnostic process. To date, the evidence relating to the confirmation belief bias for other beliefs or rules is inconclusive. On the other hand, data gathering for neutral material appears to be similar in patients with psychological disorders and non-patient controls with the exception of schizophrenia and perhaps also OCD. As data gathering appears to operate differently across these disorders (patients with OCD gather more evidence, patients with psychotic disorder gather less evidence), data gathering appears to be a distinct process that is not common across the different disorders. In the section that follows, we will elaborate on these decisions and discuss their theoretical implications.

Definite transdiagnostic processes

The evidence, as summarized in Table 4.1, suggests that interpretative reasoning meets our criteria for definite transdiagnostic processes. The evidence indicates that all of the psychological disorders studied interpret ambiguous stimuli in a negative way, relative to non-patient controls. Further, when more than one set of ambiguous stimuli has been used, the evidence suggests that patients with psychological disorders only negatively misinterpret the stimuli specific to their particular concerns.

Similarly, there was evidence in all of the psychological disorders studied showing biases in the judgement of expectancy. When studied in more detail, these judgements of expectancy appear to be related to the use of reasoning heuristics, particularly availability and simulation heuristics. It appears that the reasoning heuristics operate in the same way across non-patient controls, patients with anxiety disorders and patients with depression. Thus, anxious patients can generate more future negative events and tend to have high levels of negative expectancy, whereas depressed patients generate fewer positive

Table 4.1 Summary of findings across the psychological disorders (first column) and the reasoning processes (top line)

	Interpretational bias	Attributions[1]	Expectancy bias	Emotional reasoning	Covariation bias	Confirmation bias	Data gathering[2]
Panic disorder with or without agoraphobia	** +	** +/−	** +	** +	** +		
Specific phobia	*** +	** +/−	** +	** +	** +	** +	+
Social phobia	** +	** +	** +	** +	* −	** +	** +
OCD	** +	** +/−	** +	** +		** −	** +
PTSD/ASD	** +	** +/−	*** +	** +		** −	** **
GAD	** +	** −	** +	** +		** +	** −
Pain disorder	** +	** +	** +				
Hypochondriasis	** +	** +	** +			** +	
Dissociative disorder							
Sexual disorder	*** +	** +	** +				
Eating disorder	*** +	** −	** +				
Sleep Disorder							
Impulse Control	* +	* +	** +	+	* +		
Unipolar depression	** +/−	*** +	** +	** +		** −	** +/−
Bipolar depression	** +	** +	+				
Psychotic disorder	* +	*** +	** +	+	** +	** +	*** +
Substance disorder	* +	** +	** +				** +

Note. [1]The evidence indicates that attributions may be biased in different ways in different disorders.

[2]The positive evidence for OCD is for gathering *more* evidence before reaching a decision, whereas the positive evidence for psychotic disorders is for gathering *less* evidence before reaching a decision (i.e. data gathering appears to operate differently across these disorders).

For each reasoning process the left hand column presents an indication of the quality of the evidence as follows: *** = good quality evidence, ** = moderate quality of evidence, * = tentative quality of evidence (see page 21–22 for further explanation) and the right hand column presents an indication of the findings as follows: + = positive findings, − = negative findings, +/− = mixed findings, blank space = the reasoning process has not been researched in this disorder.

future events and tend to have low levels of positive expectancy, suggesting the standard operation of the availability heuristic across these disorders. Also consistent with the standard operation of the availability heuristics in psychological disorders, Constans and Mathews (1993) and MacLeod and Campbell (1992) demonstrated that induced mood could bias recall latencies for positive and negative events, as well as subjective estimates of the likelihood of future events. Because patients with psychological disorders probably have easier access to memories relevant to their disorders (e.g. sad situations in depression—for more detail see Chapter 3) and can more easily simulate disorder-relevant scenarios than controls, they are likely to have biased expectancies (Öst and Csatlos 2000). Thus, the evidence is consistent with the hypothesis that the availability heuristic influences expectancy judgements.

Emotional reasoning in response to anxiety is found across all of the anxiety disorders studied but not among non-patient controls. Unfortunately, emotional reasoning has not been evaluated in other disorders. Thus, the extent to which emotional reasoning is common across psychological disorders in general or just common across the anxiety disorders is currently unknown. Nonetheless, emotional reasoning meets our criteria for a definite transdiagnostic process.

Possible transdiagnostic processes

After controlling for level of depression, positive evidence has been reported for biased attributional reasoning across 11 disorders, with null results for just two disorders. As such, attributional reasoning meets our criteria for a possible transdiagnostic process. Although, as noted previously, the evidence suggests that attributions may be biased in different ways in different disorders. Specifically, patients with depression exhibit a pessimistic attributional style that is the converse of the self-serving attributional style found in non-patient controls. In other words, patients with depression and non-patient controls have a qualitatively different style. On the other hand, patients with psychotic disorders have a stronger version of the biases seen in non-patients including the self-serving attributional style and blaming negative events on external factors. That is, patients with psychotic disorders differ quantitatively from non-patient controls. Other psychological disorders appear to be characterized by a pessimistic attributional style but in the case of anxiety disorders and eating disorders, this pessimistic attributional style may be a consequence of elevated depression. Another limitation of the majority of studies of attributional biases is that they have used the unmodified Attributional Style Questionnaire. Furthermore, it is not possible to determine whether the differences between schizophrenia and depression are the result of different attributional processes within the disorders or the same process operating differently because of different current concerns. Clearly, future research should seek to investigate attributional reasoning using items that are specifically developed to assess attributions for disorder-relevant concerns.

The availability heuristic has been found in all the disorders examined but has only been examined in three disorders, meaning that it meets our criteria for a possible transdiagnostic process. The evidence suggests that covariation bias and biases in hypothesis testing may be possible transdiagnostic processes. Covariation bias for fear-relevant stimuli is common across specific phobia and panic disorder, although it has not been examined in other disorders in studies that have used the pairing of neutral and disorder-relevant slides with aversive outcomes. Thus, covariation bias is also a possible transdiagnostic process.

With respect to the threat confirmation bias reviewed within the hypothesis testing section, the few studies that have been reported with emotionally-relevant material have found that the process occurs across more than one disorder (specific phobia and hypochrondriasis). Accordingly, threat confirmation bias meets our criteria for a possible transdiagnostic process.

Like judgements of expectancy, the mechanisms underlying covariation bias and confirmation bias also appear to be common across both non-patient controls and groups diagnosed with psychological disorders. That is, the operation of the reasoning processes in the psychological disorders studied does not appear to be either quantitatively or qualitatively different from the non-patient controls. We will now move on to examine, in more detail, the evidence and arguments supporting the idea that the mechanisms underlying covariation bias and confirmation bias are common across non-patient groups and groups diagnosed with psychological disorders.

First, the mechanism for covariation bias appears to be similar for both non-patient controls and phobic patients. For both groups, the development of a covariation bias requires matching levels of emotional response to both the cue stimuli and the associated consequence stimuli (e.g. shock) such that only cue stimuli that produces emotional arousal result in illusory correlations with shock (Tomarken et al. 1995; Amin and Lovibond 1997; Kennedy et al. 1997). This emotional matching requirement explains why only patients with spider phobia show a covariation bias for spider images, whilst analogue samples, selected for being high and low for fear both show a covariation bias for blood-injury-related stimuli and angry faces. Both blood-injury-related stimuli and angry faces may induce emotional arousal in all people, whether high or low in fear, such that all people show a covariation bias for these stimuli.

Second, patients with hypochrondriasis and phobias show the same general threat confirmation bias as non-patient controls. For both controls and patients with a psychological disorder, a danger-confirmation strategy seems to be activated by the perception of threat. Patients with phobias and hypochrondriasis differ from non-patient controls in applying the danger-confirmation strategy to additional stimuli, those specific to their fear concerns, where there is not an objective threat. Thus, the same mechanism of threat activating a danger-confirmation rule applies across controls and these patient groups. The difference is not in the operation of the process but rather in the perception of threat.

Although the common operation of these reasoning processes across both controls and patients is not proof that these reasoning processes are across disorder processes, it does suggest that the mechanism of the reasoning processes may be the same whatever the psychological state. For example, if a 'better safe than sorry' strategy for threat confirmation is the standard default response that is applied whenever there is a perception of threat, it seems reasonable to hypothesize that this strategy would be activated by the specific fear concerns of other disorders. By this reasoning, the threat confirmation bias is likely to be a transdiagnostic process.

Additionally, we speculate that future research is likely to find that covariation bias and confirmation bias are definite transdiagnostic processes because both of these biases are influenced by judgements of expectancies. Initial expectancies correlate with illusory correlations and expectancies influence the selection of information. Given that biases in reasoning about expectancies appear to be common across disorders, one might expect covariation bias and confirmation bias for disorder-related concerns to show the same pattern.

Distinct processes and inconclusive evidence

Within the domain of hypothesis testing, the evidence for data gathering processes suggest that this is not an across disorder process, with schizophrenia and OCD demonstrating distinct effects from the other disorders studied, as well as contrasting effects from each other. That is, biased data gathering appears to be a distinct process only found in some psychological disorders. Patients with psychotic disorders show a tendency to gather less data before reaching a conclusion compared to other patient groups and compared to controls for both neutral and emotional material. Similarly, there is a suggestion that patients with OCD gather more data before reaching a conclusion compared to patients with GAD and non-patient controls. These two differences clearly have potential for explaining aspects of the symptomatology of OCD and schizophrenia.

There is tentative evidence that specific phobias may be associated with a general increase in belief bias. Given that belief bias has not been examined in other disorders, the evidence is inconclusive as to whether belief bias is a transdiagnostic process. Nonetheless, it is potentially a highly significant area for future research since increased belief bias across psychological disorders would have major implications for understanding the development and maintenance of disorders, despite the presence of evidence disconfirming dysfunctional beliefs.

Do reasoning biases play a causal role?

Prospective studies

Several prospective studies have shown that expectancies, illusory correlations, interpretations of ambiguous stimuli, and attributions can predict subsequent symptoms. In an analogue sample, Constans (2001) found that negative expectancies mediate future anxiety, even after controlling for current state and trait anxiety. Positive expectancy judgements about drug or alcohol use, including predictions that substance use will facilitate arousal, relaxation, or social facilitation, predict future drinking (Stacy et al. 1991; Goldman 1999). de Jong et al. (1995a) found that among women successfully treated for spider phobia, greater covariation bias following treatment predicted more relapse over the next two years. Further, the generation of alcohol and drug-related words to ambiguous stimuli and the generation of alcohol and drug-related responses to positive cues predicted drug and alcohol use 1 month later, even after controlling for previous use of drugs (Stacy 1995, 1997; Ames and Stacy 1998). However, because this task combines both the interpretation of ambiguous cues and the association of substance abuse with positive outcomes, it is not clear to what extent each of these factors independently contributes to predicting subsequent substance use.

Numerous studies have shown that a pessimistic attributional style predicts risk for future onset of major depression (e.g. see review by Alloy et al. 1999). For example, Joseph et al. (1991) found that more internal and controllable attributions during an account of a traumatic experience (the sinking of the Herald of Free Enterprise) related to intrusive thoughts, depression, and anxiety at 8 months and 19 months after the disaster. Finally, Joseph et al. (1993) subsequently found that more internal attributions for disaster-related events during the sinking of the Jupiter cruise ship were associated with greater depression and intrusive thoughts 1 year after the disaster.

Experimental studies

Prospective studies are not sufficient to confirm a causal effect of reasoning biases on the development or maintenance of disorders because the predictive association between reasoning and symptoms could be mediated by some common third-factor. To demonstrate causality, it is necessary to demonstrate that manipulating reasoning directly influences symptoms. Hence, in this section we will review evidence from experimental studies that addresses the causal role of reasoning processes, but the majority of these studies have used analogue samples.

A number of important studies have demonstrated that manipulating interpretative bias and attributional style can modify emotional experience in non-patient controls (Grey and Mathews 2000; Mathews and Mackintosh 2000; Neumann 2000; Mathews and MacLeod 2002), indicating a possible causal role for interpretations and attributions in maintaining mood state. For example, Mathews and Mackintosh (2000) asked non-anxious community volunteers to imagine themselves in approximately 100 social scenarios, each of which ended with a sentence containing a word fragment that the participant was asked to complete. The word fragment was designed so that there was only one possible solution that resolved the ambiguous nature of the preceding scenario in either a positive or negative direction. One group were trained on sentences that always ended with positive outcomes, whilst another group were trained on sentences that always ended with negative outcomes. For example, to the sentence 'Getting ready to go, you think that the new people you will meet will find you *bor-ng/fri-ndly*'. The negative training group gave higher recognition ratings to threatening interpretations of novel ambiguous descriptions and reported increased anxiety compared to the positive training group. When the outcome was directly stated, rather than constructed by completing the word fragment, there was no change in mood ratings, suggesting that active generation of meanings is necessary for the effects of interpretation bias on mood. In another study, Neumann (2000) found that prior repeated use of internal attributions enhanced the tendency to experience guilt, whereas the repeated use of external attributions enhanced the tendency to experience anger, when participants were exposed to a negative social event (e.g. being reprimanded for interrupting an experiment).

In an analogue sample of sexually functional men, Weisberg *et al.* (2001) gave bogus feedback of poor erectile response during the viewing of sexually explicit films and provided either an internal stable cause (negative thinking about sex) or an external, transient cause (films not very arousing) for the poor response. When watching a third film, participants in the external, transient attribution condition had greater objective erectile response and self-reported arousal than participants in the internal, stable attribution condition, consistent with the suggestion that attributions may play a causal role in the development of symptoms.

These studies demonstrate that it is possible to induce reasoning biases similar to those found in patients with psychological disorders in non-patient groups. Further, inducing these reasoning biases produces symptoms. Thus, these studies suggest that reasoning biases can play a causal role on symptoms, although we recognize that this conclusion is based on analogue samples and that the generalizability of the conclusion to patient samples is yet to be determined.

In one of the few studies conducted with a patient group, Craske *et al.* (2002) demonstrated that manipulating pre-sleep attributions about physiological events during sleep contributed to the likelihood of experiencing a nocturnal panic attack in patients who regularly experienced nocturnal panic attacks. In this study, the attribution was manipulated by telling some participants that physiological changes during sleep are normal and expected and by telling other patients that physiological changes were abnormal and unexpected. Information about physiological change was induced by false audio feedback. These findings add to the evidence that interpretative bias and attributional bias can causally influence emotional state.

To date, the possible causal role of illusory correlations, confirmation bias and hypothesis testing in maintaining psychological disorders has not been experimentally tested. Experimental studies have induced illusory correlations to neutral slides by pairing the slides with electric shocks with 70% contingency, but have not examined whether inducing this correlation maintains anxiety (de Jong *et al.* 1990).

Theoretical issues

If the operation of a number of reasoning processes is common across both non-patient controls and a range of psychological disorders, why do different disorders show disorder-specific consequences of reasoning biases? For example, patients tend to overestimate the likelihood of the negative or positive events most relevant to the disorder (e.g. social threat in social anxiety, positive outcomes in addiction) but not to other negative, positive, or neutral events. We hypothesize that one reason different disorders differ from each other, and from non-patient controls is the current concerns inherent to the disorder. Patients' concerns determine what they see as important and this will influence what information is most salient and accessible, and what simulations and mental searches they perform, which in turn, will influence expectancies, covariation bias, confirmation bias, and interpretations.

As well as current concerns acting to influence the input to and the subsequent output from reasoning processes, an important factor influencing reasoning biases in patients with psychological disorders is mood state. Mood can bias expectancy judgements, at least in part, through increasing the availability of memories that are mood-congruent (Constans and Mathews 1993; see Chapter 3 for a further discussion of mood-congruent memory biases). Inducing a negative mood state by failure (as described in Box 3.2) increases internal attributions for negative events for both controls (Forgas *et al.* 1990) and for paranoid and depressed patients (Bentall *et al.* 2001), although patients became more pessimistic than the controls.

What is the origin of the differences in interpretations and hypothesis testing? One possible mechanism is that the expectancy and heuristic processes determine the biases in interpretations and hypothesis testing. Studies examining the effects of stereotypes suggest that pre-existing expectancies influence the interpretation of ambiguous situations and the search for information in a manner consistent with the expectancy (Bodenhausen 1988; Johnson 1996). Therefore, expectancies can act to influence hypothesis testing and interpretations, with people tending to confirm hypotheses or make interpretations that match their expectations. For example, Cooper (1997) argued that the availability and representativeness heuristics, interacting with beliefs about weight and shape, could explain why eating disorder patients make weight and shape interpretations for ambiguous scenarios. Indeed, this account is consistent with the observation that negative interpretations of ambiguous stimuli tend to be strongest for the stimuli relevant to the particular concerns of each disorder.

Clinical implications

What are the clinical and therapeutic implications of these reasoning biases across disorders? Research investigating reasoning biases may give us an insight into the possible routes by which psychological disorders might develop or be maintained and provide clues as to useful additional domains for clinical assessment. To give an example based on the clinical case presented at the beginning of this chapter, understanding the availability heuristic can help us to see how Jane's negative expectations about social interactions might be maintained, and how past history can influence her negative thinking. Jane has memories of bullying and social humiliation, as well as an extremely distorted self-image. These memories and her self-image are very vivid and salient to her and are highly accessible. Accordingly, by the action of the availability heuristic, they are likely to bias her expectancies about future social events in a negative direction (e.g. her judgement that social humiliation is extremely likely). This biased expectancy will influence Jane's behaviour and her mood, and is likely to influence her perception of covariation and lead to a further confirmation bias. Thus, clinically, the research on heuristic biases suggests that whenever patients report dysfunctional and unrealistic expectancies, an exploration of memories and images may prove informative.

It has been suggested that emotional reasoning, covariation, and confirmation biases are clinically important (e.g. de Jong *et al.* 1998), because they can help to explain why unhelpful beliefs persist in the face of evidence that is inconsistent with the belief. These reasoning biases might stop patients with hypochrondriasis from determining that beliefs such as 'If you have a headache, then you have a brain tumour' are untrue. Given the absence of experimental manipulations demonstrating that these biases play a causal role in disorders, this hypothesis remains untested.

What are the implications for treatment? Earlier, we suggested that the reasoning biases observed are the product of an interaction between the operation of normal reasoning processes and the particular beliefs and concerns of each disorder (with the exception of data gathering in schizophrenia). We therefore have at least three separate points of intervention: to directly attempt to reduce the biases in reasoning processes, to target the beliefs and assumptions held by patients, and to target the current concerns and goals of patients. In the section that follows we will include suggestions for each of these three separate points of intervention.

Cognitive therapy and reasoning biases

Clearly, many of the core components of cognitive therapy are consistent with targeting reasoning biases and beliefs. Providing training in critical reasoning by teaching Socratic questioning to help patients explore and identify evidence and alternative viewpoints and to challenge negative thoughts and images is one way to directly challenge reasoning biases. The use of negative automatic thought forms is likely to help in this process. The aim would be to encourage patients to focus on other reasons for why something happened and thus shift their attribution (e.g. the question 'What might be an alternative explanation for this event?' is likely to be helpful).

Alternatively, challenging can encourage people to focus on facts rather than feelings to reduce emotional reasoning. For example, the questions 'Are you basing this judgement on how you feel or on the facts?' and 'What is the evidence out in the world that this thought is true?' may well help reduce emotional reasoning. This approach is consistent with the research by Gasper and Clore (1998) suggesting that explicitly encouraging people to use factual information as the basis for judgements, rather than feelings, coupled with increasing awareness of the specific cause of the feeling should remove the emotional reasoning effect. To reduce emotional reasoning, Jane would be encouraged to move away from making judgements based on internal sensations and instead, use what she observes of other's responses to judge her social performance (for further details on shifts in attention, see Chapter 2). The therapist would discuss with Jane the possibility that 'feelings are not facts' and encourage her to examine the world around her in order to obtain more objective information about people's responses to her. It would be helpful to review previous specific social experiences, such as standing on a crowded bus. With Socratic questioning it will be possible to help Jane discover that when standing on the crowded bus she used her internal feelings to judge how she appeared to other people and did not actually look at other people (Clark and Wells 1995, 1997). In line with the strategies discussed in Chapter 2, a behavioural experiment could then examine the role of internal focus in maintaining anxiety by asking Jane to compare how anxious she felt when she focused her attention on her physical sensations (e.g. shakiness) compared to when she focused her attention externally (on what the therapist was saying).

Imagery-based techniques, such as described in Chapter 3, could be very helpful for shifting the images and memories that are most accessible. For example, generating images of different, previously unexpected outcomes, may help change expectancy biases in a positive direction by influencing the availability and simulation heuristics. Indeed, as we described in Chapter 3, there is evidence that changing the end of nightmares and rehearsing the changed version is effective in reducing nightmare frequency (Krakow *et al.* 2001). For a patient with depression who tends to think the likelihood of a positive outcome is low (e.g. successfully applying for a job), imagining in detail the successful outcome and all the relevant steps (e.g. writing out the application, going to interview) may improve the expectation of success (Taylor *et al.* 1998). Similarly, encouraging Jane to remember, and to imagine, more positive social events should help to reduce her estimates that future social events will go wrong. Changing these images should reduce the availability of negative images and memories, whilst increasing the accessibility of positive images, shifting Jane to more positive expectancies about future social events.

Other important components of cognitive therapy, such as using behavioural experiments, are likely to help demonstrate the impact of reasoning biases. By encouraging patients to make specific predictions and then to test them out directly, behavioural experiments should help reduce negative interpretations of ambiguous situations (e.g. asking someone else what they think rather than 'mind-reading'), help challenge unrealistic expectancies, and help reduce illusory correlations. The use of video feedback is a good example of an effective behavioural experiment that could impact reasoning biases (Harvey *et al.* 2000). An important part of this experiment is cognitive preparation, where the patient predicts in detail what they expect themselves to look like in the video and then watches the video as though watching a stranger. Thus, the therapist would ask Jane to rate how anxious and odd she thinks she would look out of 100, and to rate any physical signs of her anxiety (e.g. shaking) and quantify them precisely (e.g. finding a matching colour for how red she thinks her face will be). The therapist will then encourage Jane to watch a video of herself 'as if you are watching someone you had never seen before on the TV'. Such an experiment should help Jane to discover that she looks much less anxious than she feels, thereby reducing emotional reasoning and misinterpretations at that moment in time. Replacing the initial extreme image with the more realistic image seen on the video would be a powerful way for Jane to modify her extreme self-image, which should further alter her expectancies about future social interactions.

Given the effectiveness of direct feedback with the video in social phobia, it is plausible that this approach could be extended and adapted to other disorders. Consistent with this view, both video feedback and prolonged body image exposure by mirrors have been found to be beneficial in anorexia nervosa (Rushford and Ostermeyer 1997) and binge eating disorder (Hilbert *et al.* 2002). We would also expect these interventions to be useful in body dysmorphia, where there are parallel concerns with appearance and self-image. It is possible that the use of objective feedback may be usefully extended to other disorders (e.g. for sexual dysfunction, more accurate reports of physiological arousal).

What does the research on reasoning processes suggest about new or improved approaches to reduce reasoning biases in patients with psychological disorders? First, the research suggests a number of possible ways to make Socratic questioning more effective to reduce reasoning biases. The research suggests that it would be useful to focus more explicitly on the internal-external dimension of attributions. For example, it would be useful to explicitly shift patients with social phobia away from an internal attribution for negative interpersonal events or to shift patients with delusional disorder away from an external personal attribution for interpersonal events (see the case study reported by Kinderman and Bentall 1997a).

Debiasing approaches

Beyond the challenging of specific negative automatic thoughts in cognitive therapy, it may be useful to consider debiasing approaches (Turk and Salovey 1985; Hayes and Hesketh 1989), specifically designed to reduce the heuristic biases by improving people's use of statistics and probability, and by deliberately encouraging people to consider why they might be wrong (Korait *et al.* 1980). Students can become better at reasoning for ill-defined problems and everyday statistical problems by teaching them to take more account of base rates (how frequently an event normally occurs) and sample size (Fong *et al.* 1986; Kosonen and Winne 1995). Reasoning performance can also be improved by teaching critical thinking (Nisbett 1993; Halpern 1998). Critical thinking involves teaching skills relating to judgements of likelihood and uncertainty, training in the structural aspects of problems and arguments, and a metacognitive component that involves evaluating the thinking process and progress towards the goal. For example, an important skill is learning the law of large numbers, that more accurate judgements can be made from larger samples and the smaller the sample, the greater variation any measure of any variable within the sample will show. Training in these approaches could be helpful for patients, perhaps by reviewing examples that are independent of the patient's concerns to illustrate the basic biases, and then teaching principles and rules to avoid these problems. For example, alongside standard Socratic questions, the therapist might teach patients to ask questions such as: How many examples are there of this event? How often does this event happen? Is this too small a sample to be able to make a reasonable judgement? Do I need to keep gathering more information? What additional information should I require to determine whether an assertion is correct? and Which information is most important in making the decision and why?

In a similar way, use of contingency tables and teaching people to attend to all possible outcomes when considering expectancies and covariation is likely to be helpful. Figure 4.1 demonstrates the use of a contingency table with regard to one of Jane's negative expectancies. To date, such explicit 'debiasing' approaches do not seem to have been systematically applied to helping patients with psychological disorders, other than treatment for patients with gambling problems where patients are educated at length about randomness and chance, in order that they learn that each gambling event is independent of the previous gambling event (Ladouceur and Walker 1996). Ladouceur and colleagues have argued that the core cognitive error in the development and maintenance of gambling is an erroneous perception of randomness. Treatments designed to specifically correct this cognitive bias have been successful in reducing problematic gambling, both in single case studies (Ladouceur *et al.* 1998) and in a randomized controlled trial (Ladouceur *et al.* 2001). The success of this approach for pathological gambling raises the possibility that specific training to reduce reasoning biases (e.g. biased

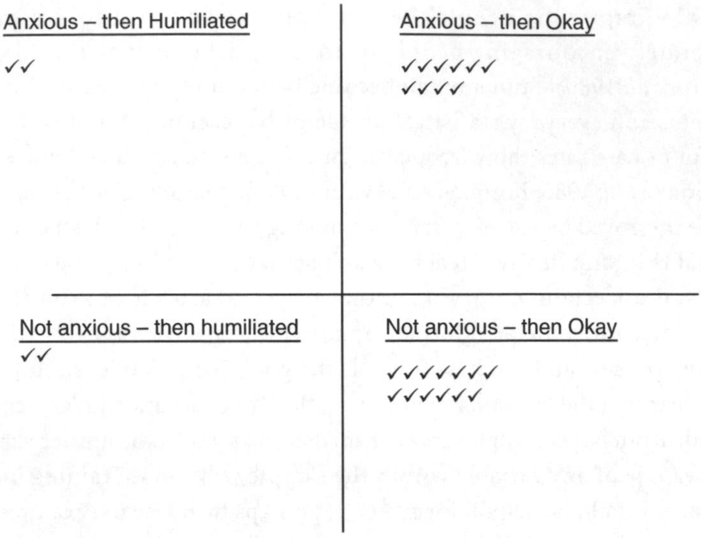

Anxious – then Humiliated	Anxious – then Okay
✓✓	✓✓✓✓✓✓ ✓✓✓✓

Not anxious – then humiliated	Not anxious – then Okay
✓✓	✓✓✓✓✓✓ ✓✓✓✓✓✓

Fig. 4.1 An example of a contingency diagram for refining expectancy judgements. Jane interprets increases in her anxiety, in particular shaking and blushing, as evidence that she will be humiliated in public. This emotional reasoning can be expressed as a expectation like 'If I feel anxious, then something humiliating will happen'. Such an expectation can be tested, and the tendency towards emotional reasoning reduced, by examining all possible contingencies relevant to the expectation over a period of time. This is done by recording the number of occasions when the expectation was confirmed (i.e. when anxiety was followed by humiliation and when not being anxious was followed by no humiliation) as well as recording the number of occasions when the expectation was not confirmed (i.e. when anxiety was not followed by humiliation and when humiliation occurred even when there was no prior anxiety). These possibilities can be usefully illustrated in a cross-shaped diagram. Over several weeks, Jane recorded how often social events fell into the different possible outcomes. The figure illustrates a completed diagram, which helped Jane to conclude that emotional reasoning leads to inaccuracy.

expectancies or emotional reasoning) might be a potent intervention for other disorders.

A continuum aims to help patients reduce 'all' and 'nothing' thinking and help them identify the 'in-between' or grey areas (Greenberger and Padesky 1995). By addressing all or nothing thinking it is possible that this will influence interpretation biases. For example, patients with bulimia nervosa will often interpret breaking a dietary rule as indicating that their eating is completely out of control (Fairburn 1997). The continuum might have at its extremes: (i) eating is completely under control at all times, in every situation and (ii) eating is completely out of control at all times, in every situation. Helping patients identify the 'in-between' (e.g. having one extra biscuit) can assist in changing the interpretation (e.g. 'I've blown it now, my eating is totally excessive').

Pie charts can be a particularly useful intervention for changing interpretations about personal responsibility (Greenberger and Padesky 1995). Pie charts involve drawing out and representing, in a diagram, the relative contribution of the factors that can influence a particular outcome or state. See Fig. 4.2 for a pie chart developed with Jane.

'Chaining' or working through probability estimates can be a helpful strategy for people who have inflated estimates of the probability of harm. Chaining involves breaking down the sequence of events necessary for the feared event to happen, and then calculating the mathematical probability of such a sequence occurring.

Another potential approach to debiasing is to consider direct training out of reasoning biases. Mathews and Mackintosh (2000) have shown that repeated priming of one style of responding (negative vs positive) causes non-patient participants to adapt their style on subsequent test scenarios, with implications for mood state. For training of this type to be useful as a therapeutic intervention we would need to demonstrate that it is robust enough to (a) persevere for weeks and (b) change biases in patients.

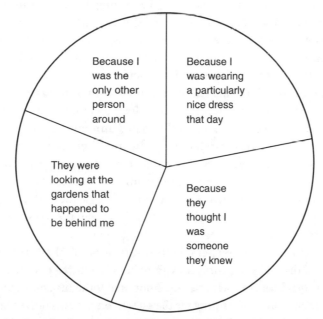

Fig. 4.2 An example of a pie chart to illustrate alternative explanations for the belief that 'people are looking at me because I look odd and crazy'.

Targeting goals and concerns

Since the reasoning biases seem to be most active with respect to the current concerns of patients, it might be worth to considering whether direct intervention at the level of patient's concerns and goals might be useful. Shifting a patient's primary concerns to more functional domains may be advantageous. A treatment approach shown to be helpful when treating drug and alcohol use is motivational counselling (Cox *et al.* 1997; Cox and Klinger 2002, 2003). The aim of this approach is to systematically explore goals. It seems likely that this approach will be relevant to a broad range of disorders. When working within a motivational counselling framework, there are a number of ways that people can structure their goals so as to reduce their motivation to change. For example, people can have goals from which they do not expect to derive much emotional satisfaction, or have unrealistic goals, or be pessimistic about achieving their goals, or have goals that are in conflict. Motivational counselling works to identify and alter these maladaptive structures through discussion and planning. It is, therefore, complementary to cognitive therapy.

Future research

As evident in Table 4.1, many gaps in our knowledge base on reasoning processes exist. The majority of studies on reasoning biases have investigated patients with anxiety disorders and depression, leaving the other disorders under-researched. Furthermore, certain paradigms, such as covariation bias and threat confirmation, have only been examined in a limited range of disorders.

The relative shift in reasoning biases between neutral and emotional material, across both patients and non-patient groups, needs to be further evaluated. It is important to recognize that the full nature of hypothesis testing across psychological disorders still remains unresolved, since confirmation biases for non-threat-related conditional beliefs and belief bias (e.g. syllogistic reasoning) for emotional material or disorder-relevant dysfunctional assumptions have not been examined. Dudley *et al.*'s (1997*a,b*, 1998) findings suggest that hypothesis testing is worse for both non-patient controls and patients with psychological disorders when the tasks incorporate emotional material.

From a cognitive therapy perspective, it is possible that proneness to psychological disorders is associated with reduced ability to 'decentre' or step back and suspend belief in self-relevant emotional thoughts and assumptions (for more discussion of decentring see the section on metacognitive regulation in Chapter 5). Reduced ability to decentre may reflect an increased confirmation bias for neutral and/or emotional beliefs. The finding of increased belief bias in women with spider phobia would be consistent with this suggestion (de Jong *et al.* 1997*b*). Determining whether this elevated belief bias can be replicated in specific phobias and whether this elevated belief bias exists in other psychological disorders is an important area for future research. Furthermore, it would be useful to examine the basic ability to shift beliefs in the light of disconfirming evidence for neutral material across both patients and controls. The interesting question is whether psychological disorders are related to a generally reduced ability to update beliefs in the light of disconfirming evidence.

Likewise, it would be useful to see how well patient groups can reach logical conclusions on syllogistic reasoning tasks for material that is both consistent and inconsistent with neutral and emotional beliefs. For example, it is possible that patients with depression would find it harder to reach accurate conclusions when the task parameters led to a conclusion inconsistent with an emotional belief like 'If I make a mistake, then I am a failure', relative to controls. It would be important to include non-patient controls in these studies to establish baseline levels of response.

There are a number of limitations to many of the existing studies of reasoning biases, which future studies will need to rectify. First, many of the studies only used non-patient controls. In the absence of one or more groups comprised of patients diagnosed with another disorder, it is difficult to judge the specificity of the reasoning bias. Second, some studies have used analogue populations (e.g. heavy drinkers in student populations as an analogue of people with diagnoses of alcohol abuse/alcohol dependence) raising questions about the generalizability of the findings. Third, studies of delusional beliefs often involved a heterogeneous range of participants who held a range of different delusions. It is possible that different results would be obtained for more homogenous groups. Fourth, at present most studies of interpretations of ambiguity and of expectancy among patients with psychological disorders have used self-report measures. Accordingly, it is not possible to rule out the the possibility that the results can be accounted for by demand or response biases. Fifth, studies of attributional style should control for level of depression and develop scenarios relevant to the specific concerns of each disorder. Finally, more studies need to examine illusory correlation by examining judgements of contingency for the pairings of disorder-relevant stimuli (e.g. a slide of a feared object) and an objective negative event (e.g. an electric shock). This paradigm is more ecologically valid and provides a more meaningful analogue of everyday responses relative to self-report measures.

The possible causal role of the various reasoning biases needs to be investigated in more detail. The paradigms manipulating attributions and interpretations of ambiguous stimuli would profitably be extended into patient samples. For example, testing the role of internal and external attributions in the context of depression. Developing the training task approach used by Mathews and Mackintosh (2000) for other biases is an important area for future research. There is also the outstanding question of whether such a training effect might have therapeutic implications. Would repeated training have sufficient impact to reduce trait anxiety or GAD? The clinical-experimental approach adopted by Harvey *et al.* (2000) could be used to ascertain whether video feedback does indeed alter reasoning biases, as we might expect.

The more refined methodologies, developed principally in the context of the anxiety disorders to reduce demand and response biases, such as the illusory correlation test (de Jong *et al.* 1992) and text comprehension for ambiguity (MacLeod and Cohen 1993) could be tested on other patient samples.

The experimental studies examining interpretations of ambiguous stimuli have tended to not include contextual information other than the context specified as an integral part of the task (e.g. the vignette provides the local context for the ambiguous sentence). In real life, ambiguous information is presented within a wider context, including the details of the situation itself, such that context may influence interpretations to a greater degree in real life. In an analogue sample, Blanchette and Richards (2003) have found that adding context in the form of presenting a word on a screen during the homophone spelling task can influence the interpretation of ambiguity. The word presented on the screen can either be an emotional or a neutral associate of the ambiguous homophone. Blanchette and Richards found a context-sensitive effect, such that visually presenting an emotional associate (e.g. 'swelling') produced more emotional spellings of the homophones (e.g. 'bruise'), whereas neutral associates (e.g. 'drink') produced more neutral spellings (e.g. 'brews') of the homophone. This context-sensitive effect was strongest in participants who had been induced into a mildly anxious mood. This preliminary research suggests the value of investigating the effect of context on reasoning biases across the psychological disorders.

Studies of emotional reasoning have focused on the anxiety disorders. It is possible that other emotions and physiological responses could play a role. Given the phenomenon of 'depression about depression' (Teasdale 1985, 1988), 'just right' experiences in OCD and the possibility that positive feelings could act as information, it would be fruitful to extend the paradigm employed by Arntz *et al.* (1995) to other psychological disorders and to examine emotional reasoning to feelings other than anxiety. Similarly, illusory correlations have been extensively studied in specific phobia and panic disorder but not in other psychological disorders. The review of the literature presented in this chapter suggests that studies investigating covariation will need to use conditioned stimuli that are emotionally relevant and an outcome that is emotionally relevant to each disorder.

The hypothesis put forward in this chapter raises the possibility that the threat-confirmation bias operates in much the same way in non-patient samples as for samples with a psychological disorder, except that the particular concerns will vary for each disorder and for the non-patient controls. Such an account predicts that anxiety and somatoform disorders would show specific threat-confirmation strategies. Thus, OCD patients might show threat-confirmation for contaminated stimuli and chronic pain patients might show threat-confirmation for items related to physical damage. For example, we might expect patients with chronic pain to show a threat confirmation bias on a Wason selection task for a conditional rule such as 'If I feel pain, then I am doing damage to myself'. It remains to be seen whether other emotional confirmation biases exist in disorders that are not centred on threat. For example, the content of beliefs in depression focus more on loss than threat. Would depressed patients show a loss-confirmation rather than success-confirmation strategy?

Finally, further research is required to investigate the way in which current concerns and goals influence reasoning biases. Understanding how concerns end up leading to further reasoning biases in particular domains will be of value across all disorders. Future research will also usefully further unpack the relationship between these different biases. For example, to what degree are biases in heuristics and expectancies able to subsequently influence the other reasoning biases? Would effectively reducing the availability and representativeness heuristics produce changes on all the other biases? Such questions are open to empirical investigation.

Key points

1. Based on the evidence reviewed in this chapter, the following reasoning processes are definite transdiagnostic processes: interpretation reasoning, expectancy reasoning, and emotional reasoning.

2. Attributional reasoning, availability heuristic, covariation bias, and confirmation bias for threat rules meet the criteria for a possible transdiagnostic process.

3. Data gathering for hypothesis testing seems to be a distinct process, with patients with psychotic disorders differing from both non-patient controls and other psychological disorders, by tending to gather less data before reaching a conclusion.

4. There is currently inconclusive evidence for the belief bias, other than for conditional rules, since hypothesis testing for emotionally relevant and disorder-congruent beliefs has not been examined, except in a few threat-confirmation studies.

5. For all of the reasoning biases, the specific information that is biased tends to reflect the personal concerns of the patients.

6. Biases in reasoning processes are common and universal (i.e. present across patient and non-patient samples). For the majority of reasoning processes, their operation seems to be similar in both non-patient controls and patients. In other words, reasoning processes appear to operate on a continuum from non-patients to patients.

7. A range of strategies is available to tackle these reasoning processes including: generating alternative reasons, exploring accessible memories and images, using imagery to create more positive images, debiasing training, teaching patients that feelings are not facts, behavioural experiments, keeping accurate contingency tables, video feedback, exploring goal structure, interpretative training.

8. Future research should aim to (a) investigate the full range of reasoning processes across the full range of psychological disorders, (b) explore the shift in reasoning biases between neutral and emotional material, and (c) investigate the ability to shift beliefs in the light of disconfirming evidence.

Chapter 5

Thought

Peter is a 40-year-old man, who previously worked in finance. He has been unemployed for 5 years, reporting constant intense anxiety, worry, and a lack of energy and pleasure. His worries include not being able to do things well enough, upsetting other people, making the wrong decisions, and never getting better. Whenever he tries to engage himself in a task, he finds it a struggle to fully concentrate; he describes his mind 'wanting' to keep thinking about possible things that could go wrong. Peter describes a history of worrying back to his early childhood, which was exacerbated by his brother suffering a severe life-threatening illness when Peter was 12. At this point, Peter recalls believing that if he did not worry about his brother it would show that he did not love his brother enough and it would reduce his brother's chances of recovery. Furthermore, Peter remembers his father being calm and matter-of-fact about his brother's illness. Peter thought that this stoic demeanour was how he should be, and so, he began to worry about his emotions and his worrisome thoughts about his brother. Furthermore, he began to try and suppress any negative thoughts and feelings and to present an outward appearance to the world of a calm and capable person. Peter stopped working 5 years ago when his anxiety escalated as he became pre-occupied over trying to make the right decision about whether to continue an intimate relationship.

Peter suffers from generalized anxiety disorder (GAD) and depression. This case provides a demonstration of the impact of thought processes on psychological distress. Peter suffers from upsetting discrete unwanted negative thoughts or *intrusions*. In response to these intrusions, Peter both dwells on their content in *recurrent negative thinking* (worry) and attempts to *suppress* negative thoughts and feelings. Furthermore, he holds both positive beliefs (e.g. the superstitious belief that worry would help his brother recover) and negative beliefs (e.g. 'it is abnormal to worry') about his thoughts. His responses to and his beliefs about his thoughts involve *metacognitive* processes. Metacognitive processes and beliefs are those concerned with the appraisal, monitoring or control of thinking itself (Flavell 1979; Nelson and Narens 1990). This chapter will examine recurrent thinking, thought suppression, and metacognition across disorders. In particular, we will seek to determine the extent to which these thought processes are relevant across the psychological disorders. Whereas Chapter 2 investigated the extent to which internal stimuli, including thoughts, capture attention at the expense of other stimuli, this chapter will explore the nature of thoughts and the chain of thinking that follows them. We will start by briefly defining and giving some background on intrusions.

Intrusions

Intrusions are spontaneous, unwanted, unbidden, uncontrollable and discrete thoughts, images, or urges that are attributed to internal origins (Rachman 1981; Wells and Morrison 1994). A negative self-critical thought like 'I am useless', an image of collapsing in the street or an urge to wash hands over again are all examples of intrusions. Many intrusive thoughts involve memories (for further details see Chapter 3).

Normal and abnormal intrusions

Intrusions are normal and universal, with unwanted intrusions being found frequently in 90% of normal non-patient populations (Rachman and de Silva 1978; Salkovskis and Harrison 1984; Clark and de Silva 1985; Freeston *et al.* 1992; Purdon and Clark 1993; Wells and Morrison 1994). What distinguishes normal and abnormal intrusions? While the content may not differ, clinical intrusions tend to be experienced as more intense, more uncomfortable, and less controllable (Rachman and de Silva 1978; Clark and de Silva 1985). The normality and universality of intrusions begs us to ask what causes intrusions to be more distressing and more frequent in psychological disorders? The cognitive view is that patients differ in their appraisals and responses to intrusions compared to controls (e.g. Salkovskis 1985; Freeston and Ladouceur 1993; Wells 1995; Wells 2000). Thus, patients tend to view intrusive thoughts as more meaningful and important, are less likely to see them as trivial and more likely to act in response to them, rather than ignore them. Two particular responses to intrusions that have been recognized as unhelpful are *recurrently dwelling* on them, as in worry or rumination, or trying to remove them, as in *thought suppression*. In this chapter we will go on to consider each of these processes, as well as the metacognitive beliefs that influence the selection of these strategies.

Forms of intrusions

Intrusions can occur in the form of a verbal thought, image, or an urge.

Images

Images are defined as contents of consciousness that possess sensory qualities, as opposed to those that are purely verbal or abstract (Paivio 1979; Kosslyn 1980, 1981; Hackmann 1997). Images usually provide a perceptual-like analogue of some or all of the sensory aspects of a real-world scene. Typically images are visual, although other sensory modalities can be represented. Images can be dynamic, allowing them to indicate a sequence or narrative of events. Images are particularly potent at evoking emotional and physiological responses (Strack *et al.* 1985; Taylor and Schneider 1989; Borkovec *et al.* 1998) and at influencing the development of coping plans and the implementation of behaviour (Taylor *et al.* 1998). Importantly, verbal thoughts and images each influence and lead onto the other (Paivio and Marschark 1991), such that a sample of thought at any one moment is rarely exclusively one form or the other.

Urges

An urge is the internal experience of a desire to perform a particular act (e.g. to eat, to drink alcohol, to neutralize an obsession). Urges can be induced by exposure to the object of the desire (e.g. drug or alcohol; Childress *et al.* 1987, 1988; Ehrman *et al.* 1991; Modell and Mountz 1995) or to contextual cues associated with the behaviour (e.g. locations and people associated with drinking; Monti *et al.* 1993). Urges can also be elicited by emotional triggers (feeling bored, depressed, or anxious; Rubonis *et al.* 1994). Urges can also be induced by imagining performing an action or imagining a desired outcome (Taylor *et al.* 2000), suggesting that images and urges interact.

Current concerns

The majority of psychological disorders are characterized by disorder-specific intrusive thoughts. Anxiety disorders are characterized by intrusive catastrophic thoughts and images. For example, patients with GAD have catastrophic concerns about what might go wrong in the future (Vasey and Borkovec 1992; Davey and Levy 1998) and patients with panic disorder have catastrophic intrusions about bodily sensations (Clark 1993). Likewise, PTSD is characterized by intrusive thoughts (De Silva and Marks 1999*b*), images (Ehlers and Steil 1995) and urges/impulses (Falsetti *et al.* 2002), typically involving the recall of the traumatic incident (Reynolds and Brewin 1999). In OCD, patients suffer from obsessive intrusions that are unacceptable and repugnant, such as concerns about being contaminated with germs, images of sexual or blasphemous acts, and urges to act inappropriately (Wang and Clark 2002).

Catastrophic intrusive thoughts have also been observed in patients with hypochrondriasis (Wells and Hackmann 1993) and patients with chronic pain (Severeijns *et al.* 2001). Substance-related disorders and eating disorders are associated with increased urges to consume drugs, alcohol, or food on exposure to relevant cues (Staiger *et al.* 2000). These self-rated urges predict substance use (Childress *et al.* 1988; Monti *et al.* 1993; Cooney *et al.* 1997) and binge eating (Steiger *et al.* 1999). Hall *et al.* (1996, 2000) reported that more intrusive thoughts are associated with taking longer to fall asleep and with poorer subjective sleep quality in patients with insomnia. Patients with major depression have pessimistic intrusions about themselves, the world and the future (Wenzlaff 1993; Clark *et al.* 1999). Morrison and Baker (2000) found that patients with schizophrenia who experience auditory hallucinations have more frequent intrusive thoughts than non-hallucinating patients with schizophrenia and normal controls.

The above evidence is consistent with intrusive thoughts being triggered by conditioned associations at either a sensory or a meaning level (Brewin 1989; Klinger 1996). That is, across all disorders and for all types of intrusions, it appears that stimulus or response cues associated with the content of the intrusion can trigger the intrusion. For example, physical reminders of a trauma lead to intrusions about the trauma (de Silva and Marks 1999*a*). The occurrence of intrusive thoughts is also consistent with the current concern model, as described in Chapter 1. Thus, in combination with conditioned associations, intrusions appear to be triggered by and reflect the current concerns of each patient group. The current concern account can explain how intrusions can spontaneously occur, whilst also explaining the specific differences in intrusion content across the disorders.

Recurrent negative thinking: worry and rumination

One response to an intrusive thought is to further dwell on the subject matter of the intrusion, trying to work through it or resolve it. This is particularly likely if the intrusion is considered to be personally important. This recurrent thinking, in response to a negative intrusion, could result in worry or rumination. Worry is defined as 'a chain of thoughts and images, negatively affect-laden and relatively uncontrollable' (Borkovec *et al.* 1983). Rumination is dysfunctional, redundant, repetitive, and stereotypical thinking (Klinger 1996). More specifically, Nolen-Hoeksema (1991) defined rumination as thoughts and behaviours that repetitively focus an individual's attention on his or her negative feelings, and the nature and implications of these feelings (including the causes, meanings, and consequences of the feelings). Box 5.1 describes some common worrying and ruminative thoughts.

Whilst worry and rumination often involve self-focused attention, they are different from self-focused attention in that they involve a chain of thoughts repeating and elaborating on a particular theme. Self-focused attention, as discussed in Chapter 2, is broader than recurrent thinking, since it can include awareness of physical state, feelings, thoughts, emotions, and memories. Another difference is that self-focused attention does not necessarily involve repetitive or perseverative thinking.

Box 5.1 Examples of worry and rumination

Worry

Worry often consists of negative thinking about the future in the form of 'What if' type questions. For example, 'What if my child is in a car crash? What if I don't get the job? What if I am late?'. Worry for both patient and non-patient groups is often concerned with the same themes: relationships, lack of confidence, aimless future, work incompetence, financial problems, and socio-political concerns (Tallis *et al.* 1992). Worries can be both about normal everyday concerns, such as completing a chore and about more unlikely but more catastrophic concerns such as 'What if I am assaulted?'. Common worries include concerns about how one will come across to other people, how well one can cope with a difficult situation, making the right decision and worry about worry itself (Wells 2000).

Rumination

Rumination often takes the form of analyzing the causes and consequences of negative events, problems, and moods. For example, 'Why did this happen to me? Why me? Why can't I get better?' (Watkins and Baracaia 2001). Rumination can involve thinking over and over past events, dwelling on what went wrong. Patients often experience an ongoing spiral of thoughts, such that dwelling on one negative event will then lead onto another negative event in a prolonged chain of negative thinking.

We will now move on to explore the extent to which recurrent negative thinking is a transdiagnostic process.

Anxiety disorders

Social phobia

The Thought Control Questionnaire has been employed as a measure of recurrent thinking. It asks each respondent to endorse which strategies he or she generally uses 'When I experience an unpleasant/unwanted thought' (Wells and Davies 1994). Items on the worry scale include 'I think about past worries instead', 'I dwell on other worries' and 'I focus on different negative thoughts'. It is important to note that the worry scale on the Thought Control Questionnaire could apply to both depressive rumination and anxious worry. The other scales on the Thought Control Questionnaire measure the strategies of distraction (e.g. 'I occupy myself with work instead', 'I think about something else'), social control ('I talk to a friend about the thought'), punishment ('I punish myself for thinking the thought') and reappraisal ('I challenge the thought's validity'). Utilizing the Thought Control Questionnaire, Abramowitz *et al.* (2003*a*) found that patients with social phobia had elevated worry and punishment scores, compared to non-patient controls. Interestingly, for those patients who successfully responded to cognitive therapy, there were decreases in the use of worry and punishment strategies.

Both Mellings and Alden (2000) and Rachman *et al.* (2000) found that compared to low-anxious controls, people high in social anxiety demonstrate significantly more post-event rumination following social interactions, in the form of performing a mental 'post-mortem' about how the interaction went and how they performed. Mellings and Alden (2000) found that this rumination predicted the extent to which negative self-related information is recalled and the extent to which self-judgements, when anticipating a social interaction on a later occasion, are negative. These findings are consistent with proposals made by Clark and Wells (1995), as discussed in Chapter 1, but as they were conducted on an analogue sample they require replication in patients diagnosed with social phobia.

Obsessive-compulsive disorder

Obsessive-compulsive disorder is characterized by recurrent obsessive intrusions, about which the patient worries and which can lead to ritualized responses. Some patients with OCD demonstrate a specific pattern of obsessive rumination concerned with doubts about whether they had previously completed an action, such as doubts about locking the door (van Oppen *et al.* 1995). Patients with OCD can also suffer from morbid pre-occupation, where they ruminate about potential negative outcomes that could have happened, but which did not happen. A number of other studies have found that patients with OCD have elevated worry scores, compared to non-patient controls, on the Thought Control Questionnaire (Amir *et al.* 1997; Abramowitz *et al.* 2001; Rassin and Diepstraten 2003).

Post-traumatic stress disorder and acute stress disorder

Nolen-Hoeksema and Morrow (1991) found that the tendency to ruminate, as assessed 2 weeks before the Lomo Prieta earthquake of 1989, predicted dysphoria and PTSD symptoms 7 weeks after the earthquake. Consistently, a series of studies conducted by James Murray and his colleagues have found that scores on brief self-report measures of rumination about a traumatic event are elevated in patients with PTSD compared to non-patient controls. Examples of the items included are 'Do you go over and over what happened again and again?' and 'Do you dwell on what happened, without really solving or deciding anything?'. Furthermore, rumination several weeks after the trauma predicted the persistence of PTSD at 6 months (Murray *et al.* 2002), 1 year (Ehlers *et al.* 1998; Clohessy and Ehlers 1999; Steil and Ehlers 2000; Holeva *et al.* 2001) and 3-year follow up (Mayou *et al.* 2002). Finally, using the Thought Control Questionnaire (Wells and Davies 1994), Gladiss Warda and Richard Bryant (1998) reported that scores on the worry scale were elevated in acute stress disorder (ASD) relative to non-patient controls.

Generalized anxiety disorder

Chronic worry is central to the diagnosis of GAD (American Psychiatric Association 2001). Several studies have indicated that worry in patients with GAD is predominantly experienced in a verbal form rather than in images (Borkovec and Inz 1990; Borkovec *et al.* 1993; Freeston *et al.* 1996).

Somatoform disorders

Pain disorder

Several studies have found that patients with chronic pain ruminate about the causes of pain (Williams and Thorn 1989; Morley and Wilkinson 1995), as well as worry about the pain and its possible consequences (Sullivan *et al.* 1995; Eccleston *et al.* 2001). Further, Eccleston and his colleagues (2001) found that for patients with chronic pain, worry about pain is experienced as more difficult to dismiss, more attention grabbing, more intrusive, and more distressing than worry about other non-pain-related concerns.

Eating disorders

Using a retrospective design, Troop and Treasure (1997) reported that the onset of bulimia nervosa was associated with rumination in response to a major life event or difficulty. In an analogue sample, Hart and Chiovari (1998) found that dieters show significantly more rumination about eating and food relative to non-dieters.

Sleep disorders

People with chronic insomnia commonly attribute their sleep disturbance to intrusive thoughts or a racing mind (Lichstein and Rosenthal 1980; Borkovec *et al.* 1983; Harvey 2000, 2001*a*). Harvey (2001*a*) found that worry, as measured by the Thought Control Questionnaire, is elevated in insomnia patients compared to non-patient controls. A number of other studies, using both questionnaires and direct sampling techniques, have reported that the pre-sleep cognitive activity of patients with insomnia is more focused on not getting to sleep, general worries, solving problems, and the time than that of good sleepers (Watts *et al.* 1994; Harvey 2000; Wicklow and Espie 2000). Nelson and Harvey (2003) found that patients with insomnia reported fewer images than good sleepers, once sleep-onset latency was controlled for, and the images they reported were more unpleasant, and more likely to be concerned with sleep.

Mood disorders

Unipolar depression

The presence of rumination has been examined in unipolar depression by the use of the Rumination scale of the Response Style Questionnaire (Nolen-Hoeksema and Morrow 1991). The Response Style Questionnaire measures the tendency to respond to a sad or depressed mood with either ruminative responses (e.g. 'Analyze why I am feeling the way I am', 'Think about how tired I feel') or with distracting responses (e.g. 'Go and see a friend'). The tendency to ruminate in response to negative moods appears to be a relatively common (Rippere 1977) and stable coping style (Nolen-Hoeksema *et al.* 1993) in the general population. Both currently depressed and recovered depressed patients show elevated rumination scores, compared to never-depressed controls (Roberts *et al.* 1998; Nolen-Hoeksema 2000). Furthermore, higher scores on rumination predicts depression. Repeated prospective studies have found that rumination predicts the onset of depressive symptoms in non-depressed groups (e.g. Nolen-Hoeksema *et al.* 1993; Nolen-Hoeksema *et al.* 1994; Just and Alloy 1997) and the maintenance of depressive symptoms in clinically-depressed patients (Kuehner and Weber 1999; Nolen-Hoeksema 2000—although note the non-replications by Kasch *et al.* 2001 and Lara *et al.* 2000). Susan Nolen-Hoeksema (2000) found that rumination predicted anxiety and depressive symptoms 1 year later in currently depressed patients. Finally, Spasojevic and Alloy (2001) found that rumination predicted the onset of major depression in an undergraduate population over 2.5 years. In this study rumination mediated the effects of several other cognitive risk factors (dysfunctional attitudes, attributional style) in predicting future depressive episodes.

Psychotic disorders

Freeman and Garety (1999) found that patients with schizophrenia and persecutory delusions have levels of worry as measured on the Penn State Worry Questionnaire and the Thought Control Questionnaire, equivalent to patients with GAD.

Discussion

Definite transdiagnostic processes

As summarized in Table 5.1, the evidence suggests that recurrent negative thinking is an important process that is common across all of the psychological disorders studied to date. All of the research reviewed in this section is based on questionnaire measures (although there is some supportive prospective and experimental evidence, which we review in the later section on the causal role of recurrent thinking) and all of the disorders investigated show elevated levels of worry and rumination. As such, recurrent negative thinking meets our criteria for a definite transdiagnostic process.

Can we distinguish between different types of recurrent thinking (worry, rumination, obsessions) or do they all reflect the same process? From the section above, it is clear that worry and rumination are very similar—both involve recurrent thinking about negative themes, both predict anxiety and depression symptoms prospectively. Further, as we will see in a moment, when worry and rumination are experimentally induced, the participant experiences increases in anxiety and depressed mood. Furthermore, measures of worry and rumination are highly correlated with each other, and with an index of the tendency to think repetitively (Segerstrom et al. 2000; Fresco et al. 2002; Harrington and Blankenship 2002; Szabo and Lovibond 2002). These similarities have led to an as-yet-unresolved debate as to whether worry and rumination only differ in the content of the recurrent thinking (i.e. that they are the same process, Borkovec et al. 1998; Segerstrom et al. 2000) or whether they involve related but distinct processes (Papageorgiou and Wells 1999, 2001).

What about distinguishing between worry and obsessions? Studies in non-patient controls have also compared worry and obsessions. Compared to worries, obsessions were more likely to be visual images and were less realistic, more involuntary, more egodystonic, more likely to be associated with a sense of responsibility, easier to dismiss, and less distracting (Wells and Morrison 1994; Langlois et al. 2000a, b). An egosyntonic thought is consistent with the individual's beliefs and values, whereas an egodystonic thought is not acceptable within the person's beliefs (e.g. a blasphemous thought for a religious person). The egodystonic quality of the intrusions is the hallmark of obsessions and appears to discriminate obsessive intrusions from worrisome or ruminative intrusions (Clark and Purdon 1993; Purdon and Clark 1993, 1999; Purdon 2001). Further research within non-patient groups suggests that there are enough similarities between obsessions and worry to consider them as lying on the same continuum and sharing many of the same appraisals and strategies (Freeston et al. 1994; Langlois et al. 2000a, b).

Table 5.1 Summary of findings across the psychological disorders (first column) and the thought processes (top line)

	Recurrent thinking	Paradoxical effect of thought suppression	Metacognitive beliefs	Metacognitive awareness	Reality /source monitoring
Panic disorder with or without agoraphobia		** +			
Specific phobia	**	*** −			
Social phobia	** +	** +/−			*** −
OCD	** +	** +/−	** +		
PTSD/ASD	*** +	*** +/−	** +		
GAD	** +	* +	** +		
Pain disorder	** +	** −			
Hypochondriasis			* +		
Dissociative disorder					
Sexual disorder					
Eating disorder	** +	* −	** +		
Sleep disorder	*** +	** +	** +	**	
Unipolar depression	*** +	** +	** +	+	** −
Bipolar depression					
Psychotic disorder	* +	**	** +		*** +
Substance disorder		* +			

Note. For each thought process the left hand column presents an indication of the quality of the evidence as follows: *** = good quality evidence, ** = moderate quality of evidence, * = tentative quality of evidence (see page 21–22 for further explanation) and the right hand column presents an indication of the findings as follows: + = positive findings, − = negative findings, +/− = mixed findings, blank space = the thought process has not been researched in this disorder.

Causal role of recurrent thinking

Prospective studies

In both depression and PTSD, prospective studies show that rumination predicts both depressed and anxious symptoms at least 1–2 years in the future (e.g. Ehlers *et al.* 1998; Clohessy and Ehlers 1999; Nolen-Hoeksema 2000; Steil and Ehlers 2000; Holeva *et al.* 2001). Rumination continues to predict future symptoms even when controlling for baseline symptoms (e.g. Nolen-Hoeksema 2000).

Experimental studies

Inducing worry, by asking participants to briefly worry about a self-chosen concern, increases depressed mood and anxiety in non-patient control participants (Andrews and Borkovec 1988), and produces a short-term increase in negative intrusive thoughts (Borkovec *et al.* 1983 ; York *et al.* 1987; Butler *et al.* 1995; Wells and Papageorgiou 1995). For example, Borkovec *et al.* (1983) found that 15 or 30 minutes of worry produced more anxiety, depression, and more negative thoughts in a subsequent 5-min period for high worriers relative to low worriers. Further, following exposure to a stressful film, verbal worrying increased cognitive intrusions over the next 3 days, relative to imagining the film or doing nothing (Butler *et al.* 1995; Wells and Papageorgiou 1995). While these studies are limited by the analogue sample employed, Nelson and Harvey (2002) replicated the finding in patients with chronic insomnia.

Experimental manipulations of distraction and rumination (described in Boxes 5.2 and 5.3) have found that rumination can exacerbate negative mood (Nolen-Hoeksema and Morrow 1993), negative thinking (Lyubomirsky and Nolen-Hoeksema 1995), negative autobiographical memory recall (Lyubomirsky *et al.* 1999) and poor problem solving (Lyubomirsky and Nolen-Hoeksema 1995; Lyubomirsky *et al.* 1999). These negative effects of rumination are only found in dysphoric participants, as opposed to non-dysphoric participants. The dysphoria can be a naturally occurring dysphoric mood or dysphoria resulting from a negative mood induction (see Box 3.2). Again, much of this research has been conducted on analogue samples. However, Watkins *et al.* (2000) and Watkins and Teasdale (2001) have reported replications in patient samples.

Together, these studies suggest that recurrent thinking may play a causal role in the maintenance of psychological disorders.

Theoretical issues

While it is clear that recurrent thinking is common across all the disorders studied, it is important to note that the content of the recurrent thinking may

Box 5.2 'Make yourself ruminate'—The experimental induction of rumination

Susan Nolen-Hoeksema and her colleagues induced rumination by asking participants to focus on the causes and consequences of their feelings. Here is an excerpt from the task to give a sense of what it involves. Nolen-Hoeksema found that rumination only had negative effects when people were already in a sad mood. An interesting experiment to try for yourself is to compare the effects of working through this task when you feel okay versus when you feel a bit sad (perhaps as a result of a mood induction, as described in Box 3.2).

For the next few minutes, try your best to focus your attention on each of the ideas listed below. Read each item slowly and silently to yourself. As you read the items, use your imagination and concentration to focus your mind on each of the ideas. Spend a few moments visualizing and concentrating on each item.

Think about the physical sensations you feel in your body
Think about your character and who you strive to be
Think about the degree of clarity in your thinking right now
Think about why you react the way you do
Think about the way you feel inside
Think about the possible consequences of your current mental state
Think about how similar or different you are relative to other people
Think about what it would be like if your present feelings lasted
Think about why things turn out the way they do
Think about trying to understand your feelings
Think about how awake or tired you feel now

differ between the disorders to reflect the particular current concerns of each disorder (and each individual patient). We have highlighted in our discussion of the differences between worry, rumination, and obsessions that for each form of recurrent thinking the particular content will differ, such that; depressive rumination is predominantly concerned with loss, anxious worry is predominantly concerned with threat, and obsessions are predominantly concerned with egodystonic thoughts (Segerstrom *et al.* 2000).

Recurrent thinking has been conceptualized as an attempt at problem solving and as a self-regulatory attempt to try to resolve unfulfilled goals (Pyszczynski and Greenberg 1987; Martin and Tesser 1989, 1996; Carver and

Box. 5.3 The experimental induction of distraction

Susan Nolen-Hoeksema and her colleagues induced distraction by asking participants to focus on visual images of non-self-related scenes. Here is an excerpt from the task to give a sense of what it involves. An interesting experiment to try for yourself is to compare the effects of working through this task when you feel okay versus when you feel a bit sad (perhaps as a result of a mood induction, as described in Box 3.2).

For the next few minutes, try your best to focus your attention on each of the ideas listed below. Read each item slowly and silently to yourself. As you read the items, use your imagination and concentration to focus your mind on each of the ideas. Spend a few moments visualizing and concentrating on each item.

Think about and imagine a boat slowly crossing the Atlantic
Think about the layout of a typical classroom
Think about the shape of a large black umbrella
Think about the movement of an electric fan on a warm day
Think about raindrops sliding down a window pane
Think about a double-decker bus driving down a street
Think about and picture a full moon on a clear night
Think about clouds forming in the sky
Think about the layout of the local shopping centre
Think about and imagine a plane flying overhead
Think about fire darting round a log in a fire-place
Think about and concentrate on the expression on the face of the Mona Lisa

When feeling stressed or low distraction often results in people feeling better (Fennell and Teasdale 1984; Fennell *et al.* 1987; Nolen-Hoeksema and Morrow 1991).

Scheier 1990; Teasdale 1999*a*). Within this conceptualization of recurrent thinking, whether thinking is useful problem solving or unhelpful rumination, it will persist until the goal is attained or the goal is discarded. More specifically, worry has been conceptualized as an attempt to avoid negative events, prepare for the worst and to problem solve (Borkovec and Roemer 1995). Likewise, rumination has been proposed to be an ineffective attempt at problem solving (Martin and Tesser 1996), as well as an attempt to make sense of depressed mood (Lyubomirsky and Nolen-Hoeksema 1993; Papageorgiou and Wells 2001; Watkins and Baracaia 2001). Consistent with the view that pathological worry is a failed attempt at problem solving, in a diary study of naturally occurring worry, Szabo and Lovibond (2002) found that 48% of worry thoughts reflected attempts at solving problems that were unsuccessful, and that high worriers reported fewer successful solutions to problems. However, it is important to note that recurrent thinking is not necessarily dysfunctional. The following section will describe two examples of when recurrent thinking might be functional.

Functional recurrent thinking

Recurrent Thinking and Problem Solving. Recurrent thinking can be helpful in resolving goals and solving problems. Indeed, worry is seen as useful for problem solving, when it is appropriate, focused on real, objective concerns and relatively brief (Davey 1994). Problem solving has been conceptualized as consisting of several stages: definition or appraisal of the problem, generation of alternative solutions, selection of alternatives, implementing the chosen solution and evaluating its effectiveness (D'Zurilla and Goldfried 1971). The definition and appraisal of a problem could involve recurrent thinking about negative or difficult situations. Whether the recurrent thinking about a problem becomes functional or dysfunctional may depend on the manner in which a person approaches the problem. A positive orientation, encompassing confidence in one's ability to solve the problem, is associated with better outcomes than a negative orientation characterized by reduced self-confidence, reduced optimism, and more extreme views of the severity and intractability of the problem (e.g. Elliot *et al.* 1994, 1995).

Emotional Processing. A second area where recurrent thinking may be functional is emotional processing. Emotional processing can be defined as 'a process whereby emotional disturbances are absorbed and decline to the extent that other experiences and behaviour can proceed without disruption' (p. 51, Rachman 1980). Rachman (1980) characterized failed emotional processing as the presence of direct signs, such as disturbing dreams, intrusive and unwanted thoughts, and incongruent expressions of emotion and the presence of indirect signs, such as distress, insomnia, inability to concentrate, and irritability. However, the elaboration and focus on an upsetting event is a critical aspect of emotional processing (Rachman 1980; Rivkin and Taylor 1999). Indeed, Rachman (1980) has suggested that prolonged and repeated exposure to upsetting stimuli is an essential component of emotional processing. Further, Foa and Kozak (1986) found that emotional and physiological responses during exposure to fearful stimuli were required in order for the exposure to successfully reduce anxiety. More recently, Rachman (2001) proposed that emotional processing would be impeded by a negative orientation and facilitated by a positive orientation.

Consistent with these theoretical viewpoints, there is now an accumulation of evidence suggesting that repeated exposure to upsetting events can be beneficial. Thus, expressive writing about an upsetting and emotional event or mental simulation of upsetting events produces long-term improvements in mental and physical health (Greenberg and Stone 1992; Pennebaker 1993; Spera *et al.* 1994; Littrell 1998; Smyth 1998; Taylor *et al.* 1998; Esterling *et al.* 1999). Furthermore, compared to writing about a distracting topic, writing about an upsetting event (e.g. false low score on an IQ test, Hunt 1998; an upcoming exam, Lepore 1997) significantly reduces negative mood or depressive symptoms over relatively short-time periods (1 month, Lepore 1997; 1 day, Hunt 1998). These findings are consistent with those of Foa and colleagues (Foa and Kozak 1986; Foa *et al.* 1995*b*) who report that controlled re-exposure to trauma memories can be beneficial for patients with PTSD.

What determines functional versus dysfunctional recurrent thinking?

Given that recurrent thinking about negative events or upsetting situations can be functional and result in effective problem solving or successful emotional processing, one important question we will need to consider is what factors determine the difference between unproductive, unhelpful rumination and functional problem solving and emotional processing. A successful account of recurrent thinking in psychological disorders will also need to explain the increased frequency and duration of negative recurrent thinking in patient groups. One factor that seems important in the use of worry and rumination seems to be the beliefs that people hold about the utility of this strategy in response to intrusive thoughts or problems. This issue will be discussed further in the section later in this chapter on metacognition. Other factors that might be important are how easy it is to solve the problem and the mode of the recurrent thinking, as well as the learning (conditioning) associated with the recurrent thinking. We'll now consider each of these factors in turn.

Insoluble Problems. The problem or question that people are attempting to resolve may be an important determinant of the duration and helpfulness of recurrent thinking. Problem solving may become stuck in rumination if the problem chosen is not easily soluble or amenable to intervention. For example, the rumination could focus on an unanswerable question like 'Why did this terrible thing happen to me?' following a loss or trauma. Similarly, one type of worry in patients with GAD is about improbable future events (e.g. family dying in a car accident, Dugas *et al.* 1997), which are not amenable to useful problem solving, and thus can become persistent, unlike worries about immediate practical problems.

Mode of Processing. Another factor that may be important in determining the frequency, duration, and usefulness of recurrent thinking is the mode of thinking used during attempts at working through or solving problems. Both worry and rumination involve more verbal thinking and less visual imagery (Borkovec *et al.* 1998). Within the *cognitive avoidance* theory of worry (Borkovec *et al.* 1998), it is proposed that verbal worrying reduces the amount of aversive imagery associated with emotional concerns, thus minimizing the physiological and emotional responses to such concerns (Vrana *et al.* 1986; Borkovec and Hu 1990). This then inhibits emotional processing. Consistent with this account, verbal worry appears to suppress the cardiovascular response to threatening images or situations (giving a speech) in women afraid of public speaking (Borkovec and Hu 1990; Borkovec *et al.* 1993; Hazlett-Stevens and Borkovec 2001; but note the only partial replication by Peasley-Miklus and Vrana 2000). By minimizing the physiological and emotional response to difficulties, verbal worrying will prevent emotional processing (Rachman 1980), which requires sufficient activation of an emotional response to upsetting events or memories in order to be successful (Foa and Kozak 1986).

As well as being associated with less visual imagery, worry and rumination are associated with a more abstract and less concrete style of thinking (Stober *et al.* 2000). Abstract thinking is defined as 'indistinct, cross-situational, equivocal, unclear, aggregated'. An example of abstract thinking is describing a problem as 'always finding it hard to get on with people'. Concrete thinking is defined as 'distinct, situationally specific, unequivocal, clear, singular'. An example of concrete thinking is describing a problem as 'finding a good way to apologize to my friend after I was rude to him yesterday evening'. By definition, if thinking is more abstract, then it is less concrete, and vice versa. Research has established that problem descriptions were significantly less concrete for worry-related problems than non-worry problems when described by a college sample (Stober *et al.* 2000) and when described by patients with GAD, relative to non-patient controls (Stober and Borkovec 2002). Furthermore, an abstract-conceptual style of thinking is characteristic of the spontaneously occurring phenomenology of rumination (Emmons 1992; Teasdale 1999; Watkins and Baracaia 2001). For example, analyzing the causes, consequences, and meanings of symptoms and asking 'Why did this happen to me?' all involve more abstract thinking as defined by Vallacher and Wegner (1987). Further, Watkins *et al.* (2000) found that compared to distraction, rumination maintains overgeneral autobiographical memories in depression. Since overgeneral memories are generic summaries of repeated events (for more detail see Chapter 3) and within Stober's definition, are examples of abstract thinking, this finding suggests that rumination induces abstract thinking.

The *reduced concreteness* theory of worry (Stober, 1998; Borkovec *et al.* 1998; Stober *et al.* 2000; Stober and Borkovec 2002) proposes that the increased abstract thinking found in worry reduces visual imagery and hence reduces physiological and emotional response because abstract thoughts evoke imagery with less vividness, speed, and ease than concrete thoughts (Paivio and Marschark 1991). The reduced concreteness theory also aims to explain impaired problem solving within worry and rumination. More abstract elaborations of problems should impair problem solving because they will be less detailed and less specific, and thus poor at generating alternatives or guiding the implementation of action (Vallacher and Wegner 1987; Stober and Borkovec 2002). Consistent with this hypothesis, Watkins and Baracaia (2002) found that inducing a more abstract thinking style by asking '*why*' type questions during problem solving (e.g. '*Why* did this problem happen?') impaired problem solving in recovered depressed patients, relative to solving the problems in the absence of any questions. Inducing a more concrete action-oriented style (e.g. asking '*How* are you deciding what to do next?') removed the problem-solving deficit normally found in currently depressed patients.

To summarize this section, the evidence suggests that by impairing emotional processing and problem solving, a less visual and less concrete reasoning style would cause the concern (whether a problem, threat, or upsetting memory) to remain unresolved, such that it would continue to trigger further rumination and worry. Furthermore, more abstract concerns, such as 'something bad will happen', are harder to correct and disconfirm by external experiences than concrete concerns, further maintaining the recurrent thinking.

Conditioning. The tendency to worry or ruminate could be further maintained by higher-order conditioning such that new associations are formed between worries and internal/external stimuli, resulting in a gradual increase and spreading of the cues that can trigger off worry. Consistent with this account, Thayer and Borkovec (1995; cited in Borkovec *et al.* 1998) found that patients with GAD developed orienting responses to conditional stimuli associated with threat words. This conditioning process may also account for the findings of selective attention to mild threat stimuli in GAD (as discussed in Chapter 2). Recurrent thinking could also be reinforced by superstitious reinforcement such that many of the things that people worry about do not occur to the extent that they predicted, leading to the worry being negatively reinforced by the non-occurrence of these feared events. That is, people associate the better-than-expected outcome with the act of worrying, such that worrying is seen as a helpful strategy.

Thought suppression

An alternative approach to managing intrusive thoughts is to attempt to get rid of them. Thought suppression is the process of deliberately attempting to prevent or remove particular thoughts from entering consciousness (Wegner 1989; see reviews by Wenzlaff and Wegner 2000; Purdon 2001). An extensive experimental literature has indicated that attempting to suppress thoughts can sometimes increase their frequency (i.e. have a paradoxical effect on thought frequency). The initial, classic finding of the paradoxical effects of thought suppression came from the 'white bear' experiment (described in Box 5.4). This study demonstrates a delayed paradoxical effect of thought suppression.

Box 5.4 The White Bear Experiment

Wegner *et al.* (1987)

Participants: Student volunteers

Conditions: Volunteers randomly allocated to either try to *not* think about a white bear (suppression) or to think quietly to themselves about a white bear (thinking control) for several minutes.

Task: Following the attempt to *suppress* thoughts about the white bear or to *think* about the white bear, the volunteers reported aloud all thoughts they had in a subsequent 'thinking aloud' period. This 'thinking aloud' period was called the expression period.

Results: The students who were asked to suppress thoughts about the bear reported more thoughts about the bear in the expression period than students who had previously thought about the bear.

Conclusion: This is the classic demonstration of the delayed enhancement effect or paradoxical effect of thought suppression. Similar effects have been found for the suppression of thoughts about green rabbits (Clark *et al.* 1991, 1993) and humorous and traumatic films (Harvey and Bryant 1998). The challenge to the field is to determine the relevance of these findings to spontaneously occurring intrusive thoughts (Purdon 1999).

A delayed paradoxical effect of thought suppression occurs when suppressing a thought leads to an increase in the frequency of the thought after suppression is discontinued (post suppression).

Subsequent studies have made a variety of attempts to control for potential confounds. One attempt has involved asking participants to either suppress thoughts about a white bear or think aloud about a white bear (an expression control). The key test was the impact of this manipulation on a subsequent 'think aloud' period (i.e. expression–expression vs suppression–expression design). Two other controls are sometimes employed. In the 'free monitoring' control, participants report whatever comes to mind. This approach is perhaps the most naturalistic (as it does not artificially elevate target thoughts), but it does not control for the cueing effects (i.e. the increased mention of the target that occurs during the suppression instructions). In the 'mention' control, this problem is resolved since the target thought is mentioned in the instructions, usually as an example of thoughts the participant may or may not think about. The frequency of the target thoughts has been measured either by participants pressing a counter button for each thought or by analyzing stream-of-consciousness verbalizations.

The delayed paradoxical effect of thought suppression effect has been replicated using both free monitoring and mention controls in non-patient populations (e.g. Clark *et al.* 1991; Wegner *et al.* 1991; Clark *et al.* 1993; Kelley and Kahn 1994; Lavy and van den Hout 1994; Wegner and Gold 1995; McNally and Ricciardi 1996; Harvey and Bryant 1998). However, it is important to note that a number of studies have failed to replicate this effect (e.g. Merckelbach *et al.* 1991; Muris *et al.* 1993; Roemer and Borkovec 1994; Purdon 2001).

Suppression has been reported to also have an immediate paradoxical enhancement effect. The immediate paradoxical enhancement effect is defined as an increase in thoughts about the suppressed target during the suppression period. This effect is much less reliable than the delayed effect, with the immediate paradoxical effect being most reliably found in the presence of additional cognitive demands, such as time pressures or concurrent memory tasks (Wegner and Erber 1992; Wenzlaff and Bates 1998, 1999; Wenzlaff and Wegner 2000; Abramowitz *et al.* 2001).

Questionnaires have also been used to index thought suppression. The White Bear Suppression Inventory (Wegner and Zanakos 1994) asks participants to rate their agreement with statements like 'There are things I prefer not to think about' on a 5-point Likert-type scale. The White Bear Suppression Inventory is reliable, has good internal consistency and good validity. A number of studies have used the Thought Control Questionnaire as a potential index of thought suppression (e.g. Amir *et al.* 1997; Morrison and Wells 2000; Abramowitz *et al.* 2001, 2003*a*), with the suggestion that the worry, punishment, and distraction strategies are related to the construct of suppression (Guthrie and Bryant 2000). However, none of the Thought Control Questionnaire subscales specifically refer to thought suppression and the use of measures of distraction, punishment, and worry to index thought suppression depends on theoretical assumptions that have not yet been empirically demonstrated. For these reasons, we do not consider scores on the Thought Control Questionnaire to provide a good index of thought suppression (Harvey 2001*a*). Having outlined the principal methodologies, we now move on to review the thought suppression findings across the disorders. Given the now vast literature on thought suppression, this review will concentrate on those studies that have employed patient samples.

Anxiety disorders

Panic disorder with agoraphobia and social phobia

Fehm and Margraf (2001) found that thought suppression produced an immediate enhancement of intrusions in patients with agoraphobia, compared to healthy controls, but only for agoraphobia-related thoughts (e.g. 'I could be completely helpless and faint in a threatening situation') and not for non-specific fears (e.g. 'I could get into financial straits without it being my fault') nor for social phobia-related thoughts (e.g. 'I could completely disgrace myself in a threatening situation'). In contrast, in the same study, patients with social phobia showed an immediate enhancement for both specific and non-specific fears. This study used a within-subject design, where each group had to suppress each type of thought but it did not include subsequent thought periods without suppression instructions, such that it was not possible to determine the relative effects of suppression versus non-suppression or determine the delayed effects of suppression. Another study by Tolin *et al.* (2002) failed to find any effect of thought suppression on lexical decisions for suppressed thoughts about white bears in patients with social phobia. However, it should be noted that this study did not use a between-subjects design comparing suppression with monitoring, but rather a sequential design where all participants monitored their thoughts, then suppressed thoughts about white bears and then monitored their thoughts again.

Specific phobias

Two studies have shown that patients with spider phobia try harder to suppress spider-related thoughts during suppression than controls but no delayed enhancement effects of suppression were detected, compared to a free monitoring control (Muris *et al.* 1997, 1998). However, the failure to see any difference between conditions could be the result of the patient group spontaneously suppressing thoughts in the free monitoring condition. To reduce this potential artefact, Wang (1998; cited in Abramowitz *et al.* 2001), compared thought suppression with a free monitoring plus 'do not suppress' control to examine the occurrence of spider-related thoughts after watching a video of a tarantula spider in high spider fearful participants. Again, no immediate or delayed paradoxical effect of suppression was detected. Muris and his colleagues (1998) found that patients with dental phobia exhibited greater levels of suppression for dentist-related thoughts than non-patient controls. In a suppression versus expression design, they found that attempts to suppress dentist-related thoughts while undergoing dental treatment increased intrusive thinking and anxiety in the non-patient control group but not in the patients with dental phobia. Thus, it would appear that the specific phobias do not show any adverse effects associated with thought suppression.

Obsessive-compulsive disorder

Mark Freeston and Robert Ladouceur (1997) found that 76% of patients with OCD reported repeated attempts to suppress their intrusive obsessions. Janacek and Calamari (1999) found that patients with OCD had more intrusive thoughts both during suppression of personally relevant thoughts and during monitoring periods, compared to normal controls. However, there was no difference between the groups for the delayed paradoxical effect of suppression. Tolin *et al.* (2002) found that the attempted suppression of thoughts about white bears led to a paradoxical increase in intrusive thoughts about white bears for patients with OCD but not for non-anxious controls or patients with social phobia. On a lexical decision task, unlike the control groups, patients with OCD were faster to decide whether a word related to the suppressed thoughts about white bears (e.g. 'bear') was an English word, relative to nontarget words (e.g. 'vine') and nonwords (e.g. 'rekm'). These results suggested that thought suppression increased the accessibility of these thoughts. Tolin *et al.* (2002) also reported that patients with OCD indicated that they held more internal and negative attributions for their suppression failure than controls. These results indicate that patients with OCD may have a deficit in inhibiting thoughts, such that attempts at thought suppression increase intrusive obsessions. However, this study was limited in not having a no-suppression control condition and only neutral thoughts were used as the to-be-suppressed material.

Post-traumatic stress disorder and acute stress disorder

Thought suppression is a common response to intrusions in PTSD (Amir *et al.* 1997) and ASD (Warda and Bryant 1998). In experimental manipulations of thought suppression, Shipherd and Beck (1999) found that rape victims with PTSD showed a delayed enhancement for rape-related thoughts compared to rape victims not suffering from PTSD. Consistent with this, Harvey and Bryant (1998) found that road traffic accident victims diagnosed with ASD showed a delayed paradoxical effect of suppression for accident-related thoughts compared to road traffic accident victims without ASD (using a mention control). However, when ASD and non-ASD trauma victims participated over longer periods (3 × 24 times h periods) there was no evidence for an increase in trauma-related thoughts for a group instructed to suppress (Guthrie and Bryant 2000). However, the ASD patients engaged in more suppression regardless of instruction condition (i.e. increased suppression in control conditions).

Generalized anxiety disorder

Becker *et al.* (1998) found that compared to non-patient controls, patients with GAD were better at suppressing white-bear thoughts than personal worries, whilst the non-patient controls were better at suppressing personal worries than white-bear thoughts. There was no post-suppression period, so this study did not test the delayed paradoxical effect of thought suppression.

Somatoform disorders

Pain disorder

Harvey and McGuire (2000) compared suppression of pain-related thoughts versus attending to pain-related thoughts versus a 'think anything' control in chronic pain patients. Attending to pain thoughts led to a greater number of pain-related thoughts during the experimental period, but there was no evidence of either an immediate enhancement or delayed enhancement effect. However, participants in the suppression condition were given specific instructions to suppress thoughts about pain by using distraction, which may have made their attempts at suppression more effective.

Eating disorders

Studies of thought suppression relevant to eating disorders are limited to studies based on analogue populations. The pattern of findings across these studies is that there were no differences in the effect of attempting thought suppression in high-risk groups (high dieters, binge eaters, chocolate cravers) relative to low-risk groups (Harnden *et al.* 1997; Johnston *et al.* 1999; Oliver and Huon 2001). One might have expected the reverse pattern: the more at-risk group showing more intrusions following thought suppression. Perhaps this paradoxical effect of thought suppression would be evident in more severe patient populations. Alternatively, the absence of a delayed enhancement effect in the at-risk group may reflect prior practice at thought suppression for the food/weight-related thoughts, such that the brief experimental period may not have had much impact.

Sleep disorders

On the Thought Control Questionnaire, adapted to refer to thinking whilst trying to get to sleep, and with additional items to index thought suppression (e.g. 'I tell myself not to think about the thought') and replacement ('I think about something else'), patients with insomnia used suppression, reappraisal and worry strategies significantly more than good sleepers (Harvey 2001*a*). In a follow-up experimental study, instructions to suppress one pre-sleep concern led to longer sleep onset and poorer sleep quality in both insomnia and good sleeper groups, compared to non-suppression instructions (Harvey in press *a*).

Mood disorders

Studies of thought suppression in depression are limited in that they have been based on analogue populations such as dysphoric students (scoring greater than 8 on the 13-item Beck Depression Inventory) rather than patient groups (Wenzlaff and Bates 1998). Furthermore, the studies have tended to use a different methodology from studies in other disorders. Specifically, they have examined the effects of a cognitive load on tasks designed to index negative thinking, rather than directly examining the effects of attempted thought suppression on subsequent thoughts (e.g. Wenzlaff and Bates 1998; Wenzlaff and Eisenberg 2001). These analogue studies indicate that more depressed participants report greater efforts to suppress their unwanted negative thoughts and have difficulty inhibiting their negative thoughts (Wenzlaff 1993; Wenzlaff and Bates 1998; Beevers *et al.* 1999; Wenzlaff and Eisenberg 2001). Compared to non-depressed participants, more depressed participants try to distract themselves by focusing on other negative thoughts, which is likely to make it hard to suppress negative thoughts (Wenzlaff *et al.* 1988). Wenzlaff and Bates (1998), Wenzlaff *et al.* (2001), and Wenzlaff and Eisenberg (2001) found that introducing a cognitive load, which is known to undermine the effectiveness of thought suppression (Wegner and Erber 1992), increased negative thinking in undergraduates who had previously, but no longer, scored greater than 8 on the 13-item Beck Depression Inventory.

Negative thinking was assessed by counting: (1) negative arrangements (e.g. 'the future looks very dismal') of scrambled sentences that could be unscrambled in either positive or negative directions ('future the dismal very bright looks') (Wenzlaff and Bates 1998); (2) negative words detected in a letter grid (Wenzlaff and Elsenberg 2001); and (3) negative interpretations of ambiguous homophones (Wenzlaff *et al.* 2001*b*) (for further details on homophones see Chapter 4). Interestingly, the increase in negative thinking was correlated with the degree of reported thought suppression. Together, these results suggest that thought suppression might increase negative thinking in people at risk for depressed mood, although the generalizability of these findings to patients diagnosed with depression remains to be tested.

Substance-related disorders

Palfai *et al.* (1997) exposed heavy social drinkers to the sight and smell of their favourite alcohol, and half were encouraged to suppress their urge to drink, while half were not. Suppression of the urge to drink alcohol increased the speed to endorse alcohol outcome expectancies, that is, the accessibility of alcohol-related information.

Discussion
Possible transdiagnostic processes

When considering whether thought suppression is common across disorders, it is important to make a distinction between attempts at thought suppression and the consequences of thought suppression. Our review of the literature indicates that thought suppression is a strategy adopted in all the psychological disorders studied. Consistent with this conclusion, Spinhoven and van der Does (1999) found that White Bear Suppression Inventory scores were significantly correlated with all symptom factors on the Symptom Checklist-90 (SCL-90; Derogatis 1998). The SCL-90 is a valid and reliable multidimensional measure for a range of psychopathology. Furthermore, the White Bear Suppression Inventory scores did not differ between anxious patients, depressed patients, or people referred for help with emotional problems who did not meet diagnostic criteria for a specific disorder.

However, it is less clear whether the consequences of thought suppression are consistent and common across all disorders. That is, whether thought suppression enhances intrusive thoughts or other symptoms. It may be that deficits in the ability to suppress are limited to only some disorders. From our review of the literature, there is evidence in PTSD, agoraphobia, and insomnia that thought suppression of disorder-related thoughts leads to paradoxical increases in intrusive thoughts and/or symptoms (e.g. sleep onset latency). In social phobia, thought suppression leads to increases in intrusions for specific fear-related thoughts and for other non-specific thoughts. In ASD and OCD, there are mixed effects of thought suppression.

In contrast, patients with specific phobias appear to show no adverse consequences associated with thought suppression (Muris *et al.* 1997, 1998). The recent demonstration of the value of real world studies to investigate selective attention and memory biases (as already highlighted in Chapters 2 and 3) suggests the importance of using ecologically valid paradigms to investigate biased processing. In the absence of real world studies, negative findings may simply be a consequence of experimental material not being sufficiently meaningful to patients. However, patients with specific phobias show no adverse effects of thought suppression even when the ecological validity of the study is improved, such as viewing a video of the feared object (Wang 1998) or when in the feared situation (undergoing dental treatment for patients with dental phobia, Muris *et al.* 1998). Thus, there may genuinely be no paradoxical effect of thought suppression in specific phobia.

Patients with GAD, somatoform disorders, eating disorders, substance-related disorders, mood disorders, and psychotic disorders have not been examined sufficiently to reach any conclusions, although the few results in somatoform disorders and in analogue groups for eating disorders fail to show any paradoxical effect of thought suppression. On the basis of the evidence, thought suppression meets our criteria for a possible transdiagnostic process.

Does thought suppression play a causal role?
Prospective studies

The suppression of trauma-related thoughts is a predictor of PTSD symptom severity for patients injured in motor vehicle accidents at one year (Ehlers *et al.* 1998) and three years (Mayou *et al.* 2002) posttrauma. A tendency towards thought suppression has been reported to be a predictor of later depressive symptoms in an analogue sample; Wenzlaff and Bates (1998) found that high levels of suppression were associated with worsening depressive symptoms over 4–6 weeks in dysphoric undergraduates.

Experimental studies

All of the studies investigating the immediate and delayed paradoxical effects of thought suppression comment on the potential causal role of thought suppression on symptoms. As described above, the findings are mixed. Attempted thought suppression produced an increase in the target thought in patients with OCD (Tolin *et al.* 2002), patients with PTSD (Shipherd and Beck 1999), and patients with social phobia and agoraphobia (Fehm and Margraf 2001). Further, attempted thought suppression led to longer sleep onset latency in patients with insomnia (Harvey in press *a*). These findings are consistent with thought suppression playing a causal role in these disorders. However, thought suppression had no effect in patients with spider phobia (Muris *et al.* 1997, 1998; Wang 1998), patients with dentist phobia (Muris *et al.* 1998) and patients with chronic pain (Harvey and McGuire 2000). There were also no effects detected in samples intended as analogues of eating disorders (Harnden *et al.* 1997; Johnston *et al.* 1999; Oliver and Huon 2001).

Other experimental manipulations have been carried out in analogue non-patient populations. These studies are generally consistent with thought suppression influencing symptoms. Davies and Clark (1998), Rassin *et al.* (1997), and Harvey and Bryant (1998) found that the suppression of thoughts about an upsetting film resulted in a delayed increase in the frequency of these intrusive thoughts. Both Cioffi and Holloway (1993) and Sullivan *et al.* (1997) found that while a volunteer's arm was immersed in ice water to induce pain, suppression of thoughts either prolonged or increased the pain reported compared to a thought monitoring condition. Several other studies have found that suppressing personally relevant negative thoughts increases negative feelings but not necessarily intrusive thoughts (Purdon 2001; Markowitz and Borton 2002). Finally, Helen Trinder and Paul Salkovskis (1994) found that non-patient controls asked to suppress personally relevant obsessional thoughts over a 4-day period had more intrusions and greater discomfort than participants who monitored or thought about their thoughts.

Theoretical issues

The majority of the studies investigating thought suppression have tended to use thoughts that are related to the current concerns of each disorder as the target thoughts to be suppressed (e.g. thoughts about spiders in patients with spider phobia). However, few studies have examined the effects of thought suppression on thoughts not relevant to the disorder (especially thoughts relevant to other disorders). Studies comparing the effects of thought suppression on target thoughts relevant to the disorder and on thoughts relevant to other disorders are necessary to determine whether the effects of thought suppression are limited to the current concerns of each disorder. To the best of our knowledge only one study has attempted to address this issue. Fehm and Magraf (2001) reported that thought suppression results in a paradoxical effect for agoraphobia-related thoughts in patients with agoraphobia, but that patients with social phobia showed paradoxical effects of thought suppression for both social phobia and agoraphobia concerns. The role of current concerns in the effects of thought suppression requires further investigation.

Let us now move on to consider whether it is possible to generate a putative account of the process of thought suppression that can explain some of the divergent findings across disorders. The experimental evidence suggests that a number of factors can influence the degree to which thought suppression produces a paradoxical effect. First, focusing people on a single distracter or changing context or mood between suppression and subsequent expression periods reduces the paradoxical effects of thought suppression (Wegner *et al.* 1987, 1991; Wenzlaff *et al.* 1991). Wenzlaff *et al.* (1991) also found a reciprocal relationship between mood and a suppressed thought, such that thinking about a suppressed topic reinstates the mood at the time of suppression, while reinstating the original mood facilitates the return of the suppressed thought. These findings suggest that suppression involves the use of distracters (other thoughts, feelings, environmental cues) to divert attention from the target thought but that associations can form between the distracter and the target thought, such that exposure to the distracter can trigger the suppressed thought. A change in environment or using a relatively circumscribed and arbitrary distracter minimizes this cueing of suppressed thoughts.

Second, a number of studies have shown that increasing cognitive demands, such as trying to remember a 6-digit number, can increase the paradoxical effects of thought suppression (Wegner and Erber 1992; Wegner *et al.* 1993; Beevers *et al.* 1999). Similarly, Brewin and Beaton (2002) found that more effective thought suppression (i.e. successfully removing unwanted thoughts) was related to greater working memory capacity. These effects of cognitive load are consistent with Wegner and his colleagues' ironic process theory (Wegner 1994*a, b,* 1997; Wegner and Wenzlaff 1996). This theory proposes that the level of mental control enjoyed by an individual at any one point in time is a function of the activities of an operating process and a monitoring process. The operating process is an intentional, effortful, and conscious process, which directs attention away from unwanted thoughts towards preferred or distracting thoughts. The monitoring process is an ironic, unconscious, automatic process, which is vigilant for failures to achieve the desired state. Monitoring for an unwanted thought is going to increase awareness of the thought and make it more salient. However, the controlled operating process will then reduce awareness of the thought by focusing on other distracters. However, within the ironic process account, cognitive demands would impair the effectiveness of the operating process, whilst the ironic process would continue to find unwanted thoughts, leading to the paradoxical effects of thought suppression on the unwanted thought.

Taking the experimental findings and this theoretical account together, the extent to which attempted thought suppression leads to a paradoxical effect in any psychological disorder will depend on:

1. The range of other thoughts, feelings or environmental cues that become associated with the suppressed thought.

2. The extent of cognitive demand on the patient.

The range of associations formed will depend on the thematic content of the thoughts, the degree to which the intrusive thought is only triggered in certain contexts, and the strategic use of specific distracters. Intrusive thoughts with broader thematic content and that occur in a wide range of situations will form associations with a greater range of possible cues than thoughts with focused content that are limited to specific situations, and thus, are more likely to be triggered. Disorders with relatively circumscribed concerns that are only triggered in specific contexts and that impose relatively little cognitive demand, might then be expected to exhibit less paradoxical effects of thought suppression. Consistent with this analysis, spider phobia has very specific thought content, is only triggered in limited contexts (e.g. reminder of spider), and no paradoxical effect of thought suppression has been reported in samples with spider phobia. In contrast, for disorders where the intrusive thoughts reflect broad themes about the self, and can be triggered in many circumstances, such as social phobia, suppressed thoughts will become associated with more internal and environmental cues and will be more likely to be activated following attempted thought suppression. Furthermore, disorders where cognitive resources are reduced would be expected to show increased paradoxical effects of thought suppression. That is, negative mood, which reduces motivation and initiative (Hertel and Hardin 1990) would be likely to deplete cognitive resources. Further, anxiety can act as a form of cognitive load (Eysenck 1982; Sarason 1984; Sarason et al. 1986), as can rumination (Watkins and Brown 2002). To give two examples that are consistent with this account, intrusive thoughts are more difficult to dismiss following a dysphoric mood induction (Sutherland et al. 1982; Edwards and Dickerson 1987). Further, disorders characterized by negative appraisals of intrusive thoughts which lead to anxiety, such as PTSD, insomnia, and OCD, are the disorders where the effect of thought suppression appears to be most robust.

Metacognitive processes

What determines the selection of recurrent thinking, suppression, or other strategies in response to an intrusive thought? The consensus amongst cognitive theorists is that the strategy selected depends on the appraisals of the intrusion (e.g. Purdon and Clark 1999; Salkovskis 1999). Since appraising any cognition involves thinking about a thought, it involves metacognition. Metacognition is defined as any knowledge or process that is involved in the appraisal, monitoring, or control of cognition (Flavell 1979; Nelson and Narens 1990). Recent theoretical accounts (Teasdale 1999a,b; Wells 2000) have emphasized that metacognition plays an important role in the maintenance of psychological disorders.

When considering metacognitive processes, it is important to distinguish between metacognitive knowledge and metacognitive regulation. Metacognitive knowledge refers to the beliefs and information that people have about their own thinking processes and how they work. Such knowledge may take the form of conscious propositional beliefs (e.g. 'rumination is advantageous for problem solving'; Watkins and Baracaia 2001) or it could reflect procedural rules or routines that have developed over time and learning to guide processing (Wells 2000). Metacognitive beliefs include positive metacognitive beliefs, which emphasize the advantages of certain types of thinking (e.g. thinking that worry is helpful for problem solving), and negative metacognitive beliefs, which emphasize the risks and negative consequences of thoughts (e.g. worry will drive me crazy). Other metacognitive beliefs focus on what it means to have certain types of thoughts. For example thought-action fusion beliefs (Shafran et al. 1996) are beliefs that 'specific intrusive thoughts can directly influence the relevant external event, and/or that having these intrusive thoughts is morally equivalent to carrying out a prohibited action' (p. 80, Rachman and Shafran 1999). The former has been referred to as 'likelihood thought-action fusion' and the latter as 'morality thought-action fusion' (p. 80, Rachman and Shafran 1999).

Metacognitive regulation involves all the processes that control and monitor cognition, such as allocation of attention, monitoring, planning, and checking discrepancies. Metacognitive regulation includes the responses or strategies which people use to try to control the activities or content of their cognitive system (Wells 2000). Both recurrent thinking and thought suppression are examples of such metacognitive control strategies.

Typically, studies of metacognitive beliefs have used self-report questionnaires. Most notably, Samantha Cartwright-Hatton and Adrian Wells (1997) created the Meta-Cognitions Questionnaire to assess positive and negative metacognitive beliefs. The Meta-Cognitions Questionnaire assesses positive worry beliefs (e.g. 'Worrying helps me to avoid problems in the future'), negative beliefs about uncontrollability and danger (e.g. 'My worrying is dangerous for me'), general negative metacognitive beliefs (e.g. 'Not being able to control my thoughts is a sign of weakness') and cognitive confidence (e.g. 'I have little confidence in my memory for words and names').

We will now move on to consider two questions. What metacognitive beliefs and processes of metacognitive regulation have been identified across disorders? and Are metacognitive beliefs and processes of metacognitive regulation common across the disorders? We will begin by concentrating on the evidence relating to metacognitive beliefs and then move on to metacognitive regulation.

Metacognitive beliefs

Anxiety disorders

Obsessive-compulsive disorder

Cognitive models of OCD have proposed that intrusions are appraised as personally significant, with patients taking too much responsibility for the possible harmful consequences imagined in obsessive thoughts (Rachman 1976b; Salkovskis 1985, 1989; Rachman *et al.* 1995). Foa *et al.* (2001) found that patients with OCD reported more personal responsibility for potential harm in low-risk (e.g. 'you see a piece of string on the ground') and obsessive-compulsive relevant (e.g. 'you see some nails on a road') situations but not in high-risk non-OCD relevant situations (e.g. 'you see a person faint in a supermarket'), compared to non-anxious controls and patients with social phobia. The patients with social phobia also showed elevated responsibility compared to non-patient controls for the obsessive-compulsive relevant items. One form of elevated responsibility involves 'thought-action fusion' beliefs (Shafran *et al.* 1996; Rachman and Shafran 1999, see definition on page-221). Patients with OCD have significantly higher levels of 'Likelihood thought action fusion' than normal controls (for a reminder of the definition of 'Likelihood thought-action fusion' see page 221; Shafran *et al.* 1996; Amir *et al.* 2001). Emmelkamp and Aardema (1999) found that endorsing thought-action fusion items was related to nearly all obsessive-compulsive behaviours in a large community sample, even when levels of depression were controlled. Further, simply writing out a negative thought [e.g. 'I hope (name of a loved one) is in a car accident'] produces anxiety and the urge to neutralize the thought in participants scoring high in thought-action fusion (Rachman *et al.* 1996), although similar findings occurred in non-selected participants (van den Hout *et al.* 2001). An elegant experimental investigation of the effects of thought-action fusion is described in Box 5.5. Intolerance of uncertainty, as will be described below, was also found to be elevated in patients with OCD with checking compulsions compared to non-checking patients with OCD and controls (Abramowitz *et al.* 2003; Tolin *et al.* 2003).

Box 5.5 Inducing thought-action fusion in control volunteers

Rassin et al. (1999)

Participants: Non-patient volunteers.

Design: All participants were connected to apparatus that measures EEG (electrical activity in the brain). This involved placing several electrodes on the head. All participants were informed that the EEG equipment would be able to detect if they had the thought 'apple'. Then the thought-action fusion-induction group, but not the control group, were told that for every 'apple'-thought detected, the equipment would cause another person in an adjoining room to receive an electric shock, which the volunteer could halt by pressing a button within 2 s of the 'apple' thought.

Results: The thought-action fusion induction led to more intrusions, discomfort and attempts to control thinking than the control condition.

Critique: However, an alternative account for these findings is that the increased emotional arousal associated with thoughts of shock produced more intrusions. An improved study would be to have a shock-mention-control condition, which did not imply that the participant influenced whether the other person was shocked.

Post-traumatic stress disorder

In PTSD, the distress caused by intrusions is related to (1) how much the intrusions are viewed as unwanted or uncontrollable (Dougall *et al.* 1999) and (2) the idiosyncratic negative meanings associated with the intrusions (e.g. thinking 'I am going crazy' in response to flashbacks, Steil and Ehlers 2000). Indeed, Engelhard *et al.* (2001) have demonstrated that patients with PTSD infer danger from the presence of intrusive thoughts, compared to controls. In addition, Rassin and his colleagues (2001) found that patients with PTSD show elevated scores on the Thought-Action fusion scale, relative to non-patient controls. Thus, metacognitive appraisals of intrusions are associated with PTSD.

Generalized anxiety disorder

Patients with GAD have positive and negative metacognitive beliefs. Several self-report studies have indicated that patients with GAD believe that worry is useful for problem solving and avoiding future difficulties and that worrying makes negative events less likely to happen (Freeston *et al.* 1994; Borkovec and Roemer 1995; Borkovec *et al.* 1999). On the Meta-Cognitions Questionnaire, patients with GAD endorsed negative metacognitive beliefs about worrying, but not positive metacognitive beliefs, significantly more than patients with panic disorder, social phobia, or non-patient controls (Davis and Valentiner 2000; Wells and Carter 2001). Consistently, GAD patients show more 'worry about worry', which Wells (1995, 1997) called meta-worry or Type 2 worry. Wells (1995, 1997) proposed that this metaworry is what distinguishes normal from pathological worry. Finally, Hazlett-Stevens *et al.* (2002) found that students meeting criteria for GAD endorsed more 'Likelihood thought-action fusion' beliefs (i.e. that a thought is practically equivalent to an action) but not more moral thought-action fusion beliefs than a non-GAD group, within a large undergraduate sample.

Patients with GAD also demonstrate elevated intolerance of uncertainty, defined as a tendency to respond negatively to an ambiguous or undefined situation, independently of the likelihood or negativity of the situation (Freeston *et al.* 1994). Compared to non-patient controls, patients with GAD show elevated intolerance of uncertainty, as indexed by questionnaire (e.g. 'The smallest doubt can stop me from acting'; Dugas *et al.* 1998) and behavioural measures (Ladouceur *et al.* 1997). Dugas *et al.* (1998) have proposed that intolerance of uncertainty is the key variable in the development and maintenance of pathological worry. In support, Ladouceur *et al.* (2000) showed that experimentally increasing uncertainty on a roulette game (stressing that odds are relatively poor) produced greater worry than reducing uncertainty (stressing that odds are relatively good) in undergraduate volunteers. However, this study manipulated degree of uncertainty rather than manipulating tolerance of uncertainty and so it is not a direct test of the intolerance of uncertainty hypothesis.

Somatoform disorders

Hypochondriasis

In a heterogeneous, non-patient sample, Bouman and Meijer (1999) found that hypochrondriacal symptoms were correlated with the Meta-Cognitions Questionnaire negative metacognitive belief scales and with specific meta-cognitive beliefs about hypochrondriasis.

Eating disorders

Metacognitions have also been investigated in eating disorders. In one of the earliest studies, eating disturbance was specifically associated with cognitions of body dissatisfaction and food pre-occupation (Clark *et al.* 1989). Although many of these cognitions were not 'metacognitive', others were, such as 'thoughts that I never stop thinking about food'. Myra Cooper and her colleagues have developed the eating disorder belief questionnaire to assess a range of assumptions and beliefs associated with eating disorders including beliefs about acceptance by others, self-acceptance, and control over eating, although it does not specifically assess metacognitions (Cooper *et al.* 1997; Cooper and Turner 2000). Work by Glen Waller and his colleagues also focuses on 'core beliefs' and they have found an association, in people with eating disorders, between such beliefs and emotions such as anger (Waller 2003; Waller *et al.* 2003). The interpretation of the ability to control urges is assessed in the 'anorectic cognitions questionnaire' (e.g. Mizes *et al.* 2000) but, like the other measures, does not specifically address metacognition.

'Thoughts about thoughts' have been assessed in studies of 'Thought-shape fusion' which is a concept derived from work on thought-action fusion (see earlier Shafran *et al.* 1999; Radomsky *et al.* 2002). Thought-shape fusion refers to the interpretation of thoughts as morally unacceptable, likely to cause actual weight gain or likely to increase feelings of fatness. Such interpretations have been found to be associated with eating difficulties in an analogue and clinical sample (Shafran *et al.* 1999; Radomsky *et al.* 2002).

Sleep disorders

While an insomnia and good sleeper group did not differ on negative beliefs about worrying in bed, patients with insomnia endorsed more positive beliefs about the benefits of worrying in bed, relative to the good sleepers (Harvey in press *b*). Further, the insomnia group exhibited a larger discrepancy between their *expectation* of what can be achieved by worrying in bed and what they actually *achieve*. An example of a positive belief was that worry in bed 'helps to sort out/put things in order in my mind'. An example of a negative belief was that worry in bed 'makes me feel confused'.

Mood disorders

Positive metacognitive beliefs (e.g. 'I need to ruminate about my problems to find answers to my depression') and negative metacognitive beliefs about rumination (e.g. 'Ruminating about my problems is uncontrollable') are found in patients with depression (Papageorgiou and Wells 1999; Papageorgiou and Wells 2001; Watkins and Baracaia 2001). On one self-report measure, the Positive Beliefs about Rumination Scale (Papageorgiou and Wells 2001), patients with major depression who had experienced recurrent episodes of depression scored significantly higher than patients with panic disorder, social phobia, and non-patient controls. Although it should be noted that the sample sizes in this study were small ($n = 12$). One limitation of the Positive

Beliefs about Rumination scale is that the items confound measuring beliefs about the value of rumination with references to depression (e.g. 'I need to ruminate about my problems to find answers to my depression'), such that depressed patients may endorse these items to a greater extent because descriptions of depression are more relevant to them than to controls.

Psychotic disorders

A number of studies using the Meta-Cognitions Questionnaire have found that patients with psychosis report increased negative beliefs about the uncontrollability and danger of worry (e.g. 'My worrying could make me go mad'), increased negative metacognitive beliefs (e.g. 'It is bad to think certain thoughts'), and greater cognitive confidence (e.g. less endorsement of items like 'my memory can mislead me at times'), relative to non-patient controls (Baker and Morrison 1998; Lobban *et al.* 2002; Morrison *et al.* 2002; Morrison and Wells 2003). However, whether the metacognitive beliefs are more closely associated with particular diagnoses (e.g. schizophrenia) or with particular patterns of symptoms (e.g. auditory hallucinations, persecutory delusions) remains unclear, because the studies used very different samples. For example, Baker and Morrison (1998) examined patients with schizophrenia, but without hallucinations, whereas Morrison and Wells (2003) compared patients with schizophrenia, who experienced auditory hallucinations, with patients with schizophrenia and persecutory beliefs. In this study patients with panic disorder and non-patients were included as the control group. Morrison and Wells (2003) reported that patients with schizophrenia who experience auditory hallucinations had more negative metacognitive beliefs and more cognitive confidence than patients with schizophrenia who had persecutory beliefs.

Metacognitive regulation

As both recurrent negative thinking and thought suppression are examples of strategies adopted during metacognitive regulation, the previous sections of this chapter provide some evidence that aspects of metacognitive regulation are common across psychological disorders. Have any other aspects of metacognitive regulation been investigated in psychological disorders?

A potentially important aspect of metacognitive regulation relevant to emotional disorders is 'decentering' or 'metacognitive awareness'. 'Decentering' or 'metacognitive awareness' is defined as the ability to view thoughts as mental events in a wider context of awareness, rather than as expressions of reality (Teasdale *et al.* 1995; Teasdale 1999*b*; Teasdale *et al.* 2002). Thus, decentering is the ability to step back from thoughts and to see them as ideas to be tested rather than as facts. Decentering has previously been discussed as a core component of cognitive therapy (Beck *et al.* 1979; Ingram and Hollon 1986). John Teasdale and his colleagues (2002) examined metacognitive awareness by asking blind raters to code descriptions of participants' feelings and responses during specific memories evoked by mildly depressing scenarios. The raters coded each memory for the extent to which the participant distances themselves from their thoughts and feelings, on a scale from 1 = 'minimal discrimination' (e.g. 'I felt awful') to 5 = 'extensive distancing' (e.g. 'I'm having the thought that I made a mistake'). Teasdale *et al.* (2002) found that patients with residual depression[1] had significantly less metacognitive awareness than matched controls. Metacognitive awareness for depressing memories from the 5 months before the time of assessment predicted the time to relapse for these patients. Furthermore, where cognitive therapy or mindfulness-based cognitive therapy were effective in reducing relapse, these treatments also increased metacognitive awareness (Teasdale *et al.* 2002).

Other aspects of metacognitive regulation include the ability to monitor one's cognitive performance. Patients with OCD seem to be impaired in their ability to monitor their memory performance. There is robust evidence that patients with OCD are less confident in the accuracy of their memories than controls, despite unimpaired performance (Foa *et al.* 1997; Merckelbach and Wessel 2000; Sookman and Pinard 2002; Hermans *et al.* 2003). Such a lack of confidence in memory could both be caused by and also maintain the repeated checking observed in some patients with OCD (van den Hout and Kindt 2003) (for further details on confidence in memory see Chapter 3 on memory processes).

As well as impairments in memory performance, it has been mooted that patients with OCD may show a reality monitoring deficit (Ecker and Engelkamp 1995). That is, that they cannot determine whether a memory originated from perception or imagination (Anderson 1984). For further details on reality monitoring and source monitoring see Chapter 4. However, a number of studies have failed to find any deficit in reality monitoring for patients with OCD, regardless of whether neutral stimuli (McNally and Kohlbeck 1993; Merckelbach and Wessel 2000), anxiety-relevant stimuli (Constans *et al.* 1995) or stimuli related to personal concerns (Hermans *et al.* 2003) are presented.

---

[1]Residual depression refers to people who have been previously diagnosed with depression but no longer met diagnostic criteria although were still symptomatic.

Patients with schizophrenia have deficits in source monitoring and reality monitoring compared to non-patient controls, as described in Chapter 4 (Harvey 1985; Harvey *et al.* 1988; Vinogradov *et al.* 1997; Keefe *et al.* 1999).

Discussion

Definite transdiagnostic processes

As summarized in Table 5.1, there is accumulating evidence that most of the psychological disorders studied are characterized by positive and negative metacognitive beliefs. As such, the evidence for metacognitive beliefs meets our criteria for a definite transdiagnostic process. We note that metacognitive beliefs are not cognitive processes in the same way as attention, memory, or reasoning. However, given the potential importance of these beliefs in influencing cognition, we decided that these beliefs needed to be discussed. It is plausible that these beliefs contribute to the high levels of rumination, worry, and thought suppression already reported across most psychological disorders.

Note that in terms of metacognitive regulation, we have already seen how one metacognitive control strategy, recurrent thinking, is common across all disorders studied, and how another metacognitive control strategy, thought suppression, has been found in a number of disorders.

Distinct processes and inconclusive evidence

There is less evidence across the disorders concerning other aspects of metacognitive regulation, but different aspects of metacognitive regulation are impaired in at least three disorders: metacognitive awareness is impaired in patients with residual depression, memory confidence is impaired in patients with OCD and reality/source monitoring is impaired in patients with schizophrenia (see Table 5.1). Without further comparisons across different disorders, it is not possible to determine whether these impairments in metacognitive regulation are common or distinct across disorders. However, given that patients with schizophrenia show source monitoring and self-monitoring deficits that are not found in either patients with OCD or depression (Blakemore *et al.* 2000), it seems likely that deficits in source monitoring are not a transdiagnostic process and may be unique to psychotic disorders.

Does metacognition play a causal role?

As described earlier, both recurrent negative thinking and thought suppression have some prospective and experimental evidence indicating that they can causally influence symptoms. That is, the selection of metacognitive strategies appears to play a causal role in maintaining psychological disorders. However, there have been very few prospective or experimental studies of metacognitive beliefs and metacognitive regulation in psychological disorders.

Prospective studies

Anke Ehlers and her colleagues (1998) found that negative interpretations of intrusive thoughts (e.g. viewing intrusive thoughts as a sign of 'going mad') three months after a traumatic event was one important predictor of PTSD symptoms 1 year later. This suggests that negative metacognitive beliefs about intrusions may be one factor contributing to the development of PTSD.

Experimental studies

Few experiments have attempted to manipulate metacognitive beliefs in order to examine their role in the development or maintenance of symptoms. However, two studies have manipulated degree of thought-action fusion in non-patient volunteers and demonstrated an effect on anxiety and behaviour. First, Zucker et al. (2002) randomly allocated non-patient participants scoring high on the Thought-Action Fusion scale to either a psychoeducation condition explaining why thought-action fusion was wrong or to a placebo control. Then all participants were asked to write down, on a blank page, 'I hope that (the name of a loved one) is in a car accident'. There was a trend for participants in the psychoeducation condition to be less anxious ($p < 0.07$) in response to the writing task and they endorsed thought-action fusion beliefs significantly less compared to participants in the control condition. Second, Rassin et al. (1999) found that inducing thought-action fusion increased anxiety (for further details see Box 5.5).

The action-oriented manipulation (e.g. asking 'how am I deciding what to do next?'), employed by Watkins and Baracaia (2002), improved social problem solving in currently depressed patients (see page 209). This manipulation was derived from instructions designed to improve metacognitive monitoring during problem solving (Berardi-Coletta et al. 1995). The success of this manipulation in improving problem solving provides preliminary evidence that manipulating metacognitive regulation can influence clinically relevant outcomes.

Summary

Because the majority of studies of metacognitive beliefs are correlational, the causal role of metacognitive beliefs remains to be determined, although there is some tentative evidence suggesting that thought-action fusion influences anxiety. Furthermore, since dysfunctional metacognitive beliefs are found across nearly all the psychological disorders studied, we do not know whether metacognitive beliefs play a causal role in all disorders or are simply a consequence of psychopathology.

Clinical implications

Given that recurrent thinking and thought suppression are common across the disorders and that these processes directly influence symptoms, there is clearly a need for treatments that directly intervene to reverse these processes. This section will consider treatment possibilities arising from the literature we have reviewed, with particular reference to the case of Peter that was presented at the beginning of this chapter.

Recurrent thinking

Starting with rumination and worry, three interventions may be particularly effective for reducing negative recurrent thinking: (a) replacing cognitive avoidance with approach towards thoughts and feelings, providing an opportunity for habituation (Vaughan and Tarrier 1992; Reynolds and Tarrier 1996), (b) shifting processing to a more concrete, less abstract level, and (c) identifying and challenging the positive and negative metacognitive beliefs hypothesized to contribute to recurrent thinking. The experimental literature suggests several potential approaches for achieving the first two interventions (i.e. (a) and (b)). First, repeated exposure, whether *in vivo* or in the imagination, to the triggers of worry and rumination, whilst developing alternative responses, such as relaxation or problem solving, could be an effective intervention. Such an approach is consistent with the current treatment approach to GAD, where patients are first taught relaxation skills and, when some mastery has been achieved, to then monitor the early signs of worry and intervene with applied relaxation (Borkovec and Ruscio 2001; Borkovec *et al.* 2002).

Second, the use of detailed and vivid imagery (Hackmann 1997) is potentially a very powerful way to reduce both cognitive avoidance and make thinking more concrete and solution-focused. Nelson and Harvey (2002) demonstrated that thinking about an emotional topic in images reduced sleep onset latency in insomnia. Similarly, Taylor *et al.* (1998) demonstrated that mental simulations in imagery of how upsetting events happened improves mood and coping responses, and that imagining the process of solving a problem (how to do it) produced better solutions and more direct action, than not imagining it or imagining just the solution. These interventions have potential to break patients out of the poor problem-solving loop that maintains worry and rumination. During therapy with Peter, the therapist encouraged him to think in a more concrete manner by asking him to create images of stressful situations and images of how he would cope with those situations, concentrating on seeing vividly how he could calm himself down and what problem solving steps he would take.

The use of planned worry periods involves delaying worry until a pre-planned time (Borkovec *et al.* 1983). These can be helpful in containing rumination and helping patients establish a sense of control. Planned worry periods can help break a seemingly endless cycle of recurrent thinking. In addition, a patient can often discover from postponing worries until later in the day that (1) it is possible to control the worry and (2) later on the worry does not seem so important.

Although mostly conducted with analogue samples, the extensive literature on the benefits of expressive writing or talking (Pennebaker 1993, 1997) suggests that such approaches would be useful for facilitating emotional processing, and again, breaking the ruminative loop. Encouraging patients to disclose their thoughts and feelings, without any concern or attempt to achieve new insights or resolutions, would bypass some of the processes maintaining rumination, whilst allowing emotional processing. Such an approach is likely to be particularly relevant for patients who report intrusive memories. Interestingly, recent advances in the treatment of GAD have added an emotional-processing/interpersonal component to the standard cognitive therapy package, with the aim of ensuring that patients express their feelings and become grounded in their direct emotional experience (Borkovec *et al.* 2002; Newman *et al.* in press). Within this integrative therapy, the rationale presented to clients is that they may have overlearned the tendency to avoid painful feelings and that this tendency has negative consequences. The interpersonal/emotional-processing aspect of the therapy focuses on getting patients in touch with feared emotions, exposing their real selves to other people, and trying out new interpersonal behaviours. The therapist will continually bring the attention of the patient back to their feelings, their behaviour and their impact on others, including the therapist. For example, the therapist will encourage the patient to stay with a negative feeling, to explore and describe their feelings, allowing the feelings to deepen and be fully expressed. Preliminary findings suggest that this additional component may improve treatment outcome.

With Peter, it became clear that he always kept his feelings to himself and was concerned about sharing his worries with other people. An important component of therapy involved encouraging Peter to let people know about his concerns. This had the consequence that his relationships improved.

Further, by talking to a friend, Peter was often able to see that his concerns were exaggerated. Likewise, Peter found it helpful to stop trying to hide his feelings and pretend he was not anxious to other people. Being more assertive in of itself reduced a number of potential triggers for his worry.

An additional way to break patients out of the ruminative loop is to encourage a more concrete action-oriented mode of thinking, by encouraging the use of more process-focused, 'How?' type questions. Watkins and Baracaia (2002) demonstrated how such questions could improve problem solving in depressed patients to the level of never depressed controls. Coaching ruminative patients to identify their frequent 'Why-type' questions and to replace them with more functional 'How-type' questions, such as 'How do I get to a useful intention or a plan?' and 'What is most likely to get me what I want?' may be an effective intervention to improve problem solving and reduce rumination. Such an intervention parallels some of the teaching that occurs within problem solving therapy (Nezu *et al.* 1989; D'Zurill and Nezu 2001), although it is couched within the framework of teaching patients' to ask themselves Socratic questions. Obviously this approach is consistent with the cognitive therapy approach to challenging negative automatic thoughts. Going back to Peter, the therapist encouraged him to consider questions like: 'What was the worst thing that could happen?', 'How can I stop this happening?' and 'What can I do to cope with this event if it happened?'. For example, Peter was concerned about who would look after his sick brother when his parents died. He would repeatedly ask himself questions like 'What if I am left to look after my brother on my own?' 'Why can't I cope?' 'Why is everything always so difficult?'. However, once he began to ask himself 'how' questions, such as 'How can I prepare for looking after my brother?' 'How can I cope?' and 'How can I make things easier?', Peter quickly focused on practical steps that could be put in place to sort out finances and recruit the help of other family members, producing a substantial decrease in anxiety.

Finally, given that recurrent thinking has been conceptualized as a self-regulatory attempt to try to resolve unfulfilled goals (Pyszczynski and Greenberg 1987; Martin and Tesser 1989, 1996; Carver and Scheier 1990; Teasdale 1999), the goals that patients set for themselves may be an important factor in determining the extent of rumination. Goals that are poorly defined, too abstract, unrealistic, or in conflict with other goals are likely to lead to more recurrent thinking. Motivational counselling, which was described in Chapter 4, helps patients to ensure that their goals are more functional and so may be beneficial for reducing recurrent thinking.

Thought suppression

The current analysis of thought suppression suggests (a) that patients need to be educated that thought suppression may be counterproductive, (b) that particular forms of distraction will be effective at reducing negative intrusions, and (c) that reducing the use of suppression will reduce negative intrusions. Psychoeducation can take the form of an explicit discussion that thought suppression contributes to the maintenance of negative thoughts and moods. This point is perhaps most clearly made in a behavioural experiment. For example, within a session Peter and his therapist tried the white bear experiment, as already described in the clinical implications section of Chapter 3. This behavioural experiment clearly illustrated how thought suppression leads to further intrusions. The pros and cons of thought suppression were then discussed with Peter. Topics covered during the conversation include that suppression was very effortful and tiring, and that suppressing thoughts and emotions prevented people close to him from knowing how he felt.

Second, distraction from intrusive thoughts is likely to be more effective when patients are provided with a new positive distracter that is unrelated to their intrusive thoughts (Wegner *et al.* 1987, 1991; Wenzlaff *et al.* 1991). For example, Harvey and Payne (2002) found that patients with insomnia who engaged in imagery distraction while trying to fall asleep reported that their thinking while trying to get to sleep was less uncomfortable and that they fell asleep more quickly relative to a distraction group who were not given specific guidance as to how to distract and a no instruction group. This finding indicates the potential value of using a positive distracter, although it should be noted that this effect was demonstrated for one night only. It is possible that this kind of intervention may be best used as a one-off behavioural experiment for patients who believe that their thoughts are out of their control. By comparing the effects of suppression versus ceasing suppression and instead directing their attention to a new positive distracter, the belief that thoughts are uncontrollable can often be disconfirmed.

Third, the ironic process account (Wegner 1994*a*, *b*) suggests that the nature of the goals selected by patients may have an impact on suppression. Ironic process theory suggests that it is better to try and think of a positive thought (approach goal) than to try and not think of a negative thought (avoidance goal). Wenzlaff and Bates (2000) found that under conditions of cognitive load, trying to suppress unwanted thoughts led to the paradoxical increase of negative thoughts, whereas concentrating on alternative desirable thoughts did not. Thus, reframing an avoidance goal (to not think about failure) as an approach goal (to think about success) may be beneficial in reducing intrusions and subsequent rumination.

Metacognitive beliefs and strategies

With respect to metacognitive strategies and beliefs, more detailed assessment of these processes can benefit treatment formulation and planning. Recent approaches to depression (behavioural activation, Martell *et al.* 2001) and developments of metacognitive approaches (Wells 2000) emphasize the usefulness of detailed functional analysis of the antecedents, consequences, and possible functions of thought control strategies, such as rumination and thought suppression. Within the behavioural activation framework, depression is viewed as a set of actions in context, such that depression is a set of emotional, cognitive, physiological, and behavioural responses that have been learned. The effectiveness of behavioural activation for major depression has been found in a component analysis of CBT, with behavioural activation proving to be as effective as full cognitive therapy (Jacobson *et al.* 1996; Gortner *et al.* 1998). The behavioural activation approach emphasizes looking at the function and consequences of thoughts and behaviours rather than their form and content. Past experience is reviewed to see which environmental factors influence the likelihood of using each strategy, and how the strategy selected might contribute to maintaining their symptoms. Within this account, rumination and thought suppression would be viewed as coping styles serving an escape and avoidance function that have been reinforced in the past by the removal of aversive experience (Ferster 1973). Possible functions of rumination in depression may include avoiding the challenges of a job, avoiding risk of failure or humiliation, pre-empting other people's criticism, and controlling one's anger in order to reduce the risk of public punishment.

In a similar way, Wells (2000) discusses modifications to clinical assessment so as to gather more information about metacognitive strategies and beliefs. Such 'metacognitive profiling' extends the scope of the questions typically used in cognitive therapy in order to assess the antecedents, beliefs, and consequences relevant to metacognitive appraisals and beliefs, coping strategies, and other aspects of metacognitive regulation (e.g. focus of attention and memory). These questions focus on how people are using their cognitive processes ('What were you paying attention to?' 'How did you decide to attend to that?' 'How did you use your memory?') and their responses to each process ('Did you do anything in response to this?'). Further questions focus on the perceived advantages and disadvantages of each strategy or response ('What are the advantages of worrying?'). Further examples of these questions are provided in Table 7.3 in the next chapter. As with Socratic questioning in general, these questions can be used for both exploring and assessing a patient's metacognitive beliefs and strategies, but also can be used to shift thinking and challenge metacognitive beliefs.

The systematic use of these questions should allow the therapist to develop an idiosyncratic case formulation of both the explicit metacognitive beliefs and the implicit metacognitive procedural rules (how and when a patient uses certain strategies, focuses attention, or retrieves memories). This formulation will then help guide the planning of future treatment interventions and behavioural experiments to challenge the metacognitive beliefs or to develop more effective strategies.

For example, for rumination, a functional analysis may reveal that a patient has different patterns of behaviour (including focus of attention and style of thinking) during the times that thinking about a problem reaches a resolution compared to the times when the person gets stuck in a ruminative loop. Such a 'cognitive' functional analysis might suggest ways for a patient to change their behaviour so as to shift the patient out of rumination. With Peter, the functional analysis revealed that his tendency to worry served the function of preventing or pre-empting possible catastrophes. Peter held metacognitive beliefs such as 'If I'm not thinking about it constantly, I'm not taking it seriously enough', 'I have to worry to avoid danger', 'Worry makes me ready for danger', 'Worry predicts bad things', 'Worry helps me to solve problems'. These played an important role in serving to maintain Peter's worry. These meta-cognitive beliefs appeared to be fuelled by a core belief that 'Life is fragile—in an instant I could be rendered helpless'. The latter reflects Peter's experience of his brother's illness. To challenge these beliefs, an ongoing behavioural experiment was set up in which Peter kept a diary in which he recorded (1) when a worry was followed by predicted negative event, (2) when a worry was not followed by a negative event (incorrect prediction), and (3) when a negative event occurred about which he had not worried. Over a period of time, this diary keeping helped Peter to learn from his own experience that worry was neither an accurate nor an effective strategy. That is, it challenged his metacognitive belief that 'Worry predicts bad things'.

The functional analysis perspective further indicates that altering environ-mental contingencies and substituting alternative, more effective, approach behaviours for the avoidant strategies will be helpful. A particular strategy that is recommended for rumination is to attend fully to experience. Peter was instructed to focus and to be aware of all sensations (including colours, shapes, sounds, smells, and textures) during an activity, for example, whilst taking a walk. This approach is designed to increase direct contact with the environment and, thereby, break the ruminative loop.

Another recent treatment development that is particularly likely to be of relevance to recurrent negative thinking and metacognition is mindfulness-based CBT (described in Chapter 3). A related treatment approach, that stresses the importance of accepting thoughts and feelings is Acceptance and Commitment Therapy (ACT; Hayes 1987; Hayes *et al.* 1999*b*) (for further details see Chapter 6).

Future research

As evident in Table 5.1, many gaps in our knowledge base on thought processes across disorders remain. Thought processes have hardly been investigated at all in sexual disorders, bipolar disorder, panic disorder, and substance-related disorders. Further, the research needs to be extended to patient populations, particularly for depression and eating disorders. Importantly, there are gaps in the quality and nature of the studies in the disorders that have been investigated. Experimental manipulations of worry and rumination have concentrated on GAD and depression, and even these studies have tended to use analogue samples rather than patients. Examining the experimental effects of recurrent thinking in other disorders will be an important next step in testing the causal role of these processes across disorders. Studies of thought suppression need to take more account of methodological issues such as cognitive load and the nature of the distracter used during thought suppression. Furthermore, studies of thought suppression could profitably include more real-world settings (e.g. thought suppression over several days) and examine the effects of suppression on both disorder-relevant and disorder-irrelevant thoughts. Likewise, the majority of metacognitive studies involved self-report measures and only indicated a correlation between symptoms and metacognition. Experimental manipulations are needed to investigate the causal role of metacognitive knowledge. Experiments are crucial for taking the work on thought suppression and metacognitive beliefs forward, as these processes have been found to be characteristic of nearly all disorders. Without experimental manipulations we cannot rule out the possibility that these processes are measures of psychopathology or secondary to disorders, rather than causal factors.

A general issue for this chapter is a concern about the veracity of self-reported mental activity. Many of the measures of recurrent thinking and metacognitive beliefs depend upon self-report and as such are susceptible to demand biases. Hence, the recent studies adopting lexical decision tasks as an index of accessibility are a welcome development (e.g. Tolin *et al.* 2002). Furthermore, the act of reporting or monitoring thinking may itself influence the process of thinking. Equally, people may not be fully aware of the mechanisms underlying their cognitive processes, such that self-report may not be sensitive for exploring some aspects of cognition. For example, people are often not aware of the strategies they use to manage their thoughts. For all of these reasons, the development of cognitive-experimental paradigms to examine thought strategies is to be encouraged. For example, the experimental studies manipulating thought-action fusion provide a good benchmark for future designs to investigate the causal role of such beliefs.

Metacognitive regulation, with the exception of thought suppression and recurrent thinking, has barely been examined at all. If deficits in metacognitive regulation are a general risk factor for psychopathology, as recent theories imply (Wells 2000), then the impairments observed in depression should be found in other disorders.

We have also suggested that the mode of thinking could be a potentially important dimension across disorders, with less concrete styles of thinking common across those disorders characterized by recurrent worry or rumination. There is already evidence consistent with this hypothesis in GAD and depression. Logically, if this hypothesis is correct, patients with PTSD, insomnia, and social phobia should display a similar pattern.

At a more theoretical level, there is the question of how intrusions, rumination, and suppression interact. The literature reviewed earlier suggests that rumination may influence suppression by reducing cognitive resources. In contrast, Gold and Wegner (1995) proposed that rumination continues because of attempts to suppress intrusive thoughts (although note that Mathews and Milroy (1994) failed to find any effect of suppression on subsequent worry in high and low worriers).

Key points

1. The two thought processes that can be regarded as definite transdiagnostic processes are: (a) recurrent thinking and (b) positive and negative metacognitive beliefs.
2. Thought suppression meets our criteria for a possible transdiagnostic process.
3. There is currently inconclusive evidence for determining whether other aspects of metacognitive regulation, such as metacognitive awareness, are common or distinct processes across disorders.
4. Deficits in source monitoring are found in schizophrenia but not in depression or OCD, making this a possible distinct process.
5. Recurrent thinking tends to reflect the current concerns of each disorder.
6. Both prospective and experimental studies indicate a causal role for recurrent thinking and thought suppression in maintaining symptoms.

7. A range of strategies is available to tackle these thought processes including: education about the adverse consequences of thought suppression, training in use of distracters, replacing avoidant strategies with approach strategies, imagery work, focusing on concrete levels of thinking, emotional expression, attentional training, and metacognitive profiling.

8. Future research needs to examine the causal role of metacognitive beliefs and metacognitive regulation in psychological disorders.

Chapter 6

Behaviour

Susan arrives at her assessment appointment with an oversized handbag. Along with the typical contents of a handbag (purse, keys, and mobile telephone), it contains multiple packets of chewing gum, mints, anti-nausea tablets, and a necklace in a plastic bag. She carries these additional items because she believes they prevent her from vomiting. Susan is terrified of vomiting. Paradoxically, she has not vomited for 40 years (a long time by anyone's standards!) yet she worries that she is highly likely to vomit. In fact, she feels that she is more likely to vomit than other people partly because she has not vomited for so many years. She feels that it must be her 'turn' to become ill at any moment after so long without being sick. In response to her concern about vomiting, she takes measures to protect herself. These measures include:

- *avoiding any situations that might actually make her ill (e.g. visiting the doctor's surgery);*
- *avoiding caring for her children when they have a stomach bug;*
- *avoiding foods that could potentially give her an upset stomach which means she ate a very narrow range of foods such as toast and pasta (Susan is significantly underweight);*
- *avoiding drinking alcohol;*
- *avoiding people who have drunk alcohol since they could vomit and she is concerned that simply looking at vomit will make her feel nauseous and induce vomiting;*
- *leaving a party if anyone is drunk;*
- *avoiding areas of town where there may be homeless people since she believes they are more likely to vomit or else there may be vomit on the ground in these areas;*

In addition to avoiding situations that could induce vomiting, she also takes active measures to prevent vomiting. These include:

- *taking an anti-nausea tablet each morning;*
- *monitoring how nauseous she feels and taking another tablet if she thinks that she feels quite sick;*
- *carrying anti-nausea tablets in her handbag;*
- *sucking mints and chewing gum constantly (much to the annoyance of her husband);*
- *touching a religious symbol on the necklace she carries in her handbag and saying a quick prayer to God to stop her from being sick.*

Since she has not been sick for such a long time, she is convinced that these measures are effective and work to prevent vomiting. She strongly believes that if she 'slipped up' and did not take these measures, she would vomit.

The core tenet of cognitive behaviour theory and therapy is that cognition, emotion, and behaviour are inter-linked and that each of these processes influences the other (Padesky and Greenberger 1995; Clark and Fairburn 1997). In particular, the cognitive processes described in the previous chapters serve to maintain dysfunctional behaviour and, in turn, such behaviour maintains cognitive processes. Consider selective attention to threat (Chapter 2).

If a threat is detected, a patient is likely to experience high levels of anxiety. Anxiety is aversive and could itself be interpreted as a sign of impending danger (emotional reasoning; see Chapter 5) so it is understandable that the patient leaves the situation, avoids it in future and believes it is dangerous. Paradoxically, such avoidance may serve to maintain unhelpful beliefs about the extreme danger of the situation as it removes an opportunity for the belief to be disconfirmed. Also, in Chapter 2 we reviewed evidence that patients who suffer from some psychological disorders attend *away* from threats (Chen *et al.* 2002; Loughland *et al.* 2002). In Chapter 3 we reviewed evidence that people with certain psychological disorders may avoid encoding or recalling certain information that is particularly distressing, leading their memory to be fragmented and poorly integrated. In Chapter 5 we outlined that recurrent thinking and thought suppression can both function to avoid thoughts about disturbing emotional material.

The aim of this chapter is to review the literature on behavioural processes and to draw conclusions about the extent to which they are transdiagnostic processes. The three behavioural processes selected for consideration are escape/avoidance, within-situation safety behaviours, and ineffective safety-signals, as the majority of specific behaviours (such as checking the stove is off in certain patients with OCD can be considered within these categories. Before going any further we will pause to define the three behavioural processes of interest in this chapter.

Escape and avoidance are the first behaviours addressed in this chapter and refer to situations in which an individual does not enter, or prematurely leaves, a fear-evoking situation. Escape and avoidance behaviours are clearly noticeable and clinically important. In fact, they are often identified as a diagnostic feature of certain disorders, including specific phobia, social phobia, and post-traumatic stress disorder (PTSD).

Secondly, the chapter addresses 'within-situation safety-seeking behaviour' or, more commonly, *safety behaviour*. Such behaviour is defined as overt or covert avoidance of feared outcomes that is carried out within a specific situation (Salkovskis 1991; Wells 1997). Note that in this chapter, for simplicity, we will mostly use the term 'safety behaviour' when refering to within-situation safety-seeking behaviour. As we will see, safety behaviours are a key feature of many disorder-focused models, including social phobia, panic disorder, OCD, and insomnia. It is worth noting at the outset that some safety behaviours are highly functional when there is a real concern and the behaviour can reduce the danger (e.g. looking before you cross the road). However, if the concern is based on a perceived threat, as opposed to an actual threat, then safety behaviours can at best be irrelevant and at worst exacerbate the person's concerns (e.g. Salkovskis 1991). In the clinical case presented above, Susan used a wide range of safety behaviours, such as carrying and consuming anti-nausea tablets and sucking mints and gum to prevent a feared outcome. Susan's feared outcome was vomiting. The safety behaviour not only caused Susan to be underweight and prevented her consulting a doctor, but they also served to perpetuate Susan's specific phobia of vomiting for a number of reasons. First, Susan believed that if she did not take such precautions then she would certainly vomit. That is, she over-estimated the risk of vomiting and by using her safety behaviours she did not get an opportunity to realize that she is overestimating the risk. Second, Susan regularly reminded herself of the list of precautions she needs to take. This safety behaviour served to fuel thoughts about vomiting which meant that Susan was constantly pre-occupied with thoughts of vomiting. Third, the safety behaviours adopted by Susan maintained her belief that vomiting is imminent and dreadful.

The third behavioural process that may contribute to the maintenance of psychological disorders is the ineffective use of safety-signals, a topic which has been addressed by a small body of research (e.g. Rachman 1984). A safety-signal is defined as a behaviour or strategy that enhances a patient's sense of safety and enables the patient to partake in activities that, without the safety signal, would have been avoided.

Now that we have briefly introduced the three behavioural processes that will be discussed in this chapter, we will move on to give a theoretical context for each of them in turn.

Escape and avoidance

People can either avoid situations before they enter them or they can 'escape' and leave situations after they have been entered. Several reasons have been suggested for why such avoidance behaviour might be problematic. First, such behaviour removes the opportunity to disconfirm negative beliefs (Salkovskis 1991). Second, it denies the person the chance for positive reinforcement and could thereby contribute to the maintenance of low mood (Ferster 1973; Lewinsohn 1975; Martell *et al.* 2001). Third, it narrows the person's interests and reduces the number of external stimuli present in the environment. Such a reduction in external stimulation may exacerbate self-focused attention (see Chapter 2) and recurrent thinking (see Chapter 5). Fourth, the habituation model of anxiety (e.g. Lader and Wing 1966) implies that decreases in anxiety will only occur after prolonged exposure and relatively brief exposure periods may actually serve to 'sensitize' patients to their feared stimuli and prove detrimental (e.g. Wilson and O'Leary 1980; Marshall 1985, 1988). Needless to say, avoidance prevents prolonged exposure by definition. An alternative model of anxiety suggests that preventing avoidance behaviour increases a sense of self-control that, in turn, promotes a reduction in anxiety (Barlow 1988). It follows that avoidance prevents the reduction in anxiety. Fifth, according to learning theory (e.g. Mowrer 1960), avoidance is negatively reinforced and can become self-perpetuating. For example, Susan has not vomited for many years which sustains her avoidance of situations that could induce vomiting. Finally and most directly, avoidance behaviour is intrinsically problematic insofar as it interferes with functioning. In Susan's case, her social life was severely restricted as she was only comfortable attending parties where she could be sure that people were not going to drink alcohol—these were few and far between!

Clinical implications of avoidance behaviour

In the clinical practice of behaviour therapy, avoidance of fear-evoking situations is gradually eliminated. The rationale for this originated from Mowrer's two-stage model of fear and avoidance (1939, 1960). According to this theory, avoidance behaviour is reinforced when it is followed by a reduction in anxiety. In essence, the avoidance persists because it works; it reduces anxiety. To reduce the undesirable avoidance behaviour, the patient is instructed to remain in the fear-evoking situation until their anxiety has decreased. Indirect support for this model comes from the plethora of studies indicating that exposure is an efficacious intervention for the treatment of a range of anxiety disorders, including specific phobias, OCD, and PTSD (see Nathan and Gorman 2002 for a review). Direct empirical support for this model comes from a study using patients with height phobia (Marshall 1985). The key result of interest was that exposure was inferior if it was terminated while the participant was in a state of high anxiety, relative to when participants only left the situation when their fear levels had declined. The explanation given for this finding was that prolonged exposure is necessary to allow cognitive reappraisals of the feared situations, and that these cognitive reappraisals are most likely to occur when the person is in a state of high anxiety.

In contrast to the results of Marshall's (1985) study, two separate but small-scale studies did not detect differences between a group of participants who had standard exposure (without any avoidance of the feared situation) and those who were permitted to escape the situation (de Silva and Rachman 1984; Rachman et al. 1986). The participants in these studies were patients diagnosed with agoraphobia. The first study compared six patients treated in the usual way ('Endurance condition') with six patients allowed to escape

('Escape') and six control patients who were not treated (de Silva and Rachman 1984). Patients who were required to escape when their anxiety reached a pre-determined high level did not show increased avoidance behaviour. This result contradicted behavioural theory and therapy and warranted replication. Hence, the second study was carried out on 14 patients and the findings were largely replicated (Rachman *et al.* 1986). It should be noted, however, that a limitation of these studies is that they may have been under-powered to detect group differences. Further, there were relatively few trials in which the participants 'escaped' compared to when they did not 'escape'.

Distraction as a form of avoidance

Distraction can be seen as a subtle form of avoidance because it involves directing attention away from feared stimuli. For this reason it was briefly covered in Chapter 2. While distraction is suggested to facilitate short-term reductions in anxiety by limiting the salience of feared stimuli, it is hypothesized to impede the long-term maintenance of anxiety reduction (Rodriguez and Craske 1993). In a review of the evidence for this hypothesis, Foa and Kozak (1986) concluded that the empirical status of the hypothesis was 'unclear' with contradictory findings being reported across a range of methodologies. For example, using a within-subjects design and 16 patients diagnosed with OCD, those patients who distracted themselves during exposure by playing video-games (the therapist was allowed to play as well!) had higher levels of fear at the start of a subsequent session than those who had focused on the stimulus and on their anxiety (Grayson *et al.* 1982). In a subsequent study that aimed to replicate and extend this finding using a between-subjects design, there was no differential impact of attention focusing (exposure) versus distraction between sessions, although heart-rate response reduced more in the attention-focusing condition but subjective anxiety reduced more during the first exposure session in the distraction condition (Grayson *et al.* 1986).

In a study of 30 patients with panic disorder and moderate to severe agoraphobia, there were no differences between those patients who focused on their somatic sensations and those who engaged in distracting tasks. This was true in the short-term and six months following the completion of treatment (Craske *et al.* 1989). That is, the findings seem to suggest that there is no therapeutic disadvantage to distracting during exposure. The latter results are consistent with the cognitive hypothesis, which we will discuss in a moment, which suggests that whether or not a behaviour is dysfunctional depends on its impact on beliefs, rather than the behaviour per se (Salkovskis 1991). According to the cognitive hypothesis, there would only be a deleterious impact of distraction during exposure if the person is unable to disconfirm the belief (e.g. Salkovskis 1991).

Within-situation safety-seeking behaviour

Simple escape and avoidance behaviour, as discussed above, is easily observable. However, more subtle forms of avoidance soon became apparent. Skilled clinicians noticed that during exposure sessions in the course of behaviour therapy, some patients were using 'response aids' (Bandura *et al.* 1974). It was suggested that response aids should be removed in order for exposure to have the desired effect. The use of 'response aids' or, as they have come to be known, 'safety behaviours' (Salkovskis 1991) explains the apparent paradox that people with emotional disorders have repeated experiences indicating that their fear is not warranted yet they fail to learn from these experiences (Clark 1999).

The cognitive hypothesis

Paul Salkovskis was among the first to articulate the question: 'Why does the panic patient who believes that she will faint still believe this after approximately 2000 attacks where fainting did not occur?' (Salkovskis 1991). As already highlighted, safety behaviours are acts that are carried out within a situation to try to avert a feared outcome. The answer to the question posed by Paul Salkovskis, according to the cognitive hypothesis, is that safety behaviours prevent disconfirmation of fears. They also change potential disconfirmations into 'near misses' (Salkovskis 1991,1999; Lovibond 2001). The patient with panic disorder may think 'I nearly fainted again! I only escaped fainting because I sat down just in time'. Furthermore, it has been suggested that some safety behaviours not only prevent exposure to disconfirmatory experiences but ironically exacerbate symptoms and increase concerns (Clark 1997). To go back to the example given in Chapter 1, a typical example of a safety behaviour is when a person with social phobia grips a glass tightly to prevent it from dropping. Paradoxically, holding the glass so tightly may increase the chance of dropping it (Clark and Wells 1995). Like avoidance, safety behaviours can also be intrinsically dysfunctional due to the amount of time that the behaviour takes to perform and the interference in cognitive, social, and work functioning. For some disorders, in particular OCD and eating disorders, some of the key behavioural features of the disorder could be considered a safety behaviour (e.g. compulsions, dieting).

The safety-signal hypothesis

The notion that people with psychological difficulties, in particular anxiety, seek safety is certainly not new. Mowrer's original (1939) theory of fear and avoidance had two stages. The first stage was the acquistion of fear via classical conditioning of a fear response to previously neutral stimuli. The second stage was the emergence of avoidance behaviour. The theory was revised (Mowrer 1960) in light of the recognition of the exaggerated emphasis placed on fear as a motivating factor in human behaviour and the need for symmetry in the theory (Rachman 1976a). To address both of these difficulties, Mowrer distinguished between danger-signals and safety-signals, arguing that conditioned stimuli associated with painful experiences could take on 'danger' signals and that conditioned stimuli associated with pleasant experiences could take on 'safety' signals; both danger and safety-signals were suggested to have motivating qualities (Mowrer 1960). Gray's (1971) influential theory incorporated the notion of safety-signals, as did Seligman and Johnston (1973) in their 'cognitive theory of avoidance learning'. The safety-signal hypothesis was expanded upon by Rachman in his analysis of agoraphobia (Rachman 1984). The suggestion was that fear generates escape and avoidance behaviour (as described above) and a search for safety; 'Reduced to simple language, the agoraphobic person balances the danger threatening him against the prevailing safety precautions and the accessibility of assistance' (p. 63, Rachman 1984). People or situations that indicate the presence of safety become highly influential and fear is seen as a result of the balance between signals of threat and signals of safety (Seligman and Binik 1977).

At the time a clear advantage of this account was that it helped to explain several aspects of agoraphobic avoidance which had previously been puzzling (Rachman 1984). In particular, it helped explain why avoidance behaviour persisted in the absence of fear. According to the safety-signal hypothesis, avoidance behaviour can persist regardless of fear once safety-signals have become established. Fluctuations in the fears can also be explained by this account since a person's sense of safety is so variable. This perspective also helps explain the clinical observations that patients seem to search for safety and that agoraphobia can be precipitated following bereavement or loss. For example, the loss of a loved one may threaten one's sense of safety, particularly in people who are anxious and dependent on the loved one. This threat to safety may alter the balance between perceived danger and perceived safety, and may trigger the onset of difficulties (Rachman 1984).

It is noteworthy that some of these features, in particular the persistence of avoidance and the theme of a search for safety, are also explained by the cognitive hypothesis. For example, losing a loved one may trigger the cognition 'If something bad happens to me, there'll be nobody to help', which could increase a person's fear of going outside.

Nevertheless, the safety-signal hypothesis provides an alternative to the cognitive hypothesis that views safety behaviours as typically dysfunctional because they prevent disconfirmation of beliefs. According to the safety-signal hypothesis, feared stimuli *should* be paired with safety cues to facilitate exposure and reduce avoidance. Specifically, it was suggested that 'any procedures which improve the agoraphobic's general sense of safety and security are likely to bring about an amelioration of the agoraphobic problem' (p. 68, Rachman 1984). We will return to these contrasting hypotheses in more detail later in the chapter.

Current concerns

Why is it that some stimuli are avoided at certain times and under particular circumstances and other stimuli (which are objectively more aversive) are not? In Susan's case, she did not avoid people with illnesses that were not connected to vomiting. Further, people with OCD, particularly children, are likely to experience multiple obsessions and compulsions that change over the course of time (Rettew *et al.* 1992). As discussed in previous chapters, Klinger's current concerns theory (1996) may help to explain which stimuli are avoided in each situation. This is a point we will return to at the end of the chapter.

Avoidance and within-situation safety-seeking behaviour across disorders

Having introduced the key concepts and provided some theoretical background, we will now move on to the disorder-by-disorder review with the aim of establishing the extent to which the behavioural processes introduced above are transdiagnostic. In keeping with the transdiagnostic perspective of the book, the chapter will discuss these behavioural processes across all of the psychological disorders, but there is a necessary focus on anxiety disorders since this is where the majority of theoretical and empirical work has been conducted. One final issue to note is that randomized controlled trials only provide indirect evidence for processes that maintain psychological disorders (Salkovskis 2002). Hence, in the review that follows we will not consider evidence from treatment research unless one of the behavioural processes of interest in this chapter was the main variable manipulated in the treatment (e.g. Morgan and Raffle 1999).

Anxiety disorders

Panic disorder with or without agoraphobia

Part of the diagnostic criteria for panic disorder and agoraphobia is avoidance of situations that might trigger panic attacks and from which escape would be difficult in the event of a panic attack, such as crowded shopping centres, restaurants, and cinemas (American Psychiatric Association 1994, 2001). Support for the cognitive hypothesis regarding safety behaviours is provided by a study of 147 patients with panic disorder (Salkovskis *et al.* 1996). The Chambless Agoraphobic Cognitions Questionnaire (Chambless *et al.* 1984) was administered as an index of specific cognitions. In addition, the Safety-Seeking Behaviours Scale was administered to index the use of safety behaviours. The latter involved asking participants to rate the frequency of a set of behaviours 'when you are at your most anxious or panicky'. Examples of the behaviours include 'hold an object', 'hold a person', 'sit down', 'keep still', 'do more exercise', 'focus', 'control behaviour', 'move slowly', 'look for an escape route' and 'ask for help'. The results confirmed 75 out of the 80 predicted associations between particular cognitions and the resultant safety behaviours. For example, cognitions about fainting were associated with holding onto objects and people; cognitions about having a brain tumour were associated with focusing attention on the body; and cognitions about choking to death were associated with asking for help and focusing attention on the body. The pattern of associations observed provided evidence that the patients were taking logical action to avert their feared outcomes and the safety-seeking behaviour adopted was meaningfully related to the threats perceived by the patients. These links were interpreted as consistent with the cognitive hypothesis that safety-seeking behaviour may maintain anxiety because it prevents disconfirmation of feared catastrophes.

A dramatic example of the role safety behaviour in the maintenance of panic disorder with agoraphobia has been provided by Salkovskis and colleagues (1999). In this innovative experimental study (see Box 6.1 for further details) eighteen people with severe panic disorder with agoraphobia were instructed to either drop their safety-seeking behaviour during a 15-min exposure session or else maintain their safety-seeking behaviour. The nine participants who dropped their safety-seeking behaviour showed significant improvement on a variety of measures relative to those who did not drop their safety behaviour (Salkovskis *et al.* 1999). These results are particularly striking considering the small sample size and the brief duration of the single exposure session.

There has also been support for the safety-signal hypothesis in an influential study that examined the effect of having a safe person present during a session in which anxiety was artificially induced following a biological challenge (a 5.5% CO_2-inhalation procedure) (Carter *et al.* 1995). The key manipulation was that participants with panic disorder underwent the inhalation procedure in the presence or absence of a safe person. The group who did not have a safe person present experienced more distress, more catastrophic

Box 6.1 An experimental investigation of safety behaviours

Salkovskis *et al.* (1999)

Aim: To test the hypothesis that safety behaviours maintain anxiety because they prevent patients from benefiting from disconfirmatory experience.

Participants: Eighteen participants with panic disorder and moderate or severe avoidance.

Procedure: At the initial assessment, all participants (1) completed questionnaires indexing their anxiety and their belief in certain catastrophic cognitions and (2) completed a 'behavioural walk' that involved walking through a shopping centre and catching a bus, to see how much of it they could complete. Participants were then randomly allocated to one of two groups. One group was given 15 minutes of exposure with instructions to drop their safety behaviours. The other group was given 15 minutes of exposure but without the instruction to drop their safety behaviours. In a second session, held within the following two days, participants repeated the initial assessment measures for a second time.

Result: The participants who were instructed to drop their safety behaviours rated their anxiety and belief in the catastrophic cognitions to be lower relative to those participants who maintained their safety behaviours. The improvement was also evident on the behavioural walk.

Conclusion: The results are consistent with the hypothesis that safety behaviours play an important role in maintaining negative beliefs and anxiety in panic disorder. Furthermore, the results are consistent with the hypothesis that some of the effectiveness of exposure may be due to the disconfirmation of threat beliefs, and that the process of belief change can be facilitated by adopting a specific focus on helping patients to reduce behaviours which maintain such beliefs.

cognitions and more physiological arousal than the group of people with panic disorder who had their safe person present. The cognitive hypothesis does not dispute that such a safety behaviour would reduce anxiety and the findings are therefore consistent with both the cognitive hypothesis and the safety-signal hypothesis. However, according to the cognitive hypothesis, in the longer-term, the presence of a 'safe' person would constitute a safety behaviour that should be eliminated for lasting recovery.

The role of a 'safe other' during therapy has also been investigated in a small study of nineteen patients with agoraphobia (Sartory *et al.* 1989). Nine of these patients were treated utilizing a safety-signal technique in which they were told that they had to approach a particular target on their own but would be met by the therapist at the point at which they had previously turned back to escape the situation. For example, patients had to approach the supermarket by themselves but were met by the therapist inside. This was compared to conventional therapist-assisted exposure in which patients carried out four agreed tasks on their own. The latter group were given instructions to complete a form indicating which of the four tasks they had carried out, how long they had stayed in the feared situation, and to rate their fear. This form was discussed in the subsequent therapy session and further exposure assignments agreed. The results indicated that the safety-signal technique resulted in a small advantage over therapist-assisted exposure on some measures, although the improvements in both groups were small. Also, there are alternative explanations of the results; perhaps the safety-signal technique was more graded and therefore led to smaller increases in anxiety during treatment and perhaps patients may have been more willing to adopt this approach.

Specific phobia

Avoidance of feared situations is part of the definition of specific phobia (American Psychiatric Association 1994, 2001) and the majority of people with specific phobia attempt to escape from any situation in which they find themselves confronted with their feared stimulus. The treatment of choice for specific phobia is exposure-based procedures, particularly *in vivo* exposure, during which escape and avoidance are reduced (Barlow *et al.* 2002). This is a highly effective treatment with over 75% of patients improving in one session (e.g. Öst *et al.* 1997).

To date, only one study has examined the effect of using safety behaviour in individuals with specific phobia (Sloan and Telch 2002). In this study, 46 students with claustrophobia were randomly assigned to one of three 30 min exposure conditions. These were:

1. Guided threat focus and reappraisal of the 'core threat': participants were asked to focus on their perceived threat and look for evidence that would weaken their belief in the threat.

2. Safety behaviour utilization: participants were given the option of utilizing safety strategies such as opening a small window, standing near the exit, ensuring the door was unlocked, and talking to the experimenter.

3. Exposure control: participants were not given instructions to focus and reappraise their threat and were not provided access to the safety strategies.

The participants who utilized safety behaviours during exposure (Condition 2) had a worse outcome than those who did not, a finding that is consistent with the cognitive hypothesis and is not compatible with the safety-signal perspective. However, an earlier study produced findings that were consistent with the safety-signal hypothesis (Telch *et al.* 1994). In this study, it was predicted that perceiving that safety resources are available will reduce anxiety and the overprediction and underprediction of fear (see Chapter 4). Thirty-seven people with claustrophobia completed a claustrophobic challenge under conditions of either low or high proximity to safety (the exit). Proximity to safety was operationalized as distance from the exit. Consistent with the prediction, the availability of safety reduced the level of fear experienced. These results were considered to support the hypothesis that people with claustrophobia do not use safety information sufficiently when confronting perceived threats.

As noted in the introduction, not all safety behaviours are necessarily dysfunctional. Indeed, whether or not safety behaviours are dysfunctional depends upon whether the fear is realistic and whether the safety-signal is of genuine value. Another point to note in relation to specific phobia is that people with blood-injury-injection phobia have a physiological reaction that leads to fainting (page 1994). During exposure treatment, patients are given a 'coping strategy' called applied tension, which temporarily sustains an increase in blood pressure and heart rate. Applied tension requires patients to alternately tense and relax all the large muscle groups of the body for 15 s before and during exposure to their feared stimulus. This method has been described in detail and appears to be efficacious (Öst and Sterner 1987). The potential importance of coping strategies in resolving theoretical debate in this area will be discussed later in this chapter.

Social phobia

The diagnostic criteria for social phobia involve the avoidance of feared social situations (American Psychiatric Association 1994, 2001). Further, of all the psychological disorders, safety behaviours in social phobia have perhaps received the most attention. This is partly due to the fact that they form an integral part of the Clark and Wells (1995) cognitive model of social phobia, as highlighted in Chapter 1. Examples of safety behaviours employed by patients with social phobia include gripping objects tightly to avoid hand shaking, avoiding eye contact, monitoring one's speech, and mentally rehearsing sentences (Wells 1997). It is not difficult to imagine how such behaviours unintentionally increase the chance of the person experiencing poor social interactions and being evaluated negatively. Indeed, in a well-designed analogue study of socially anxious students, more negative responses from other people were elicited when safety behaviours were used than when no such safety behaviours were performed (Alden and Bieling 1998). Such negative responses are likely to serve to confirm the patient's belief that they are disliked and are poor at socializing.

There is accruing evidence for the importance of addressing safety behaviours in the treatment of social phobia. The first study was a case series including eight people with social phobia (Wells *et al.* 1995). In this study, a single session of exposure treatment plus instructions to drop safety behaviours (with an appropriate rationale for this) was found to be more effective than exposure treatment (with an exposure rationale) without a change in safety behaviours. Second, in a small randomized controlled trial, thirty people with social phobia were randomly assigned to standard group cognitive behaviour therapy (CBT; 'usual') or standard group CBT treatment plus instructions to drop safety behaviours ('safety' group; Morgan and Raffle 1999). The treatment lasted for 3 weeks and there was a total of 10 days (80 h) of therapy. Both groups improved but there was a significantly greater change for symptoms of social phobia for the 'safety' group (as measured by the Social Phobia and Anxiety Inventory; Turner *et al.* 1989). Despite these encouraging findings, it should be noted that at the post-treatment assessment the reported use of safety behaviours in the 'safety' group did not reduce, relative to the 'usual' group. That is, the participants in the 'safety' group indicated that while they had dropped some safety behaviours, they held onto others. Although the extent to which this study provides support for the cognitive hypothesis has been debated (Battersby 2000; Morgan 2000), the results suggest that whilst the elimination of safety behaviour is an important component of cognitive therapy for social phobia, it may be difficult to achieve.

Obsessive-compulsive disorder

Compulsions are described as behaviours or mental acts that aim to prevent a dreaded event or situation, but are not connected in a realistic way with whatever they are designed to prevent (or else are clearly excessive) (American Psychiatric Association 1994, 2001). Hence, compulsions could be considered to be a safety behaviour. Examples of compulsions include checking, mental neutralizing, and washing. The early behavioural theories of OCD considered compulsions to be functionally similar to avoidance (Rachman and Hodgson 1980) and it was clear from the start that 'response prevention' during exposure was necessary. Exposure with response prevention is an efficacious treatment (see Franklyn and Foa 2002) and early experimental data showed that compulsions were pivotal to the maintenance of obsessional complaints (Rachman and Hodgson 1980). For example, when patients were exposed to their contamination concerns their anxiety immediately increased but gradually decreased when the compulsions were prevented. The next time the patient was exposed to the contaminated stimulus, their anxiety was slightly lower than the first time, and their anxiety decreased more quickly without performing a compulsion. This kind of result provided support for the view that eliminating compulsions was essential to the elimination of obsessional fears.

Mental neutralizing in OCD can be seen as a safety behaviour designed to 'put matters right' (Rachman 1976b) or else to reduce perceived responsibility for harm (Salkovskis 1985). Examples of mental neutralizing include saying a particular phrase repeatedly in one's head or trying to obtain a particular 'corrective' mental image. In a recent empirical study, de Silva and his colleagues showed that mental neutralizing was functionally similar to overt compulsions in that anxiety increased when the person was exposed to the obsession and it decreased dramatically with mental neutralizing (de Silva *et al.* 2003). Anxiety decreased without mental neutralizing but more slowly. These findings are consistent with mental neutralizing being a covert safety behaviour and compulsions being an overt safety behaviour. However, it must be acknowledged that there may be no clinical or theoretical advantage to viewing compulsions as safety behaviours.

Post-traumatic stress disorder and acute stress disorder

As recovery from PTSD is thought to rely on the activation and modification of all elements of the trauma memory (Foa *et al.* 1989; Litz and Keane 1989), avoidance is conceptualized as core to the maintenance of PTSD. Consistently, several studies have indicated that cognitive and behavioural avoidance is predictive of chronic PTSD (e.g. Bryant and Harvey 1995a; Ehlers et al. 1998; Dunmore *et al.* 2001).

More recent concepualizations of PTSD specify an important role for safety behaviour. Specifically, Ehlers and Clark (2000) propose that chronic PTSD is caused when a trauma survivor perceives the trauma to be currently threatening. This state of 'current threat' is proposed to be the result of negative appraisals of the trauma that remain unchanged, in part, because of the use of safety behaviours. For example, a person with PTSD might think about, and discuss, the traumatic event in a completely affect-less manner, a bit like they are giving an objective news report on the incident. They may also remove from the account any particularly upsetting and anxiety-provoking aspects of the trauma (Ehlers and Clark 2000). This safety behaviour is employed in an attempt to minimize the emotional impact of the traumatic event but is a safety behaviour because (1) it will impair the processing of the trauma and (2) may result in upsetting thoughts relating to the trauma occurring more frequently (Ehlers and Clark 2000). A full empirical investigation of the role of safety behaviour, in the context of PTSD, has yet to be conducted.

Generalized anxiety disorder

As discussed in Chapter 5 it has been hypothesized that pathological worry is a form of cognitive avoidance, designed to reduce the activation of strong affect by focusing on abstract, verbal concerns (e.g. Borkovec *et al.* 1998). In another theoretical account, Woody and Rachman (1994) have suggested that like agoraphobia, GAD is a balance between safety-signals and threatening signals. According to this account, people with GAD have insufficient and/or ineffective safety-signals. The finding that people with GAD persist in attending to threatening stimuli whereas people with other psychological disorders selectively avoid this material (see Chapter 2), can perhaps be viewed as consistent with this hypothesis. Nonetheless, relatively little work has specifically been conducted examining the behavioural processes in GAD.

Somatoform disorders

Pain disorder

Avoidance of daily activities, so as not to 're-injure' or 'exacerbate' pain, has long been implicated in the maintenance of chronic pain (e.g. Philips 1987; Rose *et al.* 1992). For example, Follick *et al.* (1985) found that patients with chronic low back pain spend approximately 30% of their waking time lying down. In a review of the evidence, Philips (1987) concluded that 'the avoidance is extensive and complex, and includes avoidance of stimulation, movement, activity, social interaction, and leisure pursuits' (p. 273). Further, there is evidence that avoidance leads to increased sensitivity to pain (Philips and Jahanshahi 1985). More recently, research by Vlaeyen and colleagues has gathered evidence that fear of experiencing pain prompts avoidance of daily activities which, in turn, maintains fear of pain. Evidence in support has been reported in a single-case cross-over design in which graded activity was compared to usual activity (Vlaeyen *et al.* 2001). Graded activity was associated with a reduction in fear of pain, catastrophizing about pain and in pain disability, relative to usual activity. Although Sharp (2001*b*) has drawn attention to the likely relevance of safety behaviours to chronic pain sufferers this proposal has yet to receive systematic investigation.

Hypochondriasis

The primary safety behaviours in hypochondriasis (or health anxiety) are avoidance, reassurance seeking, and body checking (Salkovskis 1989; Warwick and Salkovskis 1990). Patients repeatedly go to medical practitioners and seek reassurance that they are not unwell. Such people often avoid any situations that could activate their health concerns, and they frequently take precautionary measures (such as controlling their breathing) which increases the focus on the body and may intensify symptoms (e.g. through hyperventilation). Again, a detailed investigation of a role for safety behaviours in hypochondriasis is yet to be conducted.

Body dysmorphic disorder

In addition to avoiding social situations, there is evidence that patients with BDD conduct many of their safety behaviours in front of the mirror. In the comparison of patients diagnosed with BDD and a non-patient control group described in Chapter 2, a self-report mirror gazing questionnaire was used to elicit beliefs as well as behaviours conducted in front of a mirror. In addition to examining self-focused attention, it was concluded that mirror gazing in BDD consists of a series of complex safety behaviours that are likely to contribute to the maintenance of the disorder (Veale and Riley 2001). For example, people with BDD may wear excessive make-up to hide their perceived deficits. Such behaviour elicits attention from other people which can be interpreted as evidence that people are staring because of the perceived defect in their appearance, thus confirming their beliefs. For some patients with BDD, the ultimate safety behaviour is cosmetic surgery. As with the less extreme safety behaviour, however, this does not always solve the problem but can lead to patients having multiple surgeries to correct perceived defects (Sarwer 1997).

Eating disorders

Avoidance is common in people with eating disorders who will usually avoid eating fattening foods and will escape from situations where they do not know the calorie content of their food intake. Many patients either avoid weighing themselves or else weigh themselves excessively (Fairburn 1995). See Box 6.2 for an experiment you could try to examine the potential implications of such behaviour. Some theorists have suggested that binge eating can be viewed as a form of cognitive avoidance and 'escape from awareness' (Heatherton and Baumeister 1991). Note that many of the behavioural features of eating disorders (e.g. dieting, vomiting, excessive exercise) could be considered to be safety behaviours to avoid weight gain, which patients typically view as

Box 6.2 What do safety behaviours do to you?

Try your own behavioural experiment on the role of frequent weighing. First, toss a coin to randomize yourself to Condition A (heads) or Condition B (tails).

Before you start, rate your pre-occupation with your weight and your dissatisfaction with your shape on a scale of 0 ('not at all') to 100 ('maximum').

Condition A: Heads

Spend an hour weighing yourself repeatedly. Weigh yourself between 20 and 30 times in a row. What happens? Does your weight fluctuate? (It should do!) Re-rate your pre-occupation with your weight and dissatisfaction with your shape.

Reflection: Imagine what people with eating disorders make of this fluctuation? What impact would such a behaviour be likely to have on pre-occupation about weight in people with an eating disorder? And on their eating?

Condition B: Tails

Don't weigh yourself this hour. At the end of the hour, re-rate your pre-occupation with your weight and dissatisfaction with your shape.

Reflection: The chances are that not weighing yourself for an hour doesn't really impact on your thoughts and feelings about your shape and weight. Imagine though how people with eating disorders would feel if they refused to know their weight for months or even years. What would they think their weight might be doing? How would not knowing their weight for such a long time impact on their thoughts and beliefs about the importance of shape and weight?

Q. What do you think is the most helpful frequency with which to weigh yourself?

A. Once a week is suggested to be the optimal frequency and look at the pattern of weight change rather than reading too much into any single number (Fairburn 1995).

catastrophic. Safety-seeking behaviour among individuals with an eating disorder can include the repeated checking of body shape to ensure that it has not spiralled out of control (Rosen 1997; Shafran *et al.* in press). The rule-ridden dieting which characterizes patients with bulimia nervosa and anorexia nervosa can be seen as a safety behaviour designed to prevent overeating and weight gain. However, as the rules are brittle and almost impossible to follow, they usually backfire in that such dieting is a common trigger of binge eating (Fairburn 1995, 1997). As with OCD, there may be little advantage to viewing the behavioural features of eating disorders as safety behaviours.

Sleep disorders

Safety behaviours in insomnia have been identified with the use of a self-report questionnaire (Harvey 2002*b*). In this study, a questionnaire based on the Dysfunctional Beliefs and Attitudes about Sleep Scale (Morin 1993) was developed to elicit safety behaviours and was administered to 33 people meeting diagnostic criteria for primary insomnia and 33 non-patient controls. The data provide evidence that people with insomnia use a wide range of safety behaviours to prevent feared outcomes. For example, safety behaviours were found to paradoxically interfere with sleep (e.g. going to bed early, napping during the day), increase worry whilst trying to get to sleep (e.g. attempted thought suppression, trying to solve the problems that had arisen in the day) and increase pre-occupation with sleep (e.g. taking the day off from work after a poor night's sleep).

Unipolar depression

Lewinsohn was among the first to identify that people with depression have a low rate of engaging in pleasant activities and that engaging in such activities can produce a decrease in depression (e.g. Lewinsohn 1975). Ferster (1973) further argued that depression was characterized by escape and avoidance behaviour, such as withdrawal, inactivity, and rumination (as discussed in Chapter 5). Recent important work in this area has demonstrated that behavioural activation to counter the patterns of avoidance, withdrawal, and inactivity that may exacerbate depressive episodes is a highly effective treatment (Jacobson *et al.* 1996). This treatment approach (behavioural activation) predominantly focuses on replacing avoidance behaviour with approach behaviour (Martell *et al.* 2001). Indeed, behavioural activation has been found to be as effective as full cognitive therapy in a large, well conducted randomized controlled trial both at end of treatment (Jacobson *et al.* 1996) and at a one and two-year follow-up (Gortner *et al.* 1998). A large scale trial is currently attempting to replicate these findings and examine which aspects of the therapy are most useful.

Psychotic disorders

Interesting work has recently been conducted investigating avoidance and safety behaviours in people with persecutory delusions. In a study that provides evidence for the importance of avoidance and safety behaviours in psychosis, an investigation was conducted on 25 people with persecutory delusions. A detailed assessment was made of the presence of safety behaviours (including avoidance) and the content of delusions and emotional distress. Avoidance was the most common safety behaviour and higher levels of anxiety were associated with greater use of safety behaviours (Freeman *et al.* 2001). Further details of the safety behaviours identified in this study are presented in Box 6.3. As evident from Box 6.3 several of the participants in this study reported avoidance.

Substance abuse disorders

As is the case with binge eating, an 'escape from awareness' hypothesis can be applied to substance-related disorders. It is possible that 'escape from awareness' is motivated by experiential avoidance (Hayes *et al.* 1996), that is, attempts to avoid thoughts, feelings, or sensations. In other words, substances are thought to be used as a way to suppress distressing memories, thoughts, or emotions. Indirect evidence in support of this view is provided by studies demonstrating that emotions can trigger cravings (Childress *et al.* 1986) and the finding that the majority of episodes of drinking are aimed at manipulating mood (Sanchez-Craig 1984). However, a detailed investigation of safety behaviours is yet to be conducted.

Discussion

The aim of this chapter has been to establish the extent to which behavioural processes are relevant across the disorders. In doing this, we have not included indirect evidence from randomized controlled trials unless one of the behavioural processes was the main variable manipulated in the treatment. As summarized in Table 6.1, the quality of the evidence that has accrued can be greatly improved. Surprisingly, behavioural processes have not yet been investigated in several disorders. Nonetheless, avoidance and safety-seeking behaviour meet our criteria for being definite transdiagnostic processes (for a reminder of definitions, see Page 21–22). Ineffective safety-signals meet out criteria for a possible transdiagnostic process. No inconclusive or distinct processes were identified. In the section that follows we will elaborate on and justify these decisions.

Definite transdiagnostic processes

As noted at the beginning of this chapter, overt avoidance behaviour is part of the diagnostic criteria for several psychological disorders, such as phobias and

Box 6.3 Number of patients with persecutory delusions endorsing various safety behaviours (Freeman *et al.* 2001)

Safety behaviour	Number of patients ($n = 25$)
Avoidance safety behaviours	
Avoiding meeting people or attending social gathering	14
Avoiding walking on the street	13
Avoiding pubs	11
Avoiding being far from home	11
Avoiding shops	10
Avoiding public transport	9
Avoiding enclosed spaces	9
In-situation safety behaviours: posthoc inspection suggested four themes:	17

'Protection' e.g. by not answering the front door, checking locks, only going outside if accompanied by a family member, putting a chair against the bedroom door at night.
'Invisibility' e.g. wearing a hat or cycle helmet, walking quickly, keeping eyes to the ground to avoid the attention of others.
'Vigilance' e.g. watching people, looking up and down the street to see if someone is outside
'Resistance' e.g. getting ready to strike out if attacked

Other safety behaviours identified	
Escape safety behaviours e.g. leaving the aerobics class after noticing somebody looking at them	8
Compliance safety behaviours e.g. saying 'good morning' to neighbours to try to make them like me	6
Help seeking safety behaviours e.g. ask God for help in reducing the danger	9
Aggression safety behaviours e.g. approaching people and asking them to 'get off my back'	5
Delusional safety behaviours e.g. thinking of having a nice holiday in another country because British police (who were believed to be persecuting the patient) would not be present	2

Table 6.1 Summary of direct empirical evidence across the psychological disorders (first column) and the behavioural processes (top row)[1]

	Avoidance		Safety behaviour		Ineffective safety signals	
Panic disorder with or without agoraphobia			**	+	**	+
Specific phobia	**	+	*	+	**	+
Social phobia			**	+		
OCD			**2	+		
PTSD/ASD	**	+				
GAD						
Pain disorder	**	+				
Hypochondriasis						
BDD			**	+		
Dissociative disorder						
Sexual disorder						
Eating disorder			**	+		
Sleep disorder			**	+		
Unipolar depression	**	+				
Bipolar depression						
Psychotic disorder	*	+	*	+		
Substance disorder						

Note. For each behavioural process the lefthand column presents an indication of the quality of the evidence as follows: *** = good quality evidence, ** = moderate quality of evidence, * = tentative quality of evidence (see page 21–22 for criteria for each) and the righthand column presents an indication of the findings as follows: + = positive findings, – = negative findings, +/– = mixed findings, black space = the behavioural process has not been researched in this disorder.

[1]Note that indirect evidence from treatment studies involving exposure is not included as evidence in support of avoidance unless one of the behavioural processes of interest in this chapter was the main variable manipulated in the treatment.

[2] If the behavioural features of the disorder are viewed as safety behaviours.

PTSD. In addition, there is empirical evidence for the importance of avoidance behaviour across a range of psychological disorders including specific phobia, PTSD, pain disorder, unipolar depression, and psychotic disorders. As such, overt avoidance behaviour meets our criteria for a definite transdiagnostic process.

Safety behaviour also meets our criteria for a definite transdiagnostic process since it is present in *all* of the disorders in which it has been investigated including several anxiety disorders, BDD, eating disorder, insomnia, and psychosis. Although the specific content of the safety behaviour may vary across disorders (e.g. gripping a glass in social phobia, wearing a protective helmet in psychosis), their hypothesized function across the disorders is identical. In essence, the majority of disorder-focused models are consistent with the cognitive hypothesis proposed by Paul Salkovskis (1991) and suggest that avoidance and safety-seeking behaviour serves to prevent the disconfirmation of dysfunctional beliefs that maintain the disorder.

Possible transdiagnostic processes

To date, the safety-signal hypothesis of Rachman (1984) has only been applied to agoraphobia and GAD and it has only been empirically evaluated in agoraphobia and specific phobia. Future research is required to determine the extent to which it is applicable across the disorders.

Do behavioural processes play a causal role?

Relatively few prospective studies have been conducted. Several prospective studies were discussed in the previous section on PTSD. These highlighted that avoidance is predictive of the development of PTSD (e.g. Ehlers *et al.* 1998; Dunmore *et al.* 2001). In a prospective study, fear avoidance beliefs were assessed rather than avoidance behaviour per se. Fear avoidance beliefs are defined as beliefs about how physical activity, especially avoidance of it, affects pain. In this study, the authors investigated the prevalence of back pain in 415 people who completed the Fear-Avoidance Beliefs Questionnaire at baseline and one-year follow up (Linton *et al.* 2000). Fear-avoidance beliefs were found to increase the risk for a future episode of spinal pain by twofold.

Direct experimental support for a causal role for safety-seeking behaviour is evident from the experimental studies showing a reduction in symptoms if safety behaviours are eliminated (e.g. Salkovskis *et al.* 1999; Sloan and Telch 2002). Although there is evidence that exposure is not necessary for fear reduction (see de Silva and Rachman 1984 for a convincing argument), we have also covered evidence that avoidance can prevent anxiety reduction (e.g. Marshall 1985). Taken together, this evidence provides preliminary support for the proposal that avoidance behaviour and safety behaviour play a causal role in the maintenance of psychological disorders.

Theoretical issues

As already highlighted, Klinger's current concerns hypothesis (1996) may help to explain some of the differences that exist across the disorders and it appears to be obvious from the work reviewed in this chapter that people avoid the situations that are relevant to their current concerns. For example, patients with social phobia who are afraid of speaking in public due to fear of making a fool of themselves will turn down the opportunity to give a presentation. However, these people will be unlikely to avoid situations in which they do not know the calorie-content of the food that they are eating. Conversely, patients with eating disorders may not have difficulties speaking in public but the thought of eating food prepared by others, with unknown calorie content, may fill them with horror. Similarly, many of the safety behaviours identified by Dan Freeman and his colleagues (2001), in their study of people with persecutory delusions (see Box 6.3), will be specific to people who feel persecuted. The current concerns view helps explain why the safety behaviours can be so idiosyncratic. That is, it depends on the outcome one is trying to prevent and the situation and stimuli involved.

The current concerns view also has potential to explain variations in safety behaviour within a disorder across time, particularly since we consider that current concerns are highly likely to fluctuate over time. Although this proposal has not been investigated, a good example is the way in which the theme of OCD can vary according to the type of illness that is most newsworthy at the time. For example, prior to AIDS being identified, patients with OCD obviously did not complain of fear that they would catch this illness. However, cases of OCD reporting a fear of AIDS began to appear in the late 1980s after the AIDS virus had received widespread news coverage (e.g. Todd 1989; see also Box 7.1 in Chapter 7).

It is important to note that many of the cognitive processes discussed in Chapters 2–5 may have the *function* of avoiding perceived negative outcomes. Consistent with this, many of the clinical interventions discussed so far (e.g. externally focused attention) have involved reducing avoidance and encouraging the client to test the validity of their unhelpful beliefs. In this chapter the focus has been on overt avoidance or within-situation safety behaviours that people with psychological disorders may carry out to avoid danger or seek safety.

An important question is whether the mechanism by which overt avoidance and safety behaviour work is by preventing disconfirmation of beliefs, as proposed by proponents of the cognitive hypothesis (Salkovskis 1991). It is certainly an intuitively plausible hypothesis and the experimental studies show that dropping safety behaviours result in improved outcome (and decreased dysfunctional beliefs). However, it is possible that dropping safety behaviour functions by reducing anxiety (rather than beliefs) and that it is this reduction in anxiety that leads to the reduction in dysfunctional beliefs. To demonstrate unequivocally that safety behaviour prevent disconfirmation of beliefs, tightly controlled experimental manipulations are needed to manipulate safety behaviour and beliefs, while holding anxiety constant.

There have been fewer attempts to evaluate the safety-signal hypothesis and more direct experimental data is desirable. The little data that is available is consistent with the view that giving patients with panic disorder and agoraphobia a safety-signal alleviates anxiety (Telch *et al.* 1994; Carter *et al.* 1995) and agoraphobic avoidance (Sartory *et al.* 1989).

At first glance, the clinical implications derived from the cognitive and safety-signal hypotheses appear incompatible. The cognitive hypothesis predicts that the *elimination* of safety behaviours is necessary for recovery (Salkovskis 1999). It is reasonable to consider that many safety behaviours could provide a safety-signal and the safety-signal hypothesis predicts that any procedures or behaviour that improve the sense of safety will be therapeutic (in agoraphobia at least; Rachman 1984). That is, according to this hypothesis, the *introduction* of a safety behaviour can be desirable. Can these different views be reconciled?

The distinction drawn by Paul Salkovskis and his colleagues between a coping response and an avoidance response may help resolve apparent differences between the two hypotheses (Salkovskis *et al.* 1996, 1999). Salkovskis *et al.* suggest that a coping response is one that is intended by the person to control anxiety with no further beliefs about the benefits of the response. Consider the example of a patient with panic disorder who chews on gum to reduce his anxiety. If this patient believes that chewing gum is the ingredient in the situation that prevents him collapsing or going crazy, then chewing gum is a safety behaviour. However, if this patient does not believe that the gum chewing is related to him collapsing or going crazy but simply helps him deal with his nerves by distraction then chewing gum is not catastrophe-based and will not interfere with disconfirmation. In contrast, the latter scenario would enhance cognitive change because the strategy is based on an alternative, benign explanation of the symptoms and situations (i.e. 'I'm just nervous'). So the key point is that safety-signals could be considered to be a helpful coping response if they function to reduce anxiety but do not function to prevent or avoid catastrophe.

There is an alternative way of integrating the two approaches that has also remained untested. It is possible that safety behaviours can act as safety-signals and reduce both anxiety and catastrophic beliefs if they meet the following criteria:

1. They realistically prevent an actual feared consequence from arising.

2. They can be carried out reliably.

3. They can be carried out without adverse consequences.

To take a trivial example by way of illustration, looking before crossing the road realistically prevents being run over, it is a behaviour that can be reliably performed, and it can usually be carried out without any difficulty. To take a more clinical example, 'applied tension' is a technique that prevents fainting in people with blood-injury phobia, it can be carried out reliably, and it has no adverse consequence. So perhaps an efficacious long-term intervention might involve shifting the person away from the use of unreliable safety behaviours with negative consequences to the use of reliable safety behaviours that could act as safety-signals and realistically prevent the feared event without any negative consequences.

Clinical implications

It is important to note the abundance of evidence in support of exposure as the method of choice to reduce avoidance across the anxiety disorders (see Nathan and Gorman 2002). Although exposure may not be necessary for fear reduction (de Silva and Rachman 1984), it is certainly a highly effective technique. Whether its efficacy is attributed primarily to habituation, self-efficacy, change in affect, or change in cognitions has yet to be clearly established.

With regard to safety behaviours, although it appears difficult to reconcile the clinical implications of the cognitive hypothesis and safety-signal hypothesis, this need not be the case. The former advocates elimination of safety behaviour whereas the latter suggests introducing more safety-signals. However, the apparent difference in the clinical implications of the cognitive and safety-signal hypotheses could be integrated if the sequence of interventions is timed correctly. It is possible that encouraging the use of safety-signals initially allows the person to enter situations that allow the disconfirmation of certain beliefs. The therapeutic gains that result from the initial intervention may decrease the person's sense of danger, and reduce the need for safety-signals. Dropping the safety-signals will then allow the disconfirmation of the remaining beliefs that may be contributing to the maintenance of the disorder. For example, it may be useful for patients with anorexia nervosa to wear baggy clothes as they gain weight. This could disconfirm the belief that weight gain would make them extremely unhappy and they would be unable to cope. However, as their weight has stabilized at a higher level, a full wardrobe would then be encouraged so that they are able to fully accept their shape and weight.

Attempting to approach something that has been avoided can sometimes be assisted with the use of imagery and role plays. For example, one patient with social phobia felt as though people who served in shops thought that he was stupid and were likely to scold him or ridicule him if he did anything wrong. In preparing for an exposure task that involved going into a shop, this patient did an imagery task in which he imagined he was at a checkout. The therapist assisted with the development and maintenance of the image by asking what he would do at each stage. If the behaviour reported might prove counterproductive (e.g. avoiding eye contact), the therapist would suggest an alternative response (e.g. looking at her and saying 'hello'). After going through this sequence in his imagination, it was repeated in a role-play in which the therapist played the shop assistant. After this the patient was willing to try it out in reality.

Behavioural activation can be used to replace avoidance behaviour with approach behaviour designed to increase the likelihood of experiencing positive events (Martell *et al.* 2001). One patient with schizophrenia described avoiding many of his usual every day activities. One consequence of the avoidance behaviour was low mood. The patient quickly grasped that by avoiding his usual daily activities, he could be contributing to the persistence of his low mood. He agreed to produce a list of his usual activities (especially the ones he had been avoiding) and he gave each activity a rating (0 = 'not at all', 10 = 'extremely') in terms of how difficult it would be to begin this activity. This list is displayed in Box 6.4. The patient was asked to choose an activity that he had been avoiding but that he felt he would be able to try. He chose to talk to his son on the phone. The patient rated his level of depression from 0 'not at all' to 10 'extremely' both before and after he had done this. In the next session, he reported that his depressed mood had been 9 out of 10 before the phone call and 7 out of 10 afterwards. The therapist asked what he made of this, and he replied that 'doing some things can help lift my mood'.

A newer treatment approach, Acceptance and Commitment Therapy (ACT), is derived from Stephen Hayes and colleagues' (1996) work on experiential avoidance which has already been highlighted in Chapter 1 as a transdiagnostic process. ACT emphasizes within-session experiential exercises and involves assisting clients to notice and abandon attempts to avoid or suppress. Instead, the goal of therapy is to teach acceptance of unpleasant emotions, physical sensations, and cognitions. Accordingly, this approach is distinct from many other CBT approaches which involve teaching clients to purposively regulate or change emotion, physical sensations, and cognitions. 'The ubiquity of problems associated with experiential avoidance suggests that it might be safer to help clients step out of this altogether' (p. 1663, Hayes *et al.* 1996). Emphasis is also given to committing to valued outcomes and to the development of behaviour that will help achieve these outcomes. To quote the originators of the treatment, 'ACT therapists try to help clients make room for life's difficulties and to move in the direction of their chosen values. The barriers to doing this are experiential avoidance and cognitive fusion, which prevent a behavioural commitment to living a valued life' (p. 81, Hayes *et al.* 1999b). Cognitive fusion refers to the belief that the content of thought closely reflects

Box 6.4 Activity list generated during behavioural activation.

Activity	Difficulty rating
Watch TV	2
Tidy room	3
Talk to son on phone	3
Talk to ex-partner on phone	4
Talk to friend on phone	5
Go for a walk in the hospital grounds	5
Go to talk to other patients	6
Visit son	8
Visit ex-partner	8
Visit friend	9
Eat with other patients	10
Go shopping	10
Re-decorate flat	10

Note. The difficulty rating ranged from 0 'not at all difficult' to 10 'extremely difficult'.

reality. The early research evidence for ACT has been promising. For example, Bach and Hayes (2002) found that four sessions of ACT was superior to 'treatment as usual' in the prevention of rehospitalization in clients with positive psychotic symptoms who had previously been hospitalized for these symptoms.

Susan

After her assessment session, a personalized formulation of the maintenance of Susan's difficulties was drawn up by Susan and the therapist. It was agreed that avoidance and the safety behaviours might be maintaining her difficulties and specifically contributing to the persistence of her beliefs that she was highly likely to vomit. It was agreed to start by trying not to avoid relatively benign situations, such as going to the doctor's surgery. This seemed particularly relevant since Susan had a growth on her arm that she needed to be checked out by a physician. She reluctantly agreed to do this and, after some hesitation, also agreed *not* to eat mints and chew gum during the visit. She insisted on taking an anti-nausea tablet first though. She went to the doctor and this 'behavioural experiment' went well—she did not vomit afterwards. She was sufficiently motivated to try going to other more difficult situations, and she combined this with dropping the safety behaviour of rubbing her necklace and taking an anti-nausea pill in the morning. After several sessions, she was able to enter all situations that she previously avoided and she no longer engaged in safety behaviour.

She was also able to watch a video in which someone was vomiting and although she was somewhat disgusted by it she was able to cope with. Another major change was that if her daughter became unwell Susan was able to look after her. She no longer thought it was highly likely that she was going to vomit, but she acknowledged that it was likely that she would vomit at some point in the future. She was uncertain as to how she might cope if she did vomit but thought she would be able to just about manage.

Future research

As evident in Table 6.1, many gaps in our knowledge on behavioural processes across disorders exist. This is surprising. Perhaps clinicians and researchers are already convinced of the importance of behavioural processes, hence the research has not accumulated. We suggest that future research on behavioural processes is important, particularly since much of the evidence has accumulated from questionnaire or interview studies (and indirect treatment studies in the case of avoidance). The disadvantages of self-report data have been highlighted at several points throughout this book and include that self-report measures can be open to biases and inaccuracies in memory and they rely on the patient having full knowledge and insight into the processes that are functioning to maintain their disorder. The latter point is likely to be particularly relevant as behavioural processes can be subtle and covert. Accordingly, it will be important to conduct research with the broadest range of psychological disorders using experimental paradigms that fully activate the behavioural processes of interest.

Empirical work is needed to compare the predictions from the cognitive hypothesis and safety-signal hypothesis, and also to identify the mechanism of action of avoidance. In order to investigate the mechanisms of action studies need to be designed that can distinguish between moderators and mediators. Such studies could be conducted within the context of large randomized controlled trials (e.g. Kraemer *et al.* 2002) but cross-sectional, longitudinal, and particularly experimental designs lend themselves to the efficient testing of hypotheses regarding the role of safety behaviour. If support is found for the cognitive hypothesis then further questions remain. Is this true of all safety behaviour? Do all safety behaviours work in the same way? Are there differences in the operation of safety behaviour across psychological disorders? Is there ever a time when using a safety behaviour is desirable? The example of blood-injury-injection phobia suggests that the answer to the latter question may be 'yes.'

Future research needs to expand beyond identifying the specific content of the safety behaviour among the disorders. Questions that require answers include: Does such behaviour prevent the disconfirmation of beliefs turning each panic attack into a 'near miss' heart attack? Is it the case that such behaviour prevents optimal exposure? Is there a causal role for safety behaviours? Why are safety behaviours so idiosyncratic (as illustrated by some of the behaviours reported by the patients with psychotic disorders in Box 6.3) and at other times so prototypical (as is the case with averting eye-gaze in social phobia)? These are useful and interesting avenues worthy of further exploration. Perhaps, though, the most important questions are clinical ones. Should patients sometimes be encouraged to seek safety as the safety-signal hypothesis would indicate? Or should patients be encouraged to drop all safety behaviours as the cognitive hypothesis would suggest? If so, is there an optimal time to drop safety behaviour and avoidance strategies within therapy? And, critically, how can we best help our patients to do this?

Key points

1. Two definite transdiagnostic processes have been identified: overt avoidance and safety behaviour.

2. One possible transdiagnostic process has been identified: ineffective safety-signals.

3. Current concerns may help explain the specific form of the avoidance and safety behaviours.

4. Theoretically, the cognitive hypothesis is that safety behaviours should be eliminated as they prevent disconfirmation of dysfunctional beliefs. An alternative hypothesis, the 'safety-signal' hypothesis, suggests that increasing the availability of safety-signals can be therapeutic.

5. All of the behavioural processes discussed, including experiential avoidance, require further research. Future research should attempt to integrate the cognitive hypothesis and the safety-signal hypothesis by considering the timing of the interventions and the nature and quality of the safety behaviours adopted.

Chapter 7

Conclusions

The aim of this book has been to examine the extent to which the cognitive and behavioural processes that maintain psychological disorders are trans-diagnostic. The hypothesis that we sought to test was that psychological disorders are more similar than different in terms of the cognitive and behavioural processes that maintain them. We have attempted to evaluate this hypothesis by reviewing the scientific literature, across the adult Axis 1 disorders, on attentional processes (Chapter 2), memory processes (Chapter 3), reasoning processes (Chapter 4), thought processes (Chapter 5), and behavioural processes (Chapter 6). A summary of our findings is presented in Table 7.1. In support of the hypothesis tested, and as evident in Table 7.1, we conclude that there are vast similarities across the disorders. Further, within the limits of the processes and disorders that we have reviewed, there appear to be more similarities than differences in terms of the cognitive behavioural processes that maintain psychological disorders. Specifically, 12 definite transdiagnostic processes and 9 possible transdiagnostic processes have been identified. In contrast, only 2 distinct processes were identified. Although the evidence for experiential avoidance has not been considered in this book, it has been presented elsewhere (Hayes *et al.* 1996). Furthermore, in each of Chapters 3, 5, and 6 we have discussed evidence for avoidance of thoughts and memories across disorders, consistent with the experiential avoidance account. As such, experiential avoidance is included in Table 7.1 as a definite transdiagnostic process, bringing the tally to 13 definite transdiag-nostic processes.

In Chapter 1 we suggested that the field is currently dominated by a 'disorder-focus'. By this we mean that there has been a tendency for researchers and clinicians to focus on and specialize in one specific disorder, seeking to understand its aetiology and maintenance and to maximize the success of the treatment for it. The clear advantage of the disorder-focus is that it has led to important developments in our understanding of, and ability to treat, several psychological disorders. However, in Chapter 1 we identified a number of disadvantages to a disorder-focus including (1) that it does not cater well for patients presenting with comorbidity and (2) that progress made in the understanding or treatment of one disorder has been relatively slow to be

Table 7.1 Summary of the definite, possible, inconclusive, and distinct transdiagnostic processes

Attentional processes (Chapter 2)	Memory processes (Chapter 3)	Reasoning processes (Chapter 4)	Thought processes (Chapter 5)	Behavioural processes (Chapter 6)
Definite transdiagnostic processes[3]				
Selective attention to external stimuli	Explicit selective memory	Interpretation reasoning	Recurrent thinking	Avoidance behaviour
Selective attention to internal stimuli	Recurrent memory	Expectancy reasoning	Positive and negative metacognitive beliefs	Safety behaviour
Avoidance and attention towards safety		Emotional reasoning		Experiential avoidance
Possible transdiagnostic processes[3]				
	Implicit selective memory	Attributional reasoning[1]	Thought suppression	Ineffective safety signals
	Overgeneral memory	Availability heuristic		
	Avoidant encoding and retrieval	Covariation bias		
		Confirmation bias for threat rules		
Inconclusive processes				
Reduced self-protective bias	Processes of working memory	Belief bias	Metacognitive awareness	
	Memory distrust			
Distinct processes				
		Data-gathering deficit[2] (psychotic disorders)	Source monitoring (psychotic disorders)	

[1] The evidence indicates that attributions may be biased in different ways in different disorders.

[2] The positive evidence for OCD is for gathering *more* evidence before reaching a decision, whereas the positive evidence for psychotic disorders is for gathering *less* evidence before reaching a decision (i.e. data gathering appears to operate differently across these disorders).

[3] See page 24 for definitions.

disseminated to researchers working on other disorders for which the discovery may be directly relevant. We suggested in Chapter 1 that this disorder-focus is driven, at least partly, by the DSM and ICD classification systems as these use groups of signs and symptoms to identify specific and discrete disorders that are assumed to have a clear cause and treatment. We noted in Chapter 1 that these classification systems have advantages (e.g. facilitating communication between clinicians, facilitating research) and disadvantages (e.g. most psychological disorders do not have a known cause and treatment, the system assumes each disorder is a discrete entity). In response to these disadvantages, several researchers have proposed alternative approaches. For example, Stephen Hayes and his colleagues have suggested that common processes of aetiology and maintenance should become the basis for research and clinical practice. The term 'functional diagnostic dimensions' was used to describe these common processes and Hayes et al. (1996) convincingly demonstrated the utility of this approach with experiential avoidance. Other researchers, such as Ingram (1990) for self-focused attention and Ladouceur and colleagues (2000) for strategies used to manage intrusive thoughts, have noted the common occurrence of these specific processes *across* disorders. Based on the evidence presented in Chapters 2–6, our conclusion that there is considerable overlap in the maintaining processes that characterize various psychological disorders, is consistent with these proposals and moves them forward in that we have considered a broader range of processes across a broader range of psychological disorders.

Accounting for the differences

If the majority of cognitive and behavioural processes that maintain psychological disorders are transdiagnostic then this raises an obvious and important dilemma; namely, how do we explain the differences between the psychological disorders? Why is it that a patient with OCD, a patient with chronic insomnia and a patient diagnosed with schizophrenia can present with such different symptoms? We would like to suggest that there are at least three possible solutions to this dilemma. First, the disorders differ in their characteristic current concerns. Second, the disorders may differ in their relative balance of different common processes. Third, the cognitive and behavioural processes that are distinct to particular disorders may account for the differences. Let us move on to consider each of these three possible solutions in more detail. But before doing so, note that these solutions are unlikely to be distinct from each other. Rather, they may make a parallel contribution to the different presentations of the different psychological disorders.

Current concerns

Throughout Chapters 2–6, it has become clear that current concerns influence cognitive and behavioural processes. Current concerns appear to determine the specific stimuli that are attended to and remembered, the specific situations that are misinterpreted, the content of thought and the specific behaviours that are used to avert danger (e.g. Lavy and van den Hout 1994; Klinger 1996; for a similar point within the anxiety disorders see also Wells 1997). For example, consider two disorders that display common processes but differ in their current concerns. A sub-group of people with OCD fear contamination (the current concern). These patients selectively attend to contamination-related words (Tata *et al.* 1996), selectively remember contaminated objects (Creschi *et al.* 2003) and will attempt to avoid contamination by repetitive washing. In contrast, people with eating disorders are excessively concerned about their weight and shape (the current concern). Such patients selectively attend to words relating to their weight and shape (e.g. Reiger *et al.* 1998), selectively remember weight and shape-related words (e.g. Hermans *et al.* 1998) and attempt to avoid putting on weight by avoiding certain foods (dieting). Thus, both groups of patients show the same cognitive and behavioural processes (selective attention, selective memory, and avoidance behaviours) but the different concerns of the disorders mean that patients with an eating disorder and patients with OCD typically present very differently. To flesh out this point, refer back to Box 1.7 in Chapter 1 for a list of the typical current concerns of a range of psychological disorders.

The next significant question is: Why do people with different psychological disorders have different current concerns? Although not a topic for consideration in this book, it is likely that a variety of factors determine this, including biology (e.g. genes), personality, learning history, traumatic experiences, and culture. For examples of the way in which culture has influenced current concerns see Box 7.1.

Balance of common processes

A general conclusion from Chapters 2–6 is that many of the cognitive and behavioural processes that we have discussed exist on a continuum with normal functioning (e.g. Matt *et al.* 1992). Our proposal is that a person with a psychological disorder could show any one of the cognitive behavioural processes at any point along the continuum. Accordingly, perhaps the different psychological disorders may be, at least partly, distinguished by their relative balance of the cognitive behavioural processes. For example, as discussed in Chapter 2, Jostes *et al.* (1999) explored private self-consciousness across social

Box 7.1 Examples of culture influencing current concerns

It is evident that certain psychological disorders are specific to certain cultures, or they may appear and disappear as a function of changes within a culture. This may be a product of the current concerns that are available to the individual within a particular culture, at a particular time. For example:

1. A review commisioned by the British Medical Association on eating disorders pointed to their association with cultural values of weight and shape inherent to western culture (BMA 2000).

2. Throughout history there have been many examples of large-scale phobic/anxiety reactions in the form of fears of mass poisoning, vampire attacks, and witch hunts (Mackay 1841; Showalter 1997).

3. 'Jerusalem Syndrome' is a disorder characterized by a delusional belief that the person is a prominent biblical figure. This is triggered within a short period of arriving in Jerusalem (Bar-El *et al.* 1991).

See Mansell (2003) for further discussion of cultural influences on current concerns and the way in which they can be integrated into cognitive models of psychological disorders.

phobia, panic disorder, OCD, bulimia, and non-patient controls. The results indicated that people with social phobia reported the highest levels of private self-consciousness, with patients diagnosed with bulimia reporting no difference relative to the non-patient controls, and the panic and OCD groups reporting intermediate levels. While this study is limited by its reliance on a self-report scale, it illustrates the point that different disorders may lie on a process continuum. Thus, in principle, differences in the relative balance of these processes may contribute to the differences between the disorders. This proposal remains to be directly investigated.

Distinct processes

We have concluded that some cognitive and behavioural processes are distinct processes. That is, they appear to be specific to certain disorders or certain groups of disorders (see Table 7.1). Clearly, it may be the presence of a distinct process that contributes to the differences between disorders. Psychotic disorders are the most prominent example. The empirical evidence suggests that psychotic disorders are associated with a data-gathering bias and a bias to make external attributions for internally generated thoughts and sensations (as described in Chapters 4 and 5). These processing biases have not been found in the other psychological disorders investigated to date and may, therefore, be partly responsible for why psychotic disorders have traditionally been separated from the 'neuroses'. However, it is important to note that even the comparisons made between psychotic disorders and non-clinical populations may be made on along a continuum such that some individuals without a psychotic disorder may show the same processing biases under certain conditions. Furthermore, there is good evidence that psychotic symptoms can also be maintained by the processes that we have identified to be common across disorders (e.g. internally focused attention, see Chapter 2; safety behaviours, see Chapter 6).

It is also noteworthy that certain processes may be common to a number of different psychological disorders, yet be absent in other disorders. In other words, the processes would be transdiagnostic in the sense of being common across a range of disorders, but would not be universally transdiagnostic, in that the process does not occur in *every* disorder. For example, overgeneral memory has been identified in unipolar depression, bipolar disorder, post-traumatic stress disorder (PTSD), acute stress disorder (ASD), psychosis, and eating disorders but is not evident in generalized anxiety disorder (GAD), social phobia, or OCD. As discussed in Chapter 3, it is possible that overgeneral memory may only be found in the cluster of disorders that are strongly associated with the experience of trauma or abuse (e.g. Kuyken and Brewin 1995; Dalgleish *et al.* 2003). Similarly, the paradoxical effects of thought suppression may be common across a number of psychological disorders, but do not appear to occur in specific phobias.

Summary

We have proposed three accounts for why the psychological disorders may present differently despite sharing common maintaining processes; that the disorders may differ in their characteristic current concerns, that the disorders may differ in their relative balance of different common processes and that there may be distinct cognitive behavioural processes. Remember that we are suggesting that it is likely that these explanations are not mutually exclusive and that they can operate in parallel and interact. Note also that the three potential explanations do not compromise the view that many cognitive and behavioural processes are common to all psychological disorders.

Comorbidity

Despite different psychological disorders having specific presentations, the reality of clinical practice is that most patients present with more than one diagnosable disorder. As discussed in Chapter 1, the results from epidemiological studies (Regier *et al.* 1990; Robins *et al.* 1991; Kessler *et al.* 1994; Ustun *et al.* 1995) and from studies of point prevalence (Sanderson *et al.* 1990; Brown and Barlow 1992; Carter *et al.* 2001) make a clear and cogent case for the relative rarity of 'pure' cases. In fact, Kessler and his colleagues (1994) noted that, on average, patients present with 2.1 disorders. Furthermore, even those patients who only meet criteria for one psychological disorder often present with patterns of symptoms consistent with other disorders. For example, symptoms of anxiety and depression are common to many patients with a broad range of psychological disorders.

As discussed in Chapter 1, there are several possible ways of accounting for the high rates of comorbidity. We suggest that the literature reviewed in Chapters 2–6, and summarized in Table 7.1, constitutes evidence in support of the account that states that one reason why psychological disorders co-occur is because they share overlapping maintaining processes. We suggest that there are at least two routes by which transdiagnostic processes might contribute to the maintenance of comorbidity. First, one transdiagnostic process may maintain more than one disorder. Second, one transdiagnostic process may increase the likelihood of the onset of another process. We will discuss these two pathways with reference to the case of Bill, who was diagnosed with several comorbid disorders, as described back in Chapter 1 in Box 1.2.

1. *One transdiagnostic process may maintain more than one psychological disorder.* When Bill avoids attending to external social information (in Box 1.2—'he keeps his eyes to the ground') he misses out on experiences that could disconfirm the beliefs that (a) he will be negatively evaluated by other people, which maintains the social phobia, and that (b) he will be attacked by a stranger, which maintains the PTSD. It is possible that during his psychosis the same process served to maintain his fear that strangers in the street were talking about him.

2. *One transdiagnostic process may increase the likelihood of the onset of another process.* When Bill avoids eye contact for fear of being attacked, he comes to focus on his internal state; he notices he feels hot, sweaty, and anxious. This, in turn, triggers emotional reasoning; Bill uses his feelings of anxiety to judge that he is under threat and that someone is likely to attack him. In this example, attending away from threat maintained self-focused attention and self-focused attention contributed to emotional reasoning.

If it turns out that the comorbidity between the psychological disorders is, at least partly, accounted for by the disorders sharing overlapping maintaining processes it is possible that clients presenting with comorbid problems might be better assisted if a transdiagnostic process perspective to assessment and treatment is adopted. The following section will explore this possibility.

Clinical implications

At the outset we emphasize that we advocate an evidence-based approach to treatment. That is, as a first choice we suggest using a treatment protocol that has demonstrated efficacy for the disorder in question, as evaluated in well-executed randomized controlled trials (e.g. cognitive behavioural therapy (CBT) to treat bulimia nervosa; Wilson and Fairburn 2002). Having said that, we note that many cognitive behavioural treatments have tended to be explicitly content-focused in that they seek to identify and challenge negative thoughts and unhelpful assumptions. In this section we suggest that there is likely to be utility in a process-focused approach to treatment that seeks to target the cognitive and behavioural processes that maintain psychological disorders. However, we recognize that CBT treatments that do not explicitly target processes are efficacious and often change processes. For example, there is evidence that despite not explicitly targeting selective attention, successful CBT has reduced attentional biases in patients with GAD (Mathews *et al.* 1995; Mogg *et al.* 1995*b*), specific phobia (Lavy and van den Hout 1993; van den Hout *et al.* 1997) and OCD (Foa and McNally 1986). Thus, successful CBT may indirectly or implicitly change transdiagnostic processes. However, it is possible that by directly and explicitly changing transdiagnostic processes, treatments may be more efficient and possibly more effective. Consistent with this suggestion are the findings reported from randomized controlled trials of cognitive behavioural treatments that have explicitly sought to reverse maintaining processes. Such treatments have proven to be highly effective (e.g. panic disorder—Clark *et al.* 1994; social phobia—Clark *et al.* in press; PTSD—Ehlers *et al.* in press). Accordingly, we suggest that further moving towards a process-focused approach, in addition to the standard content-focused CBT, may be beneficial. In particular, a process-focused approach may be beneficial for:

1. Patients who do not get better with the current evidence-based treatments.

2. Patients for whom there is no evidence-based psychological treatment. Unfortunately, there are many psychological disorders without a strong evidence-base in support of a particular psychological therapeutic approach.

3. For complex cases, particularly those patients who present with considerable comorbidity. These are the patients for whom it may be difficult to

determine which disorder is primary, which disorder to focus on treating, and/or which treatment model to adopt as a guide to treatment. As many randomized controlled trials have excluded patients with comorbid disorders, there may be no evidence-base for the particular combination of psychological disorders with which the patient presents. Accordingly, targeting transdiagnostic processes, as part of a process-based approach, may be one way to resolve the tricky question of how to structure therapy in these cases.

Process as a barrier to change

To further flesh out the potential importance of developing a process-focused approach to assessment and treatment, one of the reasons why patients do not respond to therapy is likely to be that one or more of the cognitive behavioural processes may present a barrier to change. Indeed, in Chapters 2–6 we presented evidence that many of the cognitive behavioural processes play a causal role in maintaining the disorder. Thus, it is likely that the more severe manifestations of these processes could prevent or limit recovery. For example, Salkovskis (1991, 1999) proposed that the use of safety behaviours prevents disconfirmation of unwarranted fears. Consistent with this suggestion, a therapeutic intervention produces better results if safety behaviours are eliminated (Salkovskis et al. 1999; Morgan and Raffle 1999; Sloan and Telch 2001). Likewise, Peter de Jong and his colleagues (1998) proposed that reasoning biases, such as confirmation bias and covariation bias, explain how unhelpful beliefs can persist even in the face of contradictory evidence. Finally, negative recurrent thinking, in the form of depressive rumination, has been found to impair the effectiveness of therapy. Siegle et al. (1997) reported that higher levels of rumination predicted slower response to cognitive therapy for depression.

The processes may also interfere with the basics of therapy itself, such as the development of a collaborative therapeutic alliance and accurate communication between patient and therapist. For example, a patient with social phobia who avoids eye contact with the therapist and who constantly scans the room, and looks out the window, may not be able to pay close attention to the content of therapy. At the very least, this will minimize the patient's ability to consider what is discussed and may increase the risk of misunderstanding. Furthermore, such processes may well limit the patient's sense of 'being present' there in the session and of connecting with the therapist, impeding the development of good rapport and a strong collaborative relationship.

In the following two sections we pull together some initial ideas as to how a process-based assessment and treatment could be conducted. However, we emphasize that this approach should be considered speculative and tentative until it is properly and fully specified, piloted, and then tested within case series and randomized controlled trials.

Assessment and formulation

Given the evidence that transdiagnostic processes may play a maintaining role in psychological disorders and act as a barrier to change, it will be useful to include consideration of these processes during the assessment and formulation stages of therapy. Three broad questions, for each transdiagnostic process, should be considered during the initial assessment:

1. Is the process present?

2. How is the process relevant to the presenting problem?

3. Is the process likely to act as a barrier to change? If so, how?

Careful questioning, diary-keeping, and behavioural experiments are likely to be helpful when establishing the answers to these questions. As such, the assessment and formulation for some processes is likely to take more than one session. Note also that many patients will not be fully aware of the presence of the process. That is, many of these processes operate automatically and without conscious decision making. Accordingly, the therapist has to develop creative ways to establish the importance of cognitive behavioural processes. Here are some preliminary suggestions:

1. Drawing on analogies (see Box 7.2).

2. The therapist may also gain helpful information from accompanying the patient, and observing him or her, in the problematic situation. For example, on accompanying Bill (case described in Box 1.2) on a trip to a shopping centre, a new safety behaviour was discovered. When Bill tried to purchase a cup of coffee, a small scene was created because Bill looked to the ground and quietly mumbled his order. The man serving at the counter lost his patience with Bill after a third attempt to complete the order. Bill was not aware that he used this safety behaviour so without the opportunity to observe Bill in this 'real world' setting the safety behaviour may have remained undiscovered.

3. Wells and Matthews (1994) and Wells (2000) have outlined specific questions to assess for the presence of attentional processes, memory processes, and metacognitive processes. Building on these, Box 7.3 presents a detailed set of assessment questions specifically designed for each of the transdiagnostic processes that we have discussed in this book. These questions are likely to be most informative when they are asked with

reference to a very specific problematic or emotional situation as this is when the processes will be most active and most salient. But note that it can also be helpful to ask these questions with reference to a less emotional or less problematic situation as this will help to clarify how these processes operate normally.

4. Encouraging the patient to keep a daily diary can help to further clarify which processes might be present and whether they are associated with symptoms. For example, patients can be asked to fill in modified daily automatic thoughts records for situations they found upsetting or difficult. In addition to asking patients to note the situation, their thoughts, and their emotions, it may be helpful to add columns that specifically enquire about processes. For example, 'What were you paying attention to in the situation?', 'What memories came to mind in the situation?', or 'What did you do?'. Discussing the content of these diaries with patients will help to flag up important maintaining processes, as well as possible relationships between processes. We emphasize to patients that it is most helpful if diaries are completed in 'real-time' (i.e. during or immediately following the situation) rather than retrospectively (i.e. one week later or just before the therapy session).

5. Behavioural experiments can be very helpful for establishing if a process directly contributes to symptoms. For example, many patients with insomnia monitor/scan their body for signs of tiredness during the day (e.g. sore eyes, aching muscles) and when these body sensations are detected they often trigger worries such as 'I'm exhausted', 'how am I going to cope' and 'I can't go on'. As monitoring of body sensations tends to occur automatically (a bit like a virus scanner, see Box 7.2), a behavioural experiment can be helpful for demonstrating the potential importance of the process. For example, one patient with chronic insomnia was finding it difficult to grasp these ideas. As he was going on a six-hour walk in the mountains at the weekend with his wife he agreed to conduct an experiment. He agreed to spend 30 min of the walk monitoring his body sensations by asking himself the following questions 'how do my legs feel right now?', 'how does my torso feel right now?' and 'what about my shoulders and head, how do they feel?' After 30 min he rated, in a small pocket sized notebook, his level of tiredness and his enjoyment of the walk. Then, in the following 30 min he did the opposite, he directed his attention to the environment around him (i.e. away from his body sensations) by asking himself the following questions: 'what can I see?', 'is the scenery pleasant?' and 'are the wild flowers out?' Again, after 30 min he rated his tiredness and enjoyment of the walk.

Box 7.2 Helpful analogies to illustrate cognitive and behavioural processes

Process	Analogy
Selective attention	It is like your attention is a spotlight and it just gets focused on one thing. You miss out on other things because the spotlight is always being drawn to one part of the situation (e.g. the negative part) like a magnet. Our goal is to try to broaden the spotlight to see the whole situation, realistically and in an unbiased way.
Selective memory	I find that when I am trying to remember a song that I have heard many times before, I can only remember the chorus. That is the only bit that comes to mind. I have a 'selective memory' for only the most prominent part of the song.
Disorganized memory	Imagine 'a cupboard in which many things have been thrown in quickly and in a disorganized fashion, so it is impossible to fully close the door and things fall out at unpredictable times. Organizing the cupboard will mean looking at each of the things and putting them into their place. Once this is done, the door can be closed and remains shut' (p. 337, Ehlers and Clark 2000).
Expectancy, interpretation and heuristic biases	Here is a personal example from RS. When I was writing my thesis, I was pretty nervous about the first chapter I handed in and thought it was rubbish. When I got it back, the comment was 'I've stopped reading for the writing style from hell'. It was only after I had calmed down a bit that I re-read it and realized that it said 'I've stopped reading for the writing style from here.' It was partly because I expected to see criticism that I got it!
Emotional reasoning	It is like being on a stormy sea in a tiny boat and being jolted around, afraid that you are going to sink. We are not trying to stop the sea from being stormy, because we cannot control the weather. Instead we will try to equip the boat with a sail, a rudder, a map, and a compass, and try to help you navigate your way through the sea. We cannot get rid of your emotions but we can try to understand them better and help you deal with them. [can also be used for intrusive thoughts or voices]

Box 7.2 Helpful analogies to illustrate cognitive and behavioural processes *(continued)*

Process	Analogy
Recurrent thinking	It is like when you have had an argument with someone. The contents of the argument go round and round in your head, you replay it, thinking of all the things you could have said. Has that ever happened to you?
Safety behaviour	An example from Paul Salkovskis. Builders wanted to play a joke on a young, naïve apprentice so they asked him to hold up a wall: 'What ever you do, don't let go of this wall or it will collapse to the ground and be ruined!'. The apprentice was very keen and did so, even when the other builders went off for lunch, and even though it was raining. He would have stayed there all night except for one of the builders took pity on him and told him to try to let go. The apprentice was terrified of the consequences but he did so. What do you think happened? The apprentice was still hovering near the wall, so he was told to step away, and see what happened. He was even told to push the wall. It was still standing. The point here is that he thought he was preventing something that would never have happened anyway, and sometimes you have to push hard to find out that the bad thing would not happen.
Automaticity of processes	It is like the way that your computer works when you turn it on in the morning. It whirs away for several minutes until it is ready for you to log on. During this time, although you are not really aware of it, your virus scanner is scanning your computer to check for viruses that could threaten the safety of your computer files. In a similar way, many people find that they scan their body or their mind to check for things, like thoughts or feelings, that could be threatening. Sometimes this scanning takes place without us being fully aware of it.
Changing an automatic process	Do you drive a car? Do you find that you have to think consciously about exactly how to change gear, use the pedals, and turn the steering wheel? Most people are not aware of themselves doing these tasks. But what about when you first learned to drive? Did you have to concentrate much harder then? So it seems that many things we do are automatic but we need to put in some effort and control our behaviour to learn new things. But when we have learned them, these new behaviours or ways of thinking become more automatic too. [could phrase in terms of riding a bicycle or baking a cake]

Box 7.3 Examples of useful questions for assessing transdiagnostic processes

Selective attention: What were you paying most attention to/listening to/looking at/noticing/focusing on in the situation? How did you divide your attention? Did you concentrate your attention on anything in particular? Were you paying attention to your thoughts, your feelings, or the situation? What was happening just before you paid attention to this? What happened when you looked at this/listened to this/focused on him/her? What were the consequences of paying attention to this? How do you decide what you are going to pay attention to?

Selective and recurrent memory: What memories came up in this situation? Do they come into your mind unbidden or are you trying to remember them? Do the same or similar memories come up again and again in other situations? Are there memories that are relevant to this situation that do not come up? How do you feel when these memories come to mind? What effect do these memories have on you? How long have you tended to recall this memory? Has it become more or less frequent over time? As the memory has become more/less frequent, have your problems become better or worse? What happens if you recall a different memory in a similar situation? How do you use your memory? What are the advantages and disadvantages of remembering this?

Expectancy and interpretation biases: What do you expect to happen here? What judgements are you making about this situation? How are you evaluating this situation? What is the effect of making this prediction/judgement? What sort of evidence do you look for? How do you weigh up the different information? How do you know what happened/will happen exactly? Was your decision influenced by your memories, feelings, or your imagination? What would change your conclusions? What is different between the situations when you make more pessimistic or more optimistic judgements?

Box 7.3 Examples of useful questions for assessing transdiagnostic processes *(continued)*

Recurrent thinking: Do you ever ruminate/become pre-occupied/seem to get things stuck in your mind and can not get rid of them? What sort of things did you say to yourself in your head? What sort of things trigger this recurrent kind of thinking? What types of things do you become pre-occupied with? What happens when you dwell on things? What effect does it have on your mood or your actions? What differences do you notice in your thinking patterns when you are having a bad day in comparison to when you are having one of your better days? What helps to stop you dwelling on things? Are there any strategies you use to try and avoid ruminating/dwelling on things? What was different between the times that dwelling on things quickly reached a useful conclusion and the times that it went on and on, without getting anywhere? Do you have any pictures or images come to mind?

Avoidance and safety behaviour: When you feel under threat, are there certain things that you do to cope with the situation? Are there things that you do just in case something happens? What activities, situations, or people do you avoid? What would happen if you stopped doing this? How much does the avoidance stop you doing what you want? What are the short-term effects of trying to cope with this way? What effect does it have on you in the longer term? Have you ever done something different? What happened then? What helped you to do something different?

Note: Many of the questions suggested for one process could be adapted to be used for the other processes.

This experiment helped to establish that internally directed selective attention contributed substantially to daytime tiredness for this patient. The conclusion the patient drew was that monitoring for tiredness increases tiredness.

6. Quantitative measures, such as rating scales and questionnaires, can also be helpful. Many therapists administer ratings and questionnaires at the beginning, in the middle, and at the end of treatment as a way to inform the therapeutic process and so as to evaluate treatment outcome. It is worth considering the inclusion of ratings of: the frequency of the process (How often does it happen?), the duration of the process (How long does it last?), how long the patient has displayed the process (When did it start?), the controllability of the process, and the disruption caused by the process. Importantly, there are many established questionnaires specifically designed to measure processes, including those listed in Box 2.1 of Chapter 2. Other examples include the Penn State Worry Questionnaire (Meyer *et al.* 1990) and the Thought Control Questionnaire (Wells and Davies 1994). The advantage of using these measures over ratings you make up yourself is that the established psychometric properties of these measures ensures that they are adequately and appropriately measuring the concepts you are interested in.

Once the processes that are present and seem to be involved in maintaining the disorder have been established, we can incorporate these processes into a formulation. This formulation will need to relate processes to content. That is, it will be a formulation of both process and content. Figure 7.1 illustrates a content and process formulation for Bill. Of course, the aim of a formulation is that it guides the intervention by systematically removing obstacles to recovery. For further helpful information on case formulation see Jacqueline Persons' classic book (Persons 1989).

Treatment

At the outset we note that when attempting to treat transdiagnostic processes, as with any cognitive behavioural intervention, the engagement of the client and establishing a strong collaborative alliance will be crucial. Further, the core elements of CBT, such as collaborative empiricism, agenda-setting, and homework are all going to be important and are well-described elsewhere (e.g. Beck 1995). Likewise, core to any attempt to treat transdiagnostic processes will be: a personalized formulation, providing a strong rationale for treatment, Socratic questioning and guided discovery, monitoring the relevant process(es), diary keeping, psychoeducation including illustrative analogies to clarify the nature of the process (see Box 7.2), and behavioural experiments.

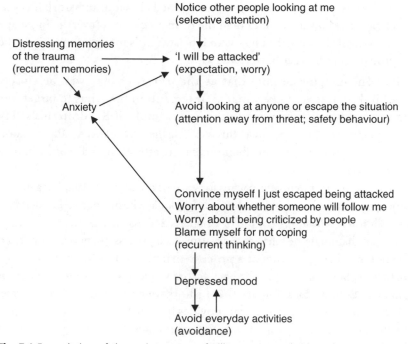

Fig. 7.1 Formulation of the maintenance of Bill's symptoms (with each process in parentheses).

What if more than one process is identified in the formulation, which process should be tackled first? Which process, if any, is primary? In most cases there will not be a clear-cut answer to these questions. To resolve this issue it may be worth considering the following:

1. Which process seems to be causing the patient the most distress and which does the patient wish to address first? It will obviously increase the acceptability of the treatment and the patient's interest in the treatment if the answer/s to this question is tackled early on in treatment.

2. Which processes are most closely related to the primary concern hypothesized to maintain the disorder? For example, for panic disorder, where catastrophic misinterpretation of threat is considered the primary concern, it seems sensible to target the appraisal of bodily sensations.

3. Another point of view is that it may be more fruitful to target processes that are not so closely related to the primary concern of the disorder, when those processes are more concrete and easier to tackle. Early success in therapy may promote engagement for future interventions that are more challenging or require more perseverance. For example, CBT treatments

for bulimia nervosa start by targeting the behavioural disturbances of dieting and bingeing, rather than the primary concern (overvaluing shape and weight) because the binge eating behaviour is thought to maintain the primary concern (Fairburn *et al.* 1993).

It is encouraging to note that as the processes may well be closely inter-linked, it is very likely that an intervention that aims to target one process will modify other processes. For example, if Bill drops his safety behaviour of avoiding eye contact this will have the effect of decreasing attention to internal cues and perhaps then increasing attention to disconfirmatory information.

The various treatment approaches for each of the cognitive and behavioural processes that we have discussed in this book have been reviewed in detail in the 'Clinical implications' section of Chapters 2–6. As an aide memoire for the strategies that might be relevant to treating each process, we have summarized the potential components of a process-orientated treatment below. For further explanation please refer back to the 'clinical implications' section of Chapters 2–6. In the summary that follows we have included a reference, wherever possible, to a source that provides helpful 'how to' advice for implementing the treatment component. Note that many of these suggestions that link treatment components to specific cognitive and behavioural processes have yet to be empirically verified.

Attentional processes

1. Giving a rationale and education (analogies can be helpful, see Box 7.2).
2. Behavioural experiments in which attention is directed externally/to the environment (Bennett-Levy *et al.* in press).
3. Attention training (Wells 2000).
4. Mindfulness training to focus and sustain attention to the external environment (Segal *et al.* 2002).
5. Cognitive rehabilitation to improve attentional performance for patients with schizophrenia (Wykes *et al.* 2003).
6. Computer-based training to train attention to non-negative stimuli (MacLeod *et al.* 2002).
7. Positive data log to reduce the tendency to only attend to one category of information, such as negative information (Greenberger and Padesky 1995).
8. Negative automatic thought records to encourage attention to a broader range of information (Beck 1995; Greenberger and Padesky 1995).

Memory processes

1. Giving a rationale and education (analogies can be helpful, see Box 7.2).

2. Imaginal and *in vivo* exposure to improve the organization and clarity of memory (Rothbaum and Schwartz 2002).

3. White bear experiment to demonstrate the adverse consequences of suppressing memories (Wegner 1994).

4. Arrange to obtain factual information to improve the organization and clarity of memory.

5. Gain a historical perspective such that a clear 'line' can be drawn between the present and the unpleasant events that happened in the past (Ehlers and Clark 2000).

6. Write down nightmares, change the ending, and rehearse the changed ending (Krakow *et al.* 2001).

7. Imagery work (Hackmann 1997).

8. Modify negative observer perspective images (Hirsch *et al.* 2003*a*; in press).

9. Negative automatic thought records to encourage the recall of specific memories (Beck 1995; Greenberger and Padesky 1995).

10. Mindfulness training to reduce overgeneral memory (Segal *et al.* 2002).

11. Behavioural experiments to address selective memory and memory distrust (Bennett-Levy *et al.* in press).

Reasoning processes

1. Giving a rationale and education (analogies can be helpful, see Box 7.2).

2. Negative automatic thought records to help patients explore and identify evidence and alternative view points (Beck 1995; Greenberger and Padesky 1995).

3. Training in critical reasoning.

4. Encouraging patients to focus on facts rather than feelings.

5. Imagery-based techniques to reduce the accessibility of unhelpful images and memories.

6. Behavioural experiments including video feedback (e.g. Rushford and Ostermeyer 1997 for eating disorders; Harvey *et al.* 2000 for social anxiety).

7. Socratic questioning (Beck 1995) to address attributional biases.

8. Debiasing approaches (Hayes and Hesketh 1989).

9. Contingency tables (see Fig. 4.1).

10. Computerized task to train a person out of reasoning biases (Mathews and Mackintosh 2000).

11. Shifting the goals and current concerns that fuel reasoning biases with motivational counselling (Cox and Klinger 2003).

12. Continua to reduce 'all or nothing thinking' (Greenberger and Padesky 1995).

13. Pie charts to draw out the relative contribution of all of the factors involved (Greenberger and Padesky 1995; see also Fig. 4.2).

14. Chaining or working through probability estimates to show the true probability of an event (nearly always very low!).

Thought processes

1. Giving a rationale and education (analogies can be helpful, see Box 7.2).

2. Negative automatic thought records to help patients evaluate the evidence for their recurrent thoughts and identify themes in their recurrent thoughts (Beck 1995; Greenberger and Padesky 1995).

3. Replace cognitive avoidance with approach towards thoughts and feelings to promote habituation.

4. Shift information processing to a more concrete, less abstract level (e.g. by encouraging thinking in images; Nelson and Harvey 2002).

5. Identify and challenge positive and negative metacognitive beliefs.

6. Expressive writing to promote emotional processing (Pennebaker 1997).

7. Train in the use of process focused 'how?' type questions and reduce 'why?' type questions (Watkins and Baracaia 2002).

8. Problem-solving therapy to promote resolution of problems and concerns (D'Zurilla and Nezu 2001).

9. Motivational counselling to review goals (Cox and Klinger 2003).

10. Behavioural experiments, such as the white bear experiment, to demonstrate the counterproductive effects of thought suppression (Wegner 1994). For ideas of other behavioural experiments for recurrent thinking see Bennet-Levey et al. (in press).

11. Distraction with a new positive distractor (Harvey and Payne 2002).

12. Assessing metacognitive beliefs (Wells 2000; Box 7.3).

13. Functional analysis to detect possibilities for behavioural change so as to help reduce rumination.

14. Mindfulness training to attend fully to experience and reduce rumination (Segal *et al.* 2002).

15. Acceptance and Commitment Therapy (ACT; Hayes *et al.* 1999*a*).

16. Planned worry periods (Borkovec *et al.* 1983).

17. Relaxation training.

Behavioural processes

1. Giving a rationale and education (analogies can be helpful, see Box 7.2).

2. *In vivo* and imaginal exposure to reduce avoidance (Nathan and Gorman 2002).

3. Dropping safety behaviours (Wells *et al.* 1995; Salkovskis *et al.* 1999).

4. Use of safety signals early on in therapy (Rachman 1984).

5. Acceptance and Commitment Therapy (ACT; Hayes *et al.* 1999*a*).

6. Use of imagery.

7. Behavioural activation (Martell *et al.* 2001).

Limitations

In this chapter we have summarized some of the clinical implications, in terms of assessment and treatment, of a transdiagnostic perspective. As we stated earlier, these suggestions represent some very early thoughts about the way in which a transdiagnostic process perspective may translate into clinical practice. Much research remains to be done in terms of fully specifying a process-orientated treatment, piloting it, and then establishing its efficacy. We emphasize that many of the suggestions in the previous section that link treatment components to specific cognitive and behavioural processes have yet to be empirically verified.

In this section we wish to take a step back from treatment considerations and reflect on a number of limitations inherent to the transdiagnostic process perspective that has been discussed in this book. First, our evaluation of the utility of the transdiagnostic process perspective is limited in several ways. Most obviously, we have reviewed a restricted range of adult Axis 1 disorders. This decision was motivated, in part, by a concern not to produce a long and unreadable book and in part by the research evidence; the cognitive and behavioural processes we have discussed have mainly been examined in the adult Axis 1 disorders. However, we recognize that the extent to which the conclusions we have drawn would be upheld if a broader range of psychological disorders were considered, including disorders suffered in childhood, remains to be determined.

The transdiagnostic process perspective proposed here is by no means a panacea. Disorder-focused approaches are clearly valuable in that they have generated well-validated treatments for a range of psychological disorders. One might argue that the disorder-focused approaches will be less relevant to patients with high levels of comorbidity. But at least in the context of PTSD, there is evidence against this proposal (Gillespie *et al.* 2002). Having said that, we recognize that patients with comorbid disorders are often excluded from randomized controlled trials. As such, following the trials described in Chapter 1 (e.g. Tsao *et al.* 2002), future trials should consider including patients with comorbid conditions so as to evaluate the extent to which a disorder-focused approach reduces the presence of other disorders and to determine whether a transdiagnostic process perspective is more helpful.

Finally, we have developed criteria for evaluating the quality of the evidence of the research reviewed (page 21–22) and for evaluating the extent to which each process is relevant across the disorders (page 24). We have already highlighted some of the limitations of the Quality of Evidence criteria (page 22). Here we would like to draw attention to the limitations of our definition for a definite versus possible transdiagnostic process. A definite transdiagnostic process was defined as positive evidence for the presence of the process across four or more psychological disorders. Note that one limitation of this definition is that it is possible to meet criteria if all four positive findings were reported within one category of disorders (i.e. four anxiety disorders). For example, whilst emotional reasoning has been found in all the disorders studied, it has only been investigated in the anxiety disorders (panic disorder, specific phobia, OCD, social phobia, and PTSD). So it is possible that emotional reasoning is unique to the anxiety disorders (Arntz *et al.* 1995; Engelhard *et al.* 2001). We made this decision due to a concern that the boundaries for categories of disorders in the DSM are often debated (e.g. should PTSD and ASD be included as a dissociative disorder rather than an anxiety disorder; Davidson and Foa 1993) and also to make the definitions more digestible and memorable. Clearly though, further research is required to confirm that the processes that we have declared 'definite transdiagnostic processes' are indeed 'definite'.

Finally, we also note that our declaration that some processes are distinct to specific disorders should be treated with caution. To truly demonstrate a distinct effect, the majority of disorders need to be investigated. In fact, for both of the processes we found to be distinct only a limited selection of disorders have been examined. Furthermore, there is the issue of matching for severity and chronicity. For example, the data gathering bias has not been examined in detail in many severe and chronic psychological disorders, other than psychotic disorders. It may be that more severe and chronic depression would also be associated with impaired data gathering.

Future directions

Towards the end of each of Chapters 2–6 we have included possible future research directions. In addition to the specific suggestions made in each chapter, several other future directions are noteworthy. In this book we have limited ourselves to an examination of the cognitive behavioural processes that *maintain* psychological disorders. Although the evidence for cognitive and behavioural processes involved in *predisposing* and *precipitating* disorders is currently sparse, we hope that in the future a similar exercise to the one undertaken in this book will be possible for predisposing and precipitating processes. Such work will be important for facilitating preventative interventions.

Another key issue is that experimental research is urgently required to confirm that the cognitive and behavioural processes discussed within this book are causally related to disorders, rather than simply epiphenomenal. In addition, the specificity of the processes and the role of current concerns would be better evaluated in research that compares, within the one study, a range of patient groups on tasks that involve stimuli that reflect a range of disorder-relevant concerns. Several experiments have taken this approach (e.g. Arntz *et al.* 1995; Becker *et al.* 2001) but further work is required.

In this chapter we have suggested three accounts for why the psychological disorders present differently despite having common maintaining processes. These possibilities require empirical testing. We have also made an attempt to outline some aspects of a transdiagnostic process-focused assessment and treatment. Importantly, the relationship between the various cognitive and behavioural processes requires detailed exploration. With this it will be possible to determine the extent to which there is conceptual overlap between the processes. If so, this will present new and significant opportunities for theoretical advances and will validate the hunch that targeting treatment at one process will modify others.

Many other fascinating questions remain to be unravelled. Which cognitive and behavioural processes are necessary and sufficient for the maintenance of psychological disorders? Are some processes more core than others? If one process is successfully treated do the others go too? How do the cognitive and behavioural processes fit together? Answering questions such as these will facilitate the development of the treatment implications of a transdiagnostic perspective. Clearly, there is much to be done such that research into cognitive behavioural processes and treatments are likely to remain high on the research agenda for many years to come.

Summary

In this book we have aimed to systematically examine the utility of a trans-diagnostic process perspective. That is, we aimed to determine the extent to which the cognitive and behavioural processes that maintain psychological disorders are common across the disorders. The cognitive and behavioural processes that we have examined in Chapters 2–6 are attentional processes, memory processes, reasoning processes, thought processes, and behavioural processes. In support of our hypotheses, we have found that the majority of the processes examined meet our criteria for definite or probable trans-diagnostic processes (as summarized in Table 7.1). In this chapter we have attempted to outline three proposals for why the different psychological disorders can present so differently. To recap, we have suggested that the disorders may differ in their characteristic current concerns, that the disorders may differ in their relative balance of different common processes and that the cognitive and behavioural processes that are distinct to particular disorders may account for the differences. Further, we have outlined some preliminary ideas about the implications of a transdiagnostic process perspective for assessing and treating patients. Perhaps most importantly we have concluded that a transdiagnostic process perspective has sufficient utility that future research is warranted to extend our conclusions and develop their implications for treatment.

References

Abramowitz, J.S., Tolin, D.F., and Street, G.P. (2001). Paradoxical effects of thought suppression: a meta-analysis of controlled studies. *Clinical Psychology Review*, 21, 683–703.

Abramowitz, J.S., Whiteside, S., Kalsy, S.A., and Tolin, D.F. (2003). Thought control strategies in obsessive-compulsive disorder: a replication and extension. *Behaviour Research and Therapy*, 41, 529–40.

Abramowitz, J.S., Dorfan, N.M., and Tolin, D.F. (2003*a*). Thought control strategies in generalized social phobia. *Behaviour Research and Therapy*, 41, 529–40.

Abramowitz, J.S., Whiteside, S., Lynam, D., and Kalsy, S. (2003*b*). Is thought-action fusion specific to obsessive-compulsive disorder?: a mediating role of negative affect. *Behaviour Research and Therapy*, 41, 1069–79.

Abramson, D.J., Barlow, D.H., and Abrahamson, L.S. (1989). Differential effects of performance demand and distraction on sexually dysfunctional males. *Journal of Abnormal Psychology*, 98, 241–7.

Abramson, L.Y., Alloy, L.B., and Metalsky, G.I. (1989*b*). Hopelessness depression: a theory-based subtype of depression. *Psychological Review*, 96, 358–72.

Abramson, L.Y., Seligman, M.E.P., and Teasdale, J.D. (1978). Learned helplessness in humans: critique and reformulation. *Journal of Abnormal Psychology*, 87, 49–79.

Adams, H.E., Doster, J.A., and Calhoun, K.S. (1977). A psychologically based system of response classification. In A.R. Ciminero, K.S. Calhoun, and H.E. Adams, Eds. *Handbook of behavioural assessment*, pp. 47–8. New York: Wiley.

Alden, L.E. and Bieling, P. (1998). Interpersonal consequences of the pursuit of safety. *Behaviour Research and Therapy*, 36, 53–64.

Alloy, L.B. and Abramson, L.Y. (1988). Depressive realism: four theoretical perspectives. In L.B. Alloy, Ed. *Cognitive processes in depression*, pp. 223–65. New York: Guilford Press.

Alloy, L.B. and Ahrens, A.H. (1987). Depression and pessimism for the future: biased use of statistically relevant information in predictions for self versus others. *Journal of Personality and Social Psychology*, 52, 366–78.

Alloy, L.B. and Tabachnik, N. (1984). Assessment of covariation by humans and animals: the joint influence of prior expectations and current situational information. *Psychological Review*, 91, 112–49.

Alloy, L.B., Abramson, L.Y., and Whitehouse, W.G., *et al.* (1999). Depressogenic cognitive styles: predictive validity, information processing and personality characteristics, and developmental origins. *Behaviour Research and Therapy*, 37, 503–31.

American Psychiatric Association (1987). *Diagnostic and statistical manual of mental disorders*, 3rd Edition (revised). Washington, DC: Author.

American Psychiatric Association (1994). *Diagnostic and statistical manual of mental disorders*, 4th Edition. Washington, DC: American Psychiatric Association.

American Psychiatric Association (2001). *Diagnostic and statistical manual of mental disorders*, 4th Edition (text revision). Washington, DC: Author.

Ames, S.L. and Stacy, A.W. (1998). Implicit cognition in the prediction of substance use among drug offenders. *Psychology of Addictive Behaviors*, 12, 272–81.

Amin, J.M. and Lovibond, P.F. (1997). Dissociations between covariation bias and expectancy bias for fear-relevant stimuli. *Cognition and Emotion*, 11, 273–89.

Amir, N., McNally, R.J., Riemann, B.C., Burns, J., Lorenz, M., and Mullen, J.T. (1996a). Suppression of the emotional Stroop effect by increased anxiety in patients with social phobia. *Behaviour Research and Therapy*, 34, 945–8.

Amir, N., McNally, R.J., Riemann, B.C., and Clements, C. (1996b). Implicit memory bias for threat in panic disorder. *Behaviour Research and Therapy*, 34, 157–62.

Amir, N., McNally, R.J., and Wiegartz, P.S. (1996c). Implicit memory bias for threat in posttraumatic stress disorder. *Cognitive Therapy and Research*, 20, 625–35.

Amir, N., Cashman, L., and Foa, E.B. (1997). Strategies of thought control in obsessive-compulsive disorder. *Behaviour Research and Therapy*, 35, 775–7.

Amir, N., Foa, E.B., and Coles, M.E. (1998a). Negative interpretation bias in social phobia. *Behaviour Research and Therapy*, 36, 945–57.

Amir, N., Foa, E.B., and Coles, M.E. (1998b). Automatic activation and strategic avoidance of threat-relevant information in social phobia. *Journal of Abnormal Psychology*, 107, 285–90.

Amir, N., Stafford, J., Freshman, M.S., and Foa, E.B. (1998c). Relationship between trauma narratives in trauma pathology. *Journal of Traumatic Stress*, 11, 385–92.

Amir, N., Foa, E.B., and Coles, M.E. (2000). Implicit memory bias for threat-relevant information in generalized social phobia. *Journal of Abnormal Psychology*, 109, 713–20.

Amir, N., Coles, M.E., Brigidi, B., and Foa, E.B. (2001a). The effect of practice on recall of emotional information in individuals with generalized social phobia. *Journal of Abnormal Psychology*, 110, 76–82.

Amir, N., Freshman, M., Ramsey, B., Neary, E., and Bartholomew, E. (2001b). Thought-action fusion in individuals with OCD symptoms. *Behaviour Research and Therapy*, 39, 765–76.

Amir, N., Coles, M.E., and Foa, E.B. (2002). Automatic and strategic activation and inhibition of threat-relevant information in posttraumatic stress disorder. *Cognitive Therapy and Research*, 26, 645–55.

Andersen, S.M. and Limpert, C. (2001). Future-event schemas: automaticity and rumination in major depression. *Cognitive Therapy and Research*, 25, 311–33.

Andersen, S.M., Spielman, L.A., and Bargh, J.A. (1992). Future-event schemas and certainty about the future: automaticity in depressives' future-event predictions. *Journal of Personality & Social Psychology*, 63, 711–23.

Anderson, R.E. (1984). Did, I, do it or did I only imagine doing it? *Journal of Experimental Psychology: General*, 113, 594–613.

Andrews, G. (1996). Comorbidity in neurotic disorders: the similarities are more important than the differences. In R.M. Rapee, Ed. *Current controversies in the anxiety disorders*, pp. 3–20. New York: Guildford.

Andrews, V.H. and Borkovec, T.D. (1988). The differential effects of induction of worry, somatic anxiety and depression on emotional experience. *Journal of Behavior Therapy and Experimental Psychiatry*, 19, 21–6.

Arntz, A., Lavy, E., van den Berg, G., and van Rijsoort, S. (1993). Negative beliefs of spider phobics: a psychometric evaluation of the spider phobia beliefs questionnaire. *Advances in Behaviour Research and Therapy*, 15, 257–77.

Arntz, A., Hildebrand, M., and van den Hout, M.A. (1994). Overprediction of anxiety and disconfirmatory processes in anxiety disorders. *Behaviour Research and Therapy*, 32, 709–22.

Arntz, A., Rauner, M., and van den Hout, M.A. (1995). 'If I feel anxious, there must be a danger': ex-consequentia reasoning in inferring danger in anxiety disorders. *Behaviour Research and Therapy*, 33, 917–25.

Asmundson, C.J.G. and Stein, M.B. (1994). Selective processing of social threat in patients with generalized social phobia: evaluation using a dot-probe paradigm. *Journal of Anxiety Disorders*, 8, 107–17.

Asmundson, C.J.G., Kuperos, J.L., and Norton, C.T. (1997). Do patients with chronic pain selectively attend to pain-related information? Preliminary evidence for the mediating role of fear. *Pain*, 72, 27–32.

Austin, D.W. and Richards, J.C. (2001). The catastrophic misinterpretation model of panic disorder. *Behaviour Research and Therapy*, 39, 1277–91.

Bach, P. and Hayes, S.C. (2002). The use of acceptance and commitment therapy to prevent the rehospitalization of psychotic patients: a randomized controlled trial. *Journal of Consulting and Clinical Psychology*, 70, 1129–39.

Baddeley, A.D. (1994). *Your memory: a users guide*, 2nd edition. Harmondsworth, Middlesex: Penguin books.

Baddeley, A.D. (1997). *Human memory: theory and practice*, revised edition. Sussex, UK: Psychology Press.

Baddeley, A.D. and Hitch, G. (1974). Working memory. In G.H. Bower, Ed. *The psychology of learning and motivation*, Vol. 8. London: Academic Press.

Baker, C.A. and Morrison, A.P. (1998). Cognitive processes in auditory hallucinations: attributional biases and metacognition. *Psychological Medicine*, 28, 1199–1208.

Bandura, A., Jeffery, R.W., and Wright, C.L. (1974). Efficacy of participant modeling as a function of response induction aids. *Journal of Abnormal Psychology*, 83, 56–64.

Banos, R.M., Medina, P.M., and Pascual, J. (2001). Explicit and implicit memory biases in depression and panic disorder. *Behaviour research and therapy*, 39, 61–74.

Baptista, A., Figueira, M.L., Lima, M.L., and Matos, F. (1990). Bias in judgment in panic disorder patients. *Acta Psiquiatrica Portuguesa*, 36, 25–35.

Bar-El Kalian, M., Eisenberg, B., and Schneider, S. (1991). Tourists and psychiatric hospitalisation with reference to psychiatric aspects concerning management and treatment. *Medicine and Law*, 10, 487–92.

Bargh, J.A. (1982). Attention and automaticity in the processing of self-relevant information. *Journal of Personality and Social Psychology*, 43, 425–36.

Bargh, J.A. and Pratto, F. (1986). Individual construct accessibility and perceptual selection. *Journal of Experimental Social Psychology*, 22, 293–311.

Barlow, D.H. (1986). Causes of sexual dysfunction: the role of anxiety and cognitive interference. *Journal of Consulting and Clinical Psychology*, 54, 140–8.

Barlow, D.H. (1988). *Anxiety and its disorders: the nature and treatment of anxiety and panic*. New York: Guilford Press.

Barlow, D.H. (2001). *Clinical handbook of psychological disorders: a step-by-step treatment manual*. New York: Guildford Press.

Barlow, D.H., Sahheim, D.K., and Beck, J.G. (1983). Anxiety increases sexual arousal. *Journal of Abnormal Psychology*, 92, 49–54.

Barlow, D.H., Raffa, S.D., and Cohen, E.M. (2002). Psychosocial treatments for panic disorders, phobias, and generalized anxiety disorder. In P.E. Nathan and J.M. Gorman,

Eds. *A guide to treatments that work,* 2nd Edition, pp. 301–35. London: Oxford University Press.

Barr, L.C., Goodman, W.K., and Price, L.H. (1993). The serotonin hypothesis of obsessive compulsive disorder. *International Clinical Psychopharmacology,* Suppl 2, 79–82.

Barsky, A.J., Goodson, J.D., Lane, R.S., and Cleary, P.D. (1988). The amplification of somatic symptoms. *Psychosomatic Medicine,* 50, 510–19.

Barsky, A.J., Wyshak, G., and Klerman, G.L. (1990). The somatosensory amplification scale and its relationship to hypochondriasis. *Journal of Psychiatric Research,* 24, 323–34.

Barsky, A.J., Coeytaux, R.R., Sarnie, M.K., and Cleary, P.D. (1993). Hypochondriacal patient's beliefs about good health. *American Journal of Psychiatry,* 150, 1085–9.

Barsky, A.J., Ahern, D.K., Bailey, E.D., Saintfort, R., Liu, E.B., and Peekna, H.M. (2001). Hypochondriacal patients' appraisal of health and physical risks. *American Journal of Psychiatry,* 158, 783–7.

Bartlett, F.C. (1932). *Remembering: a study in experimental and social psychology.* Cambridge: Cambridge University Press.

Battersby, M. (2000). Response to 'does reducing safety behaviours improve treatment response in patients with social phobia?' *Australian and New Zealand Journal of Psychiatry,* 34, 871–3.

Beck, A.T. (1967). *Depression.* New York: Harper and Row.

Beck, A.T. (1976). *Cognitive therapy and the emotional disorders.* New York: International Universities Press.

Beck, A.T., Rush, A.J., Shaw, B.F., and Emery, G. (1979). *Cognitive therapy of depression.* New York: Guilford Press.

Beck, A.T., Emery, G., and Greenberg, R.L. (1985). *Anxiety disorders and phobias: a cognitive perspective.* New York: Basic Books

Beck, J.G., Barlow, D.H., and Sakheim, D.K. (1983). The effects of attentional focus and partner arousal on sexual responding in functional and dysfunctional men. *Behaviour Research and Therapy,* 21, 1–8.

Beck, J.S. (1995). *Cognitive therapy: basics and beyond.* New York: Guilford Press.

Becker, E.S., Rinck, M., Roth, W.T., and Margraf, J. (1998). Don't worry and beware of white bears: thought suppression in anxiety patients. *Journal of Anxiety Disorders,* 12, 39–55.

Becker, E.S., Roth, W.T., Andrich, M., and Margraf, J. (1999). Explicit memory in anxiety disorders. *Journal of Abnormal Psychology,* 108, 153–63.

Becker, E.S., Rinck, M., Margraf, J., and Roth, W.T. (2001). The emotional Stroop effect in anxiety disorders: general emotionality or disorder specificity? *Journal of Anxiety Disorders,* 15, 147–59.

Beevers, C.G., Wenzlaff, R.M., Hayes, A.M., and Scott, W.D. (1999). Depression and the ironic effects of thought suppression. *Clinical Psychology: Science and Practice,* 6, 133–48.

Bélanger, L., Morin, C.M., Langlois, F., and Ladouceur, R. (in press). Insomnia and generalized anxiety disorder: effects of cognitive behavior therapy for GAD on insomnia symptoms. *Journal of Anxiety Disorders.*

Bennett-Levy, J., Butler, G., Fennell M.J.V., Hackmann, A., Mueller, M., and Westbrook, D. (in press). *Oxford Guide to Behavioural Experiments in Cognitive Therapy.* Oxford: Oxford University Press.

Bentall, R.P. (1990). The illusion of reality: a review and integration of psychological research on hallucinations. *Psychological Bulletin*, 107, 82–95.

Bentall, R.P. and Kaney, S. (1989). Content-specific information processing and persecutory delusions: an investigation using the emotional Stroop test. *British Journal of Medical Psychology*, 62, 355–64.

Bentall, R.P. and Kaney, S. (1996). Abnormalities of self-representation and persecutory delusions: a test of a cognitive model of paranoia. *Psychological Medicine*, 26, 1231–7.

Bentall, R.P. and Kinderman, P. (1998). Psychological processes and delusional beliefs: implications for the treatment of paranoid states. In T. Wykes, N. Tarrier and S. Lewis, Eds. *Outcome and innovation in psychological treatment of schizophrenia*, pp. 119–44. Chichester: Wiley.

Bentall, R.P. and Young, H.F. (1996). Sensible hypothesis testing in deluded, depressed and normal subjects. *British Journal of Psychiatry*, 168, 372–5.

Bentall, R.P., Kaney, S., and Dewey, M.E. (1991). Persecutory delusions: an attribution theory analysis. *British Journal of Clinical Psychology*, 30, 13–23.

Bentall, R.P., Corcoran, R., Howard, R., Blackwood, N., and Kinderman, P. (2001). Persecutory delusions: a review and theoretical integration. *Clinical Psychology Review*, 21, 1143–92.

Berardi-Coletta, B., Buyer, L.S., Dominowski, R.L., and Rellinger, E.R. (1995). Metacognition and problem solving: a process-oriented approach. *Journal of Experimental Psychology: Learning, Memory and Cognition*, 21, 205–23.

Beutler, L.E. and Malik, M.L. (2002). *Rethinking the DSM: a psychological perspective.* Washington: American Psychological Association.

Bianchi, R. (1971). The origins of disease phobia. *Australia and New Zealand Journal of Psychiatry*, 5, 241–57.

Blakemore, S.-J., Smith, J., Steel, R., Johnstone, E.C., and Frith, C.D. (2000). The perception of self-produced sensory stimuli in patients with auditory hallucinations and passivity experiences: evidence for a breakdown in self-monitoring. *Psychological Medicine*, 30, 1131–9.

Blanchette, I. and Richards, A. (2003). Anxiety and the interpretation of ambiguous information: beyond the emotion-congruent effect. *Journal of Experimental Psychology: General*, 132, 294–309.

Blashfield, R.K. (1990). Comorbidity and classification. In J.D. Maser and C.R. Cloninger, Eds. *Comorbidity of mood and anxiety disorders*, pp. 61–82. American Washington, D.C: Psychiatric Press.

Bodenhausen, G.V. (1988). Stereotypic biases in social decision making and memory: testing process models of stereotype use. *Journal of Personality and Social Psychology*, 55, 726–37.

Bögels, S.M., Mulkens, S., and De Jong, P.J. (1997). Task concentration training and fear of blushing. *Clinical Psychology and Psychotherapy*, 4, 251–8.

Brokovec, T. D., Hazlett-Stevens, H., and Diaz, M.L. (1999). The role of positive beliefs about worry in generalized anxiety disorder and its treatment. *Clinical Psychology and Psychotherapy*, 6, 126–38.

Borkovec, T.D. and Hu, S. (1990). The effect of worry on cardiovascular response to phobic imagery. *Behaviour Research and Therapy*, 28, 69–73.

Borkovec, T.D. and Inz, J. (1990). The nature of worry in generalized anxiety disorder: a predominance of thought activity. *Behaviour Research and Therapy*, 28, 153–8.

Borkovec, T.D. and Roemer, L. (1995). Perceived functions of worry among generalized anxiety disorder subjects: Distraction from more emotional topics? *Journal of Behavior Therapy and Experimental Psychiatry*, 26, 25–30.

Borkovec, T.D. and Ruscio, A.M. (2001). Psychotherapy for generalized anxiety disorder. *Journal of Clinical Psychiatry*, 62, 37–42.

Borkovec, T.D., Robinson, E., Puzinsky, T., and DePree, J.A. (1983). Preliminary exploration of worry: some characteristics and processes. *Behaviour Research and Therapy*, 21, 9–16.

Borkovec, T.D., Lyonfields, J.D., Wiser, S.L., and Diehl, L. (1993). The role of worrisome thinking in the suppression of cardiovascular response to phobic imagery. *Behaviour Research and Therapy*, 31, 321–4.

Borkovec, T.D., Abel, J.L., and Newman, H. (1995). Effects of psychotherapy on comorbid conditions in generalised anxiety disorder. *Journal of Consulting and Clinical Psychology*, 63, 479–83.

Borkovec, T.D., Ray, W.J., and Stober, J. (1998). Worry: a cognitive phenomenon intimately linked to affective, physiological, and interpersonal behavioral processes. *Cognitive Therapy and Research*, 22, 561–76.

Borkovec, T.D., Newman, M.G., Pincus, A.L., and Lytle, R. (2002). A component analysis of cognitive-behavioral therapy for generalized anxiety disorder and the role of interpersonal problems. *Journal of Consulting and Clinical Psychology*, 70, 288–98.

Bornstein, R.F. (2003). Behaviorally referenced experimentation and symptom validation: a paradigm for 21st-century personality disorder research. *Journal of Personality Disorders*, 17, 1–18.

Bouman, T.K. and Meijer, K.J. (1999). A preliminary study of worry and metacognitions in hypochondriasis. *Clinical Psychology and Psychotherapy*, 6, 96–101.

Bower, G.H. (1981). Mood and memory. *American Psychologist*, 36, 129–48.

Bower, G.H. (1987). Commentary on mood and memory. *Behaviour Research and Therapy*, 25, 443–55.

Bowley, M.P., Drevets, W.C., Ongur, D., and Price, J.L. (2002). Low glial numbers in the amygdala in major depressive disorder. *Biological Psychiatry*, 52, 404–12.

Bradley, B.P., Gossop, M., Brewin, C.P., *et al.* (1992). Attributions and relapse in opiate addicts. *Journal of Consulting and Clinical Psychology*, 60, 470–2.

Bradley, B.P., Mogg, K., and Williams, R. (1995). Implicit and explicit memory for emotion congruent information in clinical depression and anxiety. *Behaviour Research and Therapy*, 33, 755–70.

Bradley, B.P., Mogg, K., White, J., Groom, C., and de Bono, J. (1999). Attentional bias for emotional faces in generalised anxiety disorder. *British Journal of Clinical Psychology*, 38, 267–78.

Bremner, J.D. and Brett, E. (1997). Trauma-related dissociative states and long-term psychopathology in posttraumatic stress disorder. *Journal of Traumatic Stress*, 10, 37–49.

Brennan, J.H. and Hemsley, D.R. (1984). Illusory correlations in paranoid and non-paranoid schizophrenia. *British Journal of Clinical Psychology*, 23, 225–6.

Breslau, N., Roth, T., Rosenthal, L., and Andreski, P.S. (1997). Daytime sleepiness: an epidemiological study of young adults. *American Journal of Public Health*, 87, 1649–53.

Brewin, C.R. (1989). Cognitive change processes in psychotherapy. *Psychological Review*, 96, 379–94.

Brewin, C.R. and Andrews, B. (1998). Recovered memories of trauma. Phenomenology and cognitive mechanisms. *Clinical Psychology Review*, 18, 949–70.

Brewin, C.R. and Beaton, A. (2002). Thought suppression, intelligence, and working memory capacity. *Behaviour Research and Therapy*, 40, 923–30.

Brewin, C.R. and Holmes, E.A. (2003). Psychological theories of posttraumatic stress disorder. *Clinical Psychology Review*, 23, 339–76.

Brewin, C.R., Dalgleish, T., and Joseph, S. (1996a). A dual representation theory of posttraumatic stress disorder. *Psychological Review*, 103, 670–86.

Brewin, C.R., Hunter, E., Carroll, F., and Tata, P. (1996b). Intrusive memories in depression. *Psychological Medicine*, 26, 1271–6.

Brewin, C.R., Reynolds, M., and Tata, P. (1999). Autobiographical memory process and the course of depression. *Journal of Abnormal Psychology*, 108, 511–7.

British Medical Association (2000). *Eating disorders: body image and the media*. London, UK: BMA.

Brittlebank, A.D., Scott, J., Williams, J.M., and Perrier I.N. (1993). Autobiographical recall memory in depression: state or trait marker? *British Journal of Psychiatry*, 162, 118–21.

Brosschot, J.F. and Aarsse, H.R. (2001). Restricted emotional processing and somatic attribution in fibromyalgia. *International Journal of Psychiatry in Medicine*, 31, 127–46.

Brown, D., Scheflin, A.W., and Hammond, D.C. (1988). *Memory, trauma, treatment and the law*. New York: Norton.

Brown, G.P., MacLeod, A.K., Tata, P., and Goddard, L. (2002). Worry and the simulation of future outcomes. *Anxiety, Stress and Coping*, 15, 1–17.

Brown, T.A. (1996). Validity of the DSM-III-R and DSM-IV classification systems for anxiety disorders. In R.M. Rapee, Ed. *Current controversies in the anxiety disorders*, pp. 21–45. New York: Guildford.

Brown, T.A. and Barlow, D.H. (1992). Comorbidity among anxiety disorders: implications for treatment and DSM-IV. *Journal of Consulting and Clinical Psychology*, 60, 835–44.

Brown, T.A. and Chorpita, B.F. (1996). Reply to Andrews. on the validity and comorbidity of the DSM-III-R and DSM-IV anxiety disorders. In R.M. Rapee, Ed. *Current controversies in the anxiety disorders*, pp. 48–52. New York: Guilford.

Brown, T.A., Antony, M.M., and Barlow, D.H. (1995). Diagnostic comorbidity in panic disorder: effect on treatment outcome and course of comorbid diagnoses following treatment. *Journal of Consulting and Clinical Psychology*, 63, 408–18.

Brown, T.A., Barlow, D.H., and Chorpita, B.F. (1998). Structural relationships among dimensions of the DSM-IV anxiety and mood disorders and dimensions of negative affect, positive affect and autonomic arousal. *Journal of Abnormal Psychology*, 107, 179–92.

Brown, T.A., Di Nardo, P.A., Lehman, C.L., and Campbell, L.A. (2001). Reliability of DSM-IV anxiety and mood disorders: Implications for the classification of emotional disorders. *Journal of Abnormal Psychology*, 110, 49–58.

Bryant, R.A. (1993). Memory for pain and affect in chronic pain patients. *Pain*, 54, 347–51.

Bryant, R.A. and Harvey, A.G. (1995a). Avoidant coping style and post-traumatic stress following motor vehicle accidents. *Behaviour Research and Therapy*, 33, 631–5.

Bryant, R.A. and Harvey, A.G. (1995b). Processing threatening information in posttraumatic stress disorder. *Journal of Abnormal Psychology*, 104, 537–41.

Bryant, R.A. and Harvey, A.G. (1997). Attentional bias in posttraumatic stress disorder. *Journal of Traumatic Stress*, 10, 635–44.

Bryant, R.A., Harvey, A.G., Gordon, E., and Barry, R.J. (1995). Eye movement and electrodermal responses to threat stimuli in post-traumatic stress disorder. *International Journal of Psychophysiology*, 20, 209–13.

Buckley, T.C., Blanchard, E.B., and Hickling, E.J. (2002). Automatic and strategic processing of threat stimuli: a comparison between PTSD, panic disorder and nonanxiety controls. *Cognitive Therapy and Research*, 26, 97–115.

Buhlmann, U., McNally, R.J., Wilhelm, S., and Florin, I. (2002). Selective processing of emotional information in body dysmorphic disorder. *Journal of Anxiety Disorders*, 16, 289–98.

Burke, M. and Matthews, A. (1992). Autobiographical memory and clinical anxiety. *Cognition and Emotion*, 6, 23–35.

Butler, G. and Mathews, A. (1983). Cognitive processes in anxiety. *Advances in Behaviour Research and Therapy*, 5, 51–62.

Butler, G., Wells, A., and Dewick, H. (1995). Differential effects of worry and imagery after exposure to a stressful stimulus: a pilot study. *Behavioural and Cognitive Psychotherapy*, 23, 45–56.

Byrne, A. and MacLeod, A.K. (1997). Attributions and accessibility of explanations for future events in anxiety and depression. *British Journal of Clinical Psychology*, 36, 505–20.

Byrne, D.G. (1976). Choice reaction times in depressive states. *British Journal of Clinical Psychology*, 15, 149–56.

Candido, C.L. and Romney, D.M. (1990). Attributional style in paranoid versus depressed patients. *British Journal of Medical Psychology*, 63, 355–63.

Carter, M.M., Hollon, S.D., Carson, R., and Shelton, R.C. (1995). Effects of a safe person on induced distress following a biological challenge in panic disorder with agoraphobia. *Journal of Abnormal Psychology*, 104, 156–63.

Carter, R.M., Wittchen, H.U., Pfister, H., and Kessler, R.C. (2001). One-year prevalence of subthreshold and threshold DSM-IV generalized anxiety disorder in a nationally representative sample. *Depression and Anxiety*, 13, 78–88.

Cartwright-Hatton, S. and Wells, A. (1997). Beliefs about worry and intrusions: the metacognitions questionnaire and its correlates. *Journal of Anxiety Disorders*, 11, 279–96.

Carver, C.S. and Scheier, M.F. (1982). Control theory: a useful conceptual framework for personality-social, clinical and health psychology. *Psychological Review*, 97, 19–35.

Carver, C.S. and Scheier, M.F. (1990). Origins and functions of positive and negative affect: a control-process view. *Psychological Bulletin*, 92, 111–35.

Ceschi, G., Van der Linden, M., Dunker, D., Perround, A., and Bredart, S. (2003). Further exploration memory bias in compulsive washers. *Behaviour Research and Therapy*, 41, 737–48.

Chadwick, P. and Taylor, G. (2000). Are deluded people unusually prone to illusory correlation? *Behavior Modification*, 24, 130–41.

Chambless, D.L. (1996). In defense of dissemination of empirically supported psychological interventions. *Clinical psychology: science and practice*, 3, 230–5.

Chambless, D.L., Caputo, G.C., Bright, P., and Gallagher, R. (1984). Assessment of fear of fear in agoraphobics: the body sensations questionnaire and the agoraphobic cognitions questionnaire. *Journal of Consulting and Clinical Psychology*, 52, 1090–7.

Chapman, L.J. and Chapman, J.P. (1967). Genesis of popular but erroneous psychodiagnostic observations. *Journal of Abnormal Psychology*, 72, 193–204.

Chapman, L.J. and Chapman, J.P. (1969). Illusory correlation as an obstacle to the use of valid diagnostic signs. *Journal of Abnormal Psychology*, 74, 271–80.

Chapman, L.J. and Chapman, J.P. (1982). Test results are what you think they are. In D. Kahneman, P. Slovic, and A. Tversky, Eds. *Judgment under uncertainty: heuristics and biases*. pp. 239–49. Cambridge: Cambridge University Press.

Chemtob, C.M., Roitblat, H.L., Hamada, R.S., Muraoka, M.Y., Carlson, J.G., and Bauer, G.B. (1999). Compelled attention: the effects of viewing trauma-related stimuli on concurrent task performance in posttraumatic stress disorder. *Journal of Traumatic Stress*, 12, 309–26.

Chen, Y.P., Ehlers, A., Clark, D.M., and Mansell, W. (2002). Patients with generalized social phobia direct their attention away from faces. *Behaviour Research and Therapy*, 40, 677–87.

Childress, A.R., McLellan, A.T., Natale, M., and O'Brien, C.P. (1986). Mood states can elicit conditioned withdrawal and cravings in opiate abuse patients. In L. Harris, Ed. *Problems of drug dependence*. National Institute of Drug Abuse Monograph Series No. 76, pp. 137–44. US Washington DC: Government Printing Office.

Childress, A.R., McLellen, A.T., Natale, M., and O'Brien, C.P. (1987). Mood states can elicit conditioned withdrawal and craving in opiate abuse patients. *NIDA Research Monographs*, 76, 137–44.

Childress, A.R., Ehrman, R., McLellen, A.T., and O'Brien, C. (1988). Conditioned craving and arousal in cocaine addiction: a preliminary report. *NIDA Research Monographs*, 81, 74–80.

Christianson, S.-A. and Nilsson, L-G. (1989). Hysterical amnesia: a case of aversively motivated isolation of memory. In T.-Archer and L.-G. Nilsson, Eds. *Aversion, avoidance, and anxiety: perspectives on aversively motivated behaviour*, pp. 289–310. Hillsdale, N.J.: Lawrence Erlbaum Assoc.

Cioffi, D. and Holloway, J. (1993). Delayed costs of suppressed pain. *Journal of Personality and Social Psychology*, 64, 274–82.

Cipher, D.J. and Fernandez, E. (1997). Expectancy variables predicting tolerance and avoidance of pain in chronic pain patients. *Behaviour Research and Therapy*, 35, 437–44.

Clancy, S.A., Schachter, D.L., McNally, R. J., and Pitman, R.K. (2000). False recognition in women reporting recovered memories of sexual abuse. *Psychological Science*, 11, 26–31.

Clancy, S.A., McNally, R.J., Schacter, D.L., Lezenweger, M.F., and Pitman, R.K. (2002). Memory distortion in people reporting abduction by aliens. *Journal of Abnormal Psychology*, 111, 455–61.

Clark, D.A. and de Silva, P. (1985). The nature of depressive and anxious thoughts: Distinct or uniform phenomena? *Behaviour Research and Therapy*, 23, 383–93.

Clark, D.A. and Purdon, C. (1993). New perspectives for a cognitive theory of obsessions. *Australian Psychologist*, **28**, 161–7.

Clark, D.A. and Purdon, C.L. (1995). The assessment of unwanted intrusive thoughts: a review and critique of the literature. *Behaviour Research and Therapy*, **33**, 967–76.

Clark, D.A., Feldman, J., and Channon, S. (1989). Dysfunctional thinking in anorexia and bulimia nervosa. *Cognitive Therapy and Research*, **13**, 377–87.

Clark, D.A., Beck, A.T., and Alford, B.A. (1999). *Scientific foundations of cognitive theory and therapy of depression*. New York, N.Y., USA: John Wiley & Sons, Inc.

Clark, D.M. (1986). A cognitive approach to panic. *Behaviour Research Therapy*, **24**, 461–70.

Clark, D.M. (1993). Cognitive mediation of panic attacks induced by biological challenge tests. *Behaviour Research and Therapy*, **15**, 75–84.

Clark, D.M. (1997). Panic disorder and social phobia. In D.M. Clark and C.G. Fairburn, Eds. *Science and practice of cognitive behaviour therapy*, pp. 119–54. Oxford: Oxford University Press.

Clark, D.M. (1999). Anxiety disorders: why they persist and how to treat them. *Behaviour Research and Therapy*, **37** Suppl 1: S5–27.

Clark, D.M. and Fairburn, C.G. (1997). *Science and practice of cognitive behaviour therapy*. Oxford: Oxford University Press.

Clark, D.M. and Teasdale, J.D. (1982). Diurnal variation in clinical depression and accessibility of memories of positive and negative experiences. *Journal of Abnormal Psychology*, **91**, 87–95.

Clark, D.M. and Wells, A. (1995). A cognitive model of social phobia. In R. Heimberg, M. Liebowitz, D.A. Hope, and F.R. Schneier, Eds. *Social phobia: diagnosis, assessment and treatment*, pp. 69–93. New York: Guilford.

Clark, D. M. and Wells, A. (1997). Cognitive therapy for anxiety disorders. In L. J. Dickstrein, M. B. Riba, *et al.*, Eds. *American Psychiatric Press Review of Psychiatry* 16, pp. I-9–I-43. American Psychiatric Press.

Clark, D.M., Ball, S. and Pape, D. (1991). An experimental investigation of thought suppression. *Behaviour Research and Therapy*, **29**, 253–7.

Clark, D.M., Winton, E., and Thynn, L. (1993). A further investigation of thought suppression. *Behaviour Research and Therapy*, **31**, 207–10.

Clark, D.M., Salkovskis, P.M., Hackmann, A., Middleton, H., Anastasiades, P., and Gelder, M.G. (1994). A comparison of cognitive therapy, applied relaxation, and imipramine in the treatment of panic disorder. *British Journal of Psychiatry*, **164**, 759–69.

Clark, D.M., Salkovskis, P.M., and Öst, L. (1997). Misinterpretations of body sensations in panic disorder. *Journal of Consulting and Clinical Psychology*, **65**, 203–13.

Clark, D.M., Ehlers, A., McManus, *et al.* (in press). Cognitive therapy vs. fluoxetine plus self exposure in the treatment of generalized social phobia (social anxiety disorder): a randomised controlled trial. *Journal of Consulting and Clinical Psychology*.

Clark, L., Iversen, S.D., and Goodwin, G.M. (2001). A neuropsychological investigation of prefrontal cortex involvement in acute mania. *American Journal of Psychiatry*, **158**, 1605–11.

Clayton, I.C., Richards, J.C., and Edwards, C.J. (1999). Selective attention in obsessive-compulsive disorder. *Journal of Abnormal Psychology*, **108**, 171–5.

Clohessy, S. and Ehlers, A. (1999). PTSD symptoms, response to intrusive memories and coping in ambulance service workers. *British Journal of Clinical Psychology*, **38**, 251–65.

Cloitre, M. and Leibowitz, M.R. (1991). Memory bias in panic disorder: an investigation of the cognitive avoidance hypothesis. *Cognitive Therapy and Research*, 15, 371–86.

Cloitre, M., Shear, M.K., Cancienne, J., and Zeitlin, S.B. (1994). Implicit and explicit memory for catastrophic associations to bodily sensations words in panic. *Cognitive Therapy and Research*, 18, 225–40.

Cloitre, M., Cancienne, J., Heimberg, R.G., Holt, C.S., and Liebowitz, M. (1995). Memory bias does not generalise across anxiety disorders. *Behaviour Research and Therapy*, 33, 305–7.

Cohen, J. and Cohen, P. (1983). *Applied multiple regression/correlation analysis for the behavioural sciences*, 2nd Edition. Hillsdale, NJ: Erlbaum.

Cohen, N.J. and Squire, L.R. (1980). Preserved learning and retention of pattern analyzing skill in amnesia: Dissociation of knowing how and knowing that. *Science*, 210, 207–10.

Coles, M.E. and Heimberg, R.G. (2002). Memory biases in the anxiety disorders: current status. *Clinical Psychology Review*, 22, 587–627.

Coles, M.E., Turk, C.L., Heimberg, R.G., and Fresco, D.M. (2001). Effects of varying levels of anxiety within social situations: relationship to memory perspective and attributions in social phobia. *Behaviour Research and Therapy*, 39, 651–65.

Coles, M.E., Turk, C.L., and Heimberg, R.G. (2002). The role of memory perspective in social phobia: immediate and delayed memories for role-played situations. *Behavioural and Cognitive Psychotherapy*, 30, 415–25.

Coles, M.E., Frost, R.O., Heimberg, R.G., and Rheaume, J. (2003). 'Not just right experiences': perfectionism, obsessive-compulsive features and general psychopathology. *Behaviour Research and Therapy*, 41, 681–700.

Coloumbe, A., Ladouceur, R., Deshairnais, R., and Jobin, J. (1992). Erroneous perceptions and arousal amongst regular and irregular video poker players. *Journal of Gambling Studies*, 11, 221–42.

Compton, R.J. (2000). Ability to disengage attention predicts negative affect. *Cognition and Emotion*, 14, 401–15.

Constans, J.I. (2001). Worry propensity and the perception of risk. *Behaviour Research and Therapy*, 39, 721–9.

Constans, J.I. and Mathews, A. (1993). Mood and the subjective risk of future events. *Cognition and Emotion*, 7, 545–60.

Constans, J.I., Foa, E.B., Franklin, M.E., and Mathews, A. (1995). Memory for actual and imagined events in OC checkers. *Behaviour Research and Therapy*, 33, 665–71.

Constans, J.I., Penn, D.L., Ihen, G.H., and Hope, D.A. (1999). Interpretive biases for ambiguous stimuli in social anxiety. *Behaviour Research and Therapy*, 37, 643–51.

Conway, M.A. (1996). Autobiographical memories and autobiographical knowledge. In D.C. Rubin, Ed. *Remembering our past: studies in autobiographical memory*, p. 68. England: Cambridge University Press.

Conway, M.A. and Pleydell-Pearce, C.W. (2000). The construction of autobiographical memories in the self-memory system. *Psychological Review*, 107, 261–88.

Conway, M.A. and Rubin, D.C. (1993). The structure of autobiographical memory. In A.E. Collins, S.E. Gathercole, M.A. Conway, and E.M. Morris, Eds. *Theories of memory*, pp. 103–37. Hillsdale, NJ: Erlbaum.

Cooney, N.L., Litt, M.D., Morse, P.A., Bauer, L.O., and Gaupp, L. (1997). Alcohol cue reactivity, negative mood reactivity, and relapse in treated alcoholic men. *Journal of Abnormal Psychology*, 106, 243–50.

Cooper, M. (1997). Bias in interpretation of ambiguous scenarios in eating disorders. *Behaviour Research and Therapy*, 35, 619–26.

Cooper, M. and Turner, H. (2000). Underlying assumptions and core beliefs in anorexia nervosa and dieting. *British Journal of Clinical Psychology*, 39, 215–8.

Cooper, M., Cohen-Tovée, E. Todd, G., Wells, A., and Tovée, M. (1997). The eating disorder belief questionnaire: preliminary development. *Behaviour Research and Therapy*, 35, 381–8.

Corney, W.J. and Cummings, W.T. (1985). Gambling behavior and information processing biases. *Journal of Gambling Behavior*, 3, 190–201.

Cox, W.M. and Klinger, E. (1988). A motivational model of alcohol use. *Journal of Abnormal Psychology*, 97, 168–80.

Cox, W.M. and Klinger, E. (2002). Motivational structure: relationships with substance use and processes of change. *Addictive Behaviors*, 27, 925–40.

Cox, W.M. and Klinger, E. Eds. (2003). *Handbook of motivational counselling*. New York: Wiley and Sons.

Cox, W.M., Klinger, E., and Blount, J.P. (1997). *Systematic motivational counselling: a treatment manual*. Copyrighted manual available from W.M. Cox.

Cranston-Cuebas, M.A., Barlow, D.H., Mitchell, W., and Athanasiou, R. (1993). Differential effects of a misattribution manipulation on sexually functional and dysfunctional males. *Journal of Abnormal Psychology*, 102, 525–33.

Craske, M.G., Street, L., and Barlow, D.H. (1989). Instructions to focus upon or distract from internal cues during exposure treatment of agoraphobic avoidance. *Behaviour Research and Therapy*, 27, 663–72.

Craske, M.G., Lang, A.J., Rowe, M., *et al.* (2002). Presleep attributions about arousal during sleep: nocturnal panic. *Journal of Abnormal Psychology*, 111, 53–62.

Croll, S. and Bryant, R.A. (2000). Autobiographical memory in postnatal depression. *Cognitive Therapy and Research*, 24, 419–26.

Crombez, G., Vervaet, L., Baeyens, F., Lysens, R., and Eelen, P. (1996). Do pain expectancies cause pain in chronic low back pain patients? a clinical investigation. *Behaviour Research and Therapy*, 34, 919–25.

Crombez, G., Eccleston, C., Baeyens, F., van Houdenhove, B. and van den Broeks, A. (1999). Attention to chronic pain is dependent upon pain-related fear. *Journal of Psychosomatic Research*, 47, 403–10.

Crombez, G., Eccleston, C., van den Broeks, A., van Houdenhove, B., and Goubert, L. (2002). The effects of catastrophic thinking about pain on attentional interference by pain: No mediation of negative affectivity in healthy volunteers and in patients with low back pain. *Pain Research and Management*, 7, 31–9.

Dalgleish, T. (1995). Performance on the emotional Stroop task in groups of anxious, experts and control subjects: a comparison of computer and card presentation formats. *Cognition and Emotion*, 9, 341–62.

Dalgleish, T. and Watts, F.N. (1990). Biases of attention and memory in disorders of anxiety and depression. *Clinical Psychology Review*, 10, 589–604.

Dalgleish, T., Spinks, H., Yiend, J., and Kuyken, W. (2001a). Autobiographical memory style in seasonal affective disorder and its relationship to future symptom remission. *Journal of Abnormal Psychology*, 110, 335–40.

Dalgleish, T., Tchanturia, K., Serpell, L., Hems, S., de Silva, P., and Treasure, J. (2001*b*). Perceived control over events in the world in patients with eating disorders: a preliminary study. *Personality and Individual Differences*, 31, 453–60.

Dalgleish, T., Tchanturia, K., Serpell, L., Hems, S., Yiend, J., de Silva, P., and Treasure, J. (2003). Self-reported parental abuse relates to autobiographical memory style in patients with eating disorders. *Emotion*, 3, 211–22.

Dar, R., Rish, S., Hermesh, H., Taub, M., and Fux, M. (2000). Realism of confidence in obsessive-compulsive checkers. *Journal of Abnormal Psychology*, 109, 673–8.

Darwin, C. (1872). *The expression of emotions in man and animals*. London: John Murray.

Davey, G.C.L. (1994). Pathological worrying as exacerbated problem solving. In G.C.L. Davey and F. Tallis, Eds. *Worrying: perspectives on theory, assessment and treatment*. Chichester: John Wiley and Sons.

Davey, G.C.L. and Levy, S. (1998). Catastrophic worrying: personal inadequacy and a perseverative iterative style as features of the catastrophizing process. *Journal of Abnormal Psychology*, 107, 576–86.

Davey, G.C.L., Tallis, F., and Capuzzo, N. (1996). Beliefs about the consequences of worrying. *Cognitive Therapy and Research*, 20, 499–520.

Davidson, J.R. and Foa, E.B. (1993). *Posttraumatic stress disorder in review: recent research and future developments*. Washington, DC: American Psychiatric Press.

Davies, M.I. and Clark, D.M. (1998). Thought suppression produces a rebound effect with analogue post-traumatic intrusions. *Behaviour Research and Therapy*, 36, 571–82.

Davis, R.N. and Valentiner, D.P. (2000). Does meta-cognitive theory enhance our understanding of pathological worry and anxiety? *Personality and Individual Differences*, 29, 513–26.

Day, S.J., Holmes, E.A., and Hackmann, A. (in press). Occurrence of imagery and its link with early memories in agoraphobia. *Memory*.

de Decker, A., Hermans, D., Raes, F., and Eelen, P. (2003). Autobiographical memory specificity and trauma in inpatient adolescents. *Journal of Clinical Child and Adolescent Psychology*, 32, 22–31.

de Jong, P.J. and Merckelbach, H. (2000). Phobia-relevant illusory correlations: the role of phobic responsivity. *Journal of Abnormal Psychology*, 109, 597–601.

de Jong, P.J., Merckelbach, H., and Arntz, A. (1990). Illusory correlations, on-line probability estimates and electrodermal responding in a quasi-conditioning paradigm. *Biological Psychiatry*, 31, 201–12.

de Jong, P.J., Merckelbach, H., Arntz, A., and Nijman, H. (1992). Covariation detection in treated and untreated spider phobics. *Journal of Abnormal Psychology*, 101, 724–7.

de Jong, P.J., Merckelbach, H., and Arntz, A. (1995*a*). Covariation bias in phobic women: the relationship between a priori expectancy, on-line expectancy, autonomic responding and a posteriori contingency judgement. *Journal of Abnormal Psychology*, 104, 55–62.

de Jong, P.J., van den Hout, M.A., and Merckelbach, H. (1995*b*). Covariation bias and the return of fear. *Behaviour Research and Therapy*, 33, 211–3.

de Jong, P.J., Mayer, B., and van den Hout, M. (1997*a*). Conditional reasoning and phobic fear: evidence for a fear-confirming reasoning pattern. *Behaviour Research and Therapy*, 35, 507–16.

de Jong, P.J., Weertman, A., Horselenberg, R., and van den Hout, M.A. (1997*b*). Deductive reasoning and pathological anxiety: evidence for a relatively strong 'belief bias' in phobic subjects. *Cognitive Therapy and Research*, 21, 647–62.

de Jong, P.J., Haenen, M.A., Schmidt, A., and Mayer, B. (1998*a*). Hypochondriasis: the role of fear-confirming reasoning. *Behaviour Research and Therapy*, 36, 65–74.

de Jong, P.J., Merckelbach, H., Bogels, S., and Kindt, M. (1998*b*). Illusory correlation and social anxiety. *Behaviour Research and Therapy*, 36, 1063–73.

De Silva, P. (2001). Impact of trauma on sexual functioning and sexual relationships. *Sexual and Relationship Therapy*, 16, 269–78.

De Silva, P. and Marks, M. (1999*a*). Intrusive thinking in post-traumatic stress disorder. In W. Yule, Eds. *Post-traumatic stress disorders: concepts and therapy*, pp. 161–75. New York: John Wiley and Sons.

De Silva, P. and Marks, M. (1999*b*). The role of traumatic experiences in the genesis of obsessive-compulsive disorder. *Behaviour Research and Therapy*, 37, 941–51.

De Silva, P. and Marks, M. (2001). Traumatic experiences, post-traumatic stress disorder and obsessive-compulsive disorder. *International Review of Psychiatry*, 13, 172–80.

De Silva, P. and Rachman, S. (1984). Does escape behaviour strengthen agoraphobic avoidance? A preliminary study. *Behaviour Research and Therapy*, 22, 87–91.

De Silva, P., Menzies, R.G., and Shafran, R. (2003). Spontaneous decay of compulsive urges: the case of covert compulsions. *Behaviour Research and Therapy*, 41, 129–37.

Denny, E. and Hunt, R. (1992). Affective valence and memory in depression: dissociation of recall and fragment completion. *Journal of Abnormal Psychology*, 101, 575–82.

Derogatis, L.R. (1998). *SCL-90 Administration, scoring and procedures manual 1 for the revised version and other instruments of the psychopathology rating scale series.* Baltimore. M.D.: Clinical Psychometrics Research Unit, Johns Hopkins University School of Medicine.

Di Nardo, P.A., Brown, T.A., and Barlow, D.H. (1994). *Anxiety disorders interview schedule for DSM-IV: lifetime version (ADIS-IV-L).* San Antonio, TX: Psychological Corporation.

Dibartolo, P.M., Brown, T.A., and Barlow, D.H. (1997). Effects of anxiety on attentional allocation and task performance: an information processing analysis. *Behaviour Research and Therapy*, 35, 1101–11.

Dolan, R.J., Fletcher, P.C., McKenna, P.J., Frith, C.D., and Grasby, P.M. (1997). A functional imaging study of memory impairment in schizophrenia. *Brain and Cognition*, 35, 346–8.

Dougall, A.L., Criag, K.J., and Baum, A. (1999). Assessment of characteristics of intrusive thoughts and their impact on distress among victims of traumatic events. *Psychosomatic Medicine*, 61, 38–48.

Dowd, T.E., Lawson, G.W., and Petosa, R. (1986). Attributional style of alcoholics. *International Journal of the Addictions*, 21, 589–93.

Drevets, W.C., *et al.* (1999). PET imaging of serotonin 1A receptor binding in depression. *Biological Psychiatry*, 46, 1375–87.

Dudley, R.E.J., John, C.H., Young, A.W., and Over, D.E. (1997*a*). Normal and abnormal reasoning in people with delusions. *British Journal of Clinical Psychology*, 36, 243–58.

Dudley, R.E.J., John, C.H., Young, A.W., and Over, D.E. (1997*b*). The effect of self-referent material on the reasoning of people with delusions. *British Journal of Clinical Psychology*, 36, 575–84.

Dudley, R.E.J., Young, A.W., John, C.H., and Over, D.E. (1998). Conditional reasoning in people with delusions: performance on the Wason selection task. *Cognitive Neuropsychiatry*, 3, 241–58.

Dugas, M.J., Freeston, M.H., and Ladouceur, R. (1997). Intolerance of uncertainty and problem orientation in worry. *Cognitive Therapy and Research*, 21, 593–606.

Dugas, M.J., Gagnon, F., Ladouceur, R., and Freeston, M.H. (1998). Generalized anxiety disorder: a preliminary test of a conceptual model. *Behaviour Research and Therapy*, 36, 215–26.

Dunmore, E., Clark, D.M., and Ehlers, A. (2001). A prospective investigation of the role of cognitive factors in persistent posttraumatic stress disorder (PTSD) after physical or sexual assault. *Behaviour Research and Therapy*, 39, 1063–84.

Dunning, D. and Story, A.L. (1991). Depression, realism, and the overconfidence effect: are the sadder wiser when predicting future actions and events? *Journal of Personality and Social Psychology*, 61, 521–32.

D'Zurilla, T.J. and Goldfried, M.R. (1971). Problem solving and behavior modification. *Journal of Abnormal Psychology*, 78, 107–26.

D'Zurilla, T.J. and Nezu, A.M. (2001). Problem-solving therapies. In K.S. Dobson, ed. *Handbook of cognitive-behavioral therapies*, 2nd Edition, pp. 211–41. New York: Guilford Press.

Earleywine, M. (1994). Cognitive bias covaries with alcohol consumption. *Addictive Behaviors*, 19, 539–44.

Eccleston, C. and Crombez, G. (1999). Pain demands attention: a cognitive-affective model of the interruptive function of pain. *Psychological Bulletin*, 125, 356–66.

Eccleston, C., Crombez, G., Aldrich, S., and Stannard, C. (2001). Worry and chronic pain patients: a description and analysis of individual differences. *European Journal of Pain*, 5, 309–18.

Ecker, W. and Engelkamp, J. (1995). Memory for actions in obsessive-compulsive disorder. *Behavioural and Cognitive Psychotherapy*, 23, 349–71.

Edelmann, R.J. and Baker, S.R. (2002). Self-reported and actual physiological responses in social phobia. *British Journal of Clinical Psychology*, 41, 1–14.

Edwards, L., Pearce, S., Collett B.J. and Pugh, R. (1992). Selective memory for sensory and affective information in chronic pain and depression. *British Journal of Clinical Psychology*, 31, 239–48.

Edwards, L.C. and Pearce, S.A. (1994). Word completion in chronic pain: evidence for schematic representation of pain? *Journal of Abnormal Psychology*, 103, 379–82.

Edwards, L.C., Pearce, S.A., and Beard, R.W. (1995). Remedication of pain-related memory bias as a result of recovery from chronic pain. *Journal of Psychosomatic Research*, 39, 175–81.

Edwards, S. and Dickerson, M. (1987). Intrusive unwanted thoughts: a two-stage model of control. *British Journal of Medical Psychology*, 60, 317–28.

Ehlers, A. and Breuer, P. (1992). Increased cardiac awareness on panic disorder. *Journal of Abnormal Psychology*, 101, 371–82.

Ehlers, A. and Breuer, P. (1995). Selective attention to physical threat in subjects with panic attacks and specific phobias. *Journal of Anxiety Disorders*, 9, 11–31.

Ehlers, A. and Clark, D.M. (2000). A cognitive model of posttraumatic stress disorder. *Behaviour Research and Therapy*, 38, 319–45.

Ehlers, A. and Steil, R. (1995). Maintenance of intrusive memories in posttraumatic stress disorder: a cognitive approach. *Behavioural and Cognitive Psychotherapy*, 23, 217–49.

Ehlers, A., Margraf, J., Davies, S., and Roth, W.T. (1988a). Selective processing of threat cues in subjects with panic attacks. *Cognition and Emotion*, 2, 201–19.

Ehlers, A., Mayou, R.A., and Bryant, B. (1998b). Psychological predictors of chronic posttraumatic stress disorder after motor vehicle accidents. *Journal of Abnormal Psychology*, 107, 508–19.

Ehlers, A., Hackmann, A., Steil, R., Clohessy, S., Wenninger, K., and Heike, W. (2002). The nature of intrusive memories after trauma: the warning signal hypothesis. *Behaviour Research and Therapy*, 40, 995–1002.

Ehlers, A., Mayou, R.A., and Bryant, R. (2003). Cognitive predictors of posttraumatic stress disorder in children: results of a prospective longitudinal study. *Behaviour Research and Therapy*, 41, 1–10.

Ehlers, A., Clark, D.M., Hackmann, A., McManus, F., Fennell, M., Herbert, C., and Mayou, R. (2003). A randomized controlled trial of cognitive therapy, self-help booklet, and repeated assessment as early interventions for posttraumatic stress disorder. *Archives of General Psychiatry*, 60, 1024–32.

Ehrman, R.N., Robbins, S.J., Childress, A.R., and O'Brien, C.P. (1991). Conditioned responses to cocaine-related stimuli in cocaine abuse patients. *Psychopharmacology (Berl)*, 107, 523–9.

Eich, E. (1995). Searching for mood dependent memory. *Psychological Science*, 6, 67–75.

Eich, E., Macaulay, D., and Lam, R.W. (1997). Mania, depression, and mood dependent memory. *Cognition and Emotion*, 11, 607–18.

Elliot, T.R., Herrick, S.M., MacNair, R.R., and Harkins, S.W. (1994). Personality correlates of self-appraised problem solving ability: problem orientation and trait affectivity. *Journal of Personality Assessment*, 63, 489–505.

Elliot, T.R., Sherwin, E., Harkins, S.W., and Marmarosh, C. (1995). Self-appraised problem solving ability, affective states and psychological distress. *Journal of Counseling Psychology*, 42, 105–15.

Ellis, A. (1958). Rational psychotherapy. *Journal of General Psychology*, 59, 35–49.

Ellis, H.C. and Moore, B.A. (1999). Mood and memory. In T. Dalgleish and M. Power, Eds. *Handbook of cognition and emotion*, pp. 193–211. Chichester: John Wiley and Sons,

Elzinga, B.M., de Beurs, E., Sergeant, J.A., van Dyck, R. and Phaf, R. (2000). Dissociative style and directed forgetting. *Cognitive Therapy and Research*, 24, 279–95.

Emmelkamp, P.M.G. and Aardema, A. (1999). Metacognitive, specific obsessive-compulsive beliefs and obsessive-compulsive behaviour. *Clinical Psychology and Psychotherapy*, 6, 139–46.

Emmons, R.A. (1992). Abstract versus concrete goals: personal striving level, physical illness, and psychological well-being. *Journal of Personality and Social Psychology*, 62, 292–300.

Engelhard, I.M., Macklin, M.L., McNally, R.J., van den Hout, M.A., and Arntz, A. (2001). Emotion- and intrusion-based reasoning in Vietnam veterans with and without chronic posttraumatic stress disorder. *Behaviour Research and Therapy*, 39, 1339–48.

Ensum, I. and Morrison, A.P. (2003). The effects of focus of attention on attributional bias in patients experiencing auditory hallucinations. *Behaviour Research and Therapy*, 41, 895–907.

Erblich, J., and Earleywine, M. (1995). Distraction does not impair memory during intoxication: support for the attention-allocation model. *Journal of Studies on Alcohol*, 56, 444–8.

Esterling, B.A., L'Abate, L., Murray, E.J., and Pennebaker, J.W. (1999). Empirical foundations for writing in prevention and psychotherapy: mental and physical health outcomes. *Clinical Psychology Review*, 19, 79–96.

Evans, J., St, B.T. (2002). Logic and human reasoning: an assessment of the deduction paradigm. *Psychological Bulletin*, 128, 978–96.

Evans, J., St, B.T. and Over, D.E. (1996). Rationality in the selection task: epistemic utility versus uncertainty reduction. *Psychological Review*, 103, 356–63.

Evans, J., St, B.T., Barston, J.L., and Pollard, P. (1983). On the conflict between logic and belief in syllogistic reasoning. *Memory and Cognition*, 11, 295–306.

Evans, J., St, B.T., Over, D.E., and Manktelow, K.I. (1993). Reasoning, decision making and rationality. *Cognition*, 49, 164–87.

Evans, J., Williams, J.M.G., O'Loughlin, S., and Howells, K. (1992). Autobiographical memory and problem-solving strategies of parasuicide patients. *Psychological Medicine*, 22, 399–405.

Eysenck, H.J. (1973). Personality, learning, and 'anxiety'. *Handbook of abnormal psychology*, pp. 390–419. San Diego, CA: EdITs Publishers.

Eysenck, M. and Byrne, A. (1994) Implicit memory bias, explicit memory bias and anxiety. *Cognition and Emotion*, 8, 415–32.

Eysenck, M.W. (1982). *Attention and arousal*. New York: Springer-Verlag.

Eysenck, M.W. (1992). *Anxiety: The cognitive perspective*. London: Lawrence Erlbaum Associates Ltd.

Eysenck, M.W., MacLeod, C., and Mathews, A. (1987). Cognitive functioning in anxiety. *Psychological Research*, 49, 189–95.

Eysenck, M.W., Mogg, K., May, J., Richards, A., and Mathews, A. (1991). Bias in interpretation of ambiguous sentences related to threat in anxiety. *Journal of Abnormal Psychology*, 100, 144–50.

Fairburn, C. (1997). Eating disorders. In D.M. Clark and C.G. Fairburn, Eds. *Science and practice of cognitive behaviour therapy*, pp. 209–42. Oxford: Oxford University Press.

Fairburn, C., Shafran, R., and Cooper, Z. (1999). A cognitive behavioural theory of anorexia nervosa. *Behaviour Research and Therapy*, 37, 1–13.

Fairburn, C.G. (1995). *Overcoming binge eating*. New York: Guildford Press.

Fairburn, C.G., Marcus, M.D., and Wilson, G.T. (1993). Cognitive-behavioral therapy for binge eating and bulimia nervosa: a comprehensive treatment manual. In C.G. Fairburn and G.T. Wilson, Eds. *Binge eating: nature, assessment, and treatment*, pp. 361–404.

Fairburn, C.G., Cooper, Z., and Shafran, R. (2003). Cognitive behaviour therapy for eating disorders: a 'transdiagnostic' theory and treatment. *Behaviour Research and Therapy*, 41, 509–28.

Falsetti, S.A. and Resick, P.A. (1995). Causal attributions, depression and post-traumatic stress disorder in victims of crime. *Journal of Applied Social Psychology*, 25, 1027–42.

Falsetti, S.A., Monnier, J., Davis, J.L., and Resnick, H.S. (2002). Intrusive thoughts in posttraumatic stress disorder. *Journal of Cognitive Psychotherapy*, 16, 127–43.

Farrell, M., Howes, S., Bebbington, P., *et al.* (2001). Nicotine, alcohol and drug dependence and psychiatric comorbidity. Results of a national household survey. *British Journal of Psychiatry*, **179**, 432–37.

Fassino, S., Pieró A Daga, G.A., Leombruni, P., Mortara, P., and Rovera, G.G. (2002). Attentional biases and frontal functioning in anorexia nervosa. *International Journal of Eating Disorders*, **31**, 274–83.

Fear, C. and Healy, D. (1997). Probabilistic reasoning in obsessive-compulsive and delusional disorders. *Psychological Medicine*, **27**, 199–208.

Fear, C., Sharp, H., and Healy, D. (1996). Cognitive processes in delusional disorders. *British Journal of Psychiatry*, **168**, 61–7.

Fehm, L. and Margraf, J. (2001). Thought suppression: specificity in agoraphobia versus broad impairment in social phobia? *Behaviour Research and Therapy*, **40**, 57–66.

Fenigstein, A., Scheier, M.F., and Buss, A.H. (1975). Public and private self-consciousness: Assessment and theory. *Journal of Consulting and Clinical Psychology*, **43**, 522–7.

Fennell, M.J.V. and Teasdale, J.D. (1984). Effects of distraction on thinking and affect in depressed patients. *British Journal of Clinical Psychology,* **23**, 65–6.

Fennell, M.J.V., Teasdale, J.D., Jones, S., and Damle, A. (1987). Distraction in neurotic and endogenous depression: an investigation of negative thinking in major depressive disorder. *Psychological Medicine*, **17**, 441–52.

Ferster, C.B. (1973). A functional analysis of depression. *American Psychologist*, **28**, 857–70.

Fichten, C.S., Spector, I., and Libman, E. (1988). Client attributions for sexual dysfunction. *Journal of Sex and Marital Therapy*, **14**, 208–24.

Flavell, J.H. (1979). Metacognition and cognitive monitoring: a new area of cognitive developmental inquiry. *American Psychologist*, **34**, 906–11.

Fleck, D.E., Sax, K.W., and Strakowski, S.M. (2001). Reaction time measures of sustained attention differentiate bipolar disorder from schizophrenia. *Schizophrenia Research*, **52**, 251–9.

Foa, E.B. and Hearst-Ikeda, D. (1996). Emotional dissociation in response to trauma: an information-processing approach. In L.K. Michelson and W.J. Ray, Eds. *Handbook of dissociation: theoretical and clinical perspectives,* pp. 207–22. New York: Plenum Press.

Foa, E.B. and Kozak, M.J. (1986). Emotional processing and fear: exposure to corrective information. *Psychological Bulletin*, **99**, 20–35.

Foa, E.B. and McNally, R.J. (1986). Sensitivity to feared stimuli in obsessive-compulsives: a dichotic listening analysis. *Cognitive Therapy and Research*, **10**, 477–86.

Foa, E.B. and Meadows, E.A. (1997). Psychosocial treatments for posttraumatic stress disorder: a critical review. *Annual Review of Psychology*, **48**, 449–80.

Foa, E.B., Steketee, G., and Rothbaum, B.O. (1989). Behavioral/cognitive conceptualizations of post-traumatic stress disorder. *Behavior Therapy*, **20**, 155–76.

Foa, E.B., Feske, U., Murdock, T.B., Kozak, M.J., and McCarthy, P.R. (1991). Processing of threat-related information in rape victims. *Journal of Abnormal Psychology*, **100**, 156–62.

Foa, E.B., Ilai, D., McCarthy, P.R., Shoyer, B., and Murdoch, T. (1993). Information processing in obsessive-compulsive disorder. *Cognitive Therapy and Research*, **17**, 173–89.

Foa, E.B., Molnar, C., and Cashman, L. (1995a). Change in rape narratives during exposure therapy for posttraumatic stress disorder. *Journal of Traumatic Stress*, **8**, 675–90.

Foa, E.B., Riggs, D.S., Massie, E.D., and Yarczower, M. (1995*b*). The impact of fear activation and anger on the efficacy of exposure treatment for posttraumatic stress disorder. *Behavior Therapy*, 26, 487–99.

Foa, E.B., Franklin, M.E., Perry, K.J., and Herbert, J.D. (1996). Cognitive biases in generalized social phobia. *Journal of Abnormal Psychology*, 105, 433–9.

Foa, E.B. Amir, N., Gershuny, B.S., Molnar, C., and Kozak, M.J. (1997). Implicit and explicit memory in obsessive compulsive disorder. *Journal of Anxiety Disorders*, 11, 119–29.

Foa, E.B., Amir, N., Bogert, K.V., Molnar, C., and Przeworski, A. (2001). Inflated perception of responsibility for harm in obsessive-compulsive disorder. *Journal of Anxiety Disorders*, 15, 259–75.

Follette, W.C. and Houts, A.C. (1996). Models of scientific progress and the role of theory in taxonomy development: a case study of the DSM. *Journal of Consulting and Clinical Psychology*, 64, 1120–32.

Follick, M.J., Ahern, D.K., Laser-Wolston, N., Adams, A.E., and Molloy, A.J. (1985). Chronic pain: electromechanical recording device for measuring patients' activity patterns. *Archives of Physical and Medical Rehabilitation*, 66, 75–9.

Fong, G.T., Krantz, D.H., and Nisbett, R.E. (1986). The effects of statistical training on thinking about everyday problems. *Cognitive Psychology*, 18, 253–92.

Ford, D. and Kamerow, D. (1989). Epidemiologic study of sleep disturbances and psychiatric disorders. *Journal of the American Medical Association*, 262, 1479–84.

Forgas, J.P., Bower, G.H., and Moylan, S.J. (1990). Praise or blame? Affective influences on attributions for achievement. *Journal of Personality and Social Psychology*, 59, 809–19.

Fox, E., Lester, V., Russo, R., Bowles, R.J., Pichler, A., and Dutton, K. (2000). Facial expressions of emotion: are angry faces detected more efficiently? *Cognition and Emotion*, 14, 61–92.

Franken, I.H.A., Kroon, L.Y., and Hendriks, V.M. (2000). Influence of individual differences in craving and obsessive cocaine thoughts on attentional processes in cocaine abuse patients. *Addictive Behaviours*, 25, 99–102.

Franklyn, M.E. and Foa, E.B. (2002). Cognitive behavioral treatments for obsessive compulsive disorder. In P.E. Nathan and J.M. Gorman, Eds. *A guide to treatments that work*, 2nd edition, pp. 367–96. Oxford: Oxford University Press.

Freed, S., Craske, M.G., and Greher, M.R. (1999). Nocturnal panic and trauma. *Depression and Anxiety*, 9, 141–5.

Freeman, D. and Garety, P.A. (1999). Worry, worry processes and dimensions of delusions: an exploratory investigation of a role for anxiety processes in the maintenance of delusional distress. *Behavioural and Cognitive Psychotherapy*, 27, 47–62.

Freeman, D., Garety, P.A., and Kuipers, E. (2001). Persecutory delusions: developing the understanding of belief maintenance and emotional distress. *Psychological Medicine*, 31, 1293–1306.

Freeman, R., Touyz, S., Sara, G., Rennie, *et al.* (1991). In the eye of the beholder: processing body shape information in anorexic and bulimic patients. *International Journal of Eating Disorders*, 10, 709–14.

Freeston, M.H. and Ladouceur, R. (1993). Appraisal of cognitive intrusions and response style: replication and extension. *Behaviour Research and Therapy*, 31, 181–91.

Freeston, M.H. and Ladouceur, R. (1997). What do patients do with their obsessive thoughts? *Behaviour Research and Therapy*, 35, 335–48.

Freeston, M.H., Ladouceur, R., Thibodeau, N., and Gagnon, F. (1992). Cognitive intrusions in a non-clinical population. Associations with depressive, anxious, and compulsive symptoms. *Behaviour Research and Therapy*, **30**, 263–71.

Freeston, M.H., Rheaume, J., Letarte, H., Dugas, M.J., and Ladouceur, R. (1994). Why do people worry? *Personality and Individual Differences*, **17**, 791–802.

Freeston, M.H., Dugas, M.J., and Ladouceur, R. (1996). Thoughts, images, worry and anxiety. *Cognitive Therapy and Research*, **20**, 265–73.

Fresco, D.M., Frankel, A.N., Mennin, D.S., Turk, C.L., and Heimberg, R.G. (2002) Distinct and overlapping features of rumination and worry: the relationship of cognitive production to negative affective states. *Cognitive Therapy and Research*, **26**, 179–88.

Friedman, B.H., Thayer, J.F., and Borkovec, T.D. (2000). Explicit memory bias for threat words in generalized anxiety disorder. *Behaviour Therapy*, **31**, 745–56.

Frith, C.D. (1992). *The cognitive neuropsychology of schizophrenia*. Hove: Lawrence Erlbaum.

Frodl, T., *et al.* (2003). Larger amygdala volumes in first depressive episode as compared to recurrent major depression and healthy control subjects. *Biological Psychiatry*, **53**, 338–44.

Fromholt, P., Larsen, P., and Larsen, S. (1995). Effect of late-onset depression and recovery on autobiographical memory. *Journal of Gerentology: Psychological and Social Sciences*, **50**, 74–81.

Gaboury, A. and Ladouceur, R. (1989). Erroneous perceptions and gambling. *Journal of Social Behaviour and Personality*, **4**, 411–20.

Galinsky, A.D. and Moskowitz, G.B. (2000). Counterfactuals as behavioral primes: Priming the simulation heuristic and consideration of alternatives. *Journal of Experimental Social Psychology*, **36**, 384–409.

Ganellen, R.J. (1988). Specificity of attributions and overgeneralization in depression and anxiety. *Journal of Abnormal Psychology*, **97**, 83–6.

Garcia-Campayo, J., Larrubia, J., Lobo, A., Perez-Echeverria, M.J., and Campos, R. (1997). Attribution in somatizers: stability and relationship to outcome at 1-year follow-up. *Acta Psychiatria Scandinavia*, **95**, 433–8.

Garety, P.A. and Freeman, D. (1999). Cognitive approaches to delusions: a critical review of theories and evidence. *British Journal of Clinical Psychology*, **38**, 113–54.

Garety, P.A., Hemsley, D.R., and Wessely, S. (1991). Reasoning in deluded schizophrenic and paranoid patients: biases in performance on a probabilistic inference task. *Journal of Nervous and Mental Disease*, **179**, 194–201.

Garety, P.A., Kuipers, E., Fowler, D., Freeman, D., and Bebbington, P.E. (2001). A cognitive model of the positive symptoms of psychosis. *Psychological Medicine*, **31**, 189–95.

Garner, D.M. (1991). *Eating disorders inventory 2: professional manual*. Odessa, F.L: Psychological Resources.

Gasper, K. and Clore, G.L. (1998). The persistent use of negative affect by anxious individuals to estimate risk. *Journal of Personality and Social Psychology*, **74**, 1350–63.

Gigerenzer, G., Todd, P.M., and the A.B.C Research Group (1999). *Simple heuristics that make us smart*. Oxford: Oxford University Press.

Gilboa-Schechtman, E., Foa, E.B., and Amir, N. (1999). Attentional biases for facial expressions in social phobia: the face-in-the-crowd paradigm. *Cognition and Emotion*, **13**, 305–18.

Gilboa-Schechtman, E., Franklin, M.E., and Foa, E.B. (2000). Anticipated reactions to social events: differences among individuals with generalized social phobia, obsessive compulsive disorder and nonanxious controls. *Cognitive Therapy and Research*, 24, 731–6.

Gillespie, K., Duffy, M., Hackmann, A., and Clark, D.M. (2002). Community based cognitive therapy in the treatment of post-traumatic stress disorder following the Omagh bomb. *Behaviour Research and Therapy*, 40, 345–57.

Gilligan, S.G. and Bower, G.H. (1984). Cognitive consequences of emotional arousal. In C.E. Izard, J. Kagan, and R.B. Zajonc, Eds. *Emotions, cognition and behaviour*, pp. 47–58. Cambridge: Cambridge University Press.

Goddard, L., Dritschel, B., and Burton, A. (1997). Role of autobiographical memory in social problem solving and depression. *Journal of Abnormal Psychology*, 105, 609–16.

Goebel, M., Spathoff, G., Schulze, C., and Florin, I. (1990). Dysfunctional cognitions, attributional style and depression in bulimia. *Journal of Psychosomatic Research*, 33, 747–52.

Gold, D.B. and Wegner, D.M. (1995). Origins of ruminative thought: trauma, incompleteness, nondisclosure and suppression. *Journal of Applied Social Psychology*, 25, 1245–61.

Goldman, M.S. (1999). Risk for substance abuse: memory as a common etiological pathway. *Psychological Science*, 10, 196–8.

Goldman, M.S., Brown, S.A., Christiansen, B.A., and Smith, G.T. (1991). Alcoholism and memory: broadening the scope of alcohol-expectancy research. *Psychological Bulletin*, 110, 137–46.

Golier, J.A., Yehuda, R., Lupien, S.J., Harvey, P.D., Grossman, R., and Elkin, A. (2002). Memory performance in Holocaust survivors with posttraumatic stress disorder. *American Journal of Psychiatry*, 159, 1682–8.

Goodwin, R.D., Amador, X.F., Malaspina, D., Yale, S.A., Goetz, R.R., and Gorman, J.M. (2003). Anxiety and substance use cormorbidity among inpatients with schizophrenia. *Schizophrenia Research*, 61, 89–95.

Gortner, E.T., Gollan, J.K., Dobson, K.S., and Jacobson, N.S. (1998). Cognitive-behavioral treatment for depression: relapse prevention. *Journal of Consulting and Clinical Psychology*, 66, 377–84.

Gotlib, I.H. and McCann, C.D. (1984). Construct accessibility and depression: an examination of cognitive and affective factors. *Journal of Personality and Social Psychology*, 47, 427–39.

Gotlib, I.H. and Cane, D.B. (1987). Construct accessibility and clinical depression: A longitudinal investigation. *Journal of Abnormal Psychology*, 96, 199–204.

Gotlib, I.H., McLachlan, A.L., and Katz, A.N. (1988). Biases in visual attention in depressed and nondepressed individuals. *Cognition and Emotion*, 2, 185–200.

Gray, J.A. (1971). *The psychology of fear and stress*. England: Mcgraw-Hill Book Company.

Grayson, J.B., Foa, E.B., and Steketee, G. (1982). Habituation during exposure treatment: distraction vs attention-focusing. *Behaviour Research and Therapy*, 20, 323–8.

Grayson, J.B., Foa, E.B., and Steketee, G.S. (1986). Exposure in vivo of obsessive-compulsives under distracting and attention-focusing conditions: replication and extension. *Behaviour Research and Therapy*, 24, 475–9.

Greenberg, M.A. and Stone, A.A. (1992). Emotional disclosure about traumas and its relation to health: Effects of previous disclosure and trauma severity. *Journal of Personality and Social Psychology*, 63, 75–84.

Greenberger, D. and Padesky, C.A. (1995). *Mind over mood: a cognitive therapy treatment manual for clients.* New York: Guilford Press.

Greening, L., Dollinger, S.J., and Pitz, G. (1996). Adolescents' perceived risk and personal experience with natural disasters: an evaluation of cognitive heuristics. *Acta Psychologica,* **91,** 27–38.

Greisberg, S. and McKay, D. (2003). Neuropsychology of obsessive-compulsive disorder: a review and treatment implications. *Clinical Psychology Review,* **23,** 95–117.

Grey, N., Young, K., and Holmes, E. (2002). Cognitive restructuring within reliving: a treatment for peritraumatic emotional 'hotspots' in posttraumatic stress disorder. *Behavioural and Cognitive Psychotherapy,* **30,** 37–56.

Grey, S. and Mathews, A. (2000). Effects of training on interpretation of emotional ambiguity. *Quarterly Journal of Experimental Psychology,* **53,** 1143–62.

Griffiths, M.D. (1994). The role of cognitive bias and skill in fruit machine gambling. *British Journal of Psychology,* **85,** 351–69.

Guthrie, R. and Bryant, R. (2000). Attempting suppression of traumatic memories over extended periods in acute stress disorder. *Behaviour Research and Therapy,* **38,** 899–907.

Hackmann, A. (1997). The transformation of meaning on cognitive therapy. In M. Power and C.R. Brewin, Eds. *Transformation of meaning in psychological therapies,* pp. 125–40. Chichester: Wiley.

Hackmann, A., Surawy, C., and Clark, D.M. (1998). Seeing yourself through others' eyes: a study of spontaneously occurring images in social phobia. *Behavioural and Cognitive Psychotherapy,* **26,** 3–12.

Hackmann, A., Clark, D., and McManus, F. (2000). Recurrent images and early memories in social phobia. *Behaviour Research and Therapy,* **38,** 601–10.

Hadjistavropoulos, H.D., Hadjistavropoulos, T., and Quine, A. (2000). Health anxiety moderates the effects of distraction versus attention to pain. *Behaviour Research and Therapy,* **38,** 425–38.

Haenen, M.A., Schmidt, A.J.M., Kroeze, S., and van den Hout, M.A. (1996). Hypochondriasis and symptom reporting – the effect of attention versus distraction. *Psychotherapy and Psychosomatics,* **65,** 43–48.

Haenen, M.A., Schmidt A.J.M., Schoenmakers, M., and van den Hout, M.A. (1997). Tactual sensitivity in hypochondriasis. *Psychotherapy and Psychosomatics,* **66,** 128–32.

Haenen, M.A., de Jong, P.J., Schmidt, A.J., Stevens, S., and Visser, L. (2000). Hypochondriacs' estimation of negative outcomes: Domain-specific and responsiveness to reassuring and alarming information. *Behaviour Research and Therapy,* **38,** 819–33.

Hall, M., Buysse, D.J., Reynolds, C.F., Kupfer, D.J., and Baum, A. (1996). Stress-related intrusive thoughts disrupt sleep-onset and continuity. *Sleep Research,* **25,** 163.

Hall, M., Buysse, D.J., Nowell, P.D., *et al.* (2000). Symptoms of stress and depression as correlated of sleep in primary insomnia. *Psychosomatic Medicine,* **62,** 227–30.

Halligan, S.L., Clark, D.M., and Ehlers, A. (2002). Cognitive processing, memory, and the development of PTSD symptoms: two experimental analogue studies. *Journal of Behavior Therapy and Experimental Psychiatry,* **33,** 73–89.

Halligan, S.L., Michael, T., Clark, D.M., and Ehlers, A. (2003). Posttraumatic stress disorder following assult: the role of cognitive processing, trauma memory, and appraisals. *Journal of Consulting and Clinical Psychology,* **71,** 419–31.

Halpern, D.F. (1998). Teaching critical thinking for transfer across domains: dispositions, skills, structure training and metacognitive monitoring. *American Psychologist*, 53, 449–55.

Harnden, J.L., McNally, R.J., and Jimerson, D.C. (1997). Effects of suppressing thoughts about body weight: a comparison of dieters and nondieters. *International Journal of Eating Disorders*, 22, 285–90.

Harrington, J.A. and Blankenship, V. (2002). Ruminative thoughts and their relation to depression and anxiety. *Journal of Applied Social Psychology*, 32, 465–85.

Hart, K.E. and Chiovari, P. (1998). Inhibition of eating behavior: negative cognitive effects of dieting. *Journal of Clinical Psychology*, 54, 427–30.

Harvey, A.G. (2000). Pre-sleep cognitive activity: a comparison of sleep-onset insomniacs and good sleepers. *British Journal of Clinical Psychology*, 39, 275–86.

Harvey, A.G. (2001a). I can't sleep, my mind is racing! an investigation of strategies of thought control in insomnia. *Behavioural and Cognitive Psychotherapy*, 29, 3–12.

Harvey, A.G. (2001b). Insomnia: symptom or diagnosis? *Clinical Psychology Review*, 21, 1037–59.

Harvey, A.G. (2002a). A cognitive model of insomnia. Behaviour Research and Therapy, 40, 869–93.

Harvey, A.G. (2002b). Identifying safety behaviors in insomnia. *Journal of Nervous and Mental Disease*, 190, 16–21.

Harvey, A. G. (in press a). The attempted suppression of pre-sleep cognitive activity in insomnia. *Cognitive Therapy and Research*.

Harvey, A.G. (in press b). Beliefs about the utility of pre-sleep worry: an investigation of individuals with insomnia and good sleepers. *Cognitive Therapy and Research*.

Harvey, A.G. and Bryant, R.A. (1998). The effect of attempted thought suppression in acute stress disorder. *Behaviour Research and Therapy*, 36, 757–63.

Harvey, A.G. and Bryant, R.A. (1999a). Brief report a qualitative investigation of the organization of traumatic memories. *British Journal of Clinical Psychology*, 38, 401–5.

Harvey, A.G. and Bryant, R.A. (1999b). The role of anxiety in attempted thought suppression following exposure to distressing or neutral stimuli. *Cognitive Therapy and Research*, 23, 39–52.

Harvey, A.G. and Bryant, R.A. (2000). Memory for acute stress disorder symptoms: a two year prospective study. *Journal of Nervous and Mental Disease*, 188, 602–7.

Harvey, A.G. and Bryant, R.A. (2002). Acute stress disorder: a synthesis and critique. *Psychological Bulletin*, 128, 886–902.

Harvey, A.G. and McGuire, B.E. (2000). Suppressing and attending to pain-related thoughts in chronic pain patients. *Behaviour Research and Therapy*, 38, 1117–24.

Harvey, A.G. and Payne, S. (2002). The management of unwanted pre-sleep thoughts in insomnia: distraction with imagery versus general distraction. *Behaviour Research and Therapy*, 40, 267–77.

Harvey, A.G., Bryant, R.A., and Rapee, R.M. (1996). Preconscious processing of threat in posttraumatic stress disorder. *Cognitive Therapy and Research*, 20, 613–23.

Harvey, A.G., Bryant, R.A., and Dang, S.T. (1998). Autobiographical memory in acute stress disorder. *Journal of Consulting and Clinical Psychology*, 66, 500–6.

Harvey, A.G., Clark, D.M., Ehlers, A., and Rapee, R.M. (2000). Social anxiety and self-impression: cognitive preparation enhances the beneficial effects of video feedback following a stressful social task. *Behaviour Research and Therapy*, 38, 1183–92.

Harvey, A.G., Bryant, R.A., and Tarrier, N. (2003a). Cognitive behaviour therapy for posttraumatic stress disorder. *Clinical Psychology Review*, 23, 501–22.

Harvey, A.G., Jones, C., and Schmidt, A.D. (2003b). Sleep and posttraumatic stress disorder: a review. *Clinical Psychology Review*, 23, 377–407.

Harvey, J.M., Richards, J.C., Dziadosz, T., and Swindell, A. (1993). Misinterpretation of ambiguous stimuli in panic disorder. *Cognitive Therapy and Research*, 17, 235–48.

Harvey, P.D. (1985). Reality monitoring in mania and schizophrenia: the association between thought disorder and performance. *Journal of Nervous and Mental Disease*, 173, 67–73.

Harvey, P.D., Earle-Boyer, E.A., and Levinson, J.C. (1988). Cognitive deficits and thought disorder: a retest study. *Schizophrenia Bulletin*, 14, 57–66.

Hayes, B. and Hesketh, B. (1989). Attribution theory, judgmental biases, and cognitive behavior modification: prospects and problems. *Cognitive Therapy and Research*, 13, 211–30.

Hayes, S.C. (1987). A contextual approach to therapeutic change. In N. Jacobson, Ed. *Psychotherapists in clinical practice: cognitive and behavioral perspectives*, pp. 327–87. New York: Guilford Press.

Hayes, S.C. and Follette, W.C. (1992). Can functional analysis provide a substitute for syndromal classification. *Behavioural Assessment*, 14, 345–65.

Hayes, S.C., Wilson, K.G., Strosahl, K., Gifford, E.V., and Follette, V.M. (1996). Experiential avoidance and behavioral disorders: a functional dimensional approach to diagnosis and treatment. *Journal of Consulting and Clinical Psychology*, 64, 1152–68.

Hayes, S.C. Bissett, R.T., Korn, Z., *et al.* (1999a).The impact of acceptance versus control rationales on pain tolerance. *Psychological Record*, 49, 33–47.

Hayes, S.C., Strosahl, K.D., and Wilson, K.G. (1999b). *Acceptance and commitment therapy: an experiential approach to behavior change.* New York: Guilford Press.

Haynes, S.N. and O'Brien, W.H. (1990). Functional analysis in behaviour therapy. *Clinical Psychology Review*, 10, 649–68.

Hayward, P., Ahmad, T., and Wardle, J. (1994). Into the dangerous world: an in vivo study of information processing in agoraphobics. *British Journal of Clinical Psychology*, 33, 307–15.

Hazlett-Stevens, H. and Borkovec, T.D. (2001). Effects of worry and progressive relaxation on the reduction of fear in speech phobia: an investigation of situational exposure. *Behavior Therapy*, 32, 503–17.

Hazlett-Stevens, H., Zucker, B.G., and Craske, M.G. (2002). The relationship of thought-action fusion to pathological worry and generalized anxiety disorder. *Behaviour Research and Therapy*, 40, 1199–1204.

Heatherton, T.F. and Baumeister, R.F. (1991). Binge eating as escape from self-awareness. *Psychological Bulletin*, 110, 86–108.

Heimberg, R.G., Vermilyea, J.A., Dodge, C.S., *et al.* (1987). Attributional style, depression and anxiety: an evaluation of the specificity of depressive attributions. *Cognitive Therapy and Research*, 11, 537–50.

Heimberg, R.G., Klosko, J.S., Dodge, C.S., *et al.* (1989). Anxiety disorders, depression, and attributional style: a further test of the specificity of depressive attributions. *Cognitive Therapy and Research*, 13, 21–36.

Hellawell, S.J. and Brewin, C.R. (2002). A comparison of flashback and ordinary autobiographical memories of trauma: cognitive resources and behavioural observations. *Behaviour Research and Therapy*, 40, 1143–56.

Hemsley, D.R. (1987). An experimental psychological model for schizophrenia. In H. Hefner, W.F. Gattaz, and W. Janzarik, Eds. *Search for the causes of schizophrenia* pp. 179–88. Berlin: Springer-Verlag.

Hemsley, D.R. (1993). A simple (or simplistic?) cognitive model for schizophrenia. *Behaviour Research and Therapy*, 31, 633–45.

Hermans, D., Pieters, G., and Eelen, P. (1998). Implicit and explicit memory for nondieting controls. *Journal of Abnormal Psychology*, 107, 193–202.

Hermans, D., Martens, K., DeCort, K., Pieters, G., and Eelen, P. (2003). Reality monitoring and metacognitive beliefs related to cognitive confidence in obsessive-compulsive disorder. *Behaviour Research and Therapy*, 41, 383–401.

Henderson, D., Hargreaves, I., Gregory, S., and Williams, J.M. (2002). Autobiographical memory and emotion in a non-clinical sample of women with and without a reported history of childhood sexual abuse. *British Journal of Clinical Psychology*, 41, 129–41.

Hertel, P.T. and Hardin, T.S. (1990). Remembering with and without awareness in a depressed mood: Evidence of deficits in initiative. *Journal of Experimental Psychology: General*, 119, 45–59.

Hilbert, A., Tuschen-Caffier, B., and Vogele, C. (2002). Effects of prolonged and repeated body image exposure in binge-eating disorder. *Journal of Psychosomatic Research*, 52, 137–44.

Hill, A.B. and Knowles, T.H. (1991). Depression and the emotional Stroop effect. *Personality and Individual Differences*, 12, 481–5.

Hirsch, C.R. and Mathews, A. (1997). Interpretive inferences when reading about emotional events. *Behaviour Research and Therapy*, 35, 1123–32.

Hirsch, C.R. and Mathews, A. (2000). Impaired positive inferential bias in social phobia. *Journal of Abnormal Psychology*, 109, 705–12.

Hirsch, C.R., Clark, D.M., Mathews, A., and Williams, R. (2003a). Self-images play a causal role in social phobia. *Behaviour Research and Therapy*, 41, 909–21.

Hirsch, C.R., Clark, D.M., Mathews, A., and Williams, R. (in press). Negative self-imagery in social anxiety contaminates social interactions. *Memory*.

Hirsch, C.R., Mathews, A., Clark, D.M., Williams, R.M., and Morrison, J. (2003b). Negative self-imagery blocks inferences. *Behaviour Research and Therapy*, 41, 1383–96.

Hodgson, R. and Rachman, S. (1977). Obsessional compulsive complaints. *Behaviour Research and Therapy*, 15, 389–95.

Hoelscher, T.J., Klinger, E., and Barta, S.G. (1981). Incorporation of concern- and nonconcern-related verbal stimuli into dream content. *Journal of Abnormal Psychology*, 90, 88–91.

Hofmann, S.G., Ehlers, A., and Roth, W.T. (1995). Conditioning theory: a model for the etiology of public speaking anxiety? *Behaviour Research and Therapy*, 33, 567–71.

Hohlstein, L.A., Smith, G.T., and Atlas, J.G. (1998). An application of expectancy theory to eating disorders: development and validation of measures of eating and dieting expectancies. *Psychological Assessment*, 10, 49–58.

Holeva, V., Tarrier, N., and Wells, A. (2001). Prevalence and predictors of acute stress disorder and PTSD, following road traffic accidents: thought control strategies and social support. *Behavior Therapy*, 32, 65–83.

Holmes, E.A., Brewin, C.R., and Hennessy, R.G. (in press). Trauma films, information processing and intrusive memory development. *Journal of Experimental Psychology: General*.

Hooker, W.D. and Jones, R.T. (1987). Increased susceptibility to memory intrusions and the Stroop interference effect during acute marijuana intoxication. *Psychopharmacology*, 91, 20–4.

Hope, D.A., Gansler, D.A., and Heimberg, R.G. (1989). Attentional focus and causal attributions in social phobia: Implications from social psychology. *Clinical Psychology Review*, 9, 49–60.

Hope, D.A., Rapee, R.M., Heimberg, R.G., and Dombeck, M.J. (1990). Representations of the self in social phobia: vulnerability to social threat. *Cognitive Therapy and Research*, 14, 177–89.

Horenstein, M. and Segui, J. (1997). Chronometrics of attentional processes in anxiety disorders. *Psychopathology*, 30, 25–35.

Horley, K., Williams, L.M., Gonsalvez, C., and Gordon, E. (2003). Social phobics do not see eye to eye: a visual scanpath study of emotional expression processing. *Journal of Anxiety Disorders*, 17, 33–44.

Horowitz, M.J. (1986). Stress response syndromes, 2nd Edition. New York: Jason Aronson.

Hunt, J. and Cooper, M. (2001). Selective memory bias in women with bulimia nervosa and women with depression. *Behavioural and Cognitive Psychotherapy*, 29, 93–102.

Hunt, M.G. (1998). The only way out is through: emotional processing and recovery after a depressing life event. *Behaviour Research and Therapy*, 36, 361–84.

Hunter, E.C.M., Phillips, M.L., Chalder, T., Sierra, M., and David, A.S. (2003). Depersonalisation disorder: a cognitive-behavioural conceptualization. *Behaviour Research and Therapy*, 41, 1451-67.

Huq, S.F., Garety, P.A., and Hemsley, D.R. (1988). Probabilistic judgements in deluded and non-deluded subjects. *Quarterly Journal of Experimental Psychology*, 40A, 801–12.

Hyman, I.E. and Loftus, E.F. (1998). Errors in autobiographical memory. *Clinical Psychology Review*, 18, 933–47.

Ingram, R.E. (1990). Self-focused attention in clinical disorders: review and a conceptual model. *Psychological Bulletin*, 109, 156–76.

Ingram, R.E. and Hollon, S.D. (1986). Cognitive therapy for depression from an information processing perspective. In R.E. Ingram, Ed. *Information processing approaches to clinical psychology*, pp. 259–81. Orlando Florida: Academic Press.

Ingram, R.E. and Smith, T.W. (1984). Depression and internal versus external focus of attention. *Cognitive Therapy and Research*, 8, 139–52.

Isen, A.M., Shalker, T.E., Clark, M., and Carp, L. (1978). Affect, accessibility of material in memory, and behaviour: a cognitive loop? *Journal of Personality and Social Psychology*, 48, 1413–26.

Ito, L.M., de Araujo, L.A., Tess, V.L., de Barros Neto, T.P., Asbahr, F.R., and Marks, I. (2001). Self-exposure therapy for panic disorder with agoraphobia: randomised controlled study of external vs. interoceptive self-exposure. *British Journal of Psychiatry*, 178, 331–6.

Jackman, L.P., Williamson, D.A., Netemeyer, R.G., and Anderson, D.A. (1995). Do weight-preoccupied women misinterpret ambiguous stimuli related to body size? *Cognitive Therapy and Research*, 19, 341–55.

Jacobson, N.S., Dobson, K.S., Truax, P.A., *et al.* (1996). A component analysis of cognitive-behavioral treatment for depression. *Journal of Consulting and Clinical Psychology*, 64, 295–304.

James, W.A. (1890/1950). *The principles of psychology*. New York: Dover.

Janacek, A. and Calamari, J. (1999). Thought suppression in obsessive-compulsive disorder. *Cognitive Therapy and Research*, 23, 497–509.

Janet, P. (1907). *The major symptoms of hysteria*. New York: McMillan.

Jimerson, D.C., Lesem, M.D., Hegg, A.P., and Brewerton, T.D. (1990). Serotonin in human eating disorders. *Annals of the New York Academy of Science*, 600, 532–44.

John, C.H. and Dodgson, G. (1994). Inductive reasoning in delusional thought. *Journal of Mental Health*, 3, 31–49.

Johnsen, B.H., Laberg, J.C., Cox, W.M., Vaksal, A., and Hugdahl, K. (1994). Alcohol abusers' attentional bias in the processing of alcohol-related words. *Psychology of Addictive Behaviours*, 8, 111–15.

Johnson, D. J. (1996). Information seeking an organizational dilemma. Westport, CT: Quorum Books.

Johnson, H.M. (1994). Processes of successful intentional forgetting. *Psychological Bulletin*, 116, 274–92.

Johnson, M.K. and Hirst, W. (1993). MEM: Memory subsystems as processes. In A.F. Collins, S.E. Gathercole, M.A. Conway, and P.E. Morris, Eds. *Theories of memory* pp 241–86. Hove, UK: Lawrence Erlbaum Associated Ltd.

Johnston, L., Bulik, C.M., and Anstiss, V. (1999). Suppressing thoughts about chocolate. *International Journal of Eating Disorders*, 26, 21–7.

Johnston, W.A., Hawley, K.J., Plewe, S.H., Elliott, J.M., *et al.* (1990). Attention capture by novel stimuli. *Journal of Experimental Psychology: General*, 119, 397–411.

Joiner, T.E. (2001). Negative attributional style, hopelessness depression and endogenous depression. *Behaviour Research and Therapy*, 39, 139–49.

Jones, B.T., Corbin, W., and Fromme, K. (2001). A review of expectancy theory and alcohol consumption. *Addiction*, 96, 57–72.

Jones, M.K. and Menzies, R.G. (2000). Danger expectancies, self-efficacy and insight in spider phobia. *Behaviour Research and Therapy*, 38, 585–600.

Joseph, S.A., Brewin, C.R., Yule, W., and Williams, R.M. (1991). Causal attributions and psychiatric symptoms in survivors of the Herald of Free Enterprise disaster. *British Journal of Psychiatry*, 159, 542–6.

Joseph, S., Yule, W., and Williams, R. (1993). Post-traumatic stress: attributional aspects. *Journal of Traumatic Stress*, 6, 501–13.

Jostes, A., Pook, M., and Florin, I. (1999). Public and private self-consciousness as specific psychopathological features. *Personality and Individual Differences*, 27, 1285–95.

Judd, L.L., Kessler, R.C., Paulua, M.P., Zeller, P.V., Wittchen H-U and Kunovac, J.L. (1998). Comorbidity as a fundamental feature of generalised anxiety disorders: results from the Nationale Comorbidity Study (NCS). *Acta Psychiatrica Scandinavia*, **98**(Suppl 393), 6–11.

Just, N. and Alloy, L.B. (1997). The response styles theory of depression: tests and an extension of the theory. *Journal of Abnormal Psychology*, **106**, 221–9.

Kabat-Zinn, J. (1994). *Wherever you go, there you are: mindfulness meditation in everyday life*. New York: Hyperion.

Kahneman, D. and Tversky, A. Eds. (2000). *Choices, values, and frames*. Cambridge: Cambridge University Press.

Kahneman, D., Slovic, P., and Tversky, A. (1982). *Judgment under uncertainty: heuristics and biases*. Cambridge: Cambridge University Press.

Kamieniecki, G.W., Wade, T., and Tsourtos, G. (1997). Interpretive bias for benign sensations in panic disorder with agoraphobia. *Journal of Anxiety Disorders*, **11**, 141–56.

Kamphuis, J.H. and Telch, M.J. (2000). Effects of distraction and guided threat appraisal on fear reduction during exposure-based treatments for specific fears. *Behaviour Research and Therapy*, **38**, 1163–81.

Kampman, M., Keijsers, G.P.J., Verbraak, M.J.P.M., Näring, G, and Hoogduin, C.A.L. (2002). The emotional Stroop: a comparison of panic disorder patients, obsessive-compulsive patients, and normal controls, in two experiments. *Journal of Anxiety Disorders*, **16**, 425–41.

Kaney, S. and Bentall, R.P. (1989). Persecutory delusions and attributional style. *British Journal of Medical Psychology*, **62**, 191–8.

Kaney, S. and Bentall, R.P. (1992). Persecutory delusions and the self-serving bias: evidence from a contingency judgement task. *Journal of Nervous and Mental Disease*, **180**, 773–80.

Kaney, S., Bowen-Jones, K., Dewey, M.E., and Bentall, R.P. (1997). Two predictions about paranoid ideation: deluded, depressed and normal participants' subjective frequency and consensus judgements for positive, neutral and negative events. *British Journal of Clinical Psychology*, **36**, 349–64.

Kaney, S., Bowen-Jones, K., and Bentall, R.P. (1999). Persecutory delusions and autobiographical memory. *British Journal of Clinical Psychology*, **38**, 97–102.

Kapur, S. and Remington, G. (1996). Serotonin-dopamine interaction and its relevance to schizophrenia. *The American Journal of Psychiatry*, **153**, 466–76.

Kasch, K.L., Klein, D.N., and Lara, M.E. (2001). A construct validation study of the response styles questionnaire rumination scale in participants with a recent-onset major depressive episode. *Psychological Assessment*, **13**, 375–83.

Kaspi, S.P., McNally, R.J., and Amir, N. (1995). Cognitive processing of emotional information in posttraumatic stress disorder. *Cognitive Therapy and Research*, **19**, 433–44.

Keefe, R.S.E., Arnold, M.C., Bayen, U.J., and Harvey, P.D. (1999). Source monitoring deficits in patients with schizophrenia; a multinomial modelling analysis. *Psychological Medicine*, **29**, 903–14.

Kelley, A.E. and Kahn, J.H. (1994). Effects of suppression of personal intrusive thoughts. *Journal of Personality and Social Psychology*, **66**, 998–1006.

Kendell, R. and Jablensky, A. (2003). Distinguishing between validity and utility of psychiatric diagnoses. *American Journal of Psychiatry*, **160**, 4–12.

Kennedy, S.J., Rapee, R.M., and Mazurski, E.J. (1997). Covariation bias for phylogenetic versus ontogenetic fear-relevant stimuli. *Behaviour Research and Therapy*, 35, 415–22.

Kessler, R.C., *et al.* (1994). Lifetime and 12-month prevalence of DSM-III-R psychiatric disorders in the United States. *Archives of General Psychiatry*, 51, 8–19.

Kihlstrom, J.F. (1995). The trauma-memory argument. *Consciousness and Cognition*, 4, 63–7.

Kihlstrom, J.F. (1998). Exhumed memory. In S.J. Lynn and K.M. McConkey, Eds. *Truth in memory*, pp. 3–31. New York: Guilford Press.

Kinderman, P. (1994). Attentional bias, persecutory delusions and the self-concept. *British Journal of Medical Psychology*, 67, 53–66.

Kinderman, P. and Bentall, R.P. (1997*a*). Attribution therapy for paranoid delusions: a case study. *Behavioural and Cognitive Psychotherapy*, 25, 269–80.

Kinderman, P. and Bentall, R.P. (1997*b*). Causal attributions in paranoia and depression: internal, personal and situational attributions for negative events. *Journal of Abnormal Psychology*, 106, 341–5.

Kindt, M. and Brosschot, J.F. (1997). Phobia-related cognitive bias for pictorial and linguistic stimuli. *Journal of Abnormal Psychology*, 106, 644–8.

Kirby, K.N. (1994). Probabilities and utilities of fictional outcomes in Wason's four-card selection task. *Cognition*, 51, 1–28.

Kirsch, I. (1997). Response expectancy theory and application: a decennial review. *Applied and Preventive Psychology*, 6, 67–79.

Kirsch, I. Ed. (1999). *How expectancies shape experience*. American Psychological Association.

Klerman, G. (1990). Approaches to the phenomena of comorbidity. In J.D. Maser and C.R. Cloninger, Eds. *Comorbidity of mood and anxiety disorders*, pp. 13–37. Washington, DC: American Psychiatric Press.

Klinger, E. (1975). Consequences of commitment to and disengagement from incentives. *Psychological Review*, 82, 1–25.

Klinger, E. (1977). *Meaning and void: inner experience and the incentives in people's lives.* Minneapolis: University of Minnesota Press.

Klinger, E. (1987). Current concerns and disengagement from incentives. In F. Halisch and J. Kuhl, Eds. *Motivation, intention and violition*, pp. 337–47. Berlin: Springer-Verlag.

Klinger, E. (1996). Emotional influences on cognitive processing, with implications for theories of both. In P.M. Gollwitzer and J.A. Bargh, Eds. *The psychology of action: linking cognition and motivation to behaviour*, pp 168–89. New York: Guilford.

Klinger, E. and Kroll-Mensing (1995). Idiothetic assessment: experience sampling and motivational analysis. In J.N. Butcher, Ed. *Practical considerations in clinical personality assessment*, pp. 267–77. New York: Oxford University Press.

Koriat, A., Lichtenstein, S., and Fischhoff, B. (1980). Reasons for confidence. *Journal of Experimental Psychology: Human Learning and Memory*, 6, 107–18.

Kosaka, H., *et al.* (2002). Differential amygdala response during facial recognition in patients with schizophrenia: an fMRI study. *Schizophrenia Research*, 57, 87–95.

Kosonen, P. and Winne, P.H. (1995). Effects of teaching statistical laws on reasoning about everyday problems. *Journal of Educational Psychology*, 87, 33–46.

Kosslyn, S.M. (1980). *Image and mind.* Cambridge: Harvard University Press.

Kosslyn, S.M. (1981). The medium and the message in mental imagery: a theory. *Psychological Review*, 88, 46–66.

Kraemer, H.C., Wilson, G.T., Fairburn, C.G., and Agras, W.S. (2002). Mediators and moderators of treatment effects in randomized clinical trials. *Archives of General Psychiatry*, 59, 877–83.

Krakow, B., Hollifield, M., Johnston, L., *et al.* (2001). Imagery rehearsal therapy for chronic nightmares in sexual assault survivors with posttraumatic stress disorder. *Journal of the American Medical Association*, 286, 537–45.

Kramer, T., Buckhout, R., and Eugenio, P. (1990). Weapon focus, arousal, and eyewitness memory: Attention must be paid. *Law and Human Behavior*, 14, 167–84.

Krantz, S. and Hammen, C. (1979). Assessing cognitive bias in depression. *Journal of Abnormal Psychology*, 88, 611–19.

Kring, A.M. (2001). Emotion and psychopathology. In T.J. Mayne and G.A. Bonanno, Eds. *Emotions: current issues and future directions. Emotions and social behaviour*. New York: Guilford.

Kring, A.M. and Bachorowski, J.-A. (1999). Emotions and psychopathology. *Cognition and Emotion*, 13, 575–99.

Kroeze, S. and van den Hout M.A. (2000a). Selective attention for hyperventilatory sensations in panic disorder. *Journal of Anxiety Disorders*, 14, 563–81.

Kroeze, S. and van den Hout M.A. (2000b). Selective attention for cardiac information in panic patients (2000). *Behaviour Research and Therapy*, 38, 63–72.

Krstev, H., Jackson, H., and Maude, D. (1999). An investigation of attributional style in first-episode psychosis. *British Journal of Clinical Psychology*, 38, 181–94.

Kuehner, C. and Weber, I. (1999). Responses to depression in unipolar depressed patients: an investigation of Nolen-Hoeksema's response styles theory. *Psychological Medicine*, 29, 1323–33.

Kuhajda, M.C., Thorn, B.E., Klinger, M.R., and Rubin, N.J. (2002). The effect of headache pain on attention (encoding) and memory (recognition). *Pain*, 97, 213–21.

Kuipers, E. (1992). Expressed emotion research in Europe. *British Journal of Clinical Psychology*, 31, 429–42.

Kuyken, W. and Brewin, C.R. (1994). Intrusive memories of childhood abuse during depressive episodes. *Behaviour Research and Therapy*, 32, 525–8.

Kuyken, W. and Brewin, C.R. (1995). Autobiographical memory functioning in depression and reports of early abuse. *Journal of Abnormal Psychology*, 104, 585 91.

Kuyken, W. and Dalgleish, T. (1995). Autobiographical memory in depression. *British Journal of Clinical Psychology*, 34, 89–92.

Kyrios, M. and Iob, M.A. (1998). Automatic and strategic processing in obsessive-compulsive disorder: Attentional bias, cognitive avoidance, or more complex phenomena? *Journal of Anxiety Disorders*, 12, 271–92.

Lader, M.H. and Wing, L. (1966). *Physiological measures, sedative drugs and morbid anxiety*. Oxford: Oxford University Press.

Ladouceur, R. and Mayrand, M. (1986). Psychological characteristics of monetary risk-taking by gamblers and non-gamblers in roulette. *International Journal of Psychology*, 21, 433–43.

Ladouceur, R. and Walker, M. (1996). A cognitive perspective on gambling. In Salkovskis, P.M., Ed. *Trends in cognitive and behavioural therapies*, pp. 89–120. New York: Wiley.

Ladouceur, R., Dube, D., Giroux, I., *et al.* (1995). Cognitive biases in gambling: American roulette and 6/49 lottery. *Journal of Social Behavior and Personality*, 10, 473–9.

Ladouceur, R., Paquet, C., and Dube, D. (1996). Erroneous perceptions in generating sequences of random events. *Journal of Applied Social Psychology*, 26, 2157–66.

Ladouceur, R., Talbot, F., and Dugas, M.J. (1997). Behavioral expressions of intolerance of uncertainty in worry. *Behavior Modification*, 21, 355–71.

Ladouceur, R., Sylvain, C., Letarte, H., Giroux, I., and Jacques, C. (1998). Cognitive treatment of pathological gamblers. *Behaviour Research and Therapy*, 36, 1111–20.

Ladouceur, R., Freeston, M., Rheaume, J., *et al.* (2000a). Strategies used with intrusive thoughts: a comparison of OCD patients with anxiety and community controls. *Journal of Abnormal Psychology*, 109, 179–87.

Ladouceur, R., Gosselin, P., and Dugas, M.J. (2000b). Experimental manipulation of intolerance of uncertainty: a study of a theoretical model of worry. *Behaviour Research and Therapy*, 38, 933–41.

Ladouceur, R., Sylvain, C., Boutin, C., Lachance, S., Doucet, C., Leblond, J., and Jacques, C. (2001).Cognitive treatment of pathological gambling. *Journal of Nervous and Mental Disease*, 189, 774–80.

Lambie, J.A. and Marcel, A.J. (2002). Consciousness and the varieties of emotion experience: a theoretical framework. *Psychological Review*, 109, 219–59.

Langlois, F., Freeston, M.H., and Ladouceur, R. (2000a). Differences and similarities between obsessive intrusive thoughts and worry in a non-clinical population: study 1. *Behaviour Research and Therapy*, 38, 157 73.

Langlois, F., Freeston, M.H., and Ladouceur, R. (2000b). Differences and similarities between obsessive intrusive thoughts and worry in a non-clinical population: study 2. *Behaviour Research and Therapy*, 38, 175–89.

Lara, M.E., Klein, D.N., and Kasch, K.L. (2000). Psychosocial predictors of the short-term course and outcome of major depression: a longitudinal study of a nonclinical sample with recent-onset episodes. *Journal of Abnormal Psychology*, 109, 644–50.

Lavie, N. (1995). Perceptual load as a necessary condition for selective attention. *Journal of Experimental Psychology: Human Perception and Performance*, 21, 451–68.

Lavy, E.H. and van den Hout, M.A. (1990). Thought suppression induces intrusions. *Behavioural Psychotherapy*, 18, 251–8.

Lavy, E., van den Hout, M.A., and Arntz, A. (1993a). Attentional biases and spider phobia: conceptual and clinical issues. *Behaviour Research and Therapy*, 31, 17–24.

Lavy, E.H., van den Hout, M., and Arntz, A. (1993b). Attentional bias and facilitated escape: a pictorial test. *Advances in Behaviour Research and Therapy*, 15, 279–89.

Lavy, E.H. and van den Hout, M. (1993c). Attentional bias for appetitive cues: effects of fasting on normal subjects. *Behaviour Research and Therapy*, 31, 297–310.

Lavy, E.H. and van den Hout, M.A. (1994). Cognitive avoidance and attentional bias: causal relationships. *Cognitive Therapy and Research*, 18, 179–91.

Lavy, E.H., van Oppen, P., and van den Hout, M. (1994). Selective processing of emotional information in obsessive compulsive disorder. *Behaviour Research and Therapy*, 32, 243–6.

Lawson, C. and MacLeod, C. (1999). Depression and the interpretation of ambiguity. *Behaviour Research and Therapy*, 37, 463–74.

Lawson, C., MacLeod, C., and Hammond, G. (2002). Interpretation revealed in the blink of an eye: depressive bias in the resolution of ambiguity. *Journal of Abnormal Psychology*, 111, 107–23.

Layden, M., Newman, C., Freeman, A., and Morse, S.B. (1993). *Cognitive therapy of borderline personality disorder*. USA: Allyn and Bacon.

Leafhead, K.M., Young, A.W., and Szulecka, T.K. (1996). Delusions demand attention. *Cognitive Neuropsychiatry*, 1, 5–16.

Leckman, J.F., Walker, D.E., Goodman, W.K., Pauls, D.L., and Cohen, D.J. (1994). 'Just right' perceptions associated with compulsive behavior in Tourette's syndrome. *American Journal of Psychiatry*, 151, 675–80.

Lefebvre, J.C. and Keefe, F.J. (2002). Memory for pain: the relationship of pain catastrophizing to the recall of daily rheumatoid arthritis pain. *The Clinical Journal of Pain*, 18, 56–63.

Lepore, S.J. (1997). Expressive writing moderates the relation between intrusive thoughts and depressive symptoms. *Journal of Personality and Social Psychology*, 73, 1030–7.

Lewisohn, P.M. (1975). Engagement in pleasant activities and depression level. *Journal of Abnormal Psychology*, 84, 729–31.

Lichstein, K.L. and Rosenthal, T.L. (1980). Insomniacs' perception of cognitive versus somatic determinants of sleep disturbance. *Journal of Abnormal Psychology*, 89, 105–7.

Lindsay, D.S. and Read, J.D. (1994). Psychotherapy and memories of childhood sexual abuse: a cognitive perspective. *Applied Cognitive Psychology*, 8, 281–338.

Lindsay, M., Crino, R., and Andrews, G. (1997). Controlled trial of exposure and response prevention in obsessive-compulsive disorder. *British Journal of Psychiatry*, 171, 135–9.

Linney, Y., Peters, E., and Ayton, P. (1998). Reasoning biases in delusion-prone individuals. *British Journal of Clinical Psychology*, 37, 247–370.

Linton, S.J., Buer, N., Vlaeyen, J., and Hellsing, A.L. (2000). Are fear-avoidance beliefs related to the inception of an episode of back pain? A prospective study. *Psychology and Health*, 14, 1051–9.

Lister, R.G., Eckardt, M. J., and Weingartner, H. (1987). Ethanol intoxication and memory. Recent developments and new directions. *Recent developments in alcoholism*, 5, 111–26.

Littrell, J. (1998). Is the reexperience of painful emotion therapeutic? *Clinical Psychology Review*, 18, 71–102.

Litz, B.T. and Keane, T.M. (1989). Information processing in anxiety disorders: application to the understanding of post-traumatic stress disorder. *Clinical Psychology Review*, 9, 243–57.

Liu, S.K., Chiu, C.H., Chang, C.J., Hwang, T.J., Hwu, H.G., and Chen, W.J. (2002). Deficits in sustained attention in schizophrenia and affective disorders: stable versus state-dependent markers. *American Journal of Psychiatry*, 159, 975–82.

Lobban, F., Haddock, G., Kinderman, P., and Wells, A. (2002). The role of metacognitive beliefs in auditory hallucinations. *Personality and Individual Differences*, 32, 1351–63.

Loftus, E.F. (1979). *Eyewitness testimony*. Cambridge MA: Harvard University Press.

Loftus, E.F. (1993). The reality of repressed memories. *American Psychologist*, 48, 518–37.

Loughland, C.M., Williams, L.M. and Gordon, E. (2002). Schizophrenia and affective disorder show different visual scanning behaviour for faces: a trait versus state-based distinction. *Biological Psychiatry*, 52, 338–48.

Lovibond, P.F. (2001). The 'near miss' pathway as a fourth pathway to anxiety. *Behavioural and Cognitive Psychotherapy*, **29**, 35–43.

Lubman, D.I., Peters, L.A., Mogg, K., Bradley, B.P., and Deakin, J.F.W. (2000). Attentional bias for drug cues in opiate dependence. *Psychological Medicine*, **30**, 169–75.

Luck, S.J. and Thomas, S.J. (1999). What variety of attention is automatically captured by peripheral cues? *Perception and Psychophysics*, **61**, 1424–35.

Lucock, M. and Salkovskis, P.M. (1988). Cognitive factors in social anxiety and its treatment. *Behaviour Research and Therapy*, **26**, 297–302.

Lundh, L.-G. (1998). Cognitive-behavioural analysis and treatment of insomnia. *Scandinavian Journal of Behaviour Therapy*, **27**, 10–29.

Lundh, L.-G. and Öst, L.-G. (1996). Recognition bias for critical faces in social phobics. *Behaviour Research and Therapy*, **34**, 787–94.

Lundh, L.-G. and Öst, L.-G. (1997). Explicit and implicit memory bias in social phobia. The role of subdiagnostic type. *Behaviour Research and Therapy*, **35**, 305–17.

Lundh, L.-G., Cyzykow, S., and Öst, L.-G. (1997*a*). Explicit and implicit memory bias in panic disorder with agoraphobia. *Behaviour Research and Therapy*, **35**, 1003–14.

Lundh, L.-G., Fröding, A., Gyllenhammar, L., Broman, J.E., and Hetta, J. (1997*b*). Cognitive bias and memory performance in patients with persistent insomnia. *Scandinavian Journal of Behaviour Therapy*, **26**, 27–35.

Lundh, L.-G., Thulin, U., Cyzykow, S., and Öst, L.-G. (1998). Recognition bias for safe faces in panic disorder with agoraphobia. *Behaviour Research and Therapy*, **36**, 323–37.

Lundh, L.-G., Wikstrom, J., Westerlund, J., and Öst, L.-G. (1999). Preattentive bias for emotional information in panic disorder with agoraphobia. *Journal of Abnormal Psychology*, **108**, 222–32.

Lyon, H.M., Kaney, S., and Bentall, R.P. (1994). The defensive functions of persecutory delusions: evidence from attribution tasks. *British Journal of Psychiatry*, **164**, 637–46.

Lyon, H.M., Startup, M., and Bentall, R.P. (1999). Social cognition and the manic defense: attributions, selective attention and self-schema in bipolar affective disorder. *Journal of Abnormal Psychology*, **108**, 273–82.

Lyubomirsky, S. and Nolen-Hoeksema, S. (1993). Self-perpetuating properties of dysphoric rumination. *Journal of Personality and Social Psychology*, **65**, 339–49.

Lyubomirsky, S. and Nolen-Hoeksema, S. (1995). Effects of self-focused rumination on negative thinking and interpersonal problem solving. *Journal of Personality and Social Psychology*, **69**, 176–90.

Lyubomirsky, S., Caldwell, N.D., and Nolen-Hoeksema, S. (1998). Effects of ruminative and distracting responses to depressed mood on retrieval of autobiographical memories. *Journal of Personality and Social Psychology*, **75**, 166–77.

Lyubomirsky, S., Tucker, K.L., Caldwell, N.D., and Berg, K. (1999). Why ruminators are poor problem solvers: clues from the phenomenology of dysphoric rumination. *Journal of Personality and Social Psychology*, **77**, 1041–60.

Maas, A. and Kohnken, G. (1989). Eyewitness identification. *Law and Human Behaviour*, **11**, 397–408.

Mackay, C. (1841). *Extraordinary popular delusions and the madness of crowds*. Reprinted (1996). New York, NY: Wiley.

Mackinger, H.F., Pachinger, M.M., Leibetseder, M.M., and Fartacek, R.R. (2000). Autobiographical memories in women remitted from major depression. *Journal of Abnormal Psychology*, 109, 331–4.

MacLeod, A., Mathews, A., and Tata, P. (1986). Attentional bias in emotional disorders. *Journal of Abnormal Psychology*, 95, 15–20.

MacLeod, A.K. and Byrne, A. (1996). Anxiety, depression and the anticipation of future positive and negative experiences. *Journal of Abnormal Psychology*, 105, 286–9.

MacLeod, A.K. and Salaminiou, E. (2001). Reduced positive future thinking in depression: cognitive and affective factors. *Cognition and Emotion*, 15, 99–107.

MacLeod, A.K., Williams, J.M.G., and Bekerian, D.A. (1991). Worry is reasonable: the role of explanations in pessimism about future personal events. *Journal of Abnormal Psychology*, 100, 478–86.

MacLeod, A.K., Rose, G.S., and Williams, J.M.G. (1993). Components of hopelessness about the future in parasuicide. *Cognitive Therapy and Research*, 17, 441–5.

MacLeod, A.K., Tata, P., Kentish, J., and Jacobsen, H. (1997a). Retrospective and prospective cognitions in anxiety and depression. *Cognition and Emotion*, 11, 467–79.

MacLeod, A.K., Pankhania, B., Lee, M., and Mitchell, D. (1997b). Parasuicide, depression and the anticipation of positive and negative future experiences. *Psychological Medicine*, 27, 973–7.

MacLeod, A.K., Haynes, C., and Sensky, T. (1998). Attributions about common bodily sensations: their associations with hypochondriasis and anxiety. *Psychological Medicine*, 28, 225–8.

MacLeod, C. and Campbell, L. (1992). Memory accessibility and probability judgements: an experimental evaluation of the availability heuristic. *Journal of Personality and Social Psychology*, 63, 890–902.

MacLeod, C. and Cohen, I. (1993). Anxiety and the interpretation of ambiguity: a text comprehension study. *Journal of Abnormal Psychology*, 102, 238–47.

MacLeod, C. and Hagan, R. (1992). Individual differences in the selective processing of threatening information, and emotional responses to a stressful life event. *Behaviour Research and Therapy*, 30, 151–61.

MacLeod, C. and McLaughlin, K. (1995). Implicit and explicit memory bias in anxiety: a conceptual replication. *Behaviour Research and Therapy*, 33, 1–14.

MacLeod, C., Tata, P., and Mathews, A. (1987). Perception of emotionally valenced information in depression. *British Journal of Psychology*, 26, 67–68.

MacLeod, C., Rutherford, E., Campbell, L., Ebsworthy, G., and Holker, L. (2002). Selective attention and emotional vulnerability: assessing the causal basis of their association through the experimental manipulation of attentional bias. *Journal of Abnormal Psychology*, 111, 107–23.

MacLeod, C.M. (1989). Word context during initial exposure influences degree of priming in word fragment completion. *Journal of Experimental Psychology: Learning Memory and Cognition*, 15, 398–406.

Maidenberg, E., Chen, E., Craske, M., Bohn, P., and Bytritsky, A. (1996). Specificity of attentional bias in panic disorder and social phobia. *Journal of Anxiety Disorders*, 10, 529–41.

Mandler, G., Mandler, J.M., and Uviller, E.T. (1958). Autonomic feedback: the perception of autonomic activity. *Journal of Abnormal and Social Psychology*, 56, 367–73.

Manktelow, K.L. and Over, D.E. (1991). Social rules and utilities in reasoning with deontic conditionals. *Cognition*, 39, 85–105.

Mansell, W. (2000). Conscious appraisal and the modification of automatic processes in anxiety. *Behavioural and Cognitive Psychotherapy*, 28, 99–120.

Mansell, W. (2003). Universal selection theory: implications for multidisciplinary approaches to clinical psychology and psychiatry. *New Ideas in Psychology*, 21, 121–40.

Mansell, W. and Clark, D.M. (1999). How do I appear to others? Social anxiety and processing of the observable self. *Behaviour Research and Therapy*, 37, 419–34.

Mansell, W. and Lam, D. (in press). A preliminary study of autobiographical memory in remitted bipolar disorder and the role of imagery in memory specificity. *Memory*.

Mansell, W., Clark, D.M., Ehlers, A., and Chen, Y. (1999). Social anxiety and attention away from emotional faces. *Cognition and Emotion*, 13, 673–90.

Mansell, W., Clark, D.M., and Ehlers, A. (2003). Internal versus external attention in social anxiety: an investigation using a novel paradigm. *Behaviour Research and Therapy*, 41, 555–72.

Margo, A., Hemsley, D.R., and Slade, P.D. (1981). The effects of varying auditory input on schizophrenic hallucinations. *British Journal of Psychiatry*, 139, 122–27.

Markowitz, L. J. and Borotn, J. L. S. (2002). Suppression of negative self-reference and neutral thoughts: a preliminary investigation. *Behavioural and Cognitive Psychotherapy*, 30, 271–77.

Marlatt, G.A. and Gordon, J.R. Eds. (1985). *Relapse prevention: maintenance strategies in the treatment of addictive behaviors*. New York: Guilford Press.

Marmar, C.R., Weiss, D.S., Schlenger, W.E., *et al.* (1994). Peritraumatic dissociation and posttraumatic stress in male Vietnam theater veterans. *American Journal of Psychiatry*, 151, 902–7.

Marshall, P.S., Forstot, M., Callies, A., Peterson, P.K., and Schenck, C.H. (1997). Cognitive slowing and working memory difficulties in chronic fatigue syndrome. *Psychosomatic Medicine*, 59, 58–66.

Marshall, W.L. (1985). The effects of variable exposure in flooding therapy. *Behavior Therapy*, 16, 117–35.

Marshall, W.L. (1988). Behaviour therapy. In C.G. Last and M. Hersen M., Eds. *Handbook of anxiety disorders. Pergamon General Psychology Series*, Vol. 151, pp. 338–61. Elmsford, US: Pergamon Press, Inc.

Martell, C.R., Addis, M.E., and Jacobson, N.S. (2001). *Depression in context: strategies for guided action*. W. W. New York: Norton and Co, Inc.

Martin, J.A. and Penn, D.L. (2002). Attributional style in schizophrenia: an investigation in outpatients with and without persecutory delusions. *Schizophrenia Bulletin*, 28, 131–42.

Martin, L.L. and Stoner, P. (1995). Mood as input: what we think about how we feel determines how we think. In L.L. Martin and A. Tesser, Eds. *Striving and feeling: interactions between goals, affect and self-regulation*. Hillsdale NJ: Lawrence Erlbaum Associates.

Martin, L.L. and Tesser, A. (1989). Towards a motivational and structural theory of ruminative thought. In J.S. Uleman and J.A. Bargh, Eds. *Unintended thought* pp. 306–26. New York: Guilford.

Martin, L.L. and Tesser, A. (1996). Some ruminative thoughts. In R.S. Wyer Eds. *Ruminative thoughts. Advances in social cognition*, Vol. 9, pp. 1–47. USA: Lawrence Erlbaum Associates.

Martin, L.L., Ward, D.W., Achee, J.W., and Wyer, R.S. (1993). Mood as input: people have to interpret the motivational implications of their moods. *Journal of Personality and Social Psychology*, **64**, 317–26.

Mathews, A. (1990). Why worry? The cognitive function of anxiety. *Behaviour Research and Therapy*, **28**, 455–68.

Mathews, A. (1997). Information-processing biases in anxiety disorders. In D.M. Clark and C.G. Fairburn, Eds. *Science and practice of cognitive behaviour therapy*, pp. 47–66. Oxford: OUP.

Mathews, A. and Bradley, B. (1983). Mood and the self reference bias in recall. *Behaviour Research and Therapy*, **21**, 247–78.

Mathews, A. and Mackintosh, B. (2000). Induced emotional interpretation bias and anxiety. *Journal of Abnormal Psychology*, **109**, 602–15.

Mathews, A. and MacLeod, C. (1985). Selective processing of threat cues in anxiety states. *Behaviour Research and Therapy*, **23**, 563–9.

Mathews, A. and MacLeod, C. (1986). Discrimination of threat cues without awareness in anxiety states. *Journal of Abnormal Psychology*, **95**, 131–8.

Mathews, A. and MacLeod, C. (1994). Cognitive approaches to emotion. *Annual Review of Psychology*, **45**, 25–50.

Mathews, A. and MacLeod, C. (2002). Induced processing biases have causal effects on anxiety. *Cognition and Emotion*, **16**, 331–54.

Mathews, A. and Milroy, R. (1994). Effects of priming and suppression of worry. *Behaviour Research and Therapy*, **32**, 843–50.

Mathews, A., May, J., Mogg, K., and Eysenck, M. (1990). Attentional bias in anxiety: selective search or defective filtering? *Journal of Abnormal Psychology*, **99**, 166–73.

Mathews, A., Mogg, K., Kentish, J., and Eysenck, M. (1995). Effect of psychological treatment on cognitive bias in generalized anxiety disorder. *Behaviour Research and Therapy*, **33**, 293–303.

Mathews, A., Mogg, K., May, J., and Eysenck, M. (1989*a*). Implicit and explicit memory bias in anxiety. *Journal of Abnormal Psychology*, **98**, 236–40.

Mathews, A., Richards, A., and Eysenck, M. (1989*b*). Interpretation of homophones related to threat in anxiety states. *Journal of Abnormal Psychology*, **98**, 31–4.

Mathews, A., Ridgeway, V., and Williamson, D.A. (1996). Evidence for attention to threatening stimuli in depression. *Behaviour Research and Therapy*, **34**, 695–705.

Matt, G., Vacquez, C., and Campbell, W.K. (1992). Mood-congruent recall of affectively toned stimuli: a meta-analytical review. *Clinical Psychology Review*, **12**, 227–55.

Mattia, J.L., Heimberg, R.G., and Hope, D.A. (1993). The revised Stroop colour-naming task in social phobics. *Behaviour Research and Therapy*, **31**, 305–13.

Maxwell, S.E. and Delaney, H.D. (1990). *Designing experiments and analyzing data: a model comparison perspective*. Belmont, CA: Wadsworth.

Mayou, R.A., Ehlers, A., and Bryant, B. (2002). Posttraumatic stress disorder after motor vehicle accidents: 3-year follow up of a prospective longitudinal study. *Behaviour Research and Therapy*, **40**, 665–75.

McCabe, S.B. and Gotlib, I.H. (1995). Selective attention and clinical depression: performance on a deployment of attention task. *Journal of Abnormal Psychology*, 104, 241–45.

McCabe, S.B. and Toman, P.E. (2000). Stimulus exposure duration in a deployment-of-attention task: effects on dysphoric, recently dysphoric, and nondysphoric individuals. *Cognition and Emotion*, 14, 125–42.

McCabe, S.B., Gotlib, I.H., and Martin, R.A. (2000). Cognitive vulnerability for depression: deployment of attenton as a function of history of depression and current mood state. *Cognitive Therapy and Research*, 24, 427–44.

McCracken, L.M. (1997). Attention to pain in persons with chronic pain: a behavioural approach. *Behavior Therapy*, 28, 271–84.

McFarlane, A.C. (1986). Posttraumatic morbidity of a disaster. *Journal of Nervous and Mental Disease*, 174, 4–14.

McFarland, C. and Buehler, R. (1998). The impact of negative affect on autobiographical memory: the role of self-focused attention to moods. *Journal of Personality and Social Psychology*, 75, 1424–40.

McManus, F., Waller, G., and Chadwick, P. (1996). Biases in the processing of different forms of threat in bulimic and comparison women. *Journal of Nervous and Mental Disease*, 184, 547–54.

McNally, R.J. (1997). Memory and anxiety disorders. *Philosophical Transactions of the Royal Society of London. Series B*, 352, 1755–9.

McNally, R.J. (2003). *Remembering trauma.* Cambridge MA: Harvard University Press.

McNally, R.J. and Amir, N. (1996). Perceptual implicit memory for trauma-related information in post-traumatic stress disorder. *Cognition and Emotion*, 10, 551–6.

McNally, R.J. and Foa, E.G. (1987). Cognition and agoraphobia: bias in the interpretation of threat. *Cognitive Therapy and Research*, 11, 567–81.

McNally, R.J. and Kohlbeck, P.A. (1993). Reality monitoring in obsessive-compulsive disorder. *Behaviour Research and Therapy*, 31, 249–53.

McNally, R.J. and Ricciardi, J.N. (1996). Suppression of negative and neutral thoughts. *Behavioural and Cognitive Psychotherapy*, 24, 17–25.

McNally, R.J., Foa, E.B., and Donnell, C.D. (1989). Memory bias for anxiety information in patients with panic disorder. *Cognition and Emotion*, 3, 27–44.

McNally, R.J., Riemann, B.C., Louro, C.E., Lukach, B.M., and Kim, E. (1992). Cognitive processing of emotional information in panic disorder. *Behaviour Research and Therapy*, 30, 143–9.

McNally, R.J., English, G.E., and Lipke, H.J. (1993). Assessment of intrusive cognition in PTSD: use of the modified Stroop paradigm. *Journal of Traumatic Stress*, 6, 33–41.

McNally, R.J., Litz, B.T., Prassas, A., Shin, L.M., and Weathers, F.W. (1994). Emotional priming of autobiographical memory in post-traumatic stress disorder. *Cognition and Emotion*, 8, 351–67.

McNally, R.J., Lasko, N.B., Macklin, M.L., and Pitman, R.K. (1995). Autobiographical memory disturbance in combat-related posttraumatic stress disorder. *Behaviour Research and Therapy*, 33, 619–30.

McNally, R.J., Amir, N., and Lipke, H.J. (1996). Subliminal processing of threat cues in posttraumatic stress disorder? *Journal of Anxiety Disorders*, 10, 115–28.

McNally, R.J., Metzger, L.J., Lasko, N.B., Clancy, S.A., and Pitman, R.K. (1998). Directed forgetting of trauma cues in adult survivors of childhood sexual abuse with and without posttraumatic stress disorder. *Journal of Abnormal Psychology*, 107, 596–601.

Mellings, T. and Alden, L.E. (2000). Cognitive processes in social anxiety: the effects of self-focus, rumination and anticipatory processing. *Behaviour Research and Therapy*, 38, 243–57.

Merckelbach, H. and Wessel, I. (2000). Memory for actions and dissociation in obsessive-compulsive disorder. *Journal of Nervous and Mental Disease*, 188, 846–8.

Merckelbach, H., Muris, P., van den Hout, M., and de Jong, P. (1991). Rebound effects of thought suppression: instruction dependent? *Behavioural Psychotherapy*, 19, 225–38.

Metalsky, G.I., Joiner, T.E., Wonderlich, *et al.* (1997). When will bulimics be depressed and when not? The moderating role of attributional style. *Cognitive Therapy and Research*, 21, 61–72.

Meyer, T.J., Miller, M.L., Metzger, R.L., and Borkovec, T.D. (1990). Development and validation of the Penn State Worry Questionnaire. *Behaviour Research and Therapy*, 28, 487–95.

Michelson, L.K., Bellanti, C.J., Testa, S.M., and Marchione, N. (1997). The relationship of attributional style to agoraphobia severity, depression and treatment outcome. *Behaviour Research and Therapy*, 35, 1061–73.

Miguel, E.C., Rosario-Campos, M.C., Prado, H.D., *et al.* (2000). Sensory phenomena in obsessive-compulsive disorder and Tourette's Disorder. *Journal of Clinical Psychiatry*, 61, 150–6.

Mikulincer, M. and Solomon, Z. (1988). Attributional style and combat-related posttraumatic stress disorder. *Journal of Abnormal Psychology*, 97, 308–13.

Miller, G.A., and Chapman, J.P. (2001). Misunderstanding analysis of covariance. *Journal of Abnormal Psychology*, 110, 40–8.

Mizes, J.S., Christiano, B., Madison, J., Post, G., Seime, R., and Varnado, P. (2000). Development of the mizes anorectic cognitions questionnaire-revised: psychometric properties and factor structure in a large sample of eating disorder patients. *International Journal of Eating Disorders*, 28, 415–21.

Modell, J.G. and Mountz, J.M. (1995). Focal cerebral blood flow changes during craving for alcohol measured by SPECT. *Journal of Neuropsychiatry and Clinical Neuroscience*, 7, 15–22.

Mogg, K. and Bradley, B.P. (1998). A cognitive-motivational analysis of anxiety. *Behaviour Research and Therapy*, 36, 809–48.

Mogg, K. and Bradley, B.P. (2002). Selective orienting of attention to masked threat faces in social anxiety. *Behaviour Research and Therapy*, 40, 1403–14.

Mogg, K., Bradley, B.P., Williams, R., and Mathews, A. (1993). Subliminal processing of emotional information in anxiety and depression. *Journal of Abnormal Psychology*, 102, 304–11.

Mogg, K., Bradley, B.P., and Williams, R. (1995a). Attentional bias in anxiety and depression: the role of awareness. *British Journal of Clinical Psychology*, 34, 17–36.

Mogg, K., Bradley, B.P., Millar, N., and White, J. (1995b). A follow-up study of cognitive bias in generalized anxiety disorder. *Behaviour Research and Therapy*, 33, 927–35.

Mogg, K., Bradley, B.P., de Bono, J., and Painter, M. (1997). Time course of attentional bias for threat information in non-clinical anxiety. *Behaviour Research and Therapy*, 35, 297–303.

Mogg, K., Mathews, A., and Weinman, J. (1987). Memory bias in clinical anxiety. *Journal of Abnormal Psychology*, 96, 94–98.

Mogg, K., Matthews, A., and Weinman, J. (1989). Selective processing of threat cues in anxiety states: a replication. *Behaviour Research and Therapy*, 27, 317–23.

Mogg, K., Bradley, B.P., Hyare, H., and Lee, S. (1998). Selective attention to food-related stimuli in hunger: are attentional biases specific to emotional and psychopathological states, or are they also found in normal drive states? *Behaviour Research and Therapy*, 36, 227–37.

Mogg, K., McNamara, J., Powys, M., Rawlinson, H., Seiffer, A., and Bradley, B. (2000*a*). Selective attention to threat: a test of two cognitive models of anxiety. *Cognition and Emotion*, 14, 375–99.

Mogg, K., Millar, N., and Bradley, B.P. (2000*b*). Biases in eye movements to threatening facial expressions in generalized anxiety disorder and depressive disorder. *Journal of Abnormal Psychology*, 109, 695–704.

Mohlman, J. and Zinbarg, R.E. (2000). What kind of attention is necessary for fear reduction? An empirical test of the emotional processing model. *Behavior Therapy*, 31, 113–33.

Molina, S., Borkovec, T.D., Peasely, C., and Person, D. (1998). Content analysis of worrisome streams of consciousness in anxious and dysphoric participants. *Cognitive Therapy and Research*, 22, 109–23.

Monti, P.M., Rohsenow, D.J., Rubonis, A.V., *et al.* (1993). Alcohol cue reactivity: effects of detoxification and extended exposure. *Journal of Studies in Alcohol*, 54, 235–45.

Moore, R.G., Watts, F.N., and Williams, J.M.G. (1988). The specificity of personal memories in depression. *British Journal of Psychology*, 72, 479–83.

Morgan, H. (2000). Response to Dr. Battersby. *Australian and New Zealand Journal of Psychiatry*, 34, 872–3.

Morgan, H. and Raffle C. (1999). Does reducing safety behaviours improve treatment response in patients with social phobia? *Australian and New Zealand Journal of Psychiatry*, 33, 503–10.

Morin, C.M. (1993). *Insomnia: psychological assessment and management.* New York: Guildford Press.

Morley, S. and Wilkinson, L. (1995). The pain beliefs and perceptions inventory: a British replication. *Pain*, 61, 427–33.

Morrison, A.P. (2001). The interpretation of intrusions in psychosis: an integrative cognitive approach to hallucinations and delusions. *Behavioural and Cognitive Psychotherapy*, 29, 257–76.

Morrison, A.P. and Baker, C.A. (2000). Intrusive thoughts and auditory hallucinations: a comparative study of intrusions in psychosis. *Behaviour Research and Therapy*, 38, 1097–106.

Morrison, A.P., Haddock, G., and Tarrier, N. (1995). Intrusive thoughts and auditory hallucinations: a cognitive approach. *Behavioural and Cognitive Psychotherapy*, 23, 265–80.

Morrison, A.P. and Haddock, G. (1997a). Cognitive factors in source monitoring and auditory hallucinations. *Psychological Medicine*, 27, 669–79.

Morrison, A.P. and Haddock, G. (1997b). Self-focused attention in schizophrenic patients and normal subjects: a comparative study. *Personality and Individual Differences*, 23, 937–41.

Morrison, A.P. and Wells, A. (2000). Thought control strategies in schizophrenia: a comparison with non-patients. *Behaviour Research and Therapy*, 38, 1205–9.

Morrison, A.P. and Wells, A. (2003). A comparison of metacognitions in patients with hallucinations, delusions, panic disorder and non-patient controls. *Behaviour Research and Therapy*, 41, 251–6.

Morrison, A.P., Wells, A., and Nothard, S. (2000). Cognitive factors in predisposition to auditory and visual hallucinations. *British Journal of Clinical Psychology*, 39, 67–78.

Morrison, A.P., Beck, A.T., Glentworth, D., *et al.* (2003). Imagery and psychotic symptoms: a preliminary investigation. *Behaviour Research and Therapy*, 40, 1053–62.

Morrison, A.P., Bentall, R.P., French, P., *et al.* (2004). Randomised controlled trial of early detection and cognitive therapy for preventing transition to psychosis in high-risk individuals. *British Journal of Psychiatry*, 181 (s43), s78–s84.

Morrow, J. and Nolen-Hoeksema, S. (1990). Effects of responses to depression on the remediation of depressive affect. *Journal of Personality and Social Psychology*, 58, 519–27.

Moulds, M.L. (2002). *Memory processes in acute stress disorder.* Unpublished doctoral dissertation.

Moulds, M.L. and Bryant, R.A. (2002). Directed forgetting in acute stress disorder. *Journal of Abnormal Psychology*, 111, 175–9.

Mowrer, O.H. (1939). Anxiety and learning. *Psychological Bulletin*, 36, 517–8.

Mowrer, O.H. (1960). *Learning theory and behavior.* Oxford: Wiley.

Muris, P., Merckelbach, H., and de Jong, P. (1993). Verbalization and environmental cueing in thought suppression. *Behaviour Research and Therapy*, 31, 609–12.

Muris, P., Merckelbach, H., Horselemberg, R., Sijsenaar, M. and Leeuw, I. (1997). Thought suppression in spider phobia. *Behaviour Research and Therapy*, 35, 769–74.

Muris, P., Jongh, A.D., Merckelbach, H., Postema, S., and Vet, M. (1998). Thought suppression in phobic and non-phobic dental patients. *Anxiety, Stress and Coping*, 11, 275–87.

Murphy, F.C., Sahakian, B.J., Rubinsztein, J.S., Michael, A., Rogers, R.D., *et al.* (1999). Emotional bias and inhibitory control processes in mania and depression. *Psychological Medicine*, 29, 1307–21.

Murray, J., Ehlers, A., and Mayou, R.A. (2002). Dissociation and post-traumatic stress disorder: two prospective studies of road traffic accident survivors. *British Journal of Psychiatry*, 180, 363–8.

Musa, C., Lépine J.P., Clark, D.M., Mansell, W., and Ehlers, A. (2003). Selective attention in social phobia and the moderating effect of a concurrent depressive disorder. *Behaviour Research and Therapy*, 41, 1043–54.

Nash, M.R. (1994). Memory distortion and sexual trauma: the problem of false negatives and false positives. *The International Journal of Clinical and Experimental Hypnosis*, 42, 346–62.

Nathan, P.E. and Gorman, J.M. (2002). *A guide to treatments that work* 2nd Edition. London: Oxford University Press.

Neely, J.H. (1977). Semantic priming and retrieval from lexical memory: roles on inhibitionless spreading activation and limited capacity attention. *Journal of Experimental Psychology: General*, 106, 226–54.

Neitzert Semler, C. and Harvey, A.G. (in press-*a*). An investigation of monitoring for sleep-related threat in primary insomnia. *Behaviour Research and Therapy*.

Neitzert Semler, C. and Harvey, A.G. (in press-*b*). Monitoring for sleep-related threat: development and validation of the sleep associated monitoring index (SAMI). *Psychosomatic Medicine*.

Nelson, J. and Harvey, A.G. (2002). The differential functions of imagery and verbal thought in insomnia. *Journal of Abnormal Psychology*, 111, 665–9.

Nelson, J. and Harvey, A.G. (2003). Pre-sleep imagery under the microscope: a comparison of patients with insomnia and good sleepers. *Behaviour Research and Therapy*, 41, 273–84.

Nelson, K. and Gruendel, J. (1981). General event representations: basic building blocks of cognitive development. In *Advances in developmental psychology*, Vol. 1. New York: Academic Press.

Nelson, T.O. and Narens, L. (1990). Metamemory: a theoretical framework and new findings. In G. Bower, Ed. *The psychology of learning and motivation* Vol. 26. New York: Academic Press.

Neria, Y., Bromet, E.J., Sievers, S., Lavelle, J., and Fochtmann, L.J. (2002). Trauma exposure and posttraumatic stress disorder in psychosis: findings from a first-admission cohort. *Journal of Consulting and Clinical Psychology*, 70, 246–51.

Neumann, O. (1984). Automatic processing: a review of recent findings and a plea for an old theory. In W. Prontz and A. Sanders, Eds. *Cognition and motor processes*. Berlin: Springer.

Neumann, R. (2000). The causal influences of attributions on emotions: a procedural priming approach. *Psychological Science*, 11, 179–82.

Newman, M.G., Castonguay, L.G., Borkovec, T.D., and Molnar, C. (in press). Integrative psychotherapy for generalized anxiety disorder. To be published in R. Heimberg, Ed. *The nature and treatment of generalized anxiety disorder*. New York: Guilford Press.

Nezu, A.M. (1987). A problem-solving formulation of depression: a literature review and proposal of a pluralistic model. *Clinical Psychology Review*, 7, 121–44.

Nezu, A.M., Nezu, C.M., and Perri, M.G. (1989). *Problem-solving therapy for depression: theory, research, and clinical guidelines*. New York: Wiley and Sons.

Nickerson, R.S. (1998). Confirmation bias: a ubiquitous phenomenon in many guises. *Review of General Psychology*, 2, 175–20.

Niedenthal, P.M., Tangney, J.P., and Gavanski, I. (1994). 'If only I weren't' versus 'If only I hadn't': Distinguishing shame and guilt in counterfactual thinking. *Journal of Personality and Social Psychology*, 67, 585–95.

Nikles, C.D., Brecht, D.L., Klinger, E., and Bursell, A.L. (1998). The effects of current-concern- and nonconcern-related waking suggestions on nocturnal dream content. *Journal of Personality and Social Psychology*, 75, 242–55.

Nisbett, R.E. Ed. (1993). *Rules for reasoning*. New York: Lawrence Erlbaum.

Nolen-Hoeksema, S. (1987). Sex differences in unipolar depression: evidence and theory. *Psychological Bulletin*, 101, 259–82.

Nolen-Hoeksema, S. (1991). Responses to depression and their effects on the duration of depressive episodes. *Journal of Abnormal Psychology*, 100, 569–82.

Nolen-Hoeksema, S. (2000). The role of rumination in depressive disorders and mixed anxiety/depressive symptoms. *Journal of Abnormal Psychology,* 109, 504–11.

Nolen-Hoeksema, S. and Morrow, J. (1991). A prospective study of depression and posttraumatic stress symptoms after a natural disaster: the 1989 Loma Prieta earthquake. *Journal of Personality and Social Psychology,* 61, 115–21.

Nolen-Hoeksema, S. and Morrow, J. (1993). Effects of rumination and distraction on naturally occurring depressed mood. *Cognition and Emotion,* 7, 561–70.

Nolen-Hoeksema, S., Morrow, J., and Fredrickson, B.L. (1993). Response styles and the duration of episodes of depressed mood. *Journal of Abnormal Psychology,* 102, 20–8.

Nolen-Hoeksema, S., Parker, L.E., and Larson, J. (1994). Ruminative coping with depressed mood following loss. *Journal of Personality and Social Psychology,* 67, 92–104.

Norman, D.A. and Shallice, T. (1986). Attention to action: willed and automatic control of behaviour. In R.J. Davidson, G.E. Schwartz, and D. Shapiro, Eds. *Consciousness and self-regulation,* Vol. 4. New York: Plenum.

Nugent, K. and Mineka, S. (1994). The effect of high and low trait anxiety on implicit and explicit memory tasks. *Cognition and Emotion,* 8, 147–63.

Nunn, J.D., Mathews, A., and Trower, P. (1997). Selective processing of concern-related information in depression. *British Journal of Clinical Psychology,* 36, 489–503.

Öhman, A. and Mineka, S. (2001). Fears, phobias and preparedness: toward an evolved module of fear and fear learning. *Psychological Review,* 108, 483–522.

Öhman, A., Flykt, A., and Esteves, F. (2001). Emotion drives attention: detecting the snake in the grass. *Journal of Experimental Psychology: General,* 130, 466–78.

Oliver, K.G. and Huon, G.F. (2001). Eating-related thought suppression in high and low disinhibitors. *International Journal of Eating Disorders,* 30, 329–37.

Öst, L.-G. and Sterner, U. (1987). Applied tension. a specific behavioral method for treatment of blood phobia. *Behaviour Research and Therapy,* 25, 25–9.

Öst, L.-G. and Csatlos, P. (2000). Probability ratings in claustrophobic patients and normal controls. *Behaviour Research and Therapy,* 38, 1107–16.

Öst, L.-G., Ferebee, I., and Furmark, T. (1997). One-session group therapy of spider phobia: direct versus indirect treatments. *Behaviour Research and Therapy,* 35, 721–32.

Otto, M.W., McNally, R.J., Pollack, M.H., Chen, E., and Rosenbaum, J.F. (1994). Hemispheric laterality and memory bias for threat in anxiety disorders. *Journal of Abnormal Psychology,* 103, 828–31.

Padesky, C.A. and Greenberger, D. (1995). *Clinician's guide to 'mind over mood'.* New York: Guilford Press.

Page, A.C. (1994). Blood-injury phobia. *Clinical Psychology Review,* 14, 443–61.

Paivio, A. (1979). Psychological processes in the comprehension of metaphor. In A. Ortony, Ed. *Metaphor and thought.* Cambridge: Cambridge University Press.

Paivio, A. (1986). *Mental representations: a dual coding approach.* New York: Oxford University Press.

Paivio, A. and Marschark, M. (1991). Integrative processing of concrete and abstract sentences. In A. Paivio, Ed. *Images in the mind: the evolution of a theory,* pp. 134–54. New York: Harvester Wheatsheaf.

Palfai, T.P., Monti, P.M., Colby, S.M., and Rohsenow, D.J. (1997). Effects of suppressing the urge to drink on the accessibility of alcohol outcome expectancies. *Behaviour Research and Therapy,* 35, 59–65.

Papageorgiou, C. and Wells, A. (1998). Effects of attention training on hypochondriasis: a brief case series. *Psychological Medicine*, 28, 193–200.

Papageorgiou, C. and Wells, A. (1999). Process and meta-cognitive dimensions of depressive and anxious thoughts and relationships with emotional intensity. *Clinical Psychology and Psychotherapy*, 6, 156–62.

Papageorgiou, C. and Wells, A. (2000). Treatment of recurrent major depression with attentional training. *Cognitive and Behavioral Practice*, 7, 407–13.

Papageorgiou, C. and Wells, A. (2001). Positive beliefs about depressive rumination: development and preliminary validation of a self-report scale. *Behavior Therapy*, 32, 13–26.

Parker, G., Roussos, J., Hadzi-Pavlovic, D., Mitchell, P., Wilhelm, K., and Austin, M.P. (1997). The development of a refined measure of dysfunctional parenting and assessment of its relevance in patients with affective disorders. *Psychological Medicine*, 27, 1193–203.

Parkin, A.J. (1999). *Memory: a guide for professionals*. Sussex, UK: Wiley.

Parrott, G.W. and Sabini, J. (1990). Mood and memory under natural conditions: evidence for mood incongruent recall. *Journal of Personality and Social Psychology*, 59, 321–36.

Pauli, P. and Alpers, G.W. (2002). Memory bias in patients with hypochondriasis and somatoform pain disorder. *Journal of Psychosomatic Research*, 52, 45–53.

Pauli, P., Montoya, P., and Martz, G.-E. (1996). Covariation bias in panic-prone individuals. *Journal of Abnormal Psychology*, 105, 658–62.

Pauli, P., Wiedemann, G., and Montoya, P. (1998). Covariation bias in flight phobics. *Journal of Anxiety Disorders*, 12, 555–65.

Paunovic, N., Lundh, L.G., and Öst, L.G. (2002). Attentional and memory bias for emotional information in crime victims with acute posttraumatic stress disorder (PTSD). *Journal of Anxiety Disorders*, 16, 675–92.

Pavlov, I.P. (1928). *Lectures on conditioned reflexes*. New York: Liveright.

Pearce, S.A., Isherwood, S., Hrouda, D., Richardson, P.H., Erskine, A. and Skinner, J. (1990). Memory and pain: tests of mood congruity and state dependent learning in experimentally induced and clinical pain. *Pain*, 43, 187–93.

Pearsall, J. and Trumble, B. (1996). *The Oxford English dictionary*, 2nd Edition. Oxford: OUP.

Peasley-Miklus, C. and Vrana, S.R. (2000). Effect of worrisome and relaxing thinking on fearful emotional processing. *Behaviour Research and Therapy*, 38, 129–44.

Peeters, F., Wessel, I., Merckelbach, H., and Boon-Vermeeren, M. (2002). Autobiographical memory specificity and the course of major depressive disorder. *Comprehensive Psychiatry*, 43, 344–50.

Pelissier, M.-C. and O'Connor, K.P. (2002). Deductive and inductive reasoning in obsessive-compulsive disorder. *British Journal of Clinical Psychology*, 41, 15–27.

Pennebaker, J.W. (1989). Confession, inhibition, and disease. In L. Berkowitz, Ed. *Advances in experimental social psychology*, Vol. 22, pp. 211–44. Orlando, F.L.: Academic Press.

Pennebaker, J.W. (1993). Putting stress into words: health, linguistic and therapeutic implications. *Behaviour Research and Therapy*, 31, 539–48.

Pennebaker, J.W. (1997). Writing about emotional experiences as a therapeutic process. *Psychological Science*, 8, 162–66.

Pennebaker, J.W. and Beall, S.K. (1986). Confronting a traumatic event: toward an understanding of inhibition and disease. *Journal of Abnormal Psychology*, 95, 274–81.

Perez-Lopez, J.P. and Woody, S.R. (2001). Memory for facial expression in social phobia. *Behaviour Research and Therapy*, **39**, 967–75.

Perowne, S. and Mansell, W. (2002). Social anxiety, self-focused attention, and the discrimination of negative, neutral and positive audience members by their non-verbal behaviours. *Behavioural and Cognitive Psychotherapy*, **30**, 11–23.

Perpina, C., Hemsley, D., Treasure, J., and de Silva, P. (1993). Is selective information processing of food and body words specific to patients with eating disorders? *International Journal of Eating Disorders*, **14**, 359–66.

Persons, J.B. (1989). *Cognitive therapy in practice: a case formulation approach.* NY: Guilford Press.

Peters, E., Day, S. and Garety, P. (1997). From preconscious to conscious processing: where does the abnormality lie in delusions? *Schizophrenia Research*, **24**, 120.

Peterson, C.R., Semmel, A., von Baeyer, C., Abramson, L.Y., Metalsky, G.I., and Seligman, M.E.P. (1982). The attributional style questionnaire. *Cognitive Therapy and Research*, **6**, 287–300.

Philippot, P., Schaefer, A., and Herbette, G. (2003). Consequences of specific processing of emotional information: impact of general versus specific autobiographical memory priming on emotion elicitation. *Emotion*, **3**, 270–83.

Philips, H.C. (1987). Avoidance behaviour and its role in sustaining chronic pain. *Behaviour Research and Therapy*, **25**, 273–9.

Philips, H.C. and Jahanshahi, M. (1985). Chronic pain: an experimental analysis of the effects of exposure. *Behaviour Research and Therapy*, **23**, 281–90.

Phillips, M.L. and David, A.S. (1997). Visual scan paths are abnormal in deluded schizophrenics. *Neuropsychologia*, **35**, 99–105.

Pincus, T., Pearce, S., McClelland, A., *et al.* (1994). Interpretation bias in responses to ambiguous cues in pain patients. *Journal of Psychosomatic Research*, **38**, 347–53.

Pincus, T., Pearce, S., and McClelland, A. (1995). Endorsement and memory bias of self-referential pain stimuli in depressed patients. *British Journal of Clinical Psychology*, **34**, 267–77.

Pincus, T., Pearce, S., and Perrott, A. (1996). Pain patients' bias in the interpretation of ambiguous homophones. *British Journal of Medical Psychology*, **69**, 259–66.

Placanica, J.L., Faunce, G.J., and Job, R.F. (2002). The effect of fasting on attentional biases for food and body/weight words in high and low eating disorder inventory scorers. *International Journal of Eating Disorders*, **32**, 79–90.

Posner, M.I., Snyder, C.R., and Davidson, B.J. (1980). Attention and the detection of signals. *Journal of Experimental Psychology: General*, **109**, 160–74.

Power, M. and Dalgliesh, T. (1997). *Cognition and emotion: from order to disorder.* Sussex, UK: Psychology Press.

Power, M.J., Dalgliesh, T., Claudio, V., Tata, P., and Kentish, J. (2000). The directed forgetting task: application to emotionally valent material. *Journal of Affective Disorders*, **57**, 147–57.

Puffet, A., Jehin-Marchot, D., Timsit-Berthier, M., and Timsit, M. (1991). Autobiographical memory and major depressive states. *European Psychiatry*, **6**, 141–5.

Purdon, C. (1999). Thought suppression and psychopathology. *Behaviour Research and Therapy*, **37**, 1029–54.

Purdon, C. (2001). Appraisal of obsessional thought recurrences: impact on anxiety and mood state. *Behavior Therapy*, 32, 47–64.

Purdon, C. and Clark, D.A. (1999). Meta-cognition and obsessions. *Clinical Psychology and Psychotherapy*, 6, 102–11 (Special issue, *Metacognition and Cognitive Behaviour Therapy*).

Purdon, C.A. and Clark, D.A. (1993). Obsessive intrusive thoughts in nonclinical subjects. 1. Content and relationship with depressive, anxious and obsessional symptoms. *Behaviour Research and Therapy*, 31, 713–20.

Purdon, C.A. and Clark, D.A. (2000). White bears and other elusive intrusions: assessing the relevance of thought suppression for obsessional phenomena. *Behaviour Modification*, 24, 425–53.

Pury, C.L.S. and Mineka, S. (1997). Covariation bias for blood-injury stimuli and aversive outcomes. *Behaviour Research and Therapy*, 35, 35–47.

Pyszczynski, T. and Greenberg, J. (1987). Self-regulatory perseveration and the depressive self-focusing style: a self-awareness theory of reactive depression. *Psychological Bulletin*, 102, 122–38.

Pyszczynski, T., Holt, K., and Greenberg, J. (1987). Depression, self-focused attention, and expectancies for positive and negative future life events for self and others. *Journal of Personality and Social Psychology*, 52, 994–1001.

Rachman, S. (1976a). The passing of the two-stage theory of fear and avoidance: fresh possibilities. *Behaviour Research and Therapy*, 14, 125–31.

Rachman, S. (1976b). The modification of obsessions: a new formulation. *Behaviour Research and Therapy*, 14, 437–43.

Rachman, S. (1980). Emotional processing. *Behaviour Research and Therapy*, 18, 51–60.

Rachman, S. (1981). Part 1: unwanted intrusive cognitions. *Advances in Behaviour Research and Therapy*, 3, 89–99.

Rachman, S. (1984). Agoraphobia: a safety-signal perspective. *Behaviour Research and Therapy*, 22, 59–70.

Rachman, S. (1994). The overprediction of fear: a review. *Behaviour Research and Therapy*, 32, 683–90.

Rachman, S. (1997). The evolution of cognitive behaviour therapy. In, D.M. Clark and C.G. Fairburn, Eds. *Science and practice of cognitive behaviour therapy*, pp. 3–22. Oxford: Oxford University Press.

Rachman, S. (2001). Emotional processing, with special reference to post-traumatic stress disorder. *International Review of Psychiatry*, 13, 164–71.

Rachman, S. (2002). A cognitive theory of compulsive checking. *Behaviour Research and Therapy*, 40, 625–39.

Rachman, S. and Arntz, A. (1991). The overprediction and underprediction of pain. *Clinical Psychology Review*, 11, 339–55.

Rachman, S. and Eyrl, K. (1989). Predicting and remembering recurrent pain. *Behaviour Research and Therapy*, 27, 621–35.

Rachman, S. and Hodgson, R. (1980). *Obsessions and compulsions*. Englewood Cliffs, NJ: Prentice-Hall Inc.

Rachman, S. and Lopatka, C. (1986a). Match and mismatch in the prediction of fear- I. *Behaviour Research and Therapy*, 24, 387–93.

Rachman, S. and Lopatka, C. (1986*b*). Match and mismatch of fear in Gray's theory–II. *Behaviour Research and Therapy*, 24, 395–401.

Rachman, S. and Lopatka, C. (1986*c*). Do fears summate?–III. *Behaviour Research and Therapy*, 24, 653–60.

Rachman, S. and Lopatka, C. (1986*d*). A simple method for determining the functional independence of two or more fears–IV. *Behaviour Research and Therapy*, 24, 661–4.

Rachman, S. and Shafran, R. (1998). Cognitive and behavioral features of obsessive-compulsive disorder. In R.P. Swinson, M.M. Antony, *et al.*, Eds. *Obsessive-compulsive disorder: theory, research, and treatment*, pp. 51–78. New York: Guilford Press.

Rachman, S. and Shafran, R. (1999). Cognitive distortions: thought-action fusion. Clinical Psychology and Psychotherapy, 6, 80–5.

Rachman, S., Craske, M., Tallman, K., and Solyom, C. (1986). Does escape behaviour strengthen agoraphobic avoidance? A replication. *Behaviour Therapy*, 17, 366–84.

Rachman, S., Levitt, K., and Lopatka, C. (1988). Experimental analyses of panic: claustrophobic subjects. *Behaviour Research and Therapy*, 26, 41–52.

Rachman, S., Thordarson, D.S., Shafran, R., and Woody, S.R. (1995). Perceived responsibility: structure and significance. *Behaviour Research and Therapy*, 33, 779–84.

Rachman, S., Shafran, R., Mitchell, D., *et al.* (1996). How to remain neutral: an experimental analysis of neutralization. *Behaviour Research and Therapy*, 34, 889–98.

Rachman, S., Gruter-Andrew, J., and Shafran, R. (2000). Post-event processing in social anxiety. *Behaviour Research and Therapy*, 38, 611–7.

Rachman, S.J. (1976). Obsessional-compulsive checking. *Behaviour Research and Therapy*, 14, 269–77.

Rachman, S.J. and de Silva, P. (1978). Abnormal and normal obsessions. *Behaviour Research and Therapy*, 16, 233–48.

Radomsky, A.S. and Rachman, S. (1999). Memory bias in obsessive-compulsive disorder. *Behaviour Research and Therapy*, 37, 605–18.

Radomsky, A.S., de Silva, P., Todd, G., Treasure, J., and Murphy, T. (2002). Thought-shape fusion in anxorexia nervosa: an experimental investigation. *Behaviour Research and Therapy*, 40, 1169–77.

Raes, F., Hermans, D., de Decker, A., Eelen, P., and Williams, J.M.G. (in press). Autobiographical memory specificity and affect regulation: an experimental approach. *Emotion.*

Raichle, M.E. (1997). Automaticity: from reflective to reflexive information processing in the human brain. In M. Ito, Y. Miyashita, and E.T. Rolls, Eds. *Cognition, computation and consciousness.* Oxford: OUP.

Rapee, R.M. (1993). The utilisation of working memory by worry. *Behaviour Research and Therapy*, 31, 617–20.

Rapee, R.M. (1994). Failure to replicate a memory bias in panic disorder. *Journal of Anxiety Disorders*, 8, 291–300.

Rapee, R.M. and Heimberg, R. (1997). A cognitive behavioural model of social phobia. *Behaviour Research and Therapy*, 35, 741–56.

Rapee, R.M. and Lim, L. (1992). Discrepancy between self and observer ratings of performance in social phobics. *Journal of Abnormal Psychology*, 101, 728–31.

Rapee, R.M., McCallum, S.L., Melville, L.F., Ravenscroft, H., and Rodney, J.M. (1994). Memory bias in social phobia. *Behaviour Research and Therapy*, 32, 89–99.

Rassin, E. and Diepstraten, P. (2003). How to suppress obsessive thoughts. *Behaviour Research and Therapy*, 41, 97–103.

Rassin, E., Merckelbach, H., and Muris, P. (1997). Effects of thought suppression on episodic memory. *Behaviour Research and Therapy*, 35, 1035–8.

Rassin, E., Merckelbach, H., Muris, P., and Spaan, V. (1999). Thought-action fusion as a causal factor in the development of intrusions. *Behaviour Research and Therapy*, 37, 231–7.

Rauch, S.L., *et al.* (2000). Exaggerated amygdala response to masked facial stimuli in posttraumatic stress disorder: a functional MRI study. *Biological Psychiatry*, 47, 769–76.

Reas, D.L., Whisenhunt, B.L., Netemeyer, R., and Williamson, D.A. (2002). Development of the body checking questionnaire: a self-report measure of body checking behaviors. *International Journal of Eating Disorders*, 31, 324–33.

Regier, D.A., *et al.* (1990). Comorbidity of mental disorders with alcohol and other drug abuse. Results from the epidemiologic catchment area (ECA) Study. *The Journal of the American Medical Association*, 264, 2511–8.

Reilly-Harrington, N.A., Alloy, L.B., Fresco, D.M., and Whitehouse, W.G. (1999). Cognitive styles and life events interact to predict bipolar and unipolar symptomatology. *Journal of Abnormal Psychology*, 108, 567–78.

Reiss, S. and McNally, R.J. (1985). Expectancy model of fear. In S. Reiss and R.R. Bootzin, Eds. *Theoretical issues in behaviour therapy*, pp. 107–21. San Diego, CA: Academic Press.

Rettew, D.C., Swedo, S.E., Leonard, H.L., Lenane, M.C., and Rapoport, J.L. (1992). Obsessions and compulsions across time in 79 children and adolescents with obsessive-compulsive disorder. *Journal of the American Academy of Child and Adolescent Psychiatry*, 31, 1050–6.

Reynolds, M. and Brewin, C.R. (1999). Intrusive memories in depression and posttraumatic stress disorder. *Behaviour Research and Therapy*, 37, 201–15.

Reynolds, M. and Tarrier, N. (1996). Monitoring of intrusions in post-traumatic stress disorder: a report of single case studies. *British Journal of Medical Psychology*, 69, 371–9.

Richards, A. and French, C.C. (1992). An anxiety-related bias in semantic activation when processing threat/neutral homographs. *Quarterly Journal of Experimental Psychology*, 45A, 503–25.

Richards, D. and Lovell, K. (1999). Behavioural and cognitive behavioural interventions in the treatment of PTSD. In W. Yule, Ed. *Post-traumatic stress disorders: concepts and therapy*. Chichester: Wiley.

Richards, J.C., Austin, D.A., and Alvarenga, M.E. (2001). Interpretation of ambiguous interoceptive stimuli in panic disorder and non-clinical panic. *Cognitive Research and Therapy*, 25, 235–46.

Ridout, N., Astell, A.J., Reid, I.C., Glen, T., and O'Carroll, R.E. (2003). Memory bias for emotional facial expressions in major depression. *Cognitive and Emotion*, 17, 101–22.

Rief, W., Hiller, W., and Margraf, J. (1998). Cognitive aspects of hypochondriasis and the somatisation syndrome. *Journal of Abnormal Psychology*, 107, 587–95.

Rieger, E., Schotte, D.E., Touyz, S.W., Beumont P.J.V., Griffiths, R., and Russell, J. (1998). Attentional biases in eating disorders: a visual probe detection procedure. *International Journal of Eating Disorders*, 23, 199–205.

Rippere, V. (1977). What's the thing to do when you're feeling depressed: a pilot study. *Behaviour Research and Therapy*, 15, 185–91.

Riskind, J.H., Castellon, C.S., and Beck, A.T. (1989). Spontaneous causal explanations in unipolar depression and generalized anxiety: content analysis of dysfunctional-thought diaries. *Cognitive Therapy and Research*, 13, 97–108.

Rivkin, I.D. and Taylor, S.E. (1999). The effects of mental simulation on coping with controllable stressful events. *Personality and Social Psychology Bulletin*, 25, 1451–62.

Roberts, J.E., Gilboa, E., and Gotlib, I.H. (1998). Ruminative response style and vulnerability to episodes of dysphoria: gender, neuroticism, and episode duration. *Cognitive Therapy and Research*, 22, 401–23.

Robins, C.J. and Hayes, A.H. (1995). The role of causal attributions in the prediction of depression. In G.M. Buchanan and M.E.P. Seligman, Eds. *Explanatory style*, pp. 71–98. Hillsdale NJ: Lawrence Erlbaum.

Robins, L.N., Locke, B.Z., and Regier, D.A. (1991). An overview of psychiatric disorders in America. In L.N. Robins and D.A. Regier, Eds. *Psychiatric disorders in America: the epidemiologic catchment area study*, pp. 328–66. New York: Free Press.

Robinson, J.A. (1986). Autobiographical memory: a historical prologue. In D.C. Rubin, Ed. *Autobiographical memory*, pp. 19–49. Cambridge: Cambridge University Press.

Rode, S., Salkovskis, P.M. and Jack, T. (2001). An experimental study of attention, labeling and memory in people suffering from chronic pain. *Pain*, 94, 193–203.

Rodriguez, B.I. and Craske, M.I. (1993). The effects of distraction during exposure to phobic stimuli. *Behaviour Research and Therapy*, 31, 549–58.

Roediger, H.L. and Blaxton, T.A. (1987). Retrieval modes produce dissociation in memory for surface information. In D. Gorfein and R.R. Hoffman, Eds. *Memory and cognitive processes: the Ebbinghaus centennial conference*. Hillsdale, N.J: Lawrence Erlbaum.

Roediger, H.L. and McDermott, K.B. (1992). Depression and implicit memory: a commentary. *Journal of Abnormal Psychology*, 101, 587–91.

Roelofs, J., Peters, M.L., Zeegers M.P.A., and Vlaayen, W.S. (2002). The modified Stroop paradigm as a measure of selective attention towards pain-related stimuli among chronic pain patients: a meta-analysis. *European Journal of Pain*, 6, 271–81.

Roemer, L. and Borkovec, T.D. (1994). Effects of suppressing thoughts about emotional material. *Journal of Abnormal Psychology*, 103, 467–74.

Roemer, L., Litz, B.T., Orsillo, S.M., Ehlich, P.J., and Friedman, M.J. (1998). Increases in retrospective accounts of war-zone exposure over time: the role of PTSD symptoms severity. *Journal of Traumatic Stress*, 11, 597–605.

Roese, N.J. (1997). Counterfactual thinking. *Psychological Bulletin*, 12, 133–48.

Rose, M.J., Klenerman, L., Atchison, L., and Slade, P.D. (1992). An application of the fear avoidance model to three chronic pain problems. *Behaviour Research and Therapy*, 30, 359–65.

Rosen, J.C. (1997). Cognitive-behavioral body image therapy. In D.M. Garner and P.E. Garfinkel, Eds. *Handbook of treatment for eating disorders*, pp. 188–201. New York: Guilford Press.

Ross, L. (1977). The intuitive psychologist and his shortcomings. In L. Berkowitz, Ed. *Advances in experimental social psychology*, Vol 10, pp. 173–220. New York: Academic Press.

Ross, M. and Sicoly, F. (1979). Egocentric biases in availability and attribution. *Journal of Personality and Social Psychology*, 37, 322–36.

Roth, D., Antony, M.M., and Swinson, R.P. (2001). Interpretations for anxiety symptoms in social phobia. *Behaviour Research and Therapy*, 39, 129–38.

Rothbaum, B.O. and Schwartz, A.C. (2002). Exposure therapy for posttraumatic stress disorder. *American Journal of Psychotherapy*, 56, 59–75.

Rubonis, A.V., Colby, S.M., Monti, P.M., Rohsenow, D.J., Gulliver, S.B., and Sirota, A.D. (1994). Alcohol cue reactivity and mood induction in male and female alcoholics. *Journal of Studies in Alcohol*, 54, 487–94.

Ruiter, C. and Brosschott, J.F. (1994). The emotional Stroop interference effect in anxiety: attentional bias or cognitive avoidance? *Behaviour Research and Therapy*, 32, 315–9.

Rushford, N. and Ostermeyer, A. (1997). Body image disturbances and their change with videofeedback in anorexia nervosa. *Behaviour Research and Therapy*, 35, 389–98.

Russo, R., Fox, E., Bellinger, L., and Nguyen-van-Tam, D.P. (2001). Mood-congruent free recall bias in anxiety. *Cognition and Emotion*, 15, 419–33.

Sackville, T., Schotte, D.E., Touyz, S.W., Griffiths, R., and Beaumont P.J.V. (1998). Conscious and preconscious processing of food, body, weight and shape, and emotion-related words in women with anorexia nervosa. *International Journal of Eating Disorders*, 23, 77–82.

Sakheim, D.K., Barlow, D.H., Abrahamson, D.A., and Beck, J.G. (1987). Distinguishing between organogenic and psychogenic erectile dysfunction. *Behaviour Research and Therapy*, 23, 379–90.

Salkovskis, P.M. (1985). Obsessional-compulsive problems: a cognitive-behavioural analysis. *Behaviour Research and Therapy*, 25, 571–83.

Salkovskis, P.M. (1989a). Cognitive-behavioral factors and the persistence of intrusive thoughts in obsessional problems. *Behaviour Research and Therapy*, 27, 677–82.

Salkovskis, P.M. (1989b). Somatic problems. In K. Hawton, P.M. Salkovskis, J. Kirk, and D.M. Clark, Eds. *Cognitive therapy for psychiatric problems a practical guide*. Oxford: Oxford University Press.

Salkovskis, P.M. (1991). The importance of behaviour in the maintenance of anxiety and panic: a cognitive account. *Behavioural Psychotherapy*, 19, 6–19.

Salkovskis, P.M. (1999). Understanding and treating obsessive-compulsive disorder. *Behaviour Research and Therapy*, 37, Suppl 1: S29–52.

Salkovskis, P.M. (2002). Empirically grounded clinical interventions: cognitive-behavioural therapy progresses through a multi-dimensional approach to clinical science. *Behavioural and Cognitive Psychotherapy*, 30, 3–10.

Salkovskis, P.M. and Campbell, P. (1994). Thought suppression induces intrusion in naturally occurring negative intrusive thoughts. *Behaviour Research and Therapy*, 32, 1–8.

Salkovskis, P.M. and Harrison, J. (1984). Abnormal and normal obsessions – a replication. *Behaviour Research and Therapy*, 22, 549–52.

Salkovskis, P.M. and Warwick, H.M.C. (1986). Morbid preoccupations, health anxiety and reassurance: a cognitive-behavioural approach to hypochondriasis. *Behaviour Research and Therapy*, 24, 597–602.

Salkovskis, P.M., Richards, H.C., and Forrester, E. (1995). The relationship between obsessional problems and intrusive thoughts. *Behavioural and Cognitive Psychotherapy*, 23, 282–99.

Salkovskis, P.M., Clark, D.M., and Gelder, M.G. (1996). Cognition-behaviour links in the persistence of panic. *Behaviour Research and Therapy*, 34, 453–8.

Salkovskis, P.M., Forrester, E., and Richards, C. (1998). The cognitive-behavioural approach to understanding obsessional thinking. *British Journal of Psychiatry*, **35**(suppl), 53–63.

Salkovskis, P.M., Clark, D.M., Hackmann, A., Wells, A., and Gelder, M.G. (1999). An experimental investigation of the role of safety-seeking behaviours in the maintenance of panic disorder with agoraphobia. *Behaviour Research and Therapy*, **37**, 559–74.

Sanchez-Craig, M. (1984). *A therapists' manual for secondary prevention of alcohol problems: procedures for teaching moderate drinking and abstinence.* Toronto: Addiction Research Foundation.

Sanderson, W.C., Di Nardo, P.A., Rapee, R.M., and Barlow, D.H. (1990). Syndrome comorbidity in patients diagnosed with a DSM-III-R anxiety disorder. *Journal of Abnormal Psychology*, **99**, 308–12.

Sarason, I.G. (1984). Test anxiety, stress, and social support. *Journal of Personality*, **49**, 101–14.

Sarason, I.G., Sarason, B.R., Keefe, D.E., Hayes, B.E., and Shearin, E.N. (1986). Cognitive interference: situational determinants and traitlike characteristics. *Journal of Personality and Social Psychology*, **51**, 215–26.

Sartory, G., Master, D., and Rachman, S. (1989). Safety-signal therapy in agoraphobics: a preliminary test. *Behaviour Research and Therapy*, **27**, 205–9.

Sarwer, D.B. (1997). The 'obsessive' cosmetic surgery patient: a consideration of body image dissatisfaction and body dysmorphic disorder. *Plastic Surgical Nursing*, **17**, 193–7.

Savage, C.R., Deckersbach, T., Wilhelm, S., Rauch, S.L., Baer, L., Reid, T., and Jenike, M.A. (2000). Strategic processing and episodic memory impairment in obsessive compulsive disorder. *Neuropsychology*, **14**, 141–51.

Sawchuk, C.N., Lohr, J.M., Lee, T.C., and Tolin, D.F. (1999). Exposure to disgust-evoking imagery and information processing biases in blood-injection-injury phobia. *Behaviour Research and Therapy*, **37**, 249–57.

Schacter, D.L. (1999). The seven sins of memory: insights from psychology and cognitive neuroscience. *American Psychologist*, **54**, 182–203.

Schienle, A., Vaitl, D., and Stark, R. (1996). Covariation bias and paranormal belief. *Psychological Reports*, **78**, 291–305.

Schlesier-Carter, B., Hamilton, S.A., O'Neil, P.M., *et al.* (1989). Depression and bulimia: the link between depression and bulimic cognitions. *Journal of Abnormal Psychology*, **98**, 322–5.

Schmidt, N.B., Lerew, D.R., and Trakowski, J.H. (1997). Bodily vigilance in panic disorder: evaluating attention to bodily perturbations. *Journal of Consulting and Clinical Psychology*, **65**, 214–20.

Schneider, W. and Shiffrin, R.M. (1977). Controlled and automatic human information processing: (1) Detection, search and attention. *Psychological Review*, **84**, 1–66.

Scholz, O.B., Ott, R., and Sarnoch, H. (2001). Proprioception in somatoform disorders. *Behaviour Research and Therapy*, **39**, 1429–38.

Schotte, D.E. and Clum, G.A. (1987). Problem-solving skills in suicidal psychiatric patients. *Journal of Consulting and Clinical Psychology*, **55**, 49–54.

Schotte, D.E., McNally, R.J., and Turner, M.L. (1990). A dichotic listening analysis of body weight concern in bulimia nervosa. *International Journal of Eating Disorders*, **9**, 109–13.

Schwalberg, M.D., Barlow, D.H., Alger, S.A., and Howard, L.J. (1992). Comparison of bulimics, obese binge eaters, social phobics, and individuals with panic disorder on comorbidity across DSM-III-R anxiety disorders. *Journal of Abnormal Psychology,* 101, 675–81.

Schwarz, N. and Clore, G.L. (1983). Mood, misattribution, and judgements of well-being: informative and directive functions of affective states. *Journal of Personality and Social Psychology,* 45, 513–23.

Schwarz, N. and Clore, G.L. (1988). How do I feel about it. The informative function of affective states. In K. Fiedler and J.P. Forgas, Eds. *Affect, cognition and social behaviour.* Toronto: Hogrefe.

Scott, J., Williams, J.M., Brittlebank, A., and Ferrier, I.N. (1995). The relationship between premorbid neuroticism, cognitive dysfunction and persistence of depression: a 1-year follow-up. *Journal of Affective Disorders,* 33, 167–72.

Scott, J., Stanton, B., Garland, A., and Ferrier, I.N. (2000). Cognitive vulnerability in patients with bipolar disorder. *Psychological Medicine,* 30, 467–72.

Sebastian, S.B., Williamson, D.A., and Blouin, D.C. (1996). Memory bias for fatness stimuli in the eating disorders. *Cognitive Therapy and Research,* 20, 275–86.

Segal, Z.V., Williams, J.M.G., and Teasdale, J.D. (2002). *Mindfulness-based cognitive therapy for depression – a new approach to preventing relapse.* New York: Guilford Press.

Segerstrom, S.C., Tsao, J.C., Alden, L.E., and Craske, M.G. (2000). Worry and rumination: repetitive thought as a concomitant and predictor of negative mood. *Cognitive therapy and Research,* 20, 13–36.

Seligman, M. and Binik, Y. (1977). The safety signal hypothesis. In H. Davis and H. Hurwitz, Eds. *Pavlovian operant interactions.* Hillsdale, NJ: Erlbaum.

Seligman, M.E. and Johnston, J.C. (1973). A cognitive theory of avoidance learning. In F.J. McGuigan and D.B. Lumsdenn, Eds. *Contemporary approaches to conditioning and learning.* Oxford: V. H. Winston and Sons.

Seligman, M.E.P. (1971). Phobias and preparedness. *Behavior Therapy,* 2, 307–20.

Seligman, M.E.P., Abramson, L.Y., Semmel, A., and von Baeyer, C. (1979). Depressive attributional style. *Journal of Abnormal Psychology,* 88, 242–7.

Seligman, M. E. P., Castellon, C., Cacciola, J., Schulman, P., Luborsky, L., Ollove, M., and Downing, R. (1988). Explanatory style change during cognitive therapy for unipolar depression. *Journal of Abnormal Psychology,* 97, 13–18.

Severeijns, R., Vlaeyen J.W.S., van den Hout, M.A., and Weber W.E.J. (2001). Pain catastrophizing predicts pain intensity, disability and psychological distress independent of the level of physical impairment. *Clinical Journal of Pain,* 17, 165–72.

Shafran, R., Thordarson, D.S., and Rachman, S. (1996). Thought-action fusion in obsessive compulsive disorder. *Journal of Anxiety Disorders,* 10, 379–91.

Shafran, R., Teachman, B.A., Kerry, S., and Rachman, S. (1999). A cognitive distortion associated with eating disorders: thought-shape fusion. *British Journal of Clinical Psychology,* 38, 167–79.

Shafran, R., Fairburn, C., Nelson, L., and Robinson, P.H. (2003). The interpretation of symptoms of severe dietary restraint. *Behaviour Research and Therapy,* 41, 887–94.

Shafran, R., Fairburn, C.G., Robinson, P., and Lask, B. (in press). Body checking and its avoidance in eating disorders. *International Journal of Eating Disorders.*

Shalev, A.Y., Peri, T., Canetti, L., and Schreiber, S. (1996). Predictors of PTSD in injured trauma survivors: a prospective study. *American Journal of Psychiatry*, **153**, 219–25.

Shalev, A.Y., Freedman, S., Peri, T., Brandes, D., and Sahar, T. (1997). Predicting PTSD in trauma survivors: prospective evaluation of self-report and clinician-administered instruments. *British Journal of Psychiatry*, **170**, 558–64.

Sharma, D., Albery, I.P., and Cook (2001). Selective attentional bias to alcohol-related stimuli in problem-drinkers and non-problem drinkers. *Addiction*, **96**, 285–95.

Sharp, H.M., Fear, C.F., and Healy, D. (1997). Attributional style and delusions: an investigation based on delusional content. *European Psychiatry*, **12**, 1–7.

Sharp, T. (2001a). Chronic pain: a reformulation of the cognitive-behavioural model. *Behaviour Research and Therapy*, **39**, 787–800.

Sharp, T.J. (2001b). The 'safety seeking behaviours' construct and its application to chronic pain. *Behavioural and Cognitive Psychotherapy*, **29**, 241–50.

Sharpe, L. (2002). A reformulated cognitive-behavioral model of problem gambling: a biopsychosocial perspective. *Clinical Psychology Review*, **22**, 1–25.

Shenton, M.E., Gerig, G., McCarley, R.W., Szekely, G., and Kikinis, R. (2002). Amygdala-hippocampal shape differences in schizophrenia: the application of 3D shape models to volumetric M.R. data. *Psychiatry Research*, **115**, 15–35.

Sherman, S.J., Cialdini, R.B., Schwartzman, D.F., and Reynolds, K.D. (1985). Imagining can heighten or lower the perceived likelihood of contracting a disease: the mediating effect of ease of imagery. *Personality and Social Psychology Bulletin*, **11**, 118–27.

Shipherd, J.C. and Beck, J.G. (1999). The effects of suppressing trauma-related thoughts on women with rape-related posttraumatic stress disorder. *Behaviour Research and Therapy*, **37**, 99–112.

Showalter, E. (1997). *Hystories*. New York: Columbia Universities Press.

Sidley, G.L., Whitaker, T.H., Calam, R., and Wells, T.H. (1997). The prediction of parasuicide repetition in a high-risk group. *British Journal of Clinical Psychology*, **38**, 375–86.

Siegle, G., Sagratti, S., and Crawford, C. (1999). *Effects of rumination and initial severity on response to cognitive therapy for depression*. Meeting of the Association for the Advancement of Behavior Therapy, Toronto, ON.

Silberman, E.K., Weingartner, H., and Post, R.M. (1983). Thinking disorder in depression. *Archives of General Psychiatry*, **40**, 775–80.

Silverman, R.J. and Peterson, C. (1993). Explanatory style in schizophrenic and depressed outpatients. *Cognitive Therapy and Research*, **17**, 457–70.

Simkins-Bullock, J., Wildman, B.G., Bullock, W.A., and Sugrue, D.P. (1992). Etiological attributions, responsibility attributions and marital adjustment in erectile dysfunction patients. *Journal of Sex and Marital Therapy*, **18**, 83–103.

Skinner, B.F. (1959). *Cumulative record*. New York: Appleton Century.

Sloan, T. and Telch, M.J. (2002). The effects of safety-seeking behaviour and guided threat reappraisal on fear reduction during exposure: an experimental investigation. *Behaviour Research and Therapy*, **40**, 235–51.

Smari, J., Stefansson, S., and Thorgilsson, H. (1994). Paranoia, self-consciousness and social cognition in schizophrenics. *Cognitive Therapy and Research*, **18**, 387–99.

Smeets, G., de Jong, P.J., and Mayer, B. (2000). If you suffer from a headache, then you have a brain tumour: domain specific reasoning "bias" and hypochondriasis. *Behaviour Research and Therapy,* **38**, 763–76.

Smith, T.W. and Greenberg, J. (1981). Depression and self-focused attention. *Motivation and Emotion,* **5**, 323–31.

Smyth, J.M. (1998). Written emotional expression: effect sizes, outcome types and moderating variables. *Journal of Consulting and Clinical Psychology,* **66**, 174–84.

Snider, B. S., Asmundson, G. J. G., and Wiese, K. C. (2000). Automatic and strategic processing of threat cues in patients with chronic pain: a modified-Stroop evaluation. *Clinical Journal of Pain,* **16**, 144–154.

Solomon, Z. (1989). A 3-year prospective study of post-traumatic stress disorder in Israeli combat veterans. *Journal of Traumatic Stress,* **2**, 59–73.

Sookman, D. and Pinard, G. (2002). Overestimation of threat and intolerance of uncertainty in obsessive compulsive disorder. In R.O. Frost and G. Steketee, Eds. *Cognitive approaches to obsessions and compulsions: theory, assessment and treatment,* pp. 63–89. Amsterdam: Pergamon/Elsevier Science.

Southwick, S.M., Morgan, C.A., Nicolaou, A.L., and Charney, D.S. (1997). Consistency of memory for combat-related traumatic events in veterans of operation desert storm. *American Journal of Psychiatry,* **154**, 173–7.

Spanos, N.P., Radtke-Bodorik, H.L., Ferguson, J.D., and Jones, B. (1979). The effects of hypnotic susceptibility, suggestions for analgesia, and the utilization of cognitive strategies on the reduction of pain. *Journal of Abnormal Psychology,* **88**, 282–92.

Spasojevic, J. and Alloy, L.B. (2001). Rumination as a common mechanism relating depressive risk factors to depression. *Emotion,* **1**, 25–37.

Spence, D.P. (1982). *Narrative truth and historical truth: meaning and interpretation in psychoanalysis.* New York: Norton.

Spera, S.P., Buhrfeind, E.D., and Pennebaker, J.W. (1994). Expressive writing and coping with job loss. *Academy of Management Journal,* **37**, 722–33.

Spiegel, D. (1993). Dissociation and trauma. In D. Spiegel, R.P. Kluft, R.J. Loewenstein, J.C. Nemiah, F.W. Putnam, and M. Steinberg, Eds. *Dissociative disorders: a clinical review,* pp. 117–31. Lutherville, MD: Sidran Press.

Spielman, A.J., Caruso, L.S., and Glovinsky, P.B. (1987). A behavioral perspective on insomnia treatment. *Psychiatric Clinics of North America,* **10**, 541–53.

Spinhoven, P. and van der Does, W.A.J. (1999). Thought suppression, dissociation and psychopathology. *Personality and Individual Differences,* **27**, 877–86.

Spitzer, R.L., Williams J.B.W., Gibbon, M., and First, M. (1996). *Structured clinical interview for DSM-IV (SCID).* Washington, DC: American Psychiatric Association.

Spurr, J.M. and Stopa, L. (2002). Self-focused attention in social phobia and social anxiety. *Clinical Psychology Review,* **22**, 947–75.

Spurr, J.M. and Stopa, L. (2003). The observer perspective: effects on social anxiety and performance. *Behaviour Research and Therapy,* **41**, 1009–28.

Squire, L.R. (1994). Declarative and nondeclarative memory: multiple brain systems supporting learning and memory. In D.L. Schacter and E. tulving, Eds. *Memory systems,* pp. 203–31. Cambridge MA: MIT Press.

Stacy, A.W. (1995). Memory association and ambiguous cues in models of alcohol and marijuana use. *Experimental and Clinical Psychopharmacology*, 3, 183–94.

Stacy, A.W. (1997). Memory activation and expectancy as prospective predictors of alcohol and marijuana use. *Journal of Abnormal Psychology*, 106, 61–73.

Stacy, A.W., Newcomb, M.D., and Bentler, P.M. (1991). Cognition, motivation and problem drug use: a 9 year longitudinal study. *Journal of Abnormal Psychology*, 100, 502–15.

Staiger, P., Dawe, S., and McCarthy, R. (2000). Responsivity to food cues in bulimic women and controls. *Appetite*, 35, 27–33.

Steiger, H., Lehoux, P.M., and Gauvin, L. (1999). Impulsivity, dietary control and the urge to binge in bulimic syndromes. *International Journal of Eating Disorders*, 26, 261–74.

Steil, R. and Ehlers, A. (2000). Dysfunctional meaning of posttraumatic intrusions in chronic PTSD. *Behaviour Research and Therapy*, 38, 537–58.

Stein, K.D., Goldman, M.S., and Del Boca, F.K. (2000). The influence of alcohol expectancy and mood manipulation on subsequent alcohol consumption. *Journal of Abnormal Psychology*, 109, 106–15.

Stephens, R.S., Curtin, L., Simpson, E.E., and Roffman, R.A. (1994). Testing the abstinence violation effect construct with marijuana cessation. *Addictive Behaviors*, 19, 23–32.

Stober, J. (1998). Worry, problem elaboration and suppression of imagery: the role of concreteness. *Behaviour Research and Therapy*, 36, 751–6.

Stober, J. and Borkovec, T. (2002). Reduced concreteness of worry in generalized anxiety disorder: findings from a therapy study. *Cognitive Therapy and Research*, 26, 89–96.

Stober, J., Tepperwien, S., and Staak, M. (2000). Worrying leads to reduced concreteness of problem elaborations: evidence for the avoidance theory of worry. *Anxiety, Stress and Coping*, 13, 217–27.

Stoler, L.S. and McNally, R.J., (1991). Cognitive bias in symptomatic and recovered agoraphobics. *Behaviour Research and Therapy*, 29, 539–45.

Stopa, L. and Clark, D.M. (1993). Cognitive processes in social phobia. *Behaviour Research and Therapy*, 3, 255–67.

Stopa, L. and Clark, D.M. (2000). Social phobia and interpretation of social events. *Behaviour Research and Therapy*, 38, 273–83.

Stopa, L. and Clark, D.M. (2001). Social phobia: comments on the viability and validity of an analogue research strategy and British norms for the fear of negative evaluation questionnaire. *Behavioural and Cognitive Psychotherapy*, 29, 423–30.

Stormark, K.M., Hugdahl, K., and Posner, M.I. (1999). Emotional modulation of attention orienting: a classical conditioning study. *Scandinavian Journal of Psychology*, 40, 91–9.

Strack, F., Schwarz, N., and Gscchneidinger, E. (1985). Happiness and reminiscing: the role of time perspective, affect and mode of thinking. *Journal of Personality and Social Psychology*, 49, 1460–9.

Streit, M., Wölwer, W., and Gaebel, W. (1997). Facial affect recognition and visual scanning behaivour in the course of schizophrenia. *Schizophrenia Research*, 24, 311–7.

Stroop, J.R. (1935). Studies of interference in serial verbal reactions. *Journal of Experimental Psychology*, 18, 643–62.

Sullivan, M.J.L., Rouse, D., Bishop, S., and Johnston, S. (1997). Thought suppression, catastrophizing and pain. *Cognitive Therapy and Research*, 21, 555–68.

Sullivan, M.L., Bishop, S.R., and Pivik, J. (1995). The pain catastrophizing scale: development and validation. *Psychological Assessment*, 7, 524–32.

Sutherland, G., Newman, B., and Rachman, S. (1982). Experimental investigations of the relations between mood and intrusive unwanted cognitions. *British Journal of Medical Psychology*, 55, 127–38.

Sweeney, P.D., Anderson, K., and Bailey, S. (1986). Attributional style in depression: a meta-analytic review. *Journal of Personality and Social Psychology*, 50, 974–91.

Szabo, M. and Lovibond, P.F. (2002). The cognitive content of naturally occurring worry episodes. *Cognitive Therapy and Research*, 26, 167–77.

Szeszko, P.R., et al. (1999). Orbital frontal and amygdala volume reductions in obsessive-compulsive disorder. *Archives of General Psychiatry*, 56, 913–9.

Tallis, F., Eysenck, M., and Mathews, A. (1992). A questionnaire for the measurement of nonpathological worry. *Personality and Individual Differences*, 13, 161–8.

Tamam, L. and Ozpoyraz, N. (2002). Comorbidity of anxiety disorder among patients with bipolar I disorder in remission. *Psychopathology*, 35, 203–9.

Tan, T., Kales, J.D., Kales, A., Soldatos, C.R., and Bixler, E.O. (1984). Biopsychobehavioral correlates of insomnia, IV: Diagnosis based on DSM-III. *American Journal of Psychiatry*, 141, 357–62.

Tarrier, N. (2002). The use of coping strategies and self-regulation in the treatment of psychosis. In A.P. Morrison, Ed. *A casebook of cognitive therapy for psychosis* pp. 79–107. Hove, UK: Brunner-Routledge.

Tata, P.R., Leibowitz, J.A., Prunty, M.J., Cameron, M., and Pickering, A.D. (1996). Attentional bias in obsessional compulsive disorder. *Behaviour Research and Therapy*, 34, 53–60.

Taylor, L.M., Espie, C.A., and White, C.A. (in press). Attentional bias in people with acute versus persistent insomnia secondary to cancer. *Behavioural Sleep Medicine*.

Taylor, R.C., Harris, N.A., Singleton, E.G., Moolchan, E.T., and Heishman, S.J. (2000). Tobacco craving: intensity-related effects of imagery scripts in drug abusers. *Experimental and Clinical Psychopharmacology*, 8, 75–87.

Taylor, S.E. and Brown, J.D. (1988). Illusion and well-being: a social psychological perspective on mental health. *Psychological Bulletin*, 102, 193–210.

Taylor, S.E. and Schneider, S.K. (1989). Coping and the simulation of events. *Social Cognition*, 7, 174–94.

Taylor, S.E., Pham, L.B., Rivkin, I.D., and Armor, D.A. (1998). Harnessing the imagination. Mental simulation, self-regulation and coping. *American Psychologist*, 53, 429–39.

Teasdale, J.D. (1985). Psychological treatments for depression: how do they work? *Behaviour Research and Therapy*, 23, 157–65.

Teasdale, J.D. (1988). Cognitive vulnerability to persistent depression. *Cognition and Emotion*, 2, 247–74.

Teasdale, J.D. (1999a). Emotional processing, three modes of mind and the prevention of relapse in depression. *Behaviour Research and Therapy*, 37, S53–S77.

Teasdale, J.D. (1999b). Metacognition, mindfulness and the modification of mood disorders. *Clinical Psychology and Psychotherapy*, 6, 146–56 (Special Issue, Metacognition and Cognitive Behaviour Therapy).

Teasdale, J. and Barnard, P. (1993). *Affect, cognition and change*. Hove UK: Lawrence Erlbaum Associates Ltd.

Teasdale, J.D., Segal, Z.V., and Williams, J.M.G. (1995). How does cognitive therapy prevent depressive relapse and why should attentional control (mindfulness) training help? *Behaviour Research and Therapy*, 33, 25–40.

Teasdale, J.D., Segal, Z., Williams, J.M.G., Ridgeway, V.A., Soulsby, J.M., and Lau, M.A. (2000). Prevention of relapse/recurrence in major depression by mindfulness-based cognitive therapy. *Journal of Consulting and Clinical Psychology*, 68, 615–23.

Teasdale, J.D., Moore, R.G., Hayhurst, H., Pope, M., Williams, S., and Segal, Z.V. (2002). Metacognitive awareness and prevention of relapse in depression: empirical evidence. *Journal of Consulting and Clinical Psychology*, 70, 275–87.

Telch, M.J., Valentiner, D., and Bolte, M. (1994). Proximity to safety and its effects on fear prediction bias. *Behaviour Research and Therapy*, 32, 747–51.

Terr, L. (1991). Childhood trauma: an outline and overview. *American Journal of Psychiatry*, 148, 10–20.

Terr, L. (1994). *Unchained memories*. New York: Basic Books.

Thayer, J.F., Friedman, B.H., and Borkovec, T.D. (1996). Autonomic characteristics of generalized anxiety disorder and worry. *Biological Psychiatry*, 39, 255–66.

Thorpe, S.J. and Salkovskis, P.M. (1995). Phobic beliefs: do cognitive factors play a role in specific phobias? *Behaviour Research and Therapy*, 33, 805–16.

Thorpe, S.J. and Salkovskis, P.M. (1997). Information processing in spider phobics: the Stroop colour naming task may indicate strategic but not automatic attentional bias. *Behaviour Research and Therapy*, 35, 131–44.

Thorpe, S.J. and Salkovskis, P.M. (1998). Selective attention to real phobic and safety stimuli. *Behaviour Research and Therapy*, 36, 471–81.

Thrasher, S.M., Dalgleish, T., and Yule, W. (1994). Information processing in post-traumatic stress disorder. *Behaviour Research and Therapy*, 32, 247–54.

Todd, J. (1989). AIDS as a current psychopathological theme. A report on five heterosexual patients. *British Journal of Psychiatry*, 154, 253–5.

Tolin, D.F., Abramowitz, J.S., Brigidi, B.D., Amir, N., Street, G.P., and Foa, E.B. (2001). Memory and memory confidence in obsessive–compulsive disorder. *Behaviour Research and Therapy*, 39, 913–27.

Tolin, D.F., Abramowitz, J.S., Hamlin, C., Foa, E.B., and Synodi, D.S. (2002). Attributions for thought suppression failure in obsessive-compulsive disorder. *Cognitive Therapy and Research*, 26, 505–17.

Tolin, D.F., Abramowitz, J.S., Brigidi, B.D., and Foa, E.B. (2003). Intolerance of uncertainty in obsessive-compulsive disorder. *Journal of Anxiety Disorders*, 17, 233–42.

Tolin, D.F., Lohr, J.M., Lee, T.C., and Sawchuk, C.N. (1999). Visual avoidance in specific phobia. *Behaviour Research and Therapy*, 37, 63–70.

Tomarken, A.J., Mineka, S., and Cook, M. (1989). Fear-relevant selective associations and covariation bias. *Journal of Abnormal Psychology*, 98, 381–94.

Tomarken, A.J., Sutton, S.K., and Mineka, S. (1995). Fear-relevant illusory correlations: what types of associations promote judgemental bias? *Journal of Abnormal Psychology*, 104, 312–26.

Toneatto, T., Blitz-Miller, T., Calderwood, T., Dragonetti, R., and Tsanos, A. (1997). Cognitive distortions in heavy gambling. *Journal of Gambling Studies*, 13, 253–66.

Trinder, H. and Salkovskis, P.M. (1994). Personally relevant intrusions outside the laboratory: long-term suppression increases intrusion. *Behaviour Research and Therapy*, 32, 833–42.

Troop, N.A. and Treasure, J.L. (1997). Psychosocial factors in the onset of eating disorders: Responses to life-events and difficulties. *British Journal of Medical Psychology*, 70, 373–85.

Tsao, J.C.I., Mystkowski, J.L., Zucker, B.G., and Craske, M.G. (2002). Effects of cognitive-behavioural therapy for panic disorder on comorbid conditions: Replication and extension. *Behaviour Therapy*, 33, 493–509.

Tulving, E. (1983). *Elements of episodic memory*. Oxford UK: Oxford University Press.

Turk, D.C. and Salovey, P. (1985). Cognitive structures, cognitive processes and cognitive-behavior modification: II. Judgements and inferences of the clinician. *Cognitive Therapy and Research*, 9, 19–33.

Turner, S.M., Beidel, D.C., Dancu, C.V., and Stanley, M.A. (1989). An empirically derived inventory to measure social fears and anxiety: the social phobia and anxiety inventory. *Psychological Assessment*, 1, 35–40.

Tversky, A. and Kahneman, D. (1973). Availability: a heuristic for judging frequency and probability. *Cognitive Psychology*, 5, 207–32.

Tversky, A. and Kahneman, D. (1974). Judgement under uncertainty: heuristics and biases. *Science*, 185, 1124–31.

Tyrer, P., Lee, I., and Alexander, J. (1980). Awareness of cardiac function in anxious, phobic and hypochondriacal patients. *Psychological Medicine*, 10, 171–4.

Ustun, T.B., Simon, G. and Sartorius, N. (1995). Discussion. In T.B. Ustun and N. Sartorius, Eds. *Mental illness in general health care: an international study*. New York: Wiley.

Vallacher, R.R. and Wegner, D.M. (1987). What do people think they're doing? Action identification and human behavior. *Psychological Review*, 94, 3–15.

van den Hout, M. and Barlow, D. (2000). Attention, arousal and expectancies in anxiety and sexual disorders. *Journal of Affective Disorders*, 61, 241–56.

van den Hout, M. and Kindt, M. (2003). Repeated checking causes memory distrust. *Behaviour Research and Therapy*, 41, 301–16.

van den Hout, M., Tenney, N., Huygens, K., Merkelbach, H., and Kindt, M. (1995). Responding to subliminal threat cues is related to trait anxiety and emotional vulnerability: a successful replication of MacLeod and Hagan (1992). *Behaviour Research and Therapy*, 33, 451–4.

van den Hout, M., Tenney, N., Huygens, K., and De Jong, P.J. (1997). Preconscious processing bias in specific phobia. *Behaviour Research and Therapy*, 35, 29–34.

van den Hout, M., van Pol, M., and Peters, M.(2001). On becoming neutral: effects of experimental neutralizing reconsidered. *Behaviour Research and Therapy*, 39, 1439–48.

van der Does, A.J.W., Antony, M.M., Ehlers, A., and Barsky, A.J. (2000). Heartbeat perception in panic disorder: a reanalysis. *Behaviour Research and Therapy*, 38, 47–62.

van der Kolk, B.A. (1994). The body keeps score: memory and the evolving psychobiology of posttraumatic stress. *Harvard Review of Psychiatry*, 1, 253–65.

van der Kolk, B.A. and van der Hart, O. (1989). Pierre Janet and the breakdown of adaptation in psychological data. *American Journal of Psychiatry*, 146, 1530–40.

van Oppen, P. Hoekstra, R.J., and Emmelkamp, P.M.G. (1995). The structure of obsessive-compulsive symptoms. *Behaviour Research and Therapy*, 33, 15–23.

Van Praag, H.M. (1998). The diagnosis of depression in disorder. *Australian and New Zealand Journal of Psychiatry*, 32, 767–72.

Vasey, M. and Borkovec, T.D. (1992). A catastrophising assessment of worrisome thoughts. *Cognitive Therapy and Research*, 16, 505–20.

Vasterling, J.J., Brailey, K., Constans, J.I., and Sutker, P.B. (1998). Attention and memory dysfunction in posttraumatic stress disorder. *Neuropsychology*, 12, 125–33.

Vaughan, K. and Tarrier, N. (1992). The use of image habituation training with post-traumatic stress disorder. *British Journal of Psychiatry*, 161, 658–64.

Veale, D. and Riley, S. (2001). Mirror, mirror on the wall, who is the ugliest of them all? The psychopathology of mirror gazing in body dysmorphic disorder. *Behaviour Research and Therapy*, 39, 1381–93.

Veale, D., Gournay, K., Dryden, W., *et al.* (1996). Body dysmorphic disorder: a cognitive behavioural model and pilot randomised controlled trial. *Behaviour Research and Therapy*, 34, 717–279.

Veale, D.M., Sahakian, B.J., Owen, A.M., and Marks, I.M. (1996). Specific cognitive deficits in tests sensitive to frontal lobe dysfunction in obsessive-compulsive disorder. *Psychological Medicine*, 26, 1261–9.

Veljaca, K.A. and Rapee, R.M. (1998). Detection of negative and positive audience behaviours by socially anxious subjects. *Behaviour Research and Therapy*, 36, 311–21.

Velten, E.A. (1968). A laboratory task for induction of mood states. *Behaviour Research and Therapy*, 6, 473–82.

Vinogradov, S., Willis-Shore, J., Poole, J.H., Marten, E., Ober, B.A., and Shenaut, G.K. (1997). Clinical and neurocognitive aspects of source monitoring error in schizophrenia. *American Journal of Psychiatry*, 154, 1530–7.

Vitousek, K. M. (1996). The current status of cognitive-behavioural models of anorexia nervosa and bulimia nervosa. In P. M. Salkovskis, Ed. *Frontiers of cognitive therapy*, pp. 383–418. New York: Guildford Press.

Vitousek, K.B. and Hollon, S.D. (1990). The investigation of schematic content and processing in eating disorders. *Cognitive Therapy and Research*, 14, 191–214.

Vlaeyen, J.W.S., de Jong, J., Geilen, M., Heuts P.H.T.G., and van Breukelen, G. (2001). Graded exposure *in vivo* in the treatment of pain-related fear: a replicated single-case experimental design in four patients with chronic low back pain. *Behaviour Research and Therapy*, 39, 151–66.

Vrana, S.R., Cuthbert, B.N., and Lang, P.J. (1986). Fear imagery and text processing. *Psychophysiology*, 23, 247–53.

Vrana, S.R., Roodman, A., and Beckham, J.C. (1995). Selective processing of trauma relevant words in posttraumatic stress disorder. *Journal of Anxiety Disorders*, 9, 515–30.

Waddell, G., Newton, M., Henderson, I., Somerville, D., and Main, C.J. (1993). A fear-avoidance beliefs questionnaire (FABQ) and the role of fear-avoidance beliefs in chronic low back pain and disability. *Pain*, 52, 157–68.

Wagenaar, W. (1988). *Paradoxes of gambling behaviour*. London: Erlbaum.

Walker, M.K., Ben-Tovim, D.I., Paddick, S., and McNamara (1995). Pictorial adaptation of Stroop measures of body-related concerns in eating disorders. *International Journal of Eating Disorders*, 17, 309–11.

Wallace, S.T. and Alden, L.-E. (1997). Social phobia and positive social events: The price of success. *Journal of Abnormal Psychology,* 106, 416–24.

Waller, G. (2003). Schema-level cognitions in patients with binge eating disorder: a case control study. *International Journal of Eating Disorders,* 33, 458–64.

Waller, G., Babbs, M., Milligan, R., Meyer, C., Ohanian, V., and Leung, N. (2003). Anger and core beliefs in the eating disorders. *International Journal of Eating Disorders,* 34, 118–24.

Walters, G.D. and Contri, D. (1998). Outcome expectancies for gambling: empirical modelling of a memory network in federal prison inmates. *Journal of Gambling Studies,* 14, 173–91.

Walton, M.A., Castro, F.G., and Barrington, E.H. (1994). The role of attributions in abstinence, lapse, and relapse following substance abuse treatment. *Addictive Behaviors,* 19, 319–31.

Wang, A. (1998). *Spider phobia: The effects of suppressing thoughts about looming vs. nonlooming spiders.* Unpublished Master's Theses.

Wang, A. and Clark, D.A. (2002). Haunting thoughts: the problem of obsessive mental intrusions. *Journal of Cognitive Psychotherapy,* 16, 193–208.

Warda, G. and Bryant, R.A. (1998). Thought control strategies in acute stress disorder. *Behaviour Research and Therapy,* 36, 1171–5.

Warwick, H.M.C. and Salkovskis, P.M. (1990). Hypochondriasis. *Behaviour Research and Therapy,* 28, 105–17.

Washburn, D.A. and Putney, R.T. (1998). Stimulus movement and the intensity of attention. *Psychological Record,* 48, 555–70.

Watkins, E. and Baracaia, S. (2001). Why do people ruminate in dysphoric moods? *Personality and Individual Differences,* 30, 723–34.

Watkins, E. and Baracaia, S. (2002) Rumination and social problem-solving in depression. *Behaviour Research and Therapy,* 40, 1179–89.

Watkins, E. and Brown, R.G. (2002) Rumination and executive function in depression: an experimental study. *Journal of Neurology, Neurosurgery and Psychiatry,* 72, 400–2.

Watkins, E. and Teasdale, J.D. (2001). Rumination and overgeneral memory in depression. Effects of self-focus and analytic thinking. *Journal of Abnormal Psychology,* 110, 353–7.

Watkins, E., Teasdale, J.D., and Williams, R.M. (2000). Decentring and distraction reduce overgeneral autobiographical memory in depression. *Psychological Medicine,* 30, 911–20.

Watkins, J.A., Sargent, R.G., Miller, P.M., Ureda, J.R., Drane, W.J., and Richler, D.L. (2001). A study of the attribution style, self-efficacy, and dietary restraint in female binge and non-binge eaters. *Eating and Weight Disorders,* 6, 188–96.

Watkins, P.C., Mathews, A., Williamson, D.A., and Uller, R.D. (1992). Mood congruent memory in depression: emotional priming or elaboration? *Journal of Abnormal Psychology,* 101, 581–86.

Watkins, P.C., Vache, K., Verney, S.P., and Mathews, A. (1996). Unconscious mood-congruent memory bias in depression. *Journal of Abnormal Psychology,* 105, 34–41.

Watkins, P.C., Martin, C.K., and Stern, L.D. (2000). Unconscious memory bias in depression: perceptual and conceptual processes. *Journal of Abnormal Psychology,* 109, 282–9.

Watts, F.N. and Coyle, K. (1993). Phobics show poor recall of anxiety words. *British Journal of Medical Psychology,* 66, 373–82.

Watts, F.N. and Dalgleish, T. (1991). Memory for phobia related words in spider phobics. *Cognition and Emotion,* 5, 313–29.

Watson, J.B. and Rayner, P. (1920). Conditioned emotional reactions. *Journal of Experimental Psychology*, 3, 1–14.

Watts, F.N., McKenna, F.P., Sharrock, R., and Trezise, L. (1986a). Colour-naming of phobia related-words. *British Journal of Psychology*, 77, 97–108.

Watts, F.N., Trezise, L., and Sharrock, R. (1986b). Processing of phobic stimuli. *British Journal of Clinical Psychology*, 25, 253–61.

Watts, F.N., Coyle, K., and East, M.P. (1994). The contribution of worry to insomnia. *British Journal of Clinical Psychology*, 33, 211–20.

Wearden, A.J., Tarrier, N., Barrowclough, C., Zastowny, T.R., and Rahill, A.A. (2000). A review of expressed emotion research in health care. *Clinical Psychology Review*, 20, 633–66.

Wegner, D.M. (1989). *White bears and other unwanted thoughts: Suppression, obsession and the psychology of mental control*. New York: Viking.

Wegner, D.M. (1994a). Ironic processes of mental control. *Psychological Bulletin*, 101, 34–52.

Wegner, D.M. (1994b). *White bears and other unwanted thoughts*. New York: Guilford Press.

Wegner, D.M. (1997). When the antidote is the poison: ironic mental control processes. *Psychological Science*, 8, 148–50.

Wegner, D.M. and Erber, R. (1992). The hyperaccessibility of suppressed thoughts. *Journal of Personality and Social Psychology*, 63, 903–12.

Wegner, D.M. and Gold, D.B. (1995). Fanning old flames: emotional and cognitive effects of suppressing thoughts of a past relationship. *Journal of Personality and Social Psychology*, 68, 782–92.

Wegner, D.M. and Wenzlaff, R.M. (1996). Mental control. In E.T. Higgins and A.W. Kruglanski, Eds. *Social psychology: handbook of basic principles*. New York: Guilford.

Wegner, D.M. and Zanakos, S. (1994). Chronic thought suppression. *Journal of Personality*, 62, 615–40.

Wegner, D.M., Schneider, D.J., Carter, S.R., and White, T.L. (1987). Paradoxical effects of thought suppression. *Journal of Personality and Social Psychology*, 53, 5–13.

Wegner, D.M., Schneider, D.J., Knutson, B., and McMahon, S.R. (1991). Polluting the stream of consciousness: the effect of thought suppression on the mind's environment. *Cognitive Therapy and Research*, 15, 141–52.

Wegner, D.M., Erber, R., and Zanakos, S. (1993). Ironic processes in the mental control of mood and mood-related thought. *Journal of Personality and Social Psychology*, 65, 1093–1104.

Weisberg, R.B., Brown, T.A., Wincze, J.P., and Barlow, D.H. (2001). Causal attributions and male sexual arousal: the impact of attributions for a bogus erectile difficulty on sexual arousal, cognitions, and affect. *Journal of Abnormal Psychology*, 110, 324–34.

Weiss, E.L., Longhurst, J.G., and Mazure, C.M. (1999). Childhood sexual abuse as a risk factor for depression in women: psychosocial and neurobiological correlates. *American Journal of Psychiatry*, 156, 816–28.

Weissman, M.M., Greenwald, S., Nino-Murcia, G., and Dement, W.C. (1997). The morbidity of insomnia uncomplicated by psychiatric disorders. *General Hospital Psychiatry*, 19, 245–50.

Wells, A. (1995). Metacognition and worry: a cognitive model of generalised anxiety disorder. *Behavioural and Cognitive Psychotherapy*, 23, 301–20.

Wells, A. (1997). *Cognitive therapy of anxiety disorders: a practice manual and conceptual guide.* Chichester: Wiley.

Wells, A. (2000). *Emotional disorders and metacognition: innovative cognitive therapy.* Chichester: Wiley.

Wells, A. and Carter, K. (2001). Further test of a cognitive model of GAD: metacognitions and worry in GAD, panic disorder, social phobia, depression and non-patients. *Behaviour Therapy*, 32, 85–102.

Wells, A. and Davies, M.I. (1994). The thought control questionnaire: a measure of individual differences in the control of unwanted thoughts. *Behaviour Research and Therapy*, 32, 871–8.

Wells, A. and Hackmann, A. (1993). Imagery and core beliefs in health anxiety: content and origins. *Behavioural and Cognitive Psychotherapy*, 21, 265–73.

Wells, A. and Matthews, G. (1994). *Attention and emotion: a clinical perspective.* Hove: Lawrence Erlbaum.

Wells, A. and Morrison, A.P. (1994). Qualitative dimensions of normal worry and normal intrusive thoughts. *Behaviour Research and Therapy*, 32, 867–70.

Wells, A. and Papageorgiou, C. (1995). Worry and the incubation of intrusive images following stress. *Behaviour Research and Therapy*, 33, 579–93.

Wells, A. and Papageorgiou, C. (1998). Social phobia: effects of external attention on anxiety, negative beliefs and perspective taking. *Behavior Therapy*, 29, 357–70.

Wells, A., Clark, D.M., Salkovskis, P., Ludgate, J., Hackmann, A., and Gelder, M. (1995). Social phobia: the role of in-situation safety behaviors in maintaining anxiety and negative beliefs. *Behavior Therapy*, 26, 153–61.

Wells, A., White, J., and Carter, K. (1997). Attention training: effects on anxiety and beliefs in panic and social phobia. *Clinical Psychology and Psychotherapy*, 4, 226–32.

Wells, A., Clark, D.M., and Ahmad, S. (1998). How do I look with my minds eye: perspective taking in social phobic imagery. *Behaviour Research and Therapy*, 36, 631–4.

Wenzel, A. and Holt, C.S. (1999). Dot probe performance in two specific phobias. *British Journal of Clinical Psychology*, 38, 407–10.

Wenzel, A. and Holt, C.S. (2002). Memory bias against threat in social phobia. *British Journal of Clinical Psychology*, 41, 73–9.

Wenzel, A., Jackson, L.C., and Holt, C.S. (2002). Social phobia and the recall of autobiographical memories. *Depression and Anxiety*, 15, 186–9.

Wenzlaff, R.M. (1993). The mental control of depression: Psychological obstacles to emotional well being. In D.M. Wegner and J.W. Pennebaker, Eds., *Handbook of mental control*, pp. 238–57. Englewood Cliffs, NJ: Prentice Hall.

Wenzlaff, R.M. and Bates, D.E. (1998). Unmasking a cognitive vulnerability to depression: how lapses in mental control reveal depressive thinking. *Journal of Personality and Social Psychology*, 75, 1559–71.

Wenzlaff, R.M. and Bates, D.E. (2000). The relative efficacy of concentration and suppression strategies of mental control. *Personality and Social Psychology Bulletin*, 26, 1200–12.

Wenzlaff, R.M. and Eisenberg, A.R. (2000). Mental control after dysphoria: evidence of a suppressed, depressive bias. *Behavior Therapy*, 32, 27–45.

Wenzlaff, R.M. and Eisenberg, A.R. (2001). Mental control after dysphoria: evidence of a suppressed, deprived bias. *Behaviour Therapy*, 32, 27–45.

Wenzlaff, R.M. and Wegner, D.M. (2000). Thought suppression. *Annual Review of Psychology*, 51, 59–61.

Wenzlaff, R.M., Wegner, D.M., and Roper, D.W. (1988). Depression and mental control: the resurgence of unwanted negative thoughts. *Journal of Personality and Social Psychology*, 55, 882–92.

Wenzlaff, R.M., Wegner, D.M., and Klein, S.B. (1991). The role of thought suppression in the bonding of thought and mood. *Journal of Personality and Social Psychology*, 60, 500–8.

Wenzlaff, R.M., Rude, S.S., Taylor, C.J., Stultz, C.H., and Sweatt, R.A. (2001). Beneath the veil of thought suppression: attentional bias and depression risk. *Cognition and Emotion*, 15, 435–52.

Wenzlaff, R.M., Meier, J., and Salas, D.M. (2002). Thought suppression and memory biases during and after depressive moods. *Cognition and Emotion*, 16, 403–22.

Wessel, I., Meeren, M., Peeters, F., Arntz, A., and Harald, M. (2001). Correlates of autobiographical memory specificity: the role of depression, anxiety and childhood trauma. *Behaviour Research and Therapy*, 39, 409–21.

Wessel, I., Merckelbach, H., and Dekkers, T. (2002). Autobiographical memory specificity, intrusive memory, and general memory skills in Dutch-Indonesian survivors of the World War II era. *Journal of Traumatic Stress*, 15, 227–34.

Wicklow, A. and Espie, C.A. (2000). Intrusive thoughts and their relationship to actigraphic measurement of sleep: towards a cognitive model of insomnia. *Behaviour Research and Therapy*, 38, 679–94.

Widiger, T.A. and Chaynes, K. (2003). Current issues in the assessment of personality disorders. *Current Psychiatry Reports*, 5, 28–35.

Wiedemann, G., Pauli, P., and Dengler, W. (2001). A priori expectancy bias in patients with panic disorder. *Journal of Anxiety Disorders*, 15, 401–12.

Wiers, R.W., Van Woerden, N., Smulders, F.T.Y., and De Jong, P. (2002). Implicit and explicit alcohol-related cognitions in heavy and light drinkers. *Journal of Abnormal Psychology*, 111, 648–58.

Wilhelm, S., McNally, R.J., Baer, L., and Florin, I. (1997). Autobiographical memory in obsessive-compulsive disorder. *British Journal of Clinical Psychology*, 35, 1–11.

Williams, D.A. and Thorn, B.E. (1989). An empirical assessment of pain beliefs. *Pain*, 36, 351–8.

Williams, J.M., Healy, H., Eade, J., *et al.* (2002). Mood, eating behaviour and attention. *Psychological Medicine*, 32, 469–81.

Williams, J.M., Teasdale, J.D., Segal, Z.V., and Soulsby, J. (2000). Mindfulness-based cognitive therapy reduces overgeneral autobiographical memory in formerly depressed patients. *Journal of Abnormal Psychology*, 109, 150–5.

Williams, J.M.G. (1996). Depression and the specificity of autobiographical memory. In D. Rubin, Ed. *Remembering our past: studies in autobiographical memory*, pp. 245–67. Cambridge: Cambridge University Press.

Williams, J.M.G. and Broadbent, K. (1986). Autobiographical memory in suicide attempters. *Journal of Abnormal Psychology*, 95, 144–9.

Williams, J.M.G. and Scott, J. (1988). Autobiographical memory in depression. *Psychological Medicine*, 18, 689–95.

Williams, J.M.G., Mathews, A., and MacLeod, C. (1996). The emotional Stroop task and psychopathology, *Psychological Bulletin*, 120, 3–24.

Williams, J.M.G., Watts, F., MacLeod, C., and Mathews, A. (1997). *Cognitive psychology and emotional disorders*, 2nd Edition. Chichester: Wiley.

Williams, J.M.G., Watts, F., MacLeod, C., and Mathews, A. (1988). *Cognitive psychology and emotional disorders*, 1st Edition. Chichester: Wiley.

Williams, L.M., Loughland, C.M., Gordon, E., and Davidson (1999). Visual scanpaths in schizophrenia: is there a deficit in face recognition? *Schizophrenia Research*, 36, 189–99.

Williams, M. and Dritschel, B. (1988). Emotional disturbance and the specificity of autobiographical memory. *Cognition and Emotion*, 5, 313–29.

Williams, S. (2002). Anxiety, associated physiological sensations, and delusional catastrophic misinterpretation: Variations on a theme? In A.P. Morrison, Ed. *A casebook of cognitive therapy for psychosis*, pp. 79–107. Hove, UK: Brunner-Routledge.

Williamson, D.A., Perrin, L., Blouin, D.C., and Barbin, J.M. (2000). Cognitive bias in eating disorders: interpretation of ambiguous body-related information. *Eating and Weight Disorders*, 5, 143–51.

Wilson, G.T. and O'Leary, D. (1980). *Principles of behavior therapy*. Englewood Cliffs, NJ: Prentice-Hall.

Wilson, G. T. and Faiburn, C. G. (2002). Treatments for eating disorders. In Nathan, P. E., Gorman, J. M., (Eds) *A guide to treatments that work* (2nd ed.), pp. 559–92. London: Oxford University Press, 2002.

Wilson, G.T., Fairburn, C.G., Agras, W.S., Walsh, B.T., and Kraemer, H. (2002). Cognitive behavioral therapy for bulimia nervosa: time course and mechanisms of change. *Journal of Consulting and Clinical Psychology*, 70, 267–74.

Wolpe, J. (1958). *Psychotherapy to reciprocal inhibition*. Stanford University Press.

Wonderlich, S.A., Crosby, R.D., Mitchell, J.E., *et al.* (2001). Eating disturbance and sexual trauma in childhood and adulthood. *International Journal of Eating Disorders*, 30, 401–12.

Woodruff-Borden, J., Brothers, A.J., and Lister, S.C. (2001). Self-focused attention: commonalities across psychopathologies and predictors. *Behavioural and Cognitive Psychotherapy*, 29, 169–78.

Woody, S. and Rachman, S. (1994). Generalized anxiety disorder (GAD) as an unsuccessful search for safety. *Clinical Psychology Review*, 14, 743–53.

Woody, S.R. (1996). Effects of focus of attention on anxiety levels and social performance of individuals with social phobia. *Journal of Abnormal Psychology*, 105, 61–9.

Woody, S.R. and Rodriguez, B.F. (2000). Self-focused attention and social anxiety in social phobics and normal controls. *Cognitive Therapy and Research*, 24, 473–88.

Woody, S.R., Chambless, D.L., and Glass, C.R. (1997). Self-focused attention in the treatment of social phobia. *Behaviour Research and Therapy*, 35, 117–30.

World Health Organization (1992). The ICD-10 classification of mental and behavioural disorder: diagnostic criteria for research (10th revision). Geneva: Author.

Wright, J. and Morley, S. (1995). Autobiographical memory and chronic pain. *British Journal of Clinical Psychology*, 34, 255–65.

Wykes, T., Reeder, C., Williams, C., Corner, J., Rice, C., and Everitt, B. (2003). Are the effects of cognitive remediation therapy (CRT) durable? Results from an exploratory trial in schizophrenia. *Schizophrenia Research*, 61, 163–74.

York, D., Borkovec, T.D., Vasey, M., and Stern, R. (1987). Effects of worry and somatic anxiety induction on thoughts, emotion and physiological activity. *Behaviour Research and Therapy*, 25, 523–6.

Young, H.F. and Bentall, R.P. (1995). Hypothesis testing in patients with persecutory delusions: Comparison with depressed and normal subjects. *British Journal of Clinical Psychology*, 34, 353–69.

Young, H.F. and Bentall, R.P. (1997a). Probabilistic reasoning in deluded, depressed and normal subjects: effects of task difficulty and meaningful versus non-meaningful material. *Psychological Medicine*, 27, 455–65.

Young, H.F. and Bentall, R.P. (1997b). Social reasoning in individuals with persecutory delusions: The effects of additional information on attributions for the observed behaviour of others. *British Journal of Clinical Psychology*, 36, 569–73.

Zack, M., Toneatto, T., and MacLeod, C. M. (1999). Implicit activation of alcohol concepts by negative affective cues distinguishes between problem drinkers with high and low psychiatric distress. *Journal of Abnormal Psychology*, 108, 518–31.

Zack, M., Toneatto, T., and MacLeod, C.M. (2002). Anxiety and explicit alcohol-related memory in problem drinkers. *Addictive Behaviours*, 27, 331–43.

Zitterl, W., Urban, C., Linzmayer, L., *et al.* (2001). Memory deficits in patients with DSM-IV obsessive-compulsive disorder. *Psychopathology*, 34, 113–7.

Zoellner, L.A., Alvarez-Conrad, J., and Foa, E.B. (2002). Peritraumatic dissociative experiences, trauma narratives, and trauma pathology. *Journal of Traumatic Stress*, 15, 49–5.

Zucker, B.G., Craske, M.G., Barrios, V., and Holguin, M. (2002). Thought action fusion: can it be corrected? *Behaviour Research and Therapy*, 40, 653–64.

Index